Theatricality of the Closet

Performance Works

SERIES EDITORS
Patrick Anderson and
Nicholas Ridout

This series publishes books in theater and performance studies, focused in particular on the material conditions in which performance acts are staged, and to which performance itself might contribute. We define "performance" in the broadest sense, including traditional theatrical productions and performance art, but also cultural ritual, political demonstration, social practice, and other forms of interpersonal, social, and political interaction that may fruitfully be understood in terms of performance.

Theatricality of the Closet

Fashion, Performance, and Subjectivity between Victorian Britain and Meiji Japan

✦

Michelle Liu Carriger

NORTHWESTERN UNIVERSITY PRESS
EVANSTON, ILLINOIS

Northwestern University Press
www.nupress.northwestern.edu

Printed in the United States of America

10 9 8 7 6 5 4 3 2 1

Library of Congress Cataloging-in-Publication Data

Names: Carriger, Michelle Liu, author.
Title: Theatricality of the closet : fashion, performance, and subjectivity between Victorian Britain and Meiji Japan / Michelle Liu Carriger.
Description: Evanston, Illinois : Northwestern University Press, 2023. | Series: Performance works | Includes bibliographical references and index.
Identifiers: LCCN 2023022540 | ISBN 9780810145894 (paperback) | ISBN 9780810145900 (cloth) | ISBN 9780810145917 (ebook)
Subjects: LCSH: Clothing and dress—Great Britain—History—19th century. | Clothing and dress—Japan—History—Meiji period, 1868–1912. | Clothing and dress—Social aspects. | Fashion—Great Britain—History—19th century. | Fashion—Japan—History—Meiji period, 1868–1912. | Fashion—Social aspects.
Classification: LCC GT737 .C37 2023 | DDC 391.00941/09034—dc23
LC record available at https://lccn.loc.gov/2023022540

CONTENTS

ACKNOWLEDGMENTS

This book was a long time coming and I am writing these acknowledgments as the last possible part of this document. I've become a bit superstitious about compiling this part—after years of work that alternately feels very lonely and very social, I've amassed an endless list of names. Trying to write them down, though, reveals the sprawling contours of what life as an academic feels like, with the obvious unmissable names trailing behind them other names and still more names. "I should like to call you all by name," wrote Anna Akhmatova, "but they have lost the lists."

The germ of this work emerged two decades ago when my undergraduate professor Julie Smith required everyone in the modern drama class to research and write a critical introduction to an out-of-print script. I ended up with "The Girls of the Period" by "A. B."[1] Those 1869 girls and their cross-dressing brother would lead me to Boulton and Park who would become the subjects of my MA thesis at University of Colorado, Boulder, where Oliver Gerland, Bud Coleman, Janet Jacobs, and Jim Symons guided my progress. Emma Sweeney, Emily Midorikawa, John Chantler, and especially Kyle Giocomo, all helped me survive that first UK research trip.

The research, writing, and publication of this book were supported by an Ogilvy Travel Grant from the University of Colorado, Boulder; a Paul Mellon Foundation Grant for Studies in British Art; Queen Mary, University of London's postgraduate research seminar; the Stanford Geballe workshop on fashion; and internal UCLA faculty grants, including two Dean's Vision Awards from the School of Theater, Film, and Television. The staff of archives and libraries around the world were incredibly helpful, especially those at the Bunka Gakuen Library and Special Collections who helped me print images from their collection; the Kanagawa Prefectural Museum of History in Yokohama who gifted me one of the books of *Yokohama-e* referenced here; and Jeanette L. Casey, head of the Mills Music Library of the University of Wisconsin, Madison. Thanks to UCLA's Marty Brennan and Diana King for clear advice and good cheer.

The cohorts of my different institutions provided the invaluable support and sounding board and occasional antagonism needed to help give my thinking a concrete form. Although there are others, I am especially thinking of Amanda Holden Giguere, Andrea Moon, Stephen Weitz, Christina Guttierez, Lisa Hall, and Jennifer Popple at CU Boulder; and Paige McGinley, Pannill Camp, Elise Morrison, Christian DuComb, Molly

Flynn, Jim Dennen, Eleanor Skimin, Hans Vermy, and Patrick McKelvey at Brown. Patricia Ybarra was a wonderful adviser and remains my role model in navigating the profession with convictions and humor intact. My other PhD mentors all continue to inspire: John Emigh, Robin Bernstein, and Rebecca Schneider.

Thanks to my UCLA colleagues Suk-Young Kim, Marike Splint, and Sylvan Oswald; magnificent faculty mentor Joseph Bristow; Mariko Hirano and Ken Shima who assisted with late-breaking Meiji research; manuscript workshop interlocutors Lisa Freeman, Karen Shimakawa, and Satoko Shimazaki; the incomparable Aaron C. Thomas; and graduate researchers Jenna Tamimi, Gwyneth Shanks, Clara Wilch, and Farrah O'Shea. Shelby Brewster provided editorial support. Thanks to series editors Patrick Anderson and Nicholas Ridout who stepped in at exactly the moment when I needed them most, the Northwestern University Press staff, and reader number 1, whose feedback was a perfect balance of encouraging and incisive. Thanks to the Rozay Working Group for the endless commiserating, troubleshooting, and trench camaraderie. Special thanks to Pavithra Prasad, Christina Owens, Erin Curtis, Matthew Abrams, Päivi Jämsä, Sarah Stewart, Keiko Nakada, Glenn Pereira, Glenn and Carol St. John Webb, and more who kept me anchored to the planet; Tara Rodman for deep dialogue on transnational Japan and life in general; and Sean Metzger for paving the way.

And finally, here's that place where we academics usually acknowledge, for a moment on a page most people won't read, that scholarship is entirely imbricated in everything else that makes a life. That we had to eat, sleep, rest, and love to make writing happen. The people who made this book possible are my parents Diana and Bill, who roll with this no matter how far it strays from where we started; my brother Greg; and Damian, who has crossed continents with me and for me.

Theatricality of the Closet

Chapter 1

✦

"Tissue of Quotations"

Fashion and Subjectivity

From the Bow Street police court witness stand in May 1870, Francis Kegan Cox, a London solicitor, related to the judge, assembled barristers, the accused, and the crowded court audience how at a London restaurant he had made the acquaintance of one Lord Arthur Clinton, the third son of the Duke of Newcastle. Cox also met Clinton's young companion who was dressed in a man's suit but behaved in such a way that Cox believed the person to be "a pretty woman who was inclined to flirt" (*Telegraph*, May 21, 1870, 6). After luncheon they all went back to Cox's office to drink champagne. When Clinton left the room, Cox kissed the person, only to find out thereafter that the "fascinating woman" in a men's suit was a young man named Ernest Boulton. Relating this scene in his testimony to the packed courtroom, Cox declared, "I kissed him, she, or it, believing at the time it was a woman." Although this caused the assembly to laugh, the joke came at the expense of Ernest Boulton's very status as human.

Two years earlier, a blistering article in London's *Saturday Review of Politics, Literature, Science and Art* (hereafter *Saturday*), "The Girl of the Period," accused the modern young woman of England of losing sight of her proper nature by imitating the demimonde in matters of dress, mimicking boys in adopting slang and fast manners, and "frizzing her hair like certain savages in Africa."[1] Although Victorian England was rich in talk about women and the state they were in, this article particularly stung, triggering an avalanche of printed and staged debate and commentary. Moreover, the substance of the critique tied fashioned appearances to transgressions of gender by invoking "male" habits, sexuality through referencing prostitutes, and race in the designation of hair like "savages in Africa."

Within months of the Girl of the Period's London debut, another teenager, Emperor Meiji of Japan, was catapulted to political control of the country as the figurehead for a new regime bent on avoiding the colonized and semicolonized fate of its Asian neighbors through a massive campaign of Westernization, under the banner of *Bunmei Kaika* ("Civilization and Enlightenment"). By 1872 (the year after the conclusion of Boulton and Park's tabloid trial), the nineteen-year-old emperor had traded his traditional long hair and silken court costume for a haircut, goatee, and braid-bedecked European-style military dress uniform. The imperial proclamation that accompanied the makeover declared "we must no longer appear before the people in these effeminate styles."[2] The emperor's proclamation thus staked the nation's political autonomy on gendered, (hetero)sexualized, and racialized notions of self-presentation—that is, a makeover.

And yet, fashion has typically been imagined as ancillary to "real" political forces. Even as the superficial, the apparently frivolous, the theatrical, and the fashionable have been deemed meaningless, whole societies have regularly obsessed over these dynamics, sometimes belying their "mereness" with obsessive attention, sometimes expending immense amounts of energy and time to confirm and reconfirm fashion's triviality. This book seeks to follow the trail of outsized—one might say dramatic—reactions to fashion controversies in the nineteenth century to weigh claims of fashion's insignificance against the force and energy these controversies commanded. Beginning with these three juxtaposed nineteenth-century fashion controversies and concluding with twenty-first-century transnational subcultural performances of an imagined Victorian past, this book draws connections (and distinctions) across discourses and experiences of gender, sexuality, nation, class, and temporality to articulate how quotidian performances of self-constitution through the theatricality and performativity of clothing have conditioned subjecthood in the modern, globalized world. I work from a basic axiom that is both commonsensical and radical: clothing matters. Clothing conditions virtually every encounter individuals have with each other, how individuals see themselves, and how individuals interface with their surroundings, natural and (especially) social. On one hand, this is an obvious fact: clothing the body is not only ubiquitous among humans, it is an activity that has historically been imagined to distinguish humans from other animals.[3] On the other hand, many cultures (especially European and so-called Western discourses) have maintained conflicting attitudes toward clothing—and especially "fashion"—for millennia because of its ambiguous relation to social values like truth, rationality, and the natural. The complicated mix of human attitudes toward clothing, especially distrust and outright hostility, I will contend, is related to how clothing works as a performance and a performative. Clothing stages a theatrical encounter within the sanctum of real life.

Clothing constitutes a very literal limen—"the frontier between the self and the not-self"—a margin wherein individuals are interpellated into society and where they often stage interventions into that society.[4] To put it another way: clothing is where individual identity and societal demands meet, mingle, and clash. In their book *Fashioning the Frame*, Alexandra Warwick and Dani Cavallaro articulate dress as both boundary and margin—a practice that demarcates the limits of the body and yet is itself indistinct from those boundaries.[5] Clothing fully alters the way a body is apprehended by others and even by oneself. Some parts of bodies (hair, fingernails, skin) are subjected to the changing dictates of fashion even as they are indisputably "natural" biological features. Decorations and alterations like piercing and tattooing are imposed "artificially" and artistically, and yet become inseparable from flesh. Moreover, clothing, while in one sense the ultimate sign of culture over nature (in the Bible, clothing is the very first concern of the postlapsarian Adam and Eve), is itself so fully naturalized in human society that to go naked comprises a shocking fashion statement. (Anthropologists note that even societies of people who regularly go without what Westerners would consider comprehensive clothing still have highly developed systems of bodily embellishment.[6]) In 1906 Karl Kraus declared, "Nakedness is still indissolubly bound to the idea of clothing. We perceive a clothed state as the natural condition and nakedness for us is primarily a state of being undressed and appears to us as bareness, as nudity."[7] Clothing, then, is the location where thoroughly naturalized discursive ideas about identity and culture are applied to the body.

Clothing inscribes a body, producing that body as legible or illegible within a given episteme. This is emphatically not, however, to argue for the value of an a priori body that comes "before" clothing (which is to say, discourse) that we might somehow aspire to liberate from discursive constraints. Although one might be able intellectually to imagine a body—a concatenation of physical flesh—separately from the discursive knowledges that work on that flesh, in writing that clothing produces the body I am declaring that clothing and bodies are hopelessly entwined with each other; they must be thought in tandem, especially when it comes to ideas about what is natural to bodies. For example, art historian Anne Hollander demonstrates in her foundational text *Seeing through Clothes* how a given society's forms of clothing shape how people perceive the nude body. She points out that the clothed and nude bodies of art subjects tend to resemble each other more within a given period than nudes resemble their counterparts from different times.[8] Evidence like this testifies against notions of the immutability, immanence, and precedence of a natural body prior to discourse. I follow Hollander in arguing that clothing and representations of clothing thus shape how bodies are understood within discourse, in addition to literally, physically shaping bodies (to greater and lesser extents in different times). Indeed, the coincidence of discursive (internalized) constraints and physical ones—like Susan Bordo's observation that corsets gave way not to unregulated feminine bodies, but to the internalized constraints of diet culture[9]—underlines the essential nondifferentiation between material clothing and ideologies of personhood.

Clothing is so intimately bound up with how people understand subjectivity that the names for body parts and clothing come to stand for each other; for example, in medieval times, women covered their torsos with "a pair of bodies" (two halves laced together to make what became known, to this day, as the bodice). Victorian sources consistently use items of clothing, particularly petticoats, as metonymic identifiers for women and femininity (seen in periodical headlines on "petticoat doctors" or "petticoat lawyers," for example). This usage may have spilled over into the twentieth-century slang for a woman as a "skirt" or a "piece of skirt."

As I have already intimated, the entanglement of clothing and body is not only discursive or intellectual—it is also a physical fact. Clothing and bodies interact—marking, shaping, and exerting force on each other. While garments leave their marks on flesh, bodies interpenetrate clothing with sweat and blood, bodies stretch and disfigure fabrics, and in so doing, they impart some of their own mortality on clothes. The proverbial blood, sweat, and tears that blur the boundaries of the human also decay the fabric that helps hold the line between subject and society. Garments that have had too much life disintegrate, and surviving garments partake of the mystification of the individual. Perhaps it is this transference of qualities that helps infuse clothing with affective charge and a sense of the uncanny. Articles of clothing are frequently endowed with fetishistic qualities. (Some of the most recognizable sexual fetishes are of course sartorial: shoes, corsets, leather, masks.) Clothing's privileged relation to the body has often led to poetic heights—knights carrying sleeves as favors, burying your face in a lost loved one's shirt, or Othello killing over a handkerchief. Even theorists have been moved to superstition when it comes to talking about clothing. Roland Barthes writes that "it is not possible to conceive a garment without the body . . . the empty garment, without the head and without limbs . . . is death, not the body's neutral absence, but the body decapitated, mutilated."[10] Elizabeth Wilson, in *Adorned in Dreams*, calls clothes "congealed memories," writing:

> We experience a sense of the uncanny when we gaze at garments that had an intimate relationship with human beings long since gone to their graves. For clothes are so much part of our living, moving selves that, frozen on display in the mausoleums of culture, they hint at something only half understood, sinister, threatening; the atrophy of the body and the evanescence of life.[11]

Whether my reader feels the thrill of the uncanny when looking at clothes, I look to clothing as an excellent place from which to attempt a historiography of bodies. In some sense, clothing artifacts carry the negative imprint of once-living and now-disappeared bodies. Clothes constitute, to crib a line from Barthes, "a tissue of quotations drawn from the innumerable centers of culture."[12] (And of course Barthes draws out the etymological relation of text to textile—a tissue, a fabric, woven of fibers.) Clothing is here examined as a material and discursive and (re)iterative—which is to say performance and performative—process through which individuals integrated with, stood out from, fought against, sought to change, constituted, and were constituted by their societies.

Fashion, Identity, Historiography

In the foregoing, I have begun to introduce the ways in which I see clothing as an important location from which to interrogate, analyze, and understand subject formation—"identity" as a performative outcome of embodied activities. This focus on subjectivity through clothing is further triangulated with historiographical concerns; by this I mean not only how we can use historical fashion controversies to understand the past (and past subjectivities) but also how fashion practices themselves might be thought of as modes of historiographical production. Fashion's remit is at first glance seemingly the opposite of history: history is about the past, and fashion is about the next, newest, future thing. But both are deeply concerned with representation and temporality. And fashion, for all that its primary association may be with the new, is itself a sort of recycling machine, continually manufacturing said new out of what came before. A lot like writing history.[13] Fashion's thorough imbrication with commodity culture and endless newness constitute it as a primary relation between modernity and temporality (we might almost say that fashion constitutes *the* primary relation of modern capitalism to temporality). At the same time fashion shares with performance a recursive bent—fashion's newness is consistently composed in repetition with a difference, just as is performance's apparent one-time-only uniqueness. Throughout the book, we will see fashion looked to as an agent of progress or devolution; nationalist anxieties over progress are encapsulated in the repetitive yet teleological trajectory of fashion.

Although it was not my intention, it is also not exactly a coincidence that my three historical case studies break down precisely into categories of identity or subjectivity that oppose the sovereign Western subject position of the nineteenth century: the straight white man. The Girl of the Period controversy centers on battles over the category of "woman" in inherent binary opposition to "man" in mid-Victorian England (while also activating ideas about sexuality in its invocation of prostitution and race in describing "frizzed" hairstyles). The Boulton and Park trial brought significant public speculation over the nascent possibilities of homosexual orientations (and therefore some of the first intimations of "straight" as a sexual category) to the British public.[14] The Meiji makeover project illuminates the messiness of the racial and national boundaries between "Oriental" and "white" peoples. My discussion of gothic lolita subcultural fashions demonstrates how highly fantasized revivals of nineteenth-century fashions have resurfaced today, critiquing the persistence of ideologies of Cartesian, liberal subjectivity and positing new ones.

Over the course of the research and thinking I've done in this project as well as much of the rest of my work as a performance studies scholar, I have become more and more convinced that it is the study of these nonstraight, nonwhite nonmen that help to reveal the fissures, irrationalities, and impossibilities of European, Cartesian, and Christian (read: Western) conceptions of identity and subjectivity. Or, in other words, the cases I examine here not only index debates over the boundaries of these femme, female, queer, and nonwhite identities but also demonstrate how much of human identity—in the sense of self-sameness, self-possession, self-determination, authenticity, seriousness, and meaningfulness—has been contingent on its white, straight, male guarantee. And if the attempts at self-presentation or self-expression or self-definition of those not-straight, not-white, and not-male subjects are repeatedly relegated to fakery, insufficiency, theatricality, then of what real use is identity as a guarantor of subjecthood anyway?

To be clear, this is not a screed about straight white men. What emerged as I thought through these cases of fashion controversy in concert was the insufficiency of liberal subjectivity models for all homo sapiens. I contend that these cases that expose the limits of inherited notions of subjectivity through their attention to so-called deviations from human subjecthood are the ones that can effectively aid us in recalibrating the norms of personhood for all people, by building difference and deviance into those definitions. The fluidity of these currently sharply divided identities can be indexed by observing historical change in other identity types: economic class, for example, was enshrined in the US Constitution through voting laws that required property ownership, yet class—while still obviously a salient factor in people's lives today—is no longer considered to be an inborn determiner of an individual's nature as gender, sexuality, and race still are.[15] The chapters of this book will index analogous changes in ideas about identity categories while working between the nineteenth and twenty-first centuries. This combination of different deviances (gender, sexuality, and race/nation) in one work is designed to build toward a comprehensive approach out of specialized interventions that have preceded mine.

This project of exposing the fissures and irrationalities of liberal subjectivity that have been historically sutured or disguised by recourse to socially policed practices like clothing the body (among innumerable other coercive social norms) is undergirded by the insights, advances, and interventions of innumerable feminist, queer, and critical race interventions into identity politics. It respects and appreciates those thinkers and activists and seeks to contribute to the ethical project of extending human flourishing to all people through an approach that undercuts and questions the primacy of social identities, rather than emphasizing them. Gothic lolita might be one incipient method of reimagining what it can mean to inhabit subjectivities without being defined by them. Perhaps even the word "inhabit" might help articulate some of the options that are becoming more clearly available today through rethinkings and revisions of how social identities (like gender, sexuality, race, ethnicity, class, and so on) might performatively work. "Inhabit" evokes the notion of living within various social identities, without necessarily being inseparable or permanently subsumed within. Further, inhabit harbors the sartorially inflected word "habit" within it, which speaks to the possibility of performative instantiation of identity or subjectivity through repetition.

It might be helpful therefore to spend a bit of time articulating how the terms "identity" and "subjectivity" work in this book. Throughout this work I refer to identity, social identities, and subjectivity when referring to the embodied and performative discourses that have shaped global, but especially Western European notions of what a human being is: gender, race, ethnicity, sexuality, ability, class, age, and so on. These different identity categories function by differing mechanisms and yet all tend to be elided into notions of personal identity, especially by my nineteenth-century interlocutors. Nineteenth-century Anglophone writers used the term "race" promiscuously as a word to describe any category of human they perceived as naturally distinct, so that Eliza Lynn Linton could declare the Girl of the Period "a race of women as utterly unlike the old insular ideal as if we had created another nation altogether." This line exemplifies how poorly race and nation were articulated. Here race is elided with gender and nationality (while also contextually invoking class and age, since the Girl of the Period was a critique particularly aimed at middle- and upper-class young women—almost definitionally unmarried—who were perceived as insufficiently performing their proper station).

Although repeatedly mixed, muddled, and transposed, important to keep in mind is that these demographic categories play out differently and were differently understood. For example, we cannot speak of a "homosexual identity" in the case of Boulton and Park, because the possibility of such a notion was precisely the matter under debate as the jurors and press struggled to determine the meaning of the many gendered and potentially sexualized activities the defendants had undertaken. Conversely to today's twenty-first-century attitudes, social class was, in both Japan and the United Kingdom, conceived of as more essentially inborn. In a larger sense, of course, the Victorian era was one in which all such identity characteristics and their locations or origins as interior essences, inborn nature, or nurtured acquisition were subjects of fierce scientific debate in both Meiji Japan and Victorian Britain.

The fact that one word, identity, subsumes all these dynamics—identities' eclectic and varying modes of instantiation *and* the widespread assumption that these traits were inborn essences—are part of what makes this inquiry complex. But it also speaks to the importance of attempting to think them in concert. In his work on Tokugawa and Meiji Japan, David Howell succinctly articulates this problematic vagueness in the English term. In *Geographies of Identity* he describes "*identity* as a relational term, meaning a way of distinguishing among groups of people based on their place in political and social institutions. Therefore, when I speak of identity I am not referring primarily to individuals' self-perceptions, although I suppose that externally marked identities and individual subjects' sense of self frequently overlapped."[16] The book you are reading now is of course partially concerned with exactly the problem of how identities migrate from external to internal and back, drawing on various theories of gender, race, and sexuality to trace those peregrinations. I will very briefly trace a few of those inspirations here.

In a general sense for this book project, I suggest that clothing functions and has functioned as the intermediary margin where externally imposed notions of identity have met, mingled, and disputed with internally generated notions of identity. That English does not have satisfactory terminology to distinguish these two distinct (if hopelessly entangled) modes of articulating human identities speaks to the ideological power that notions of essential, inborn identity have historically held to efface and confuse any endeavor to articulate socially created and enforced demographic markers from individual bodies. As Judith Butler has argued extensively, the real trick of gender (read: and other personal identity markers) is to appear as if it emanates from within the individual when in fact it is imposed from without.

Of all the social identities I examine in this work, the fashion borderland is probably most thoroughly saturated with overlapping and intersecting concerns about sex and gender since roughly the end of the eighteenth century and the advent of "The Great Masculine Renunciation," when European men's fashion took a sharp turn away from conspicuousness toward dark, plain, understated, and slowly changing colors and silhouettes.[17] The magnitude of this gender bifurcation eclipsed the other major articulating functions of fashion, such as to distinguish class, nationality, and social position. Certainly, clothing by no means ever stopped also being a vehicle for the bearing (baring) of those other social identities (from both above and below—uniforms versus hanky codes); rather, we will see these different factors influenced and entangled with each other, and especially with gendered considerations, throughout this book. Moreover, fashion's privileged connection with femininity contributes to fashion's gender trouble. As we see in the Boulton and Park case and the Meiji makeover, men are certainly not outside of fashion in that they must wear clothes, and their clothing no less than women's has been subject to the dynamic of fashionable change. And yet men's fashionability has, especially since the Victorian era, been severely policed and consistently disavowed in order to remain masculine.[18]

Closely related, and explicitly overlapping in the Boulton and Park case, sexuality and especially homosexual or queer sexual identities are imbricated in clothing in different ways. Because deviant sexuality does not follow familial relations like race, ethnicity, and class, and may not carry as strong an association with visually confirmable bodily features as sex or gender do, the social "doings" of queer or homosexual bodies come to have greater relative import. In other words, nonnormative sexualities have a different relation to performed activities in the absence of other agreed upon modes of bodily identification. The Boulton and Park case encompasses a nascent endeavor to construct a workable fantasy of identification that could link erstwhile invisible nonnormative sexualities to tangible features, like clothing choice, gesture, and so on.[19] Remember by the mid-twentieth century in the US one common policing tactic of gay spaces was to confirm whether an apprehended individual was wearing at least three pieces of gendered clothing matching their assigned sex.[20]

This book is further based on insights from theories that recognize race as nonbiologically constituted.[21] In specifically discussing representations of Asian women (whom she calls "the yellow woman" in the book), Anne Anlin Cheng writes,

> If we are willing to confront the life of a subject who lives as an object, then we will arrive not at an easy politics, but rather at an alternative track within the making of modern Western personhood, one that is not traceable to the ideal of a biological, organized, and masculine body bequeathed from a long line of Enlightenment thinkers, but is instead peculiarly synthetic, aggregated, feminine, and non-European.[22]

Cheng's analytic of "ornamental" personhood adapts the exterior-identity thesis to an elucidation of specifically Asian minoritarian experience, a focus on visuality and surfaces shared by Christopher Bush in his article "The Ethnicity of Things in America's Lacquered Age."[23]

Race, ethnicity, and nationality interact with the expressive and representative functions of fashion in yet another way than gender or sexuality. During the age of imperialism, imposition of modest and rational dress reform on exotic colonized others was a preoccupation of many

Europeans, even as the Romantic era's preoccupation with nationalism had fueled taxonomic encyclopedias that sought to identify, preserve, or lament the inevitable obsolescence of distinctive national and ethnic dress habits. These irreconcilable attitudes toward dress were by no means new in the nineteenth century. Just as fashion products were already circulating by the Middle Ages, so were anxieties raised by fashion's promiscuous tendencies to transgress national boundaries and muddle individuals' clear membership in their nation. Fashion has long unsettled national boundaries—from the earliest periods of long-distance trade, items of adornment and materials (fabrics and dyes) for making clothing have traveled extensively, retaining flavors of their foreignness even while being incorporated into their destinations' cultures. Thomas Dekker captured fashion's treasonous tendencies in 1606:

> An English-mans suit is like a traitors bodie that hath beene hanged, drawne, and quartered, and set up in severall places: the collar of his doublet and belly in France; the wing and narrow sleeve in Italy; the short waist hangs over a Dutch botchers stall in Utrich; his huge sloppes speakes Spanish; Polonia gives him his bootes; the blocke for his head alters faster than the feltmaker can fit him.[24]

Dekker's satirical claim, that the multinational provenances of the Englishman's clothes (and his apish proclivity for copying others) performatively make the Englishman himself a traitor, were further borne out by commercial factors, such as protectionist biases against importing fabrics, dyes, and other products that allowed currency to flow out of the realm.[25] Simultaneously desirable and dangerous, Orientalist and exoticist tastes seem to be a constant (always with shifting content) in fashion, exemplary of fashion's propensity to inflame desires for the Other, ensnaring some in its penumbra, even as it terrifies others with its promise to decompose identity. While the connoted nationality of fashion is the primary point I later discuss in examining the "extreme Meiji makeover," specifically and especially regarding the nation's imbrication with inchoate notions of race, nationalist concerns regarding clothing and fashion crop up throughout this work. Eliza Lynn Linton echoes Dekker's performative thinking and nationalist protectionism in "The Girl of the Period" when she declares that in the past "English girls were content to be what God and nature had made them. Of late years we have changed the pattern, and have given to the world a race of women as utterly unlike the old insular ideal as if we had created another nation altogether."[26]

Age, and particularly youth, are recurring concerns in all my case studies, perhaps not surprising for a work that focuses on fashion, which in the twentieth and twenty-first century has spiraled into an ever-escalating obsession with youth.[27] Certainly, the liminal period of youth is crucial to the sense of heightened surveillance aimed at the Girl of the Period and Boulton and Park's activities, as well as gothic lolitas' adolescent waywardness. The invocation of youth worked at cross-purposes in various accounts to excuse Boulton and Park's behaviors as mere child's play or conversely by those who argued that bad behaviors among the young would have permanent effects unlikely among other less impressionable ages. The emperor Meiji was himself a teenager when he was restored to political power in Japan, although his makeover would require downplaying or compensating for his youth as the governmental elites sought to bolster Japan's global standing. Finally, with the invocation of "Lolita" in gothic lolita subcultural fashion, the original nymphet's trademark youth becomes a sartorial property, put on and off at will by aficionados of all ages (and genders, races, and sexualities).

Class and socioeconomic status might be the most slippery of social identity categories indexed (and elided) by fashion. Indeed, the most influential early theorists of fashion, like Georg Simmel and Thorstein Veblen, trenchantly demonstrated how the very engine and origin of the European fashion system is basically status differentiation. Veblen's 1899 book *The Theory of the Leisure Class* introduced the term "conspicuous consumption."[28] In his 1904 treatise, Simmel argues that fashion "is a product of class distinction," wherein the upper classes are imitated by the lower classes, and so to maintain their status distinction must endlessly reinnovate fashion to maintain their superior position in the cycle.[29] Obviously high fashion maintains such a relation to class today, even to a great extent unifying the global bourgeoisie, aristocracy, and plutocracies in a shared fashion culture that frequently seems to eclipse other specificities of national, ethnic, and religious identities (a state that might remind us of Dekker's traitorous Englishman of 1606). We will see class inflect the following case studies in various ways; certainly, the privilege of a higher-class status (both in Japan and Britain) insulates some fashion transgressions, but not all other identity factors can be trumped by class status.

Histories of all these different markers of identity have frequently converged on notions of invisibility, silence, or being hidden from history; the phrase "hidden from history" gave a title to both a major work of women's history authored by Sheila Rowbotham in the mid-1970s, alternately subtitled *300 Years of Women's Oppression and the Fight against It* and *Rediscovering Women in History from the Sixteenth Century to the Present*, and the monumental eponymous essay collection subtitled *Reclaiming the Gay and Lesbian Past*, edited by Martin Duberman, Martha Vicinus, and George Chauncey Jr. in 1990.[30] Meanwhile, Jennifer Helgren and Colleen Vasconcellos declare in the introduction to *Girlhood: A Global History*, "children as a rule are some of history's most silent subjects."[31] Hidden from history suggests a sort of historiographical "closeting," the willful or negligent blindness or malice of authorities, as well as a sort of historical treasure-hunt mentality.

Hidden, missing, silent, invisible. Thanks to works like those noted above, histories of marginalized groups no longer require justifications of their importance or legitimacy. In undertaking my own work, I am surely in some sense abusing the special valence of the closet for queer studies by invoking it in the title of this book with only one clearly, unequivocally "queer" chapter. But, as I note in that chapter, the closet isn't only where queers are. It's where you keep your clothes. The closet, as avid readers of earlier English literature (like Shakespeare and the King James Bible) know, was originally a small room in large houses, usually off a bedroom where people (with the means) went to be alone and stored their greatest treasures. The closet then serves as a spatial and domestic metaphor for the same activities and conundrums borne out by clothing. Or, put another way, clothing has served as a mobile, body-sized closet, even in excess of clothing and closets' association with each other. The silences described by historians of minoritized subjectivities in the foregoing paragraphs, particularly those regarding queerness or same-sex sexual practices, have a complex relation to representation, which is to say both clothing and history writing. The closet expressly refers to something present but hidden away (literally or metaphorically) from exterior representation, yet both in the reasonings of the queer and gay historians quoted above and in the *Queen v. Boulton and Park* case in the Court of Queen's Bench 1871, the invisibility of closeted behaviors or (possibly) people was being groped out, indexically identified by the presence of the absence indicated by disguise and dissimulation. Relying on the convergence of different minoritized groups in tropes of historical invisibility and hiddenness in conjunction with closets' association with clothes, I am stretching the valence of the closet in my title to speak to a variety of queered (askew, disjointed) relations to clothing and subjective (and subjunctive) self-presentation. As I disclaim multiple times over the course of this text, this is not to homogenize different forms of identity, and especially not to appropriate the specificities of queer theory for the purposes of other groups of people, but to highlight through close comparison the differences (and convergences) in historical trajectory, mainstream cognizance, and performative constitution in multiple aspects of subjectivity. My ultimate goal is to demonstrate the insufficiency of received notions of identity for all individuals through examination of multiple parties for whom the system was never designed in the first place.

This work is therefore part of the tradition of hidden from history narratives, rediscovering marginalized, new additions to history: women, queers, nonwhite people, youth. Many of my subjects held more than one of those distinctions. This is, in many ways, another story of resistances to the status quo and to hegemonic societies bent on bending individuals to a straightening/straitening will. But it is also, as I will emphasize many times, about people who were already at the center of the status quo. For one (not insignificant) thing, most of them held at least the trump card of relative financial security: middle-classness for Boulton, Park, and other Girls of the Period, as well as many gothic lolitas; and upper-class and even royal status for many of my Meiji interlocutors. While their implication in the clothing controversies I trace here certainly does render them in some ways at odds with the demands of their larger societies, I will be aiming here to limn not just what made these subjects stand out (certainly what drew me to these cases initially) but also to recognize how they were fully embedded in their societies as well—we will see how hegemonies contain and manage challenges to their ideologies not just through abjecting them, but also through recourse to the designation of the "not really," the "theatrical," the superficial, the silly, the mere. That is to say, one of the largely implicit conclusions of this book is that it is time to reexamine and reconfigure narratives of heroic resistance not only because resistance so often is co-opted into feeding the machine it pitched itself against but also because such models obscure some conclusions even as they illuminate others. "Resistance model" critiques of all four of my cases exist already[32]; my task now will be in letting them speak to each other, reembedded in their own milieux.

Further, all too rarely acknowledged are the myriad pleasures and desires fulfilled by personal embodiment or inhabitation of various identities. Nevertheless, this book does not and cannot refute the power of Butler's (and others') warnings that performativity is not a halfway measure to freedom from hegemonic and socially coerced norms of identity. Performativity is not a heroic narrative of individual resistance to the status quo. I am less concerned here with individuals' attempts to create fulfilling or pleasing individual selves (which I do not doubt many of my interlocutors aimed for, and which I do not begrudge them, even as we surely are in no position to evaluate their endeavors). Rather, I am looking to these moments of rupture, failure, and dissensus at the level where society and individual meet to extract ideas about how to better articulate both the strands of personal freedom and social coercive power that constitute modern [Western] notions of subjectivity.

Empire

Empire becomes a linking thread (if not chain) in my narrative, perhaps necessarily because I start in Great Britain—in London—the epicenter by 1868 and 1870, not only of cultural and popular life in England (obviously the primary milieu of the Girl of the Period, Boulton, and Park) but also of the economic-political-cultural vortex that was (and is) British imperialism. More to the point, imperialism is definitionally a link among my studies in Britain and Japan, because imperialism is about consolidating and amassing multiple distinct territories under a singular controlling entity, and British and other Euro-American imperialisms were precisely the major threats Japan was addressing with its Meiji-era policy of Bunmei Kaika. Less obvious, perhaps, has been the linkage of young British women and men like the Girl of the Period, Boulton, Park, and their associates to the workings of the imperial system, right at the center of which they lived. And yet, when put into words, is it not also an obvious connection, if more circumstantial and spatial than direct? The Girl of the Period, Boulton, Park, and their cohort lived right at the center of the largest empire the planet has yet known, just on the cusp of the decades that would bring it to its greatest extent before the two tumultuous decades that would (officially) end it; their fashionable doings and news or gossip thereof were enabled by the widening vectors of capitalism sustained and buoyed by imperial conquest.[33]

Boulton, Park, the Girl of the Period, and Meiji elites are thus embedded in networks of culture and capital that connected them even as many strains of that culture declared (and declare) them quite separate, quite different, incomparable. Moreover, fashion itself is more or less indebted to the rise of global capital and trade. In 2019 global fashion was a $406 billion industry and even in the medieval period, the values of luxury imports (silks, wools, and other fabrics, as well as metals and stones for decorations) were driving forces behind international trade. As Marxist historians like Fernand Braudel have demonstrated, the systems of distinction (especially class) that fashion feeds were major sources of the growth of capitalism and its attendant drive to connect more places into networks for extraction of resources, creation of goods, and consumption.[34] In part, we will be looking at these networks of material goods, the actual raw resources and finished garments that were made available to my different interlocutors on the currents of burgeoning imperial capital in the nineteenth century. But we will also be looking at the circulation of representations and ideas about clothes, which can often travel faster and mean differently than material garments.

Like fashion, like identity itself, "an empire is partly a fiction," writes Thomas Richards in the *Imperial Archive*: "no nation can close its hand around the world; the reach of any nation's empire always exceeds its final grasp. An empire is by definition and default a nation in overreach."[35] Richards goes on to describe immaterial modes of establishing empire through knowledge, or as he puts it, the archive, through the endless, exhausting, if never exhaustive, compilation of knowledge about a place: "The Victorian archive appears as a prototype for a global system of domination through circulation, an apparatus for controlling territory by producing, distributing, and consuming information about it."[36] Richards's notion of archive can also be understood as a performative operation; the information and knowledge representing subjected places and peoples collected into the imperial archive itself creates the colonial subjection of those peoples.[37]

This observation is particularly important for my work on Meiji Japan, because Japan does not appear on the map of British colonies or extraterritorial holdings at any point and yet in a very material sense had to spend decades scheming and negotiating its way back out from the same kinds of unequal treaties as China, including foreign concessions with extraterritorial authority within the territory of Japan. Thus, although not colonized per se, one useful way to understand Japan's "Civilization and Enlightenment" policy could be as an indigenous deployment of imperial archival strategies on behalf of the nation threatened with colonization rather than the colonizer. Where British and other colonizers both formally and indirectly employed geographers, archaeologists, engineers, linguists, historians, journalists, curators, archivists, and so on, to produce, collect, and organize knowledge about their colonies, the Meiji government actively hired those same experts to create and employ knowledges on behalf of a (re)nascent Japanese empire. Our non–Japanese-language primary sources today are often from this army of professional consultants (*oyatoi gaikokujin* 御雇い外国人, hereafter *yatoi*) to the Japanese, rather than from diplomats or expatriates.[38] People like Erwin Baelz, the German doctor who worked at the Tokyo Imperial University medical school for over twenty years and became physician to the imperial family; W. E. Griffis and Leroy Lansing Janes, both American Civil War veterans hired to run schools by the Matsudaira and Hosokawa clans, respectively;[39] Basil Hall Chamberlain, the first great British Japanologist who taught at the Imperial Japanese Naval Academy and later as professor of Japanese at Tokyo Imperial University; and hundreds more engineers, architects, academics, and scientists were employed by the Japanese government and large institutions, diverting some of the tide of information into the archives of Japan rather than those of the Western imperial powers.

In thinking about the entangled nature of this Meiji interchange, I will spare a moment to discuss the primacy of the term "Victorian" in this book. For better or for worse, Victorian is a term I use repeatedly here, especially to describe the two British case studies, which of course took place in the middle of Queen Victoria's reign. Victoria's reign technically lasted from 1837 to 1901, the longest reign of any monarch of Great Britain until Queen Elizabeth II surpassed her 63.5-year record in 2015. Victorians already thought of themselves as Victorians during their own time.[40] High on their imperial and economic supremacy and the thrills of industrial revolution and mass modernization, "Victorian" took on valences in excess of just describing the British subjects of a diminutive but very long-lived monarch. Some of the additional connotations included imperial might, technological modernity, global mindedness, commercial proliferation, and social awareness. In the subsequent era(s) of modernity, "Victorian" has come to precisely connote conservatism, backwardness, and outmodedness. As is probably an inescapable oscillating dynamic within a paradigm of onward marching time, the Victorians who knew themselves to be at the leading edge of modern technology, politics, and economics have now, inevitably, been recoded by their own temporal logics as backward, conservative, old-fashioned, and superseded. Moreover, the moniker "Victorian," at least in Anglophone cultures, has further acquired a far more global sense of "nineteenth-century-ness" than precisely connoting British or Englishness. Maybe this is related to the twenty-first-century supremacy of the English language and therefore the outsized role that Anglophone culture encompasses within its penumbra as well as the nineteenth- and twentieth-century global dominance and influence of the British Empire across the planet.[41] Dallas Finn, writing on the architectural legacy of the Meiji era, expressly chose to subtitle his book *The Sites of Victorian Japan*. Finn explains,

> "Victorian Japan" is a convenient rather than strictly accurate way to describe the period when Japan turned deliberately to the West and within a generation successfully adopted many of its institutions, from railroads to string quartets, political parties to kindergartens, dynamos to battleships . . . Strict chronology and geography aside, the Japanese scene was palpably Victorian. Like the queen, Emperor Meiji belonged to the progressive mainstream of the nineteenth century and presided over an era so eventful that when he died his subjects felt a personal sense of grief and identification.[42]

I do not follow Finn in employing this convenient elision; I try to primarily stick with "Meiji" for Japan—a term for which a cosmopolitan student of world history should eventually assemble as thick a sense of meaning as Victorian has accrued. (With a healthy sense of the necessity of decentering the West in our historiographical thinking, we could even momentarily indulge the thought experiment of considering the last half of Britain's nineteenth century as a Meiji Britain.) But Meiji and Victorian nevertheless do not occupy a precise national equivalency because Japan's Meiji was deeply indebted to global Victorian culture and politics (among other Euro-American influences), while Meiji Japan was only one of many innumerable national influences on Victorian Britain. In the sense that Meiji Japan purposefully adopted and domesticated many ideas from Victorian Britain, including notions of teleological modern progress and even (eventually) a sense of superiority over other colonizable neighbors, a discussion of Meiji Japan does fit comfortably in a book also about (British) Victorians' debates about their own identity status. Further, my closing analysis retroactively reemphasizes fashion's inherent transnationalisms and cosmopolitanisms in examining the gothic lolita fashion phenomenon, a subcultural fashion that coalesced in Japan around the turn of the twenty-first century and which is typically described as featuring Victorian-style dresses and accessories. The appellation "Victorian" in the case of Japanese youth fashion speaks to how the modifier "Victorian" in global popular culture has escaped any narrow historiographical bound of referring to nineteenth-century Britain and now often describes a Euro-American (i.e., Western) nineteenth century and all our general ideas about culture, material culture, and attitude from that era. After all, the inherent internationalism of high fashion from the very moment of my three nineteenth-century case studies confirms that any Western fashion aesthetic already largely exceeds national boundaries.[43]

At this level of circulating imperial knowledge I see my nineteenth-century interlocutors most closely intertwined in negotiating both overarching discourses of European cultural supremacy (and the anxieties such a discourse engendered) and their material manifestation and regulation through quotidian rules of sartorial presentation. In my different contexts these ideologies may have worked sometimes at cross-purposes, but they are the same discourses, materialized in clothes, dissolved in entertainment and periodical chatter, debated by governments and proxy governments like heads of households and arbiters of taste. These circulating discourses were and are—like clothes—ubiquitous.

These cases not only come one from the distant margin and two from the pulsating center of nineteenth-century global imperialism but also deal primarily with disparate discourses: gender (Girl of the Period), sexuality (Boulton and Park), and race (Meiji). Moreover, the Girl of the Period; Boulton, Park, and confederates; and the Japanese people required different methodologies and approaches. The Girl of the Period was primarily a type or even a stereotype, existing as much or more in representation than in real life. By contrast, Boulton, Park, Lord Arthur Clinton, Louis Charles Hurt, John Safford Fiske, and the rest of the men caught up in the Boulton and Park cross-dressing scandal were very much flesh-and-blood individuals, whose symbolic meaning for the larger British society was hotly debated. My treatment of Meiji Japan necessarily reverts back to many collective observations and notions of national subjects in the abstract and plural. When individuals appear in my Meiji archive, they tend to be overdetermined ones like the emperor and empress, always burdened with at least two bodies—their own and the state's.[44] I am not attempting causal histories of these different controversies happening at different scales in different locations, but rather relying on the constant of the clothes themselves and the uncanny recurrence of the same anxieties about fashion, truth, and theatricality to let them speak to each other.

Clothes, like the bodies they fix within discourse, oscillate between meaning and materiality, between spectacularity (to-be-seen-ness) and functionality.[45] Most importantly, as I will return to again and again throughout, fashion and clothing are imbued with theatricality's uncertain, flickering relation to truth value, in part because they circulate both as images and as material things, but also because both material clothes and their representations are stained by societal anxieties about deception and individuals' failure—or refusal—to present various socially coerced identity characteristics at the level of the body. Through looking at these topics from the perspective of performance studies, I not only elucidate how anxieties over theatricality in everyday life motivated my nineteenth-century interlocutors but also how antitheatrical biases have limited other historical accounts.

Terminology

A wealth of terminology is available to describe the articles humans employ to cover, protect, and decorate their bodies, like clothing, clothes, style, dress, habit, apparel, and fashion. Although these words are frequently used interchangeably, throughout this work I will attempt to use different terms with a precision not often employed in colloquial usage, while also paying critical attention to the nuances and implications of these words' rich and ambiguous definitions and the ways in which these terms are so often interchanged. I will use the words *clothing*, *garment*, and *dress* to refer in the most general sense to the fabric things humans wear on their bodies. Habit, although rarely appearing in my sources, is a term that speaks evocatively to the repetitive, performance repertoire aspect of clothing.

Costume, on the other hand, does appear provocatively throughout this book. The meanings of the word costume have shifted since the Victorian era. Today costume tends to refer specifically to clothing donned expressly to appear as someone or something else and generally with the expectation that the costume not fully efface the wearer's true identity. A costume usually performs two identities at once: the true identity of the individual and the assumed one. But in the nineteenth century the word was used in many more situations. For instance, women's fashion magazines referred to their illustrated ensembles as costumes dedicated to certain activities or occasions, such as "walking costumes" or "morning costumes." We also see costume used in today's contemporary sense, although at least in the 1860s and 1870s this seems to have been the rarer usage. (In my British sources, the term "get up," "getup," or "get-up" appeared frequently where today we would say "costume.") A third definition of costume common in the nineteenth century is retained today as national, traditional, or folk costume. A folk costume is neither an individualized fashionable ensemble with a designated occasion nor a duplicitous representation.

National costume suggests a presumed stability over time with, like in a costume in the sense of open disguise, a regularized semiotic meaning: member of a specific cultural group or nation. Simultaneously, as in the fashion magazines' use of costume, traditional costume retains a sense of truthfulness or accuracy in representation. National costume—itself largely a Romantic-era fabrication[46]—helps to elucidate the instability of costume as a semiotic device. On, for example, an Italian peasant, "Italian folk costume" is perceived as natural, a truthful, essentialist expression of identity. But on Nora of Henrik Ibsen's *A Doll's House*, Italian folk costume comprises a costume in the sense of a get up.[47] Costume's oscillating relation to truth value will make it an important term in my analyses, and we will also see how the multiplicity of definitions it denoted and continues to denote significantly complicates attempts to settle wayward clothing practices into recognizable, acceptable modes.

The word *fashion* is the most complicated of all these terms. It is often used to describe any and all clothing, but at the same time denotes a specific system of constantly changing clothing forms, tied particularly to the rise of mercantilism and capitalism since the Middle Ages, as well as the industrial manufacturing technologies of the Industrial Revolution.[48] Moreover, the constant change associated with fashion is not rational or logical. Theorists stress that fashions seem to change for their own sake, for the sake of newness.[49] This dynamism tethers fashion to modernity's emphasis on reflexivity, progress, change, and the new, while also confounding modernity's desire for logic and clear truth value to its progress narrative. Indeed, sartorial fashion progress is also defiantly postmodern, in the sense that it is irrational and unpredictable, and composed of pastiche; it decontextualizes the past, untethers signifiers, and constantly returns and revises forms and ideas.[50] This (i.e., the theatricality of fashion), I suspect, is what causes much of the post-Enlightenment disdain for (or, to add a heavier valence, paranoia about) fashion as unreliable and superficial, unbounded by truth systems.

Although general usage privileges the sartorial connotation, fashion also functions as a more general term that describes any practices particularly notable for shifting and changing over time (usually rapidly and/or without clear rational causes). Further, the verb "to fashion" also suggests a creative power: "to give a particular form or shape to," "to make," as the dictionary puts it.[51] This verb definition resonates especially with my focus in this project: I argue that clothing fashions bodies and subjects, rendering them legible or illegible, acceptable or unacceptable, within a society's given discursive limits. When we talk about clothing and fashion we are talking about the body, and further, when we talk about the body, to a large extent we are also talking about clothing, which is thoroughly imbricated with physical flesh. In many ways clothing is the location of material discourse—the place where physical bodies and discursive knowledges and ideological injunctions meet and work on each other. I turn now to a discussion of how basic performance theories can help us understand how clothing does that ideological and discursive work on bodies.

Performance Theories of Clothing and Fashion

It is a truism of writers on fashion to declare fashion a performance, performative, or even performance art,[52] but these declarations are rarely if ever using performance as a word with its own complications. It is my contention too that fashion and performance have much in common and considering fashion and clothing within the paradigm of performance will yield many insights, but what does it mean to declare fashion a kind of performance? Certainly, it recognizes that clothes mean in relation to what is done with them. In the case of clothing, "what is done with them" almost invariably entails what bodies do in close conjunction with clothes. (On the rare occasions when clothes can't be worn, as in certain art projects perhaps, they still bear an indexical relation to bodies.) Fashion performance also suggests a sense of to-be-seen-ness, a sense of two parties' communication: a wearing message-sender and a seeing message-receiver or interpreter. Communication between a wearer and a see-er entails fashion's semiotic potential, a formula exploited by generations of fashion magazines as well as Roland Barthes and mass-market nonfiction like *The Language of Clothes* by Alison Lurie. But performance as presentation also can encompass the possibility of fakery, of false messaging, of what I will be calling "theatricality." By this I emphatically don't mean that theatricality is synonymous with falsity, but that it connotes a floating free of the signifier from the designation of true or false—a certain semiotic agnosticism. Fashion's theatricality (which is to say its nonattachment to true or false valences) is its source of pleasure and artistry even as it has also aroused strong moral condemnation. History is rife with antifashion polemics, often explicitly connected with femininity, from ancient Greece and Rome, through Jewish and Christian writings and commentary and works like Thomas Carlyle's *Sartor Resartus* (1833–34), through to contemporary works like Lars Svendsen's 2007 antifashion polemic *Fashion: A Philosophy*, which attributed to fashion nothing less than the dissolution of personal identity (if only!).[53] Some of these polemics presume that vanity distracts from or comes to replace better uses of time and wealth, whereas others betray an anxiety about the role clothing plays in the fixing of identity—for instance complaints about people dissembling their sex, class, age, or status. Still others fault fashion on aesthetic grounds (that it is ugly or causes people to look ugly) or dismiss fashion as crassly commercial and meaningless beyond its role in perpetuating circulation of capital. Many of these criticisms hinge on the apprehension of fashion as inherently irrational, changing without logical impetus, and therefore anathema to a societal structure that thinks of itself as rational and privileges structures and practices which justify themselves in such terms. In fact, the word "vanity"—to be preoccupied with one's own appearance—itself is derived from the Latin root "vanus" meaning empty. Garments are after all literally surfaces without depth, meant to be filled repeatedly by bodies, sometimes the same body, sometimes a different one. "God hath given you one face and you make yourselves another one," a "mad" Hamlet rants to Ophelia, neatly encapsulating the collapse between a Platonic suspicion of the truth value of surfaces and a Christian recapitulation of "God-given" nature over artifice all in a misogynist vein, even as he himself is feigning his disturbed mental state, possibly until the point that he becomes truly mad (*Hamlet* 3.1.131–32). Hamlet accuses another of blasphemous dissemblance when it is his "antick fashion" that may turn out to be performative, pitching not only himself but also Ophelia into madness.

My position in this book will be that theatricality is a discursive category that encompasses and exceeds performativity, functioning at the same sprawling and incoherent level as "performance." Performance and theatricality connote both truth in the sense of a mimetic representation and also falsity in usages that apprehend some representations as inventions unattached to referents. I associate theatricality with representation and creation in distinct ways—as a to-be-seen-ness that has historically attracted anxiety and derision on one hand, but also been understood as generative on the other. Even within the paradigm of Butlerian performativity, theatricality could usefully be seen as a descriptor of the "fictive norms" that come to wield the force of truth.

The ways fashion can materialize fictive norms of identity (precisely through its emptiness and its detachability from the body) mean it is equally capable of materializing other fictive norms; fashion has been absolutely indispensable to modes of fixing performative identities and, by precisely the same means that is has done so, it is capable of undoing those identities. Grasping this twinned promise and threat is key to understanding the paranoia displayed by the subjects in my studies. Many historians have expressed bewilderment at the frenzy such superficialities excited in the Victorians, but by carefully considering these events in light of clothing's ambiguous position and theatrical-performative capacity to settle or unsettle hegemonic ideals, I believe we can better understand what was so scary about the fashion controversies I trace here. In the following case studies, the individuals who weighed in on these clothing controversies repeatedly did so in terms that sought to reconcile the meaning of clothing acts or performances through recourse to a binary spectrum of true or accurate representations and performativity on one end, and assertions about acting, theater, joking, costume, vanity, disguise, fraud, (mindless or animal) mimicry, and mere appearances on the other. We will see through comparison that assertions of mere theatricality and of authentic truth were used as strategies on both sides of fashion controversies: both to shore up the hegemonic powers that sought to stop gender, sexual, raced, and classed clothing deviance and by those who sought to evade or alter social strictures and potentially rewrite the codes of subjectivity through what Judith Butler has called "a different sort of repeating."[54] Therefore, although this text recognizes multiple recurring binaries and prefers a focus on theatricality, it does not present it as an ethically exemplary term; this is not a book that reclaims theatricality from generations of the "antitheatrical prejudice," but rather we will see that the very ability to declare an act or an outfit or a person either theatrical *or* authentic is a function of power, albeit one that individuals were occasionally able to wield against larger systems of control and coercion.[55]

To recap and clarify what I've said so far: I want to highlight the centrality of a dynamic I call theatricality to the performance of clothing and fashion and clothing and fashion's centrality to the processes of human subject formation, especially but not exclusively in modern societies. Two major aspects of this argument rely on understanding clothing as accomplishing an action and clothing as a visual sign shared between a sender and a receiver. I associate the former with clothing's performative potential and the latter with clothing's semiotic potential. Importantly, I am not suggesting that these three categories (performative, semiotic, and theatrical) are equivalents, but that they constitute three different registers by which we might analyze clothing performance. Yet, because all three (and surely more) are in play at any given time, we see misunderstandings or controversies arise as subjects struggle to reconcile the irreconcilable multivalence of clothing (for example) both enjoined to truthfully express aspects of identity such as class, gender, and profession and simultaneously pitched toward fashionable display of novelty untethered to truth value. The remainder of this section will work through these three modes of understanding fashion and clothing within the paradigm of performance studies.

Performativity

Mundane, repetitive, and compulsory yet constantly varied and more or less aesthetic and artistic, transhistorically universal and simultaneously hyperlocalized, even individualized, clothing is emblematic of quotidian performance and performativity: clothing is a primary way of doing one's body. People have been getting dressed for millennia; as I mentioned earlier, in both mythology and anthropology the act of clothing or embellishing the body has been identified as a primary distinguisher between animals and humans. That is, clothing has long been understood as a foundational performative act that makes humans out of animals. Clothing has further been called on to establish various bodily truths of identity, such as status, class, position, gender, occupation, sexuality, race, nationality, religion, and age. This is more than a semiotic function (which I will return to later). For example, a coronation is an act of investiture that makes the clothing action of putting on a crown into the performative act of turning a person into a monarch: "Clothing in or enduement with attributes or qualities; establishment in any state of privilege or honour," as the *Oxford English Dictionary* puts it.[56] To "invest" means etymologically to put something on like a garment, but it is simultaneously to make a change in a person's status: "To clothe *with* or *in* the insignia of an office; hence, *with* the dignity itself; to install *in* an office or rank with the customary rites or ceremonies."[57] Ann Jones and Peter Stallybrass seize on a line from Prince Hal in *Henry IV, Part 2* to argue that clothing can be "*deeply* put on" in a manner that performatively instantiates various identity properties.[58] Following then the etymology of investiture and the reasoning of Jones and Stallybrass, we see that clothing can carry out an action—making an animal into a human, making a man into a king, making a PhD candidate into a doctor—as a performative, all of course depending on the felicitous conditions that must obtain for the performative to occur.[59]

The nineteenth-century clothing performatives I am particularly interested in here function as means of realizing "fantasies of identification"—a phrase coined by Ellen Samuels to name the imaginative strategies employed by societies increasingly anxious about properly categorizing and controlling bodies (i.e., subjects). Samuels explains, "these *fantasies of identification* seek to definitively identify bodies, to place them in categories delineated by race, gender, or ability states, and then to validate that placement through a verifiable, biological mark of identity."[60] Samuels's work demonstrates the decidedly imaginary bases of these insistences that essential identities were (or are) locatable and perceptible somewhere on or in the body (fingerprints, blood, DNA, etc.). Meanwhile, I examine the ways in which clothing—beyond the boundary of the body (indeed often binarily opposed to it)—nevertheless through its inextricable proximity to the body comes to function supplementally in the Derridean sense to fix those fantasies of identity. Since clothing comes to be an immediate and primary means of identifying bodies, it becomes a locus of many of these fantasies of identification, particularly for gender, class, sexuality, race, nationality, and modernity. Clothing thus becomes highly overdetermined, both body and NOT body, obviously detachable, liable to individual manipulation but so heavily relied on to guarantee fantasies of identification that insistence on its indexical value is not easily relinquished, even, in cases we'll see here, to the point of letting deviant behavior go rather than recognize its threat to the fantasized bond between clothing and identity.

Judith Butler's canon on gender performativity provides theoretical explication for the ways in which repetitive bodily actions provide the sense of reality to fantasies of identification (particularly, of course, gender). Butler builds on J. L. Austin's notions of linguistic performativity but broadens Austin's scope (tellingly titled *How to Do Things with Words*) beyond the linguistic to encompass a range of activities that can all function like a speech act to affect something (gender). If, as Butler writes, "the body is only known through its gendered appearance," that gendered appearance and thus that body is, I contend, known primarily through its clothes.[61] Clothes are the things that render the body socially legible and that have historically domesticated an infinite variety of bodies into one of two categories: female and male.[62] Clothing is emblematic of gender identity's "stylized repetition of acts": this is in part because clothing covers the greatest proportion of the individual body in public space, forming the largest canvas for, as discussed above, gendered display.[63] In the cases that follow, I contend that the clothes my subjects wore or talked about wearing really did have a strong performative effect on the ways gender, race, class, and other aspects of social identity were materialized. I am contending that the apparently superficial—the theatrical—shapes and reshapes the real.

Further, understanding gender and other social identities as performatively instantiated through dress (as well as other repeated acts) inherently presupposes identity as a social construction created through ideology, so that within the notion of performativity as a stylized repetition of acts there is already a paradoxical dual valence to the root notion of performance as simultaneously true and false, both the accomplishment of something real (or perhaps more specifically the creation of the real) as well as "theatrical" as something "for show," "mere performance/appearance," etc. Or perhaps more to the point, in Butler's and Austin's performativity, the theatrical appearance precedes and instantiates the authentic or real. We will see this unresolved incoherence in the function and performative injunction of fashion playing out in the following cases. The moments of rupture that I discuss here allow us to trace the ways in which Victorian British and Meiji Japanese subjects themselves negotiated the breakdown of identity's illusions of naturalness (fantasies of identification). This is not to say that the subjects I examine here were any less natural than other fashion iterations (shall we say "fashion statements"?) that did not elicit comment, but rather that they helped draw attention to how no clothed body can be considered natural or naturally proper. While obviously a precise idea of gender as a performative illusion of essence did not exist in the 1860s and 1870s, multiple moments reveal interlocutors dealing with just those issues. Applying a performance studies paradigm to the concerns documented in my case studies helps to elucidate the stakes of these controversies for those involved in them (as well as for us as future historians).

Fashion and clothing may at first also appear to fall into the trap of so many successors to Butler's theory of assuming that performativity means that individual subjects' free choice of different clothes solves the problem of gender's (and, I will contend, additional identities') immaterial tyranny. But the details of the studies to follow will corroborate the insufficiency of conceiving performativity as a matter of free individual choice. Kendall Gerdes reminds us in a keywords entry on "Performativity," "*Gender Trouble* braids speech act theory's insight into the scandalous power of language to posit what it describes together with strands of Lacanian psychoanalysis and poststructuralism that show that this positing power belongs to language, to 'discourse' in a Foucauldian register, and precisely *not* to the authority of the intending subject employing language that Austin started with."[64]

Performativity does not mean that gender (as well as other performative identity expressions) is a matter of free choice. Indeed, the term "subject" helps to capture these two simultaneous vectors: the performer is both subject to external strictures and a nominally autonomous subject who chooses her actions within that limited field. Butler's model of socially limited individual performance is amply demonstrated by the paradox of fashion: fashion appears to offer a nearly limitless panoply of options to individuals new each season, and yet has historically bristled with restrictions, including gendered rules, as well as race, class, ethnic, religious, and even temporal and seasonal rules of taste and social nicety.[65] We will see as we proceed how the intentions of those who wore the clothes that sparked the controversies I follow do not at all affect the outcomes of their cases; they are subjects who certainly made choices, who certainly did practice "a different sort of repeating," but who did not necessarily effect any change at all in the way they were perceived by those around them or the structures of power who sought to stop their deviant activities, at least in the short term.

Butler writes, "the formulation of the body as a mode of dramatizing or enacting possibilities offers a way to understand how a cultural convention is embodied and enacted."[66] Where Butler writes "the body as a mode of dramatizing or enacting possibilities," I suggest we think of the body as a mode of dramatizing *and* enacting possibilities, by which I mean that the stylizing of the body (such as with clothing) simultaneously semiotically represents and performatively fixes the possibilities of gender, sexuality, class, nation, race, and status. These two dynamics (of performativity and representation) are thoroughly mystified and elided with each other in my case studies.

Semiotics

In an opening gambit that ties theatricality to semiotics, Tracy Davis and Thomas Postlewait rhetorically note, theatricality "is a sign empty of meaning; it is the meaning of all signs."[67] Thinking of clothing as performative is not the same as thinking of clothing as semiotic or communicative, but clothing is also popularly interpreted semiotically. We read clothes all the time to make judgments about the bodies wearing them: "Long before I am near enough to talk to you on the street, in a meeting, or at a party, you announce your sex, age and class to me through what you are wearing—and very possibly give me important information (or misinformation) as to your occupation, origin, personality, opinions, tastes, sexual desires and current mood," declared Alison Lurie in 1981.[68] For the most part, Lurie is discussing clothing as a reliable and accurate language, but even on this first page, she parenthetically identifies the possibility of deception or miscommunication. After all, a black bow tie in a tuxedo outfit could be either a red-carpet partygoer or a waiter.

Clothing would not be nearly so difficult to comprehend if it didn't partake of the fashion system—another simultaneous signification scheme that is precisely not about truthfulness but about artistry, capitalism, pleasure, rapid irrational change, and bodily decoration. Any garment (and the body encased in it) is participating in at least two semiotic systems: one is aligned with clothing's performative potential that may or may not be truthfully communicating facts about an individual's identity, while simultaneously the garment and its wearer are participating in an artistic fashionable communication.[69] Even when an outfit is pitched against fashion (say, uniforms, 2010s "normcore," grandparents' clothes, ensembles of the indigent), it may be read through the fashion system anyway.

Fashion semiosis may or may not beautify (generations of antifashion polemicists agree it doesn't), but it does induct bodies, especially women's bodies, into a visual schema for consumption as an object in addition to potentially being apprehended as a human subject. Fashion evokes ideas in excess of the social identities of the body wearing it. Fashion voraciously appropriates and restages signifiers from across time, space, and fantasy. As much as a fashionable military style jacket, for example, is supposed to continue signifying militarism, power, and discipline after it appears on the runway and in the department store, it is also supposed to signify as just fashion and just beauty. To use an example from my case studies, the fashionable Girl of the Period featured an amalgam of the "Grecian bend" silhouette corset, pannier-shaped skirts revived from the Georgian period, coats and jackets adorned with braid detailing borrowed from European military uniforms, and fabrics and patterns borrowed from the perennially fascinating "Orient." A fashionable outfit in 1868 thus evoked all these images and their attendant associations, and yet the primary message was declared to mean only novelty, modern social currency (meaning up-to-dateness but also spending power), and visual piquancy.

The adamant superficiality of fashion that empties signifiers to repurpose them for newness and fascination and (sometimes) beauty, while retaining echoes of the signifieds from which the signifiers have been blithely (semi) detached, amply illustrates one way fashion constitutes a (theatrical) performance in excess of its performative potential—a fashionable outfit is quintessentially "not me, but not *not* me" in Richard Schechner's famous phrase.[70] Thus not only is clothing called on to semiotically express (or create) certain attributes of the individual wearing it, especially in the case of uniforms and other socially determined nonfashion clothes, but fashion is rich with semiattached signifiers that wearers and designers use artistically to create moods, affect, beauty, and political commentary. For example, fashion magazines frequently attach a style, say military cuts and colors, to a current social mood, such as somber resignation to a grim world-financial outlook. Fashion historians indulge in the same explanations linking silhouettes to historical events. For instance, the Christian Dior New Look, which required yards of fabric to create exaggerated feminine shapes, is often deemed a sign of the exuberance following the conclusion of World War II and women's redomestication after a period of relative freedom during wartime upheaval.[71] But these explanations are consistently lacking, frequently only attributable after the fact, and ingenuously totalizing. Historians can easily use hindsight to retrospectively semioticize their foregone conclusions. Other scholars argue that the only real pattern of fashion is change. If skirts were narrow in the early 1940s, they will billow in the late 1940s. If the miniskirt arrives in the 1960s, the maxiskirt will reemerge in the 1970s.[72] The changes of fashion indeed consistently elude rational explanation, making it both intensely pleasurable and seductive, and simultaneously threatening to the rational ordering of society.

Clearly the dynamic of constant irrational change (that is to say, *fashion*) is not confined to clothing, but rules all sorts of venues of design and commodity, literature and representation, and of course thought and theory. And yet clothing has become the example of fashion par excellence to such a great extent that the word "fashion" now refers first and foremost to clothing. One factor that may contribute to clothing's peculiar status with regard to the fashion dynamic is its reputation for detachment from message-bearing capacity. Clothing is generally thought to be without particular import as a symbol, but utilitarian first and foremost (therefore, it doesn't matter if the nominal symbolic message changes rapidly and irrationally). In contrast, literature, art, narrative, politics, and academic theory, while they may indeed in the end obey the rule of fashion, present themselves as much more carefully rationalized in their changes. In other words, it is clothing's reputation as already inconsequential or superficial that makes it particularly amenable to primary association with fashion. This reasoning does not necessarily explain why other sorts of aesthetic design practices (art, but especially architecture, interior design, and quotidian material culture) are less immediately associated with fashion. I suspect that clothing's imbrication with the transience of the body has helped to foster the association of clothing and fashion. In the Christian and Enlightenment context of privileging perceived immutability over mutability, the body, and the body's obvious mutability, ensures the debauched position of body, change, clothing, and fashion. Meanwhile, many of art and architecture's classic acts of self-legitimation have precisely discounted relation to the bodily and posed themselves as detached, intellectual, immutable, auratic.[73] It is much harder to deem a garment, its purpose contingent on being filled by a body, a work of self-contained rational intellectual achievement. What emerges here is a general association of transience, irrationality, and superficiality with the body (in the Cartesian sense of mind versus body), body with clothing, clothing with fashion, and fashion with transience, irrationality, and superficiality. Needless to say, all these things also have tended to share an association with the feminine or effeminate.

In fashion, as in performance, such a detachment and rearrangement of signifiers is not precisely untruthful, but anxieties prompted by both activities do tend to arise from the ways these signifiers are allowed to float free of discrete true essences. In the remainder of this work, we will see that the controversies I trace are often about the slippage between these two formulations of representation: semiotic representation of fantasies of identity one the one hand, and theatrical or aesthetic free-floating representation on the other. Inchoate and incompatible yet simultaneous and urgent demands were (and are) placed on clothing and fashion to truthfully express identity (deemed true both by society and by the individual wearing the clothes), to dissemble bodily contours, and to display beauty, artistry, or pleasure. In articulating the difficulty, not to say impossibility, of fulfilling all these requirements, we are able to piece apart at the seams the way fashion and performance of fashion manufactures the appearance of indivisibility, naturalness, self-sameness, and subjectivity and identity. All fashionable representation is further shot through with the (usually) inchoate, implicit suspicion that representation can and does slide into performative change. Thus, we should avoid dismissing theatrical representations as mere entertainment and accounts that relegate clothing to mere appearance. Though such analyses may recognize clothing's capacity to index real forces they often overlook clothing's potential for itself exerting force. Indeed, in this book I argue that some of the subversive or resistant or otherwise notably efficacious qualities of performance obtain precisely within the fictive, the mere of representation, where the representation can be decisively identified as for show and not for real.[74]

Theatricality

In this book I contend that theatricality is the term that can comprehend both the truths and falsities of representation. My fundamental working definition of theatricality will thus be *appearances (or representations) that float free of definite true or false value*. Theatricality, in my reasoning here, is a way to describe the base function of representation—representation itself partaking of the complex and undecidable processes of mimesis and semiosis—the substitution of one thing standing in for another, which might be invisible or otherwise ungraspable without representation.[75] Theatricality also comprehends *mis*representation or appearance without substance, but may just as equally indicate the necessity of some kind of work of representation to cause some invisible fact to appear (be represented). Theatricality describes the way fashion signifies: multiply and unreliably, with some signs meant to be believed and others meant to be appreciated without belief in their veracious attachment to some signified idea or state. Theatricality thus names a nebulous and sometimes disturbing dynamic that humans live with all the time: the fact that some representations are meant to be taken as truthful and others as just appearance; that some appearances are duplicitous or false, whereas others are necessary transmutations of otherwise imperceptible and incommunicable ideas; that appearances can also float free of individuals' intentions toward truth or fiction; and that pleasure, desire, and anxiety accrue to the experience of living within the uncertainty of appearances. In my usage then, theatricality is a dynamic that invokes theater's fundamental practice of substitution or representation but does not necessarily refer to the established tradition of theater itself. Indeed, the established rules of the cultural practice of theater ensure that confusions or suspicions about which representations are really true or really meant are largely already settled inside the theater. Kirk Williams goes so far as to say, "anti-theatricality is ultimately not about the theatre and always about something else: the stage is inevitably a mere symptom for some other, less effable social or metaphysical malady."[76]

Williams's provocative use of mere—not appended to stage art itself, but to its representational function relational to (presumably) real life—provokes me to again reiterate a key characteristic of theatricality underwriting much of the analysis across this book: that the mereness of theatricality, which I elsewhere call frivolity, superficiality, or emptiness, is one of its most important and pervasive valences. Theatricality's emptiness or superficiality is frequently comprehended as insufficiency—comprising only half of a surface-depth binary. As I will explore, theatricality's persistent association with insufficiency is a particularly Western cultural problem. Curiously, the opposite half of the binary, depth, has no such association with lack when encountered on its own; sometimes it is even construed as more important for its invisibility, a half-standing-for-the-whole metonymic importance that can be positive (as in a kernel of true identity or character) or negative (as in the modern era's exploitation of inborn homosexual tendency as "*the* secret"[77]). Finally, this frivolity, superficiality, and mereness is also bound up with femininity, as we will see throughout—and the femininity (or effeminacy) of theatricality will adhere not only to female bodies.

It might be salient that the word "theatricality" was coined in 1837—the same year that Queen Victoria ascended the British throne, commencing the Victorian era—by Thomas Carlyle in his history of the French Revolution: "By act and word he strives to do it; with sincerity, if possible; failing that, with theatricality."[78] This inaugural usage is one that immediately speaks to theatricality's problem with authenticity—posed in opposition to "sincerity" and yet still in concert with "act and word." Other variations on the word are much older however: the first appearance of theatrical in the *Oxford English Dictionary* is from 1558. In a coincidence I can barely believe, this is of course the year that Queen Elizabeth I took the throne, although her formal coronation events did not take place until January 15, 1559. While it would be easy to make too much of such deliciously theatrical coincidences in theatricality's own etymological history, at the very least, I take inspiration from these dates to hope that something could be made of the coincidence of feminine political power, British cultural transcendence, and matters of representation, appearance, and truth as mediated by the notion of theater and theatricality.

Working among these historical accounts and especially with fashion, I recognize theatricality, or more precisely anxieties or disputes about theatrical dynamics in everyday life, as deriving from appearances and representations' detachment from, or uncertain attachment to, truth and identity. My attempt to tie this term, via fashion, to issues of nineteenth- and twenty-first-century subjectivity is related to other critical turns toward "surface studies" and Austinian and especially post-Butlerian understandings of gender and other subjective performativities built from queer, feminist, and critical race theories.[79] It is my hope that this book can help bring a theater and performance studies perspective to the debates on theatricality, authenticity, and the performative that have raged in other academic fields, as well.

We've seen so far how complex and contradictory are the demands placed on clothing. It is called on to truthfully express (or better: fix, meaning both repair and stabilize or freeze in place) an individual's identity (in demographic terms of sex, age, economic and social status, or aesthetic taste) while simultaneously being beautiful and beautifying the wearer by camouflaging perceived bodily flaws, and avoiding vanity or self-indulgence. It is supposed to tell the truth about an individual's identity but dissemble the body's physical contours, as if (or implicitly connoting that) the shape of the body is not essential to identity. Over time, precisely because of the performative and representational elements of dress I've been discussing, clothing (and particularly that clothing called fashion) has been subject to a pejorative discourse employing antitheatrical arguments to deride, devalue, and delegitimize (interest in) clothing and fashion as superficial, untruthful, and deceitful. Clothing (everyone knows) is equally capable of dissemblance from essence as it is expression of essence. In a paradigm that takes certain social identities to be essences inborn in individuals (such as race, gender, sexuality, class, etc.), the manner in which clothing as easily disguises an actor as a king, or a man as a woman, leaves clothing open to ferocious anathema or (mere) dismissal as incapable of bearing serious import because it does not reliably relay truth about the individual it encompasses. Clothing's fundamental detachability from the body—its fundamental theatricality—renders it an unreliable index of precisely the characteristics (gender, class, race, status) it is often called on to fix. Called on to truthfully fix illusory essential qualities of identity and simultaneously called out as a medium of illusion and deception, it is no surprise that fashion and clothing constitute a ground where these issues consistently clash. Therefore, by looking at fashion, we can trace how nineteenth-century subjects dealt with many of the issues and questions of contemporary performance studies. In fashion, the questions of performance, expression of essence, and theatrical duplicity have always been current and pressing.

All my cases index deep concerns with how fashion and clothing come to pose a threat to clear and rigid delineations of identity between genders, classes, sexualities, nations, races, and temporalities. (These are all the more disturbing perhaps because clothing has been so heavily relied on to do the work of creating such boundaries.) We will see how fashion and clothing, and specifically people's performances of clothing, have sparked serious scrutiny and outrage, outsize reactions that some historians have had a hard time reconciling with the apparent superficiality of fashion. Using an underlying framework of performance theory, I propose that we take fashion as seriously as our Victorian- and Meiji-era interlocutors did and examine why a respectable middle-class girl's racy outfit might attract more condemnation than her model's actual profession, why a cross-dressed escapade in a London theater became a tabloid felony trial, and why an entire nation might stake their political future on a change of clothes.

I am not pursuing a resistance model in trying to articulate the activities of Girls of the Period, Boulton and Park, or Japanese elites. The challenges I speak of here occurred in the centers of respectability, not at their borders, nor did any of the three constitute overt attempts to oppose the status quo. Rather, they emerged from within the centers of acceptable behavior and were only then recategorized as threatening. Both fashion and theater occupy this heterotopic space within the respectable and I will be suggesting that it is something about the doubleness of theatricality that both renders such spaces tolerable within the status quo and sparks occasional controversies, disavowals, and abjections. I wonder what we might be able to learn from Boulton, Park, the Girl of the Period, and strategizing Meiji elites by thinking of them less as resistance fighters and more as fractious and active members of an always fluid global society.

This work is primarily concerned with fashion and performance in and of everyday life during a narrow window of time in the second half of the nineteenth century. Although I attempt to limit myself to a nearly synchronic analysis by focusing on three fashion controversies that happened in the late 1860s and early 1870s, those events took place on opposite sides of the globe—in Britain and Japan. This mixing of initially disparate-seeming cases is a deliberate attempt to pull into focus how small, local, ordinary practices were enmeshed in a global network or fabric of cultural and material surfaces. As Sean Metzger writes in *Chinese Looks*, "an ostensibly localized fashion can extend into histories of global import."[80] I am juxtaposing different strands of identity that, despite the wide acceptance of intersectional theory in the academy, are rarely considered together.[81] Placing gender, sexuality, race, ethnicity, and nationality in conjunction (with helpings of class and age consideration) is not meant to homogenize these discourses of subjectivity, but to articulate their differences and interactions, the places where they modify each other.

In the subsequent case studies, we see clothes consistently called on to truthfully express essences believed to be proper to the subjects who wore them and simultaneously we see these unruly subjects using their clothing to performatively become something else, or to perform seeming something or someone else. I do not seek a definitive answer to what fashion performatively accomplished or how it functioned as performance, but instead seek to articulate the ways in which anxieties and expectations about the performative, representational, and theatrical properties of clothing and fashion conditioned mid-Victorian understandings of gender, sexuality, race, class, and nation. A secondary concern is to trace how historians have dealt with fashion and performance in their treatments of these topics. I will be taking care to articulate the latent antitheatrical biases in the historiography of nineteenth-century fashion that may have obscured our ability to fully grasp the import of these fashion controversies. For example, in discussing the Girl of the Period controversy, Helsinger, Sheets, and Veeder write that we will "have to go beyond" questions of fashion and superficiality to understand the forces at work in women's lives.[82] I, on the other hand, want to take seriously the problems that the Victorians themselves took so seriously, even if later historians deemed them trivial. Such an approach is of course underwritten by poststructuralist, critical race, and post-Butlerian performativity theories which conceive of subjective categories of identity as nonessential, performative, and cultured features.

As much as aspects of the content of the subsequent chapters seem quite different from today's attitudes, much—painfully much—of it remains very familiar in contemporary world discourse. The fashion performance of gender, sexuality, nation, class, and so on, remain subjects of simultaneous dismissal and hysteria. In this sense, the Victorians and the ways in which they shaped the world are very much the structures within which we are still living, working, and thinking.

In chapter 2 I analyze mid-Victorian girls and young women's gendered self-performances, examining "The Girl of the Period," an anonymously published 1868 article in the *Saturday*, later revealed to have been written by Eliza Lynn Linton, a woman journalist who made a career of antifeminist writing. The article proclaimed that contemporary girls had lost sight of their true character to dress like prostitutes, talk slang like boys, and "frizz" their hair like "certain savages in Africa." In short, according to Linton, "extravagance of fashion" was a sign and indeed a cause of the moral decline of the English young lady. The initial incendiary article from the *Saturday* sparked an avalanche of rebuttals, confirmations, jokes, merchandise, stage characters, and even a monthly magazine. Through articulating the incoherency of the demands placed on fashion and women, I will be particularly concerned to elucidate the ways in which the theatricality of fashionability was unstably mapped onto anxieties over morality, gender, class, money, and entertainment. The interaction of pleasure and paranoia evinced by encountering the Girl of the Period's fashioned theatricality (allegedly) in everyday life sets the stage for my explication of how theatricality in everyday life (i.e., multiple and unreliable signification) as well as the centrality of theater theatricality to middle-class life in 1868 London (and other Anglophone regions) not only undercut and complicated but also covered over and eased the fundamental incoherence of the demands and desires placed on girls, identity, and fashion. These dynamics will reappear with additional valences in the later pages.

Just two years after Linton's article was published, two flashy girls of the period were in the audience of the Easter burlesque at the Strand Theatre in London, engaging in flirty horseplay, lighting cigarettes on the gas lights, and talking to gentlemen in the saloons. When Stella and Fanny left the theater that night, they were arrested by an officer who had been called by the theater management, taken to Bow Street Station, and accused of being men in women's clothes. Ernest ("Stella") Boulton and Frederick William ("Fanny Winifred") Park were eventually charged with the felony crime of "conspiracy to incite others to commit the crime of buggery"; it was unclear at the time whether passing as a member of the "opposite sex" was even illegal under British common law. Turning to the Boulton and Park case broadens my gender inquiry by adding the lens of sexuality. Boulton and Park's crimes of fashion became instrumental to changing notions of deviant sexuality—the trial prosecutors' attempt to identify sodomy in gender-deviant clothing constituted a largely unprecedented protoattempt at identifying a homosexual identity through tying performed signifiers (cross-dressing) to hitherto unspeakable signified ideas (illicit sexual behaviors). Building on the Girl of the Period's explication of how recourse to attributions of theatricality can suture and disguise social incoherence, we will see that attributions of mere theatricality can function as a mode of containing difference as effectively as abjection (maybe even more effectively).

Shortly after Boulton and Park's tabloid trial, in Japan the newly restored emperor Meiji traded in his own "gown" for a magnificent French-style military uniform bedecked in gold braid, cropped his long hair, and decreed that others should follow his example as part of the national campaign for "Civilization and Enlightenment" (*Bunmei Kaika*). The promulgation of *yōfuku* (Western-style clothing) was part of a massive Westernization campaign undertaken by the new governing faction of Japan as an overt attempt to achieve political parity with the West. Further, this political motivation was entwined with shifting notions of gender; the emperor himself announced in his dress reform proclamation that men "should no longer appear before the people in these effeminate styles."[83] The Meiji makeover thus constituted a theatrical and performative gambit to achieve political parity on the global imperial stage by looking the part. A major point built onto the foregoing in this chapter articulates how it requires a certain amount of social power to declare an appearance theatrical or authentic. In other words, while some may be able to harness the power of theatricality from below (as arguably Boulton and Park did), the socially and politically powerful can also use theatrical designations to maintain and enhance their own supremacy from above. In concluding this discussion, I introduce an alternative mode of evaluating the truth value of surface appearances, based on indigenous Japanese thought patterns rather than the British/Western dynamics we have examined so far, which met and clashed in Meiji Japan. The dyadic pair of common Japanese terms for aspects of human subjectivity, *honne* (true feelings 本音) and *tatemae* (facade 建前), furnishes an alternative model of subjectivity that might be less vexed by the problem of reliably connecting inner invisible qualities to proper expressions, offering one provisional option for a transnationally adaptable model of selfhood.

Nearly a century and a half after the tumultuous Meiji era began, Japan had finally closed the perceived gap between themselves and hegemonic Western modernity and even, according to many 1980s accounts, surpassed the erstwhile Western powers in technological and economic might—a feat achieved even after the fast-forward rise and fall of a military empire ending in the catastrophic defeat of World War II.[84] We couldn't say that the clothes made the empire and the second economic empire, but neither could we safely insist that it all could have been achieved without the notorious khaki military uniform, the ubiquitous salaryman's suit, the Prussian military-style boys' school uniform, the girls' sailor suit, and the final obsolescence of kimono daily wear for women.

I have spent little time so far describing the final chapter of this book. That is because it is quite different from the foregoing, most obviously because it examines a twenty-first-century fashion phenomenon, necessarily using very different evidence. But I think of this as the keystone of the book because it demonstrates the closing of an odd Victorian fashion circle.

After the bursting of Japan's bubble economy at the end of the 1980s, weird apparitions of Meiji *yōfuku* dreams began to appear on the streets of Harajuku, a postwar area of Tokyo famous for its youthful subcultural crowds and shops: young women dressed in spectacularly anachronistic nineteenth-century European dresses. Sort of. But more like Victorian clothes transfigured by popular memory, movie costumes, anime and manga, storybook illustrations, and doll fashions. Overwhelmingly girls and young women from their teens through twenties and overwhelmingly feminine with big bell-shaped crinoline knee-length dresses bedecked with ruffles, bows, and lace everything, the phrase "gothic lolita" (Goshikku Roriita ゴシック ロリータ) gave a name to a sprawling network of styles that eventually traveled outward from Harajuku to the rest of the world, reexporting a revivified, transmogrified Victoriana back to the rest of the world on the currents of burgeoning "Cool Japan" pop culture, new high-speed internet communications, global capital flows, and sheer spectacularity. I look to gothic lolita to complicate the geographical and temporal specificity of the "Victorian" and to highlight the historiographical potentiality of looking at fashion. Entertaining the idea of gothic lolita's emphatically anachronistic fashions as a kind of history making or doing also resituates expectations of not only how to do history but also who does history, by taking seriously the femme, the young, the nonwhite, and the queer who have so often been cast as victims of history in need of rescuing from obscurity.

The primary addition to my conception of theatricality here is further complication of the notion of identity expression. I particularly seek to question a typical doxa of subjective identity that imagines self-expression as synonymous with individual freedom. In contrast, testimony from both Japanese and foreign gothic lolitas habitually divorces ideologies of self-expression from the demographic identity factors typically associated with self. Gothic lolita adherents poignantly suggest and, by retroactive comparison, also articulate from the Girl of the Period; Boulton, Park, and their cohort; and the Meiji-era made-over Japanese citizens, that greater freedoms may be won from fashionably becoming someone else rather than fully and deeply embodying the demographic identity factors assigned to one by society. Such an insight drawn from subcultural practice reenergizes the clothing margin described by Warwick and Cavallaro as a location of struggle and multiplicity and builds on the Japanese psychological models I present.[85] I see these subcultural fashions as fundamentally critical of the pervasive ideologies that posit acceptance and embodied performance of socially regulated identity categories as personal freedom or self-actualization. Theatricality might give a name to the dynamic by which these alternative modes of subject formation operate.

I end this book on the nineteenth century with a twenty-first-century inquiry into gothic lolita subcultural fashion as one mode of acknowledging the unexpected, not to say odd or queer, ways that fashion persists and continues to carry out the discursive work of instantiating gender, sexuality, race, ethnicity, class, and modernity, even as those discourses mutate and change, even as the wearers of the clothes and the bystanders who apprehend them struggle to exert their subjectivity over their own subjectification. Apparently superficial, apparently silly, apparently the domain of those kids, women, Asians, and queers still all too often deemed ancillary to the real world of global politics and capital, the birth, death, rebirth, and possible redeath of this one strange fashion nevertheless partakes fully of that real world and we ignore and belittle the superficial and silly at our own peril.

Chapter 2

"Typical Modern Amazon"

Freaks of Fashion, Newspaper Nightmares, and the Girl of the Period

The article was not unique. "The Girl of the Period" appeared in the March 14, 1868, edition of the weekly magazine the *Saturday Review of Politics, Literature, Science, and Art*. The *Saturday* (as it was frequently abbreviated) was a leading news and opinion journal founded in 1855 by veteran editor John Douglas Cook. Socially conservative and caustically witty, one historian has declared it "the most smartly edited and the most brilliantly written critical journal of its time."[1] The March 14 issue of the *Saturday* led with an article on "The Irish Debate" and featured articles with utilitarian titles on mostly political issues: "America," "France," "Disraeli's Debut," "The Scotch Reform Bill," "The Debate on the *Alabama*," "The Horse Guard and the War Office," "Private Bill Legislation," "The Republic of Letters," "A Report on the Schools Inquiry Commission," "Church Rates," "Agricultural Statistics," "Meeting of Unemployed at St. James's Hall," "Army Education," "Pictures of the Year," "Crystal Palace Concerts," and "Press Scandals in France." In the midst of these assorted serious-minded articles on politics and society, "The Girl of the Period" took up scarcely a page:

> Time was when the stereotyped phrase, "a fair young English girl," meant the ideal of womanhood; to us, at least, of home birth and breeding. It meant a creature generous, capable, and modest; something franker than a Frenchwoman, more to be trusted than an Italian, as brave as an American but more refined, as domestic as a German and more graceful . . . This was in the old time, and when English girls were content to be what God and nature had made them. Of late years we have changed the pattern, and have given to the world a race of women as utterly unlike the old insular ideal as if we had created another nation altogether . . . The girl of the period is a creature who dyes her hair and paints her

> face, as the first articles of her personal religion; whose sole idea of life is plenty of fun and luxury; and whose dress is the object of such thought and intellect as she possesses . . . Nothing is too extraordinary and nothing too exaggerated for her vitiated taste.

These are old and familiar complaints. Even the most outrageous claim—that nice, well-bred English girls imitated the demimonde—had been aired years before, for instance, in 1864 when the *Westminster Review* reported that "fashionable young girls in London are reputed to make no secret that they dress and get themselves generally up after the pattern of certain more successful sisters, whom it was once accounted not nice to know."[2] The *Saturday* itself had lamented that courtesans had become "the goddesses of modern fashion" in at least two articles in 1865 (July 8, 1865, 43; July 19, 1865, 233) and discussed "fast" girls on several occasions (February 1, 1862, 43; July 8, 1865, 125).[3] Linton herself had already coined the phrase "the fast young lady" in an earlier *Saturday* article, and even used the phrase "girl of the period" in an 1864 short story published in *London Society*.[4] Indeed, ". . . of the period" was a typical phrase referring to the contemporary moment and modern things, often with a focus on fashionability.[5] Meanwhile, in the weeks leading up to March 14, the *Saturday* had featured critical essays titled "Woman and Her Critics" on January 25; "Mistress and Maid on Dress and Undress" on February 1; "Aesthetic Woman" who has "mounted from the kitchen to the studio" on February 8; "What Is Woman's Work?," suggesting that modern women were interested in every career except homemaking, on February 15; "Papal Women" and "The Priesthood of Woman" about women and religion on February 22 and March 7, respectively; and "Modern Mothers" (also by Linton), which suggested that for modern women "the tender duties of motherhood have become simply disagreeable constraints" on February 29.[6] It is particularly notable then that, in a context in which every criticism contained in the brief article had been aired before, and in a moment in which the parameters of English womanhood were in significant flux, something about the wit and extremity of "The Girl of the Period" struck a chord that other articles about women and "The Woman Question" didn't. What is remarkable about "The Girl of the Period" is not that it scandalously accused girls of talking slang like boys, dressing like courtesans, and "frizzing" their hair like "certain savages in Africa" (young women have been weathering such slurs for centuries if not millennia), but rather that the article and the term it provided to describe a certain performance of gender (and class and race) managed to become such a sensation throughout Britain and global English-speaking culture. (This although—or because—within the same few years British society saw the publication of John Stuart Mill's *The Subjection of Women* in 1869, the passing of the first Married Women's Property Act in 1870, and the first woman suffrage bill reaching Parliament in 1870 during the beginnings of Britain's fifty-year campaign for women's enfranchisement.[7])

Newspapers and magazines all over the country reprinted the column in whole or in excerpts and knowledge of the article was widely disseminated into Anglophone and colonized realms, like the United States, Ireland, and India.[8] One estimate reports that the publisher Bingham sold 40,000 copies of the pamphlet, while the *Saturday* saw fit to advertise the March 14 back issue specifically with reference to "The Girl of the Period."[9] The wide dissemination of the "Girl of the Period" did not, however, mean that readers, editors, and writers concurred with the acerbically witty and thoroughly mean sentiments of its author. Some of the newspapers appended commentary to their reprints of the article, like the *Pall Mall Gazette*, which couched their excerpt in ambiguous sarcasm, calling the description "elegant and accurate" and adding afterward, "How beautiful, how delicate is this!—and how very, very true!" (March 18, 1868, 1061). While it was unclear to whom the *Pall Mall* meant their sarcasm to apply—the infamous Girl, the author, or the infamous "Saturday Reviler" for publishing the piece—other newspapers made their judgments much more unambiguously: *Tinsley's Magazine* announced "the pinnacle of cynical impertinence has been reached" (quoted in *Trewman's Exeter Flying Post*, March 25, 1868) and the *Telegraph* called it "a dish of poisonous indecency" (quoted in *Sheffield and Rotherham Independent*, March 23, 1868, 4).[10]

The column and its reverberating popularity had sparked a vigorous debate about the state of young women and the standards of gender performance that played out across the newspapers, magazines, and music hall and lecture stages, imprinting itself on the public consciousness. The Girl of the Period (often abbreviated GOP, a convention I will also adopt here) provided a convenient sobriquet for a type of girl met with in every social class and position who was fashionable and fun-loving, selfish but highly entertaining. She became an unmistakable type in a reliably repeating selection of 1868's most faddish fashions—Grecian bend corset silhouettes, oversize chignons, monocles, cigarettes, high-heel boots—encountered in novels and on music-hall stages, pictured on a line of valentines, and named in the titles of two periodicals. The Girl of the Period also gave her name to greyhounds, racehorses, and ships. (Because—get it?—she was fast.) Composed of fads, the phrase "Girl of the Period" was itself faddish. Although an avalanche of GOPs appeared on the stage and in print within a short span, the magazine *Girl of the Period Almanack*, an annual, was printed only for 1869 and 1870, and *Girl of the Period Miscellany*, a monthly, lasted for just nine issues during 1869.[11]

Many historians who have taken up the Girl of the Period controversy have analyzed the issue in conjunction with biographical work on the author, Eliza Lynn Linton, a prolific novelist and columnist during the second half of the nineteenth century.[12] Originally publishing anonymously (like all articles in the *Saturday* and many other contemporary periodicals), Linton was a childless single woman (at thirty-six, she had married William Linton, a well-known engraver, but they had separated) who supported herself through her journalism and novels.[13] Although Linton was a prolific author, including over one thousand articles about women (making her putatively the first professional woman journalist in Britain), her career has been defined by the one-page article, "The Girl of the Period."[14] Fifteen years after its publication, Linton's volume of reprinted periodical essays would be titled *The Girl of the Period and Other Social Essays*, indicating that both that particular work still defined her career and that the phrase was perceived to retain some interest for the reading public as well.[15] Herbert van Thal, author of the second of the three major Linton biographies, titled his 1979 work *Eliza Lynn Linton: The Girl of the Period*. (This, I cannot help but assume, would have horrified Linton, considering her staunchly condemnatory view of her own creation.) For good or ill, "The Girl of the Period" was, one book declared in 1895, an "epoch-making essay."[16]

As an epoch-making essay, the Girl of the Period has been of interest to several historians of women and the Victorian era. Nana Rinehart's 1980 essay catalogs the article and its responses.[17] Kristine Moruzi's "Fast and Fashionable" focuses particularly on the short-lived magazines the *Girl of the Period Almanack* and the *Girl of the Period Miscellany*. In the *Girl's Own: Cultural Histories of the Anglo-American Girl, 1830–1915*, Christina Boufis uses "The Girl of the Period" and popular novels to describe a crisis in representations and self-representations of English Victorian girlhood.[18] One of the most thorough treatments of the controversy is in volume one of the 1983 work by Helsinger, Sheets, and Veeder, *The Woman Question*. In the chapter "Eliza Lynn Linton and the 'The Girl of the Period,'" after a description of the article, its responses, and some of the miscellaneous expressions of the fad, the authors conclude:

> The G.O.P. controversy indicates how close to the surface Victorian anxiety was, and how important surfaces were as indices of deepseated forces. To understand these forces, however, Victorians had to go beyond fashion and manners and confront the impact upon women of such enormous social realities as law, science, work, and religion.[19]

I want to linger on this statement to think through a complex of historiographic and social assumptions about how fashion worked, both as a subject of discourse and as a physical fact of life in Victorian British society. Helsinger, Sheets, and Veeder assert that, to understand the state of Victorian women, Victorians, and by extension historians have to "go beyond fashion and manners." And yet, in the first sentence, they also state that surfaces served as "indices" of those precise forces—law, science, work, and religion. So the issues were displayed on surfaces and yet not intelligible via such surfaces. For Helsinger, Sheets, and Veeder fashion is both a representation and nothing but representation (and unreliable representation at that). Implied in this paradoxical statement is the longstanding doxa that fashion is deceptive—unable (or unwilling) to truthfully convey information about "enormous social realities." The authors follow their Victorian subjects in discounting the truth value of fashion ("surfaces," as the authors put it) as a representational practice and fail to consider fashion at all as a material practice, a bodily practice, an artistic practice, a theatrical practice.

My intervention here, then, will be to consider fashion not (just) as a mirror; it does not only or accurately reflect or index "deepseated forces"—it is itself a force, which I suggest may also explain its constant failure to only reflect. In addition to representing ideas—to being a "language" as Alison Lurie's much-debated 1981 book put it—fashion does the work of ideology and resistance, social integration and distinction.[20] And via fashion's very inchoateness and doubleness (or theatricality, as I will further articulate), it often poses as not doing that work, as being "just for looks." The power of fashion was rarely underestimated by at least a significant minority of these Victorians: I take them seriously when they obsessed over frocks instead of suffrage, makeup over property rights, and hairstyles over education. Fashion (and, by extension, surfaces or appearances) was of constant concern to Victorians, even or even especially when they were decrying its primacy. (This, of course, is a fundamental aspect of Jonas Barish's durable theorization of Western civilization's "antitheatrical prejudice."[21] As Ackerman and Puchner put it, antitheatricalism constitutes "a paradoxical way of affirming the capacious powers of the theatre."[22]) In her monograph *Private Theatricals*, Nina Auerbach writes, "reverent Victorians shunned theatricality as the ultimate, deceitful mobility. It connotes not only lies, but a fluidity of character that decomposes the uniform integrity of the self."[23]

The various responses to the Girl of the Period illustrate the trouble with this unreliable connection between fashion as sign and truth. First, to seem and not to be—as the Girl of the Period seemed like a courtesan and yet was not one—is condemnable along the lines of Auerbach's reading of Victorian antitheatricality. Victorian attitudes followed Plato's in broad strokes when it came to the status of the copy or imitation as false and debauched. Linton states her preference for the authentic bluntly in the original article: "If we must have one thing, let us have it genuine; and the queens of St. John's Wood in their unblushing honesty, rather than their imitators and make-believes in Bayswater and Belgravia."[24]

Perhaps even worse than middle-class girls aping classless (yet rich and powerful) courtesans were the lower classes dressing up as (and perhaps even passing as) their betters, a perennial anxiety in Britain (as indeed most places), and the source of historical sumptuary laws as well as many forms of livery and uniform. Sumptuary law, livery, and uniform are all antifashion operations that seek to control fashion's dangerously theatrical semiosis, detached or not from signified features. By Linton's logic, if the superficial fashion sign is reliable ("not *not* the thing"), then the performer is indeed condemnable for breaking ideological rules that call for rigid distinctions between classes of people—"fallen women" and respectable middle-class girls, "our daughters and sisters." But on the other hand, the theatrical sign is also *not* the thing it represents: the Girl of the Period is not a courtesan, not a negress, not a maniac, although she (according to Linton) "resembles" one. Fashion constantly—one might say constitutively—calls on detached signifiers to create itself, wherein women can wear a Tyrolean hat, a Georgian pannier, the latest French fashions, a Grecian bend corset—all costumes cribbed from a sumptuously dressed and fêted prostitute—and yet not be one.

One of the things that facilitates the unifying "glue" of fashion is the plausible deniability that theatricality imparts to it, through its ability to signify something while simultaneously displaying that it is not that thing. (For example, wearing a fashionable military-style coat rarely fools someone into thinking that one is a military officer. Even when the coat is actual military surplus, the transmogrification of fashionability causes it to signify military and not military simultaneously.) Fashion's ability—and propensity—to signify multiply and unreliably (which is to say, theatrically) has, over its long history, never caused critics to cease calling on it to truthfully represent key attributes of the dressed subject. Despite the excess of controversy attracted by dress, fashion provided one way to negotiate or resolve, at the level of the fictive or theatrical, the divergent demands (modesty, conspicuous consumption, bodily attractiveness, self-expression, fashionability, or display of gender, class, race, prestige) placed on subjects. As Elizabeth Wilson puts it: "fashionable dress of the western world [is] one means whereby an always fragmentary self is glued together into the semblance of a unified identity."[25] Important to note is that this clothing doesn't resolve the contradictions of society and self, and both's interior "fragmentation." It subsumes them, sutures them temporarily or provisionally. And equally, a change of clothes (or habit, if you will) could, as we see throughout this book, unsettle, decompose, or lay bare the incoherencies that make up personal identity in a society.

Appearance's (and therefore fashion's) unsteady attachment to truth value in signification is not a reason to dismiss it as unworthy of study, but rather precisely a refutation of Helsinger, Sheets, and Veeder declaration that we must "go beyond fashion." The very incoherence of the attitudes expressed toward it indicates that clothing was a prime ground of negotiation between individual subjects and the inchoate, contradictory demands made on them by moral, sexual, and gendered ideologies. Clothing for Victorians was not just intimately bound up in moral issues but was itself a moral issue.

In the Girl of the Period controversy, multiple anxieties around fashion's theatrical-performative capacities as well as the control of young middle- and upper-class women converged. I contend that we can trace both containment and change in the ideology of proper womanhood through the proliferation of GOP tropes. Thus, controversies like the Girl of the Period, which overlapped and incorporated debates about tight lacing, high heels, rational dress reform, hair dyeing, makeup use, and adoption of masculine styles in women's fashion, which historians like Helsinger, Sheets, and Veeder have so often considered beside the point of the real "deepseated forces" acting on women (and of course men) are central to understanding how deep-seated forces did (and do) their work. I make no claim about the GOP as progressive or oppressive (surely, it's both), but instead seek to read the Girl of the Period controversy for how it secrets important political issues into an apparently superficial frame, hidden in plain sight. Historians have easily recognized the Girl of the Period trope as a sign or symbol of other issues but have less often considered that it is itself doing the political work of collapsing gender ideology into quotidian performance. Often the opposite has been said: that focus on fashion distracts from the important issues. I am not arguing that we should read bodily practices for what they really meant but instead suggesting that repetitive material performances, like clothing and accessorizing the body, materially shape subjectivity and further that it may be precisely their apparent disconnection from interior forces that allows these practices to work ideologically.

In the remainder of this chapter, I look at several ways in which the Girl of the Period controversy constituted a gender crisis. And one category crisis tends to precipitate another: Linton's critique of the Girl of the Period incorporates gender (talking slang like boys), class and sexuality (dressing like courtesans), and race ("frizzing" hair like "certain savages in Africa"). Dress isn't just required to performatively fix the male-female binary designation but a whole range of features conditioned by gender, such as occupation, age, marital status, class, race, status, and prestige. Thus, we see critics of fashion not just arguing that clothing insufficiently denoted male or female (although they did do that); they also and especially worried that one type of woman (affluent, middle- or upper-class, young, moral, and respectable) was indistinguishable from another type of woman (prostitutes and courtesans—unclassed in that, although they might be rich, they remained inadmissible in respectable society).

Throughout the twentieth- and twenty-first-century colloquial views of the Victorian era have too often conceived of Victorian femininity as a settled, monolithic category (if perhaps riven by a Madonna-whore binary), failing to grasp the ways in which that semblance of a singular acceptable femininity was forged from constant turmoil and difference, but also how multiple femininities constantly coexisted within the status quo of respectable middle- and upper-class womanhood. In this work, I use the Girl of the Period controversy to attend precisely to these two aspects of heterogeneity within status-quo femininity. This is not a story about resistance and liminality, although certainly "Girl of the Periodism" was sometimes conceived of as pushing at or beyond the bounds of respectability. Rather, I want to show here how the Girl of the Period persisted in the center of the status quo. Although attracting obsessive attention and even condemnation, she remained a centerpiece of middle-class femininity in discourse and representation, eliciting as much appreciation as scorn. Moreover, theater formed a fundamental location within which GOP pleasures could be safely indulged with social approval. I will demonstrate how the Girl of the Period occupied a heterotopic space within respectability, and I will argue that it is through theatrical dynamics that both the stage Girl of the Period and the (nearly mythic) street or real-life Girls of the Period were able to inhabit such a space, with strife admittedly, but not abjected from respectability. The discursive designation of theatricality is one mechanism by which societies contain their differences; this is not the same as abjection, but a belittling, a removing of substance and resignifying (or designifying) the appearance of a transgressive subject.

I begin by tracing the "birth" of the Girl of the Period in the burgeoning Victorian periodical press. I examine how the GOP in periodical print both identified and consolidated a shifting complex of appearances and behaviors into a trope. This coalescence not only gave a name to a particular form of quotidian gender performance but also simultaneously, in the process of punitively naming Girl of the Periodism, helped to spread and instantiate the very repertoire of behaviors the Girl of the Period attacks had meant to condemn. The controversy ignited serious moral discussion about gender, the state of young women, and modern society, but simultaneously many (perhaps most) of the responses seemed determined to take neither the accusations nor the accusers seriously, spoofing and trivializing the question and adopting the Girl of the Period into common parlance as a figure of affection and ridicule. In some sense, the Girl of the Period was performatively born via a magazine article and much of her vibrant subsequent life took place in the burgeoning Victorian periodical press, both literary and light. The excess with which the GOP was characterized led to a collapse of the masculine-feminine binary: simultaneously hyperfeminine in her obsession with frivolous self-indulgence and the accoutrements of feminine bodily display—makeup, extreme fashion, and accessories—and masculinized in her appropriation of male prerogatives like smoking, sport, riding, slang talking, indulgence in popular entertainments, and worldly knowingness. Next, I trace the Girl of the Period's leap from print to stage. Already possibly fictional and theatricalized through seeming without being, the stage proved a comfortable home for the GOP, where much of the anxiety that suffused the journalistic accounts could be assuaged by the theater's status as always already mere appearance.

A major premise of Linton's original article was an accusation that the Girl of the Period was mercenary—tantamount to a prostitute not only in her imitation of courtesans' fashions but also in her concern with money before domesticity or even romance. "Girl of the Period" came to denote a trope of middle-class femininity expressed precisely through fashionable commodity consumption, yet this (perception of a) frank and open relation to capitalism (as both consumer and commodity) also threw into turmoil a painstakingly maintained fantasy of a separate feminine domestic sphere insulated from the vagaries of commerce. I will point out a fundamental incoherence in the demands placed on women—which is to say their clothes—regarding appearance, desire, and the domestic sphere's imbrication with commerce. Commodities' smooth passage from public to private, street and store to domestic space, and the young women supposed to be protected there, raised the specter of prostitution deep within the heart of respectable middle- and upper-class homes, only for these troubling instabilities to be disavowed and displaced onto the apparently "superficial" (and onto a negative evaluation of feminine character). Fashion, as the locus of so many unfixable and anxiety-inducing uncertainties (femininity, capital, irrational signification, hollowness, bodiliness, sexuality, desire), was coded as dangerous even as it enticed interlocutors to consume the Girl of the Period on stage, in cheap novelty goods, as copy in a periodical, as just for fun and not really so bad. Commodity itself provided a means whereby the disagreeable aspects of the GOP were minimized and metabolized (back) into the mainstream, while some stage Girls of the Period, especially burlesque star Lydia Thompson, used the persona to openly critique the paradoxical demands placed on young Euro-American women.

Finally, I return to the notion of theatricality to help explain not only why the Girl of the Period caused such distress but also precisely how the doubleness of theatricality (seen in both real life and on stage) enabled the flexibility and ambivalence that allowed society to encompass and incorporate the Girl of the Period, not abject her. Although the apparent shallowness and superficiality of the controversy has led some scholars like Helsinger, Sheets, and Veeder to dismiss the GOP as a mere distraction from "deepseated issues," other scholars have overvalued the transgressive valence of the Girl of the Period without taking stock of the ways in which status-quo society voraciously consumed her. Cutting across both arguments that dismiss the furor on grounds of superficiality and those that exalt the GOP's resistant possibilities, I chart a continuity between the "silliness" of the Girl of the Period and the "serious" issues of the New

Woman and nascent "first wave" feminist movement—one that seemed clear to many contemporary commentators, but that is today less obvious.

I see the Girl of the Period as neither a capitulation to coercive norms nor an icon of resistance, but emblematic of the deeply riven and contradictory threads of power and compulsion and agency and pleasure that often disappear within conventional gender and sexuality discourses. Articulating the means and stakes of the GOP's ambivalent (or multivalent) status helps reveal how society could encompass disavowed varieties of gendered experience. The Girl of the Period controversy provides an example of how gender disobedience could be incorporated into the dominant ideology, admittedly with strife, but nevertheless without substantially altering the state of women (despite the alarms sounded by conservative commentators). More than this—such behaviors' deviant designation is neutralized, rendered innocuous, even attractive, through incorporation into the pantheon of commoditized entertainments. By no means do I mean to cynically advance a jeremiad proclaiming resistance futile, but rather I seek to articulate how theatrical practices of fashion on—and especially off—the stage function within their ideological and discursive context, without assigning a designation of good or bad to such practices, which after all are compulsory within society, as both we know it and the Victorians knew it.

"Newspaper Nightmares"

After the bombshell publication of Linton's short article in March 1868, some of the earliest calculated replies came from the weekly comic journals the *Tomahawk: A Saturday Journal of Satire, Echoes from the Clubs*, *Fun*, *Punch*, and *Judy*, which spread around the venom of their satirical response. The *Tomahawk* responded in its April 4 edition with a full-page illustration accompanied by a parodic letter to the "Authoress" written in "a Club library" that started by asserting the female gender of the author since "a *man* could not have written such a *very* spiteful leader, fair one with the locks of grey (they *are* grey I'm sure)" (April 4, 1868, 136, emphasis in the original). The style of the prose belies its claim to provenance in a club library (clubs being the Victorian era's masculine homosocial enclave par excellence[26]) through its obvious adoption of a hyperfeminine voice, or what passed for one in light periodical reading. The italicized emphases and circumlocutions ("they *are* grey I'm sure") read as satirically exaggerated conventional female speech. The feminine cant of the *Saturday* reviewer (and her fictional critic in the *Tomahawk*) established, the letter goes on to pit two distasteful modes of feminine behavior against each other—to "paint" (wear makeup), smoke, and "wear false hair" (chignons) versus "to splutter out venom o'er the columns of the *Saturday*

Review"—and then chooses the former as less offensive than the latter. Although, the letter states, "It is horrible to meet a young girl with false roses on her cheek, or sticky gold fringeing [*sic*] her forehead," and suggests that "the reward of their labour must be self-reproach and universal condemnation." The *Tomahawk* goes on to insist that only a small minority of girls are guilty of such crimes and that the bitter, elderly lady author allowed "malice to misguide [her] pencil." The illustration features the "prurient prude" of the *Saturday Review* drawing a devilish portrait of a complacent and pretty young woman with inks made of "venom" and "gall" at an easel with pantaloon-covered legs (fig. 1; April 4, 1868, 140). This initial defense stands in stark contrast to a short article published by the *Tomahawk* a month later, where they turn their guns onto the very maiden they had previously defended, suggesting that while the Girl of the Period was still rare, young women must beware not to allow the accusations to become a prophecy. Young women "have been walking on the edge of the abyss" that separates them, as yet unsullied, from the "odious" Girl of the Period, and have been "lately too familiar with the blight they would avoid" (May 2, 1868, 174).

Although most journalistic replies were quick to condemn the "Girl of the Period" article and its author, few condemned it outright without allowing that the abuses of the GOP did exist, but only in a few girls or to lesser extents. Like the *Pall Mall Gazette*'s ambivalent sarcasm and the *Tomahawk*'s articles, many magazines suggested that both girls and the *Saturday* were in the wrong. The major replies included a few common messages, often in combination: first, that Girls of the Period weren't so bad or so plentiful as the *Saturday* reviewer claimed. One of the earliest replies, from the London correspondent of *Trewman's Exeter Flying Post* summed up a paragraph excerpt from the essay:

> Pretty plain speaking, that? Of course, if it were true, the plainer the truth were put the better. But is it? Look around yourselves,—reckon up the girls of your set, look at your homes, and then answer the question for yourselves. Perhaps there is a grain of truth in it; in fact, I know there is. You have only to take a turn down Regent-street any afternoon to see saucy and thoughtless girls imitating the queens of the *demi-monde* as closely as they can with decency, and sometimes without decency. But that is about all. It is a calumny to say that these girls are anything more than thoughtless and indiscreet; and I quite agree with the young bucks of the *Globe*, that the *Saturday Reviewer*'s sketch is "an atrocious libel on the fair fame of the other sex." (March 25, 1868)[27]

The phrase "Girl of the Period" itself quickly came to contain an ambivalence. Respondents took exception to the sweeping generalization

"THE GIRL OF THE PERIOD!"
OR,
PAINTED BY A PRURIENT PRUDE.
[*See Sketch.*

Fig. 1. "The Girl of the Period / A Prurient Prude," *Tomahawk: A Saturday Journal of Satire*, April 4, 1868, 140. Courtesy of Library Special Research Collections, University of California Santa Barbara.

implied in the phrase—that every girl of the current period behaved in the way Linton described. Instead, in subsequent representations, Girl of the Period took on the connotation of a certain type of contemporary girl—fun loving, possibly a bit risqué, with a sporty disposition and a fondness for extreme fashion and makeup. Perhaps odder, these distinctions appear as decomposing recursions of each other: was a Girl of the Period really imitating the demimonde, or just kind of seeming to imitate the demimonde? *Trewman*'s suggests the Girl of the Period's imitation is "mere," not "serious," summing up an attitude I might call anti-antitheatrical (which, as the quotation shows, isn't precisely theatrical).

Both interpretations of the phrase Girl of the Period seem to have remained in circulation to some extent, so that sometimes the term was used by writers apparently unaware of or purposely disregarding any moral implications. For example, a book reviewer described a character as a Girl of the Period, but goes on to describe her as "so natural and so good, so gentle and simple, yet so wise . . . the fairest and brightest, the purest and the best, 'girl of the period' " (*Morning Post*, April 10, 1868, 3). Other uses "reclaimed" the term by valorizing some of the behaviors associated with the GOP: "Bradford boasts a large number of really lovely specimens of 'the girl of the period:' I mean the *real* girl of the period,—pleasure-loving, doubtless, startling in attire, often, but not, thank goodness! the immodest, masculine, half-dressed creature in the existence of which certain miserable prints would have us believe" (*Bradford Observer*, December 17, 1869, 4).

Although the term was used to describe a certain type of girl, the phrase Girl of the Period proved to be extremely flexible and capacious in its ability to describe a vast array of behaviors and appearances deemed outside the imagined social and moral norm or comprising a shifting new norm. While the major points of the original article included the GOP's disdain for conventional propriety and modesty ("moral muffishness," as Linton put it sarcastically), her outlandish fashions, adoption of masculine habits (in both senses of the word), and her avarice, this understanding expanded to include the notions of masculine "sportiness," such as riding horseback, playing croquet, or even riding new-fangled "velocipedes" (the faddish 1868 word for the soon-to-be ubiquitous bicycle), fickleness, silliness, and generalized disobedience to the status quo.[28] The Girl of the Period trope served as a label for a wide variety of behaviors and appearances attributed to modern young women, yet they tended to coalesce into a fairly stable trope.

Many rebuttals agreed that girls had gone astray, but some spread the blame for girls' unenviable state around. While the original article laid the blame squarely on the shoulders of the girls themselves—they had "placed *themselves* beyond the pale of masculine respect" (emphasis added)—many other periodicals acquiesced that girls were in a bad way, but asked, as the title of novelist Mary Elizabeth Braddon's article put it: "Whose Fault Is It?" The answer to that question, many authors agreed resoundingly, was "MEN."[29] Men fawned over courtesans, rewarded fast girls with attention, and ignored the gentle and retiring types. Braddon declared, "It was not till the moral deterioration of the modern young man had become a fact but too obvious, that any fatal change was perceived in the modern young woman," suggesting that Woman had but "meekly and dutifully copied the model [men] had set up before her eyes, and at whose shrine she has seen them prostrate and worshipping!"[30] Here, in a crypto-feminist critique, precisely the feminine virtue of subservience leads to the moral degeneracy of Girl of the Periodism.

Other reasonings offered up for why girls had gone astray was lack of education and boredom. In these arguments the Girl of the Period was tied most closely to the nascent "Woman Question." One of the most peculiar of these defenses was published under the title "Our Offense, Our Defence, and Our Petition" in *Macmillan's*. The author was identified only as "A Belgravian Young Lady" who declared that the "pointed, stinging satire on the frivolity and the vices of women" may seem pleasant to some, but "what is sport to others, is death—moral and intellectual—to us."[31] She conceded that there was "much of truth" in the accusations of the "Girl of the Period," adding, "We know—none better—the deep degradation of the life we live; but none but God and our own hearts can tell how bitter is the struggle in the most cases before we submit in utter hopelessness to the yoke imposed upon us by fashion" (February 1869, 323–31). The Belgravian young lady described the long and steady moral decline of the upper-middle-class girl, coddled and pampered, who repeatedly tries to find a useful purpose in her life—from homemaking to charity work to education, only to be supplanted by servants in the first place, disdained as a dilettante and forbidden to endanger herself among the poor in the second, and derided as a bluestocking whose knowledge can serve no useful purpose in the third. "She begins to despise herself" and out of sheer boredom and despair takes to "the weary, purposeless round of gaiety," which at least fills the hours and expends her energy, but like a drug constantly requires more extreme stimulation—from dancing to flirtation to the hinted possibility of "deeds worse than words." (Remember this phraseology of unspeakability as we will return to it in the next chapter). The Belgravian Young Lady concludes by asking for education and useful employment, "demand[ing] for girls growing to womanhood the opportunity of spending a portion of their young lives in the services of their God and of their fellow-creatures" and "release from their present bondage of idle selfishness" (February 1869, 331).

The third major rebuttal to the "Girl of the Period" accused the reviewer him- or herself of being the source of scandal rather than merely exposing it in others. "The Reviewer of the Period" in *Tinsley's Magazine* pulled no punches in accusing the eponymous reviewer of "one supreme effort" at notoriety "spiced with dirty innuendoes and suggestive nastiness" (July 1868, 618). The author of "Women of the Day" first published in *St. Paul's* had shruggingly suggested that while he himself had never met any Girls of the Period in his circles at "the salons of Westbournia, South Kensington, and Wimpole-cum-Wigmore-dom," perhaps the author had met these alleged girls in other, more rarefied echelons of society (June 1868, 309). The *Tinsley's* author went one better and suggested that the reviewer was himself "thirsting" for association with prostitutes, seizing on the notorious line from Linton's original column about preferring the genuine to the imitation: "If we must have one thing, let us have it genuine; and the queens of St. John's Wood in their unblushing honesty, rather than their imitators and make-believes in Bayswater and Belgravia" (July 1868). The *Examiner* summed up the theatrical question whether the *Saturday* reviewer had invented the whole thing with speculation about delusion: "Are not most of the girls we meet modest, intelligent, quiet in dress and demeanour? Surely the 'girl of the period,' in her supreme atrocity, is a hideous creation of some bewildered brain—a kind of newspaper nightmare" (*Examiner*, February 5, 1870).

These three types of replies indicate three ways of controlling the dangerous suggestion that young women might be out of society's control. First, divorce of fashion from morality. These arguments downplayed the gravity of the situation, suggesting that the Girl of the Period controversy amounted to a "storm in a teacup" or "breaking a butterfly on a wheel."[32] This comprises what we might call the anti-antitheatrical stance, refusing to recognize any deep (performative) import to the situation. Second, reducing women's behavior to a reaction to male prerogatives. In the scenario in which the Girl of the Period's birth is entirely attributable to men's desires and encouragement, then women remain without agency. This argument contains a double-bind for women. The more antifeminist interpretation is prescriptive: assuming that women's behaviors should and do conform only to male desires and requirements, precluding the possibility of women's independent self-determination. In the descriptive version of this argument, women's decisions can be thought of as considered, agential, strategic actions within a situation in which men hold the power, where failing to please could result in significant social setbacks. Third, employing strategic innocence by claiming never to have met a Girl of the Period allowed people to disavow her existence, thereby causing any threat of moral decay to appear to emanate from the journalist who claimed only to have reported it. Some would suggest that the Girl of the Period was performatively created from the *Saturday* article and Linton was therefore responsible for her existence—an existence soon spreading from the pages of newspapers and magazines to the comic stage, and from thence even into real life (rather than the other way around).

Serious replies and rebuttals employing these arguments appeared in newspapers all over Britain and the United States, the satire and humor journals, and women's magazines, penned by both women and men. Many of these authors considered the sex of the original article's author a salient factor in making sense of it. *St. Paul's* speculated at length on how the article did not seem to be by a woman because "a lady satirist would have known of no pity in her satire" nor could a woman "have ignored so strangely the whole element of passion, which plays so great a part in the lives of all women—even the most worldly, frivolous, and conventional" but neither did it appear to be the hand of a man, since "the fiddle-faddle, the foibles and trifles of the social aspect of female life, do not attract or interest men." The author concludes that the author must be "looked for in the list of young curates" who "ha[ve] been oppressed by the feminine protectorate" (June 1868, 305).[33] But, after a few articles deploring the author's lack of masculine chivalry, the gender of the author was soon inferred to be female, a conviction generally supported with misogynist rhetoric about woman's cruelty to woman, as in the *Tomahawk*'s illustrated riposte, the aforementioned "A Prurient Prude." Eliza Lynn Linton's name came up as early as July, although people also suspected Mary Elizabeth Braddon (ironically, since she eventually penned the "Whose Fault Is It?" rebuttal), the Marchioness of Salisbury, or Miss Alderson, the *sister* of the Marchioness of Salisbury.[34] Despite the official addition of Linton's name to the 1868 pamphlet form of the essay, newspapers were still disseminating the information about the author and alleged authors into 1869.[35] In her 1883 collection of article reprints (titled *The Girl of the Period and Other Social Essays*, indicating the continued importance of that specific article to her career and society at large), Linton claimed that, due to the *Saturday*'s policy of anonymous publishing, she had twice been introduced to the "Writer of 'The Girl of the Period.'" One was a clergyman and the other "a lady of rank well known in London society and to this hour believed by her own circle to have written" the article.[36] George Soames Layard, Linton's first biographer, reported that after being introduced to one of these alleged authors, Linton replied, "Lady——may have written the article, but I certainly received the cheque."[37]

When I began researching this controversy, I expected to track how the Victorian women and men of the age of "separate spheres" dealt with this attack on contemporary performances of gender, especially considering how interested readers were to discover the author's own gender. But I failed to find particularly distinct differences in the location and structure of their responses. Both women and men took offense at the author and the *Saturday* for publishing "a dish of poisonous indecency, disguised to look like the wholesome food of indignation."[38] (Is indignation ever really wholesome?) Both women and men used the pages of the respectable literary journals to respond to the charges, including the *Victoria Magazine*, edited by prominent women's rights activist Emily Faithfull, and Braddon's *Belgravia Magazine*, as well as the male-helmed magazines *St. Paul's* (edited by Anthony Trollope), *London Society*, *Macmillan's*, and *Tinsley's*. In the United States Henry James replied to the article in the *Nation* in his review of a collection of reprinted *Saturday* essays titled *Modern Women*, which included "The Girl of the Period." American novelist Louisa May Alcott declares in the preface to her 1869–70 novel *An Old-Fashioned Girl* that "The 'Old-Fashioned Girl' is not intended as a perfect model, but as a possible improvement upon the Girl of the Period, who seems sorrowfully ignorant or ashamed of the good old fashions which make woman truly beautiful and honored."[39] The women's magazines, like Samuel Beeton's titles the *Queen*, *Englishwoman's Domestic Magazine*, and *Young Englishwoman*, seemed interested in the controversy only in passing: the *Queen* mentioned the Girl of the Period, but only in a regular column in which the author decried the behavior of the heroines of recent novels, the *Englishwoman's Domestic Magazine* mentioned the Girl of the Period the most, but primarily as ammunition for their retort to the *Saturday Review* when it accused them of indecency in publishing their infamous "Whipping of Girls" letters around the same time.[40] The relative equality of the two sexes' access to the organs of publishing was frequently trumpeted in the articles that sought to prove that neither feminists nor mannish Girls of the Period had anything more to agitate for.[41]

Just as the GOP herself was considered a shocking mix of hypergendered behaviors, the textual sleuths who combed the article for clues betrayed the strength of their fantasy of identification centered on the conviction that the arrangement of words and phrases would indubitably indicate the gender of the notorious author. Girl of the Period–inspired instances of "textual drag" in which authors spoofed feminine styles of writing, such as in the aforementioned "Prurient Prude" letter in the *Tomahawk*, shored up the strength of this fantasy, even as such spoofs by men undercut the possibility that the gender of authorship could ever truly be confirmed. Linton had herself employed a male point of view in the original article, just as she would go on to write her three-volume autobiography in a male voice as *The Autobiography of Christopher Kirkland*.[42]

Girl of the Period gender trouble elicited a dose of nationalist race anxiety as well, indexed in provocative offhand references, like "negresses" and "savages in Africa" in reference to GOP hairstyles in Linton's original text. It could nearly go without saying that crises in middle-class English femininity at the height of imperialism constituted crises in *whiteness*.[43]

Subsequent treatments took up the question of girls' duty to uphold the national character, as in the widely reprinted news item reporting that

> An Irish lady, writing from the centre of India, says:—"Did you see that article in the *Saturday Review*, some time ago, called 'The Girl of the Period?' It was spiteful and untrue, but Captain ______ tells me that it has done an immense deal of harm out here. It has been translated into Hindustani, and the people are all saying, why should they educate their women if that is the result of education on Englishwomen." (*Birmingham Daily Post*, August 6, 1868, 3)

Following up this report, *London Society* concluded,

> It would no doubt be too much to expect that a London journalist, whenever he wished to write a sensational article, should be bound to consider its possible effect upon the natives of Bombay or Bengal. But it is well perhaps to remember that, when we make charges against ourselves, a great many foreigners, Asiatic as well as European, are very apt to believe us. (November 1869, 466–67)[44]

The Irish lady and *London Society* thus left most of the responsibility of protecting the character of the nation in this case to the fourth estate. A Lord J. Hervey used the same information to draw different connections between global women across national boundaries when referring to the same news item in a speech. He shifted responsibility for Indian enlightenment to Englishwomen, declaring, "English ladies could do more both to help and hinder the poor Hindoo women than they were aware of" before describing it as "a curious fact that the articles which appeared in the *Saturday Review*, on the 'Girl of the Period,' were actually translated into the native language in Bombay at the expense of a well-known native gentleman, with the view of hindering the spread of education among the Hindoo women, as he was of opinion that the tone of society which was developed by the education of English ladies was exceedingly injurious to their characters" (*Bury and Norwich Post*, March 23,1869). Such calls for the insubordinate members of the larger society to fall into line to maintain other subordinations accent the intertwining of privilege and oppression that sustained the Victorian status quo.[45]

The Coming Man of the Present Day

The next three sections trace the dissemination of the Girl of the Period out of "serious" journals and newspapers into humor magazines, the comic stage, and commercial merchandise. It was via these formats—especially the embodying process of the amateur stage and through material novelty goods—that the Girl of the Period seems to have entered into middle-class homes for perhaps the first time, in contradistinction to Linton and other disapproving journalists' claim to be describing an already widespread phenomenon. The Girl of the Period phenomenon and controversy exemplifies the entangled nature of theatrical representation and performative instantiation in its mystification of which came first—flesh-and-blood Girls of the Period on the street or the Girl of the Period born of "newspaper nightmare." The Girl of the Period coalesced across diverse media

Fig. 2. *Girl of the Period Miscellany*, no. 1 (March 1869), cover. Courtesy of Special Collections, Charles E. Young Research Library, UCLA.

into a recognizable silhouette with a strong dichotomy: startlingly sporty and masculine, but simultaneously hyperfeminine and fashionable (see, e.g., fig. 2). Perhaps ironically, the theme of unnaturalness and artificiality repeatedly recurred on the feminine side of the Girl of the Period trope.

While she raised serious concerns in the press (even in the satire magazines, like in the *Tomahawk*) who warned that girls had been walking a precipice, the Girl of the Period trope was also immensely amenable to

Fig. 3. "A Muscular Maiden," *Girl of the Period Miscellany*, no. 3 (1869). Courtesy of Special Collections, Charles E. Young Research Library, UCLA.

lighthearted treatments, from one-liner jokes to the full magazines *Girl of the Period Almanack* and *Girl of the Period Miscellany* and innumerable stage characters in burlesque, music halls, amateur theatricals, and pantomime. The *Almanack* and *Miscellany* made much of Girl of the Period's masculine habits and physical prowess, with numerous illustrations of girls doing male-coded activities, including an entire twelve-month spread of ladies' billiards, riding, punting, smoking, and so on. A vignette with accompanying illustration titled "A Muscular Maiden" (fig. 3) is written in epistolary format to the *Miscellany* (mock edited by "Miss Polly Glott") by a man smitten upon witnessing the eponymous muscular maiden punching out two boys who accost her on the street (May 1869, 78–79). By the time he catches up to offer assistance, the pugilist (whose "deltoid muscle stood out in a peculiarly fascinating way beneath her jacket") can modestly demur, "I think I have arranged the matter," with her two boy assailants incapacitated on the ground before her. Many of the masculine traits of the Girl of the Period were cultured and social rather than physical: *Punch* suggested that "PRESENTS FOR A GIRL OF THE PERIOD" should include "a bottle of olives and a box of cigars" (January 23, 1869, 32). A later joke ran:

> A girl of the period, belonging to a Paris theatre, gave a supper to a few gentlemen the other evening. Her mamma was present, half guest, half servant. One of the gentlemen was telling a story; he stopped on a sudden, and said, "I beg your pardon, the conclusion is scarcely fit for ladies' ears." "Your ear, mamma," said the girl of the period; "leave the room a minute; you can come in again by-and-by." (*Bristol Mercury*, January 22, 1870)

The invocation of both decadent fashion capital Paris and theaterfolk seems to insulate this particular GOP from any troubling associations with the respectable daughters and sisters of England. Eventually, the Girl of the Period's masculine predilections established, the jokes could go one further. One much-reprinted vignette from *Fun* reported that

> The following extraordinary advertisement appears in a Glasgow paper:
>
> A YOUNG GENTLEMAN of independent means, and by the beau sex considered handsome, wishing to forsake *bachelorship*, would be glad to meet a young lady *similarly disposed* and equally endowed.—Address, with *carte*, etc.
>
> Can it be possible! The girl of the period has been accused of aping manly tastes; but surely if she is "disposed to forsake bachelorship," the girl of the period must after all be a man. (February 27, 1869, 255)

Other newspapers reported (in an apparent jab at GOPs, feminists, *and* Americans) that "the *Chicago Tribune* is of the opinion that 'woman is undoubtedly the coming man of the present day'" (*Bradford Observer*, October 5, 1869, 4). A US newspaper struck back at the British with a news item claiming, "among the aristocratic equestrians in Hyde Park, London, recently, was a man carefully got up as a 'girl of the period,' who rode on a side-saddle, and acted the part of a woman to perfection. Singularly enough, the police took no notice of him, although he made his appearance daily for upward of a week" (*Evening Bulletin*, May 13, 1869). (Keep this story in mind for the next chapter.)

The Girl of the Period's masculine traits were counterbalanced, however, with descriptions of hyperfemininity—and peculiarly, it was the feminine GOP behaviors of extreme fashion, makeup, and hair styling that picked up the most concomitant valences of fakery and falsehood. "The complexion of a girl of the period differs from a railway season ticket—the one is, and the other is not, transferable" (*Judy*, December 23, 1868, 90). As the skin, so also the hair:

> A short time previous to the introduction of the chignon some of the ladies adopted masculine manners and dress. This combination might have an awkward result if they were put in the position of a woman who, at Belfast, the other day, was thought to be a man because she had, the report says, "a masculine appearance, spoke like a man, and smoked a pipe." The police were called in, and with their usual sagacity after examining the woman's face, declared, as does Signor Bosco, that there was "no deception." Alas! should they be called upon to decide whether a "girl of the period," who talked slangy and looked masculine, was an imposter, the examination of the hair would be a most unsatisfactory proceeding. (*Preston Guardian*, June 5, 1869)

The *Preston Guardian*'s mild remonstrance about the popularity of chignons (additions of false hair that volumized hairstyles) among fashionable women lodges an implicit critique of the artificial in dress and bodily behavior. Oddly, here it's the feminine accessory (the chignon) that is marked as fake and not the smoking of the pipe or "speaking like a man." (Remember, we've already noted how femininity has been historically associated with both nature and unnatural duplicity.[46])

Clearly then, the Girl of the Period is being disciplined, in both serious and comic modes, for excessive gendering on both sides of a binary structure—too male and too female, which nevertheless fails to switch the association of masculine with natural and feminine with unnatural, even though the discourse is about women.

The Original Girl of the Period

Just as humor magazines seized on the comic possibilities and the gendered excesses of the Girl of the Period, so too did the stage. Indeed, in some ways the GOP seemed tailor-made for the theater. (And as noted in the previous section, humor magazines had already placed her there too.) The stage seems to have been one place where everyone could approve the existence of the Girl of the Period and enjoy her outlandish style and behavior, as in an 1870 *Red Riding Hood* pantomime in Birmingham:

> The precocious talent of Nelly Smith, whose general acting, singing, and dancing are not less remarkable than the athletic skill displayed in her skipping-rope and bicycle performances; and the grotesque and piquant effect of the "Girl of the Period" episode, in which a corps of extravagantly attired belles, with the high heels, short skirts, paniers [*sic*], jackets, eye-glasses, and other orthodox equipments of the typical modern Amazon, go through some wonderful terpsichorean evolutions, combine to make this pantomime the most popular ever produced at this house, even by Mr. Rodgers. (*Birmingham Daily Post*, January 29, 1870)

Girls of the Period showed up on all kinds of stages, including burlesque, music-hall acts, comic monologues and songs, and holiday pantomimes.[47] The GOP quickly translated to a recognizable silhouette and manner for burlesque, and burlesque proved an ideal vehicle for the GOP. As in so many of the jokes and print anecdotes, she was both desirable and risible. Within a single review of *The Girls of the Period*, a burlesque by F. C. Burnand, the *Era* reviewer writes, "the object of the little piece is, of course, to hold up that wonderful creature, the 'girl of the period,' to derision; or, in other words, to satirise the fast tendencies of the age in one of its most repulsive forms of development," but also adds, "the dance of the chignoned, short-skirted, and handsomely-dressed girls has not lost its attraction" (February 28, 1869). The review encapsulates the same sorts of ambivalence contained in the newspaper retorts, calling the Girl of the Period both "wonderful" and "repulsive" in the same sentence, and frankly enjoying the spectacle of their dancing, all under the guise of "derision."

The plot of Burnand's "folly," however, does not particularly seem to harbor much derision or repulsion for "Calypso Rapid, Queen of the Girls of the Period," who hatches a plan to restore amity between Mr. and Mrs. Telemachus Brown after they have a fight over Mrs. T's bothering Mr. T with the tedium of household expenses and her mother's constant presence in their home. Calypso brings Mrs. T, her mother, and their friend Dr. Mentor (all three disguised, the former two as "Girls of the Period" and the latter cross-dressed as a "lady doctor") to the island of Nowarparticki-lar, the kingdom of the Girls of the Period, where they know Mr. T and his friend, the avowed bachelor "young man of the period" Mr. Coelebs, will surely stop on their canoe trip, enticed by the posted notice: "All *men* landing here will be prosecuted as trespassers. By order of Calypso, Queen of the Girls of the Period."[48] Upon their landing and capture by the girls of the period, Coelebs remarks, "In a state composed entirely of women—A man would be king." "On the contrary," Calypso replies, "he is a slave"

(18). Mr. T and Coelebs are eventually made the two prizes in a velocipede race among the girls; Mrs. T wins her husband, and Calypso takes second place, winning Mr. Coelebs who naturally is now in love with her. Calypso refuses to marry Mr. Coelebs, at least for the time being, but concedes that he may visit her at her island kingdom. There is a lot of laughter in the piece (and reviews attest to its success), but very little is at the girls' expense and the girls get no comeuppance in the end. Calypso has boldly stated a list of claims in a verse address to the council of girls:

CALY: Girls of the Period! Here we're met in session,
To give our opinions free expression.
ALL: We are, we are!
CALY: Who would be free, you know,
The poet says, themselves must strike the blow.
ALL: Brava! Brava!
CALY: Consider what's our mission—
To elevate the feminine condition—
To show that man shall not our master be.
ALL: Hear, hear.
CALY: To show that we're as good as he—
ALL: And better.
CALY: Aye, and better. 'Tis all fudge,
To think a girl a mere domestic drudge;
Born to be schooled, and ruled, and fooled—
ALL: No, no.
CALY: That we are not so, we are here to show.
Our right to row, race, ride, bowl, shoot, and smoke,
We will establish here beyond a joke.
And, more than that, the notion up has grown
That only man can go about *alone*.
ALL: Yah!
CALY: Yes, you're right; no wonder you're disgusted,
To think that girls like us cannot be trusted
To go alone, as *man* can do. 'Tis wrong,
We'll prove it so! á bas la Chaperon!
ALL: bas la Chaperon!
CALY: The pic-nic waits.[49]

In the end this hubristic antagonism toward the status quo is not corrected. Calypso finishes with precisely what she wants: continued reign of the island of Nowarpartickilar and a devoted man whom she will dispose of as she wills. Although Mrs. T. resumes her preferred guise of a "wife of the period" at play's end, she has successfully resolved her own troubles by temporarily adopting the powerful, self-indulgent costume of a GOP.

Burnand's piece, which seems to have been a very popular offering both in London and in the provinces and Ireland during 1869, offers a frank celebration of Girls of the Period, even in their extreme fashions, forward manner, and protofeminist social demands. Although called "plotless, or as nearly so as possible" and "a piece of absurdity" (apparently its official designation by Burnand), no review took exception to the social content (*Era*, February 28, 1869; *Dundee Courier and Argus*, September 4, 1869). Miss Sara Nelson as Calypso Rapid in Cork was deemed "most piquant and fascinating," and "her mimicry of the extravagant language and deportment were extremely successful and amusing" (*Era*, February 27, 1870).

Burnand's girls shared the stage with innumerable other GOPs, including Kate Santley, Miss Lou Sherrington, Amy Horton, Miss Ada Louise, the Sisters Bullen, Madge Clive, the Lydia Thompson troupe, Miss Azalia Sharp, Miss Robertha Erskine, Mlle Manzoni Reviere and the French Danseuses, Louisa and Jennie Arnott in Buffalo, NY, Fred Alford's Girl of the Period Ballet Troupe, and Grace Edgerton. But the Girl of the Period on stage turned out just as often to be a boy, including Mr. Arnott, Mr. F. Richard, Basil Rivers, Basil Young, Alfred Vance, John Rouse, Mr. J. Holmes as "Dandy Sall, a Negro girl of the period" (*Era*, January 2, 1870), Mr. Buck; Mr. Booth; Mr. Fredericks; Mr. Leffingwell in San Francisco; Mr. Tennant; Saphrini; Moe and Goodrich, the American skaters; Charles Crayon; Edward Terry in multiple pantomimes; one of the Brothers Mortimer; Mr. Du-Val; and Fred Foster. In June 1868, just three months after the Girl of the Period's *Saturday* debut, the annual St. John's Theatricals in Oxford featured a piece billed as "an Atrocious Outrage, entitled 'Romeo and Juliet; Or The Shaming of the True'" written by and starring Mr. E. Nolan as "Juliet (the Girl of the Period)" (*Jackson's Oxford Journal*, June 20, 1868). The year 1869 saw Edward Terry playing in a burlesque of *Bluebeard* as "a girl of the period" (one of the sisters from the fairy tale) at the Crystal Palace (*Daily Mail*, March 30, 1869); the Easter pantomime at the Strand Theatre, *Joan of Arc*, starring Thomas Thorne as Joan, "most decidedly a girl of the period and an exceedingly strong-minded woman, who ignores matrimony"; and Mr. Hollins riding a bicycle as a girl of the period ("working the bicycle in the position of a lady on one side of the saddle").[50]

The cross-dressed versions of the character seem to have amplified both the GOP's femininity and her masculinity. On the one hand, male Girls of the Period seem to have often exploited her reputation for sportiness with dame-style portrayals. A stage version of this sporty GOP was to be found in Mr. Arnott in a burlesque *Robin Hood* "as an Amazonian girl of the period, a lady of flaxen hair, and costume *au pannier*, combined with a Herculean biceps, and a mania for boxing gloves and tricycles" (*Nottinghamshire Guardian*, May 27, 1870, 5). Meanwhile, other men impressed reviewers with their feminine verisimilitude. The *Era* said of one Mr. Henry Franklin:

> [W]e can hardly believe even now that it was not a lady who played that character. If not, then Mr. Franklin is decidedly the most effeminate gentleman we ever met with. The mild, womanish voice, the girlish simper which served for a hearty laugh, the "girl of the period" walk, and even the "Grecian bend" which he adopted, assisted to convince us that Mr. Franklin, if a *Mr.* it really was, can not long have escaped from a ladies' College, where "deportment" was more studied than attention to the letter "h." In the latter particular Mr. Franklin was altogether at sea, and "ats and ay" served for "hats and hay." (March 19, 1871)

The battle of the sexes took a bizarre turn when both Kate Santley and Fred Foster vied for the designation "The Original Girl of the Period" in the pages of theatrical advertisements, while two famous conjurers, Rubini and Robert Heller, both debuted magic feats titled "The Girl of the Period" while playing opposite each other in Liverpool. (In Heller's trick "a Young Lady is mysteriously discovered in the Hat of one of the audience"; *Liverpool Mercury*, September 26, 1868). In Dublin, even "Professor BOYD'S EXELSIOR [*sic*] TROUPE of DOGS and MONKEYS" incorporated the Girl of the Period into their act and their advertisement (*Freeman's*, December 22, 1869).

Despite Fred Foster's and Kate Santley's claims, perhaps the most famous and important stage Girl of the Period was Lydia Thompson, whose burlesque troupe of "British Blondes" took the United States by storm in 1868.[51] Thompson's Girl of the Period survives today in numerous souvenir cartes de visite: an outlandishly dressed woman with an entire squirrel perched on her oversized chignon and long trailing plait, a fluffy bustle, a cane, monocle, and cigarette (see fig. 4). Indeed, as a Currier and Ives print and an extant cigar shop mannequin attest, it is likely the celebrity Thompson version of the GOP that had the bigger impression on the United States, since it's this unmistakable image that proliferates, with the telltale squirrel on top.[52] Introduced in the troupe's burlesque of *Sindbad the Sailor* in 1869, Thompson's Girl of the Period character gave a minstrel-style "stump speech" called "The Marriage Market," parodying the famous slave auction scene from Dion Boucicault's transatlantic hit melodrama *The Octoroon*.[53] Campaigning for her own "sale" to the highest bidder, Thompson reiterated Linton's complaint that Girls of the Period were too much like prostitutes, even to the extent that they unsentimentally sell (Linton said "barter") their persons in exchange for money. Thompson trumps Linton by adding the valence of slavery—invoking not only the slave auction but also the specific scene wherein an apparently

Fig. 4. Lydia Thompson burlesquing the "Girl of the Period" in *Sindbad*. Collection of the author.

white woman offers herself voluntarily—as an improvised stump speech, a format borrowed from blackface minstrelsy.[54] (Of course, Thompson's Girl of the Period has no intention of relinquishing control of the price of her sale or ending up dead.) Thompson may have made the continuity between slave auctions and middle-class courtship and marriage practices a little too clear; the *New York Clipper* reported that "she fail[ed] to make a hit" (June 5, 1869, 70).

The Girl of the Period trope proved a capacious moniker for any number of staged versions of youthful contemporary femininity (and feminized masculinity); outlandish appearance, penchant for slang and antics, "strong-mindedness" (and protofeminism, as in the examples of Girls of the Period who "ignore matrimony"), and mixed-up gender attributions aligned her precisely with comic stage characters to an uncanny extent. Indeed, an article in *London Society* titled "The Past and Future of the Girl of the Period" specifically suggested that life had imitated "art" in the case of the Girl of the Period: "When the journals . . . first betook themselves to drawing comedy from the present costumes, the prototypes of the girls they pictured were to be found only in burlesques" but the fashions had leaped from the satire into everyday life (November 1869).[55] Meanwhile, some stage reviews closed the stage-life-stage circuit: "Miss Madge Clive, assisted by Mr. Barton, gave a drawing-room entertainment in the Corn Exchange Rooms, Preston . . . the get-up, coolness, and assurance of her 'girl of the period' might have been mistaken for the genuine article" (*Preston Guardian*, December 4, 1869).

Art and life drew even closer in amateur performances and drawing-room theatricals: a drawing-room farce titled *Girls of the Period*, written by an author identified only as A. B., appeared in at least two forms. In Britain it was contained in Clement Scott's 1870 book *Drawing-Room Plays and Parlour Pantomimes*, and in the US a New York publisher printed a small brown-paper acting edition.[56] A. B.'s *Girls of the Period* features Arabella and Polly, who dress up Arabella's cousin Fred as a Girl of the Period to fool the lecherous old French count who wants to marry Arabella (who of course is in love with Charley Goahead). Like Burnand's *Girls*, this play features a happy ending for the girls involved, and their high spirits and hijinks solve their problems, rather than constitute them. And, with the circulation of a play like this, the Girl of the Period finally indubitably did appear in "the salons of Westbournia, South Kensington, and Wimpole-cum-Wigmore-dom," where the author of "Women of the Day" had sworn he had never met a Girl of the Period before.

The staged GOP then proved to be far more agreeable to the respectable English palate than the prospect of real Girls of the Period traipsing about the West End or appearing in upper-middle-class drawing rooms sans script. On one hand, it's no surprise that the theatrical Girl of the Period caused less uproar than the real Girl of the Period. The Girl of the Period was herself, according to Linton's formulation, damnable precisely for her theatricality—that she seemed to be one thing (a courtesan, bold, fast, worldly) while being another thing (a middle-class girl). Upon achieving the stage (even a drawing-room stage, as in A. B.'s *Girls of the Period*), the Girl of the Period perhaps then finally existed in her proper space—the space of seeming and not being, an unreality confirmed by the guarantee of the proscenium. (And yet, the authenticity of theatricality revolves around and around—while multiple sources suggest that representation, be it a newspaper nightmare or a burlesque character, gave form to her, Madge Clive is likened to "the genuine article" and A. B.'s drawing room farce put respectable young ladies in the role of pretending to be respectable young ladies who pretend to be fast and saucy.) On the other hand, Victorians had no problem condemning representations of subjects they felt to be inappropriate, and yet the Girl of the Period, who was certainly generally considered a disagreeable model, evoked primarily applause and approval on the stage. Although decried in real life, something about the GOP proved to be just right for degustation via the realms of representation (and not only stage representation). One aspect of her warm welcome was, of course, the separability of the stage from real life, but also the stage representations appear to have added their own commentaries to various definitions of the GOP. Comical turns like the men who played her as masculine catered to the notion that the Girl of the Period was a mythical invention; warmer, more sympathetic portrayals like Arabella, Polly, and Calypso Rapid rework the Girl of the Period trope into one that validates the modern girl as certainly modish and fun loving, but not "thank goodness! the immodest, masculine, half-dressed creature in the existence of which certain miserable prints would have us believe" (*Bradford Observer*, December 17, 1869, 4).

Most importantly, theatrical performance's liminal status as fundamentally not real while remaining endemic and embedded as a quotidian institution reconfuses the status of the Girl of the Period as mere newspaper nightmare or actual walking, talking embodied type of girl (even when, as in the case of Fred Fenton and other cross-dressed performers, the GOP was a man). Most especially, as drawing-room entertainments and amateur actors blurred the line between audience and stage, even if Linton hadn't copied her from real parlors, now the Girl of the Period was truly ensconced in the middle-class household, at least as parody and a beloved comic character.

A Sweetheart for One Shilling

Perhaps one of the most modern aspects of this modern girl was how heavily the designation relied on her consumption and display of a number of fashionable commodities; this included not just fancy fashionable frocks and accessories cribbed from courtesans, but her own body was supplemented with the store bought. Stock GOP features included dyed hair; big, brightly colored chignons of false hair amplifying her own coif; makeup and powder dissembling her features; the particularly exaggerated shape of corset popular in 1868 called the Grecian bend; and high-heeled boots that altered her height and pitched her weight forward. But all these accoutrements were already being used and debated by men and women separately from the Girl of the Period question. "Girl of the Period" rather provided a name for a character with a frank and open attitude to using these products (and maybe rather more of them than the average woman). Such excessive artificiality of course was one reason the Girl of the Period proved such an excellent staged persona for both men and women alike to play. We might further speculate that the endless jokes (remember back to the litany of jokes about transferable complexions, false hair, and so on) and caricatured stage portrayals functioned as one mode of managing, minimizing, and sublimating the anxieties raised by femininity's inextricable imbrication with falsity.

Comedic representations that did this work—which we might even call theatricalizing of the theatrical—could slip from addressing Girl of the Period habits of consumption to consumption of the Girl of the Period. The definition of the GOP's character in terms of commodity consumption was easily elided with the suggestion that the GOP treated herself as an object of exchange. For example, the magazine *Judy* spoofed the entry in an exhibition catalog of an 1869 painting called *A Girl of the Period* as follows:

No. 474. A Girl of the Period . . . . . . *W. Fyfe*

> To *paint and exhibit for sale* a girl of the period is superfluous work on the part of any artist. The girl of the period does both these offices for herself. (May 12, 1869, 20)

This joke cleverly combines the Girl of the Period's self-determination, risqué fashion choices (in referencing makeup), and a particularly bold reference to flesh trade, which ambivalently references both the notion of mercenary marriage and prostitution. Just as in Lydia Thompson's stump speech offering herself for sale on the "marriage market," Linton herself had claimed that "the legal barter of herself for so much money, representing so much dash, so much luxury and pleasure—that is her idea of marriage; the only idea worth entertaining." Linton went on to warn the potential husband of a Girl of the Period that "she has married his house, his carriage, his balance at the banker's, his title; and he himself is just the inevitable condition clogging the wheel of her fortune."[57]

Despite the historic ways that women have been used as media of exchange, Victorians were heavily invested in the mystification of the persistence of these economies of flesh within polite society.[58] Management techniques included the obsessive sorting of women into classes that did and did not engage in trade, and the persistence of the discourse of separate spheres (if not their actual existence) in which the coarseness of business was meant to be confined to the public sphere of men while segregating woman's private sphere of home and family. Most especially, there was the delineation and social abjection of those women who traded their flesh for money.[59] The Girl of the Period demonstrated the illusoriness of the boundary between prostitute and respectable married woman, revealing how respectable Victorian marriage practices required constant policing to avoid falling (back) into economic exchange. But at the same time the comic renderings of the GOP on stage and in print might be said to be sublimating and managing the taboo the Girl of the Period represented by rendering it ridiculous. This, remember, I argued is one function of theatricality: to derealize and render innocuous troubling associations and dynamics.

In the first issue of the *Girl of the Period Miscellany*, possible solutions to the "redundant woman" question are addressed, including the suggestion of sending unmarried women to the colonies to pursue "wifehood and motherhood" with the superfluous single men there. But this scheme breaks down in the (comically stated) equation of redundant women and commodity: "It hurts one's feelings as a man to think of exporting women; having them examined like government stores, and carried off in batches like Sheffield or Manchester goods" (March 1869, 6). (To say nothing of how it might hurt one's feelings as a woman!)

Linton claimed that girls were selling themselves only a few lines away from a paragraph accusing girls of admiring and imitating courtesans for hire, but she didn't make the more damning connection: that middle- and upper-class marriage was essentially prostitution and that it wasn't young women's attitudes that made it so. That would be a claim for radicals on the other side of the sociopolitical spectrum to make. Linton determinedly pushes a personal moral explanation for a situation that her feminist contemporaries (and also historians) would call a systemic political issue: claiming that girls themselves were responsible for the mercenary state of middle-class matrimony. Similarly, a few years previously, social commentators had pinned responsibility for the imbrication of respectable marriage and money on "Belgravian mothers"—well-to-do parents who cared only about securing the most financially eligible bachelors for their daughters. "Belgravian mothers" refers to a minor media scandal along the lines of the "Girl of the Period" scandal, apparently emanating from an 1861 article in the *Times*. In the satirical article, mothers of unmarried daughters from Belgravia (one of the most wealthy and fashionable areas of London) wrote to protest eligible young men's lack of interest in marriage, accusing them of preferring the company of courtesans: "We offer a supply of that [young highborn women] which ought to be to the nobility of our day what cotton is to Manchester, but all demand has ceased. . . . what our simple-minded daughters call 'the pretty housebreakers' occupy naughtily and temporarily where we should occupy *en permanence*."[60] The article caused immediate backlash (for instance, in a satirical reply letter two days later) in which the Belgravian mothers themselves were accused of scheming to attach their daughters to rich and powerful men. Much like the later GOP, who is accused of being obsessed with money over love, the Belgravian mother is supposedly obsessed with auctioning her daughter off like a commodity for the highest price ("Marriage Market and Belgravian Intelligence," *Saturday*, July 9, 1861). Indeed, a large number of the worries of "The Girl of the Period" had already been aired nearly verbatim in the Belgravian mothers controversy. From *Fraser's Magazine* in 1861:

> If mothers will look back to their own young days, and compare the salutary caution exercised with regard to their acquaintance with evil in any shape, with the reckless indifference with which they allow the "rampageous ponies" or "the becoming hats" of

> degraded women to be stock topics of comment and observation to their children; they will tremble for the results in a generation to come, whose mothers will be the fast girls, the pretty amazons of the modern Rotten-row; whose fathers will be men who have learned to talk of feminine purity as a myth, and of modesty and refinement as two of the great shams of the age. (September 1861, 309)

The author worries that talk of fashion and horse-riding (at least that of women of dubious character) would lead to the extinction of "feminine purity" in but one generation. Certainly, issues of marriage and money and gender were also being hotly debated in the political realm in the form of the Married Women's Property Bill, John Stuart Mill's woman suffrage bill, and changes in divorce law at the same time that Linton's article was mystifying those issues' imbrication by blaming women for mixing them together.

Despite the general opprobrium cast on the suggestion of a commercial bent to the girl of the period's love affairs, popular culture proved to be quite eager to buy and sell the GOP. The Girl of the Period gave her name to parasols and clothing, a card game, and songster; church and holiday bazaars featured "Girl of the Period" dolls (*Berrow's Worcester Journal*, June 5, 1869, 8).[61] "A SWEETHEART FOR ONE SHILLING" shouted the advertisement for Rimmel's Girl of the Period valentines in the 1870 season (*Examiner*, January 29, 1870) ("the Girl of the Period valentine being modern beauties, beautifully dressed *á la mode de Paris*, with saucy mottoes," as the *Englishwoman's Domestic Magazine* explained; February 1, 1870, 176). In a similar vein, a "Girl of the Period d'oyley," "etched on jean," was advertised in several magazines: "THE GIRL OF THE PERIOD D'OYLE [*sic*] always elicits amusing conversation at the dinner table. Six 'girls' sent free for 9s., in stamps or Post Office order, to the manager.—Ladies' Industrial Society, 20, Upper Berkeley-street West, Hyde Park-square" (*Englishwoman's Domestic Magazine*, October 1, 1869; *Bell's Life in London and Sporting Chronicle*, June 12, 1869). Here again the salability of the Girl of the Period is comfortably divorced from the hair-raising assertions that nice middle-class girls were selling themselves to the highest bidding groom and then modeling their trousseaux on courtesans' wardrobes, even as these products were being personified as girls for sale—"a sweetheart for one shilling" or six "girls" sent in exchange for postage stamps.

The exaggerated external appearance of the GOP, her reliance on commodities (hyperfashionable clothes, accessories, false hair, cigarettes) to "sustain the character," and the selling power of its consolidated recognizability as a trope dangerously imbricated the GOP with commodity and commerce, over and above Linton's original association of the Girl of the

Period with prostitution (which might be called the most fundamental entanglement of body with commerce). Although the accusation of the Girl of the Period as akin to courtesan had been inflammatory, it was clearly also deeply pleasurable to buy and sell her. Moreover, the proliferation of products suggests the valorization of the Girl of the Period, undercutting not only Linton's polemic denunciation but also the force of all the denunciations of fast ways and fashions. Just as sympathetic stage portrayals (re)integrated the GOP with middle-class playgoers, so numerous commodities brought the Girl of the Period home (again) to the "the salons of Westbournia, South Kensington, and Wimpole-cum-Wigmore-dom."

A Series of Transformations

The Girl of the Period craze, like fads do, ran its course. By 1869 mentions of the GOP frequently were prefaced like the editorial comment in *Fun*, which announced, "We are as sick—as we are sure the rest of the world is—of the mere mention of 'the Girl of the Period' " (March 27, 1869, 33). The *Girl of the Period Almanack* appeared in 1869 and at the beginning of 1870, bookending the nine-issue run of the *Girl of the Period Miscellany*. By 1871 *London Society* magazine had moved beyond satiation and reached nostalgia:

> The girl of the period! Where is she? What has become of her? We have missed her lately, and are beginning to wonder what kind or cruel fate has robbed us of the curls and chignons, Grecian bends, and Roman falls, which so lately disguised or disfigured a fair proportion of woman-kind. Are they lost utterly—dead and buried under the weight of censure that has been unsparingly hurled against them? We wonder if the species be utterly extinct, or whether, chameleon-like, they have changed their spots, and after a series of transformations, such as grubs and silkworms undergo, they have gradually developed and reappeared in the less attractive but equally reprehensible form of the strong-minded woman who now perambulates the world clamouring for "Woman's Rights,"—which, by-the-by, is a wrong expression, though generally accepted, for, as a rule, the fair claimant would become a trespasser on the rights of men, and would not only adorn or deform her mind with the masculine qualities, but would also assume his outer garment, clothe her dainty limbs in broadcloth, down to the very ankles, and even go so far as to cultivate the trim moustache,—we have positively seen the soft down shading the upper lip, as though Nature's self was treacherously aiding the work of transformation. (February 1871, 110)

In this remarkable passage, the opening lines of an article titled "Women's Rights," the frivolous Girl of the Period, who might have seemed the opposite of the humorless, shrill, dowdy reformer is presented as directly related, a late lamented progenitor of the much more disagreeable feminist killjoy.[62] Here, changes in mind lead a woman to adopt masculine clothing, but the "outer garment" in turn leads to a bizarre twist when the author suggests that biological change will ensue—the "trim moustache" is apparently already appearing on the female usurper's upper lip. Throughout the passage, the physical and biological are mixed up with the social in specifically sartorial terms: the Girl of the Period's fashionable trappings (curls, chignons, Grecian bends, and Roman falls) are described in a Darwinian language of extinction or evolution while a woman is said to "adorn" her mind with "masculine qualities." Even "adorn"—a cosmetic verb—is contrasted with "deform"—a verb indicating physical metamorphosis. Moreover, clothing, curiously "natural" and assumed (trousers are equal to a mustache in the passage), is here the guarantor of the "rights" on which the woman becomes a "trespasser." In *London Society*'s convoluted invocation of theatricality, artifice leads to performative change, à la Platonic antitheatrical prejudice.

London Society makes the link that later historians like Helsinger, Sheets, and Veeder will refuse: that to be a feminist could be directly related to being a fashionable, flighty, mercenary Girl of the Period, and that fashion might be a performative force that itself causes change rather than masking it. This is a negative connection for those who make it—both feminists and Girls of the Period are "reprehensible" in these critics' estimations, yet it highlights a continuity that has sometimes been forgotten now: the fashionable, commodity-centric girl of the moment might not be so far from the serious-minded feminist after all. I confess, one of the things that drew me to the Girl of the Period is precisely this sense of rebellion, how the GOP upended hegemonic generalizations about the state and behavior of Victorian women. The GOP's independent taste was illustrated in her outlandish fashion choices; her flouting of gendered conventions by horseback riding, slang talking, and smoking; and especially her alleged disregard for the traditional authority of parents, husband, and societal mores. I am not the only scholar who has found the Girl of the Period seductive; in her article "Fast and Fashionable" Kristine Moruzi argues:

> The Girl of the Period . . . becomes a lightning rod for anxieties about traditional roles for women as she actively makes her own decisions about how she conducts herself. Unable to control her appearance or her behaviour, the British press increasingly demonstrated its concern that the changing nature of girlhood was a sign of moral decline and degeneration.[63]

Moruzi goes on to cautiously outline "a space of subjective freedom for the Girl of the Period . . . free to dress and behave as she wishes."[64] A clear parallel can be drawn between the Girl of the Period and the 1990s (and into the present day) "girl power" feminism that emphasizes personal choice (and especially consumer choice) as liberation (especially when such choices also please those around her).[65] Twenty-first century notions of empowerment through the cultivation of a sexually attractive appearance, personal buying power, and proactive stances in heterosexual relations, echo the Girl of the Period's form of resistance to social conservatives while simultaneously embodying a popular fantasy of fun, sexy, desirable femininity.[66]

There are a number of problems with pinning a simple hope on the Girl of the Period as a resistant girl representation who could liberate Victorian girls through identificatory example. For one thing, it's not very clear how many actual girls were consuming the Girl of the Period as distinct from everyone else who was indulging: the *Miscellany* and *Almanack* were published out of the same offices as *Echoes from the Clubs*, and much of the content was aimed ambiguously toward both men and women and especially adults. Certainly, even if the magazines were intended for girls, there is piquant evidence of their circulation among other audiences: one notice published in the "Boy's Barter Bazaar" section of *Beeton's Boys Own Magazine* offers a copy of the *Girl of the Period Miscellany* for half its cover price or a model steam engine, suggesting pretty emphatically that at least this copy was traveling in decidedly male adolescent circles. The Girl of the Period publications, like their music-hall cousins, and the other proliferating versions mixed up reading and writing publics instead of articulating them, just as drawing room and amateur performances brought Girl of the Periodism into even the respectable houses where a "real" Girl of the Period (if they existed) would have been abhorred.

Evidence of the GOP's commercial popularity complicates an analysis that pins the efficacy of the Girl of the Period to a resistant position vis-à-vis the status quo. Linton claimed that a girl who pleased herself displeased everyone else (and was echoed by numerous "serious" journalists), but plenty of contemporary folks—theatergoers, shoppers, and magazine readers—seemed to find the Girl of the Period quite pleasing indeed—extreme, shocking, silly perhaps—but far more adorable than deplorable. Popular approval, even condescending, complicates the resistant quality of the Girl of the Period's challenge to entrenched modes of feminine conduct: People were *buying it*.

Commercial appeal does not in itself mean that the Girl of the Period couldn't have had a social effect. It points instead to the complicated position taking and even subjunctive imagination required to even approach social change and how capacious the status quo can be in encompassing positions that may seem to challenge the established norm. For all that

Moruzi looks to the Girl of the Period as a model of new subjective freedoms, the archive provides evidence of those new freedoms happening almost entirely at the level of the fictive—they happened on music-hall and burlesque stages. They happened in the pages of the *Girl of the Period Miscellany* and during private theatricals of A. B.'s *The Girls of the Period*. The Girl of the Period sparked a gender crisis on street, stage, and page. Herself mixed up, she inspired mixed-up responses everywhere—turning magazine authors into textual drag queens and music-hall performers into literal ones. This is not perhaps to say that she is part of a genealogy of gender outlaws, but rather points to how unstable gender has always been—always insufficient or excessive, guaranteed to fail. Both hotly debated and warmly received, I do not see the Girl of the Period as a heroine of feminism, nor as a dupe of commercial forces.

Rather, I look back to Lydia Thompson's Girl of the Period on the auction block. She may have been for sale, but this was not what commentators and reviewers found disturbing: it was that (as she declared in the speech) "we are aware of our own awarishness."[67] Being "aware of our own awarishness" is a phrase that has resonated with other historians, like Maria-Elena Buszek who linked the term to sexual self-possession.[68] I interpret the awarishness of Lydia Thompson on the marriage/auction block as a knowingness along the lines of a Rivière-esque sense of womanliness as masquerade.[69] We might also read awarishness as a sort of theatricality—a conscious choice of playing one's self on at least two levels: the personal and the public. The doubled attention of awarishness might recognize self-presentation (via fashion and behavior) as occurring in that marginal area of identity between societal expectations and personal identity, as described by Warwick and Cavallaro (see chap. 1). The theatricality of awarishness does not offer a liberation from the constraints of the situation, but instead it offers a sort of liberation from the tyranny of self-sameness, of identity. Although the choice is made within a constrained field, the theatricality of awarishness affords the performer freedom from the injunction to truthfully reproduce interior essences (and the compulsoriness of some of those essences). This knowingness introduces a separation—a space—between essence and expression. This is a space created within the status quo, a small space complicated and contested. This is the theatricality that nurtures a measure of self-possession as (perhaps ironically) a step toward subjectivity. If subjectivity is about self-realization or the suturing of a notion of selfhood onto or into a body, then for the modern girl of 1868, I suggest that it was theatricality that could forge the space for girls (and nongirls) to think about girls' self-possession—to become aware of their own awarishness. It is carved out at the level of the fictive—on stages, in magazines, and in fashionable outfits—and allowed to remain and proliferate precisely because it appeared not to really exist at all.

Awarishness might be the best-case scenario outcome of the Girl of the Period controversy. The stage, and especially the drawing room and amateur renditions of the Girl of the Period, may be a particularly valuable location wherein new versions of self-possessed, self-fashioned femininity were being tried on for size—and mostly discarded or dismissed as outlandish and silly. Even though it would be years before creeping changes led from Girl of the Periodism to more concrete feminist changes, I suggest these years of fictive Girls of the Period and the fashionable shifts they heralded were doing that work as surely as Helsinger, Sheets, and Veeder's "deepseated forces," entering middle-class drawing rooms and middle-class minds more easily and repeatedly, because they entered as mere entertainments and bits of folly.

Chapter 3

"Extraordinary Revelations of the Hermaphrodite Clique"

Boulton and Park and the Theater Defense

On April 28, 1870, two ladies and a gentleman stepped into a cab outside the Strand Theatre, where they had enjoyed the Easter pantomime *St. George and a Dragon.* Moments later, a policeman jumped into the cab and informed them that they were under arrest. Although the policeman offered to let the gentleman, Hugh Alexander Mundell, go, he elected to remain with Fanny and Stella on the way to Bow Street Station. But Mundell soon found that his gallantry had perhaps been misplaced when Fanny turned out to be Frederick William Park, a twenty-three-year-old law student, and Stella, who had rebuffed Mundell's romantic passes, admitted that his legal name was Ernest Boulton, a twenty-two-year-old gentleman of unspecified means. The prisoners caused a sensation the next morning, appearing in the dock still in their evening gowns from the night before. The *Illustrated Police News* reported that

> Boulton wore a cerise satin dress, with an "open square" body. The neck was hidden by the folds of a white lace scarf. The sleeves were short, scarcely reaching the elbow, and edged with white lace. The prisoner had a massive gold bracelet on the left arm, and an imitation pearl one on the right. Adopting the pronoun used regarding the prisoner during hearing of the case, "she" had a small signet ring on the little finger of the left hand, but did not wear earrings. Her hair—or rather wig—of golden colour, was fashionably dressed in the Grecian style, with plaited chignon. The front was bound with a narrow strip of black velvet, and a piece of the same material was worn round the neck, a locket being suspended from it. Park wore a beautiful green satin dress which was made with an "open square body" and short sleeves, like that of Boulton. It was also trimmed with white lace. The prisoner had a lace scarf thrown across her shoulders, so as to cover the open

> part of the dress. She had a handsome gold chain bracelet; on her left hand a signet ring, and in her ears imitation-pearl drops. Her hair was the same colour as that of her friend, and done in like fashion, excepting that the back part was done in curls instead of plaits; and in front was a diamond star on the velvet band. Both prisoners wore a white kid glove on the right hand. (May 7, 1870)

Boulton and Park were initially charged with "outraging public decency," a misdemeanor, and debate was raised in the court as to whether cross-dressing in public was illegal at all under common law (*Telegraph*, June 7, 1870). But the case quickly developed into a felony sodomy question when a police surgeon, Dr. James Paul, who had examined the prisoners the day after their arrest to "determine their sex," testified that the bodies of the defendants bore proof of felonious sexual activity—that is, buggery, an offense punishable by seven years to life in prison (KB 6/3).[1] Until 1861, only eight years previously, buggery was a capital offense; some newspapers erroneously reported that the defendants did face capital charges (*Pall Mall Gazette*, May 31, 1870).[2] Police searches turned up dresses, photographs, and letters from an ever-widening circle of men who seemed to make up a "hermaphrodite clique" of well-connected "gentlemen-women" (*Reynolds's*, June 5, 1870; *Lloyd's*, May 22, 1870). The formidable array of lawyers marshaled for the defense contended that Boulton and Park were just youthful middle-class amateur actors who had taken the pantomime too far: one witness called Boulton "the best amateur actress off the boards," while Park specialized in "dowagers and old women" (*Lloyd's*, May 22, 1870).

Boulton and Park are now, almost a century and a half later, celebrities in gay history books, comprising a whistle-stop on the tour of hidden homo history, just after the abolishment of the death penalty and before the Cleveland Street scandal, albeit always overshadowed by the ultimate eminent gay Victorian: Oscar Wilde. Further, Stella and Fanny's scrape with the long arm of the law began in 1870, precisely the year Michel Foucault calls the "birth" of the homosexual (in a statement Eve Kosofsky Sedgwick calls "an act of polemical bravado").[3] In *The History of Sexuality, Vol. 1*, Foucault dates the "birth" of "the psychological, psychiatric, medical category of homosexuality" to 1870, not because two cross-dressers were arrested and became a minor media sensation in London that year, but because German physician Karl Westphal published the opinion that his young female patient's "contrary sexual sensations" were rooted in her constitution.[4] Foucault explains, in an assertion that is itself now canonical, while sodomy had been "a category of forbidden acts . . . The nineteenth-century homosexual became a personage, a past, a case history, and a childhood, in addition to being a type of life, a life form, and a morphology, with an indiscreet anatomy and possibly a mysterious physiology."[5] Sodomy was an act that anyone might do, but homosexuality was an identity, a secret identity that permeated all aspects of that subject's being, not just the sex acts he (or she or they or it?) chose to perpetuate. The word "homosexuality" was coined in 1869 not by Westphal, but, according to Chris White, by "a man named Benkert who has gone down in history as a Hungarian doctor, but who was neither Hungarian, nor a doctor, but rather a Swedish campaigner for the rights of those he called 'homosexuals.' "[6] Benkert further gifted us with the word "heterosexuality" the following year.

Getting into trouble at such an (in)opportune moment, Boulton and Stella and Park and Fanny's scrape with the law provides a valuable glimpse into what appears to be a nascent (or even fully grown, but well hidden from history) homosexual underground. The trial proceedings introduced the wider public to the terms "camp" and "drag" for apparently the first time and conducted into the archive tales of cross-dressed boy actresses and the lovelorn men who adored them.[7] Despite the pride of place accorded to Boulton and Park in gay histories both academic and popular, let me reiterate: Boulton and Park were not arrested for sodomy but for crimes of fashion. Not only did their drag act attract the regulatory attention of the legal establishment, but they had also appeared in men's clothing, with open collars and waistcoats, powdered faces, and pink gloves so that people thought they must be women in men's clothes. Belying Justice Flowers's declaration that "the completeness of the disguise only made the offense the greater," testimony revealed that beadles, managers, and policemen had only interfered with them when they conspicuously failed to pass (*Pall Mall Gazette*, April 29, 1870; *Lloyd's*, May 14, 1870; *Times*, May 23, 1870). The manager of the Alhambra music hall declared, "I could not tell what they were, but I considered them improper persons" (*Globe*, May 13, 1870; *Telegraph*, May 10, 1871).

Where others have been preoccupied with peeling back the burlesque frippery of the drag queen to find a homosexual or trans forefather (or -mother), here I am interested in *what* was in the closet, not *who*. I am discussing public performances, not private acts—because, crucially, the acts that the prosecution eventually had to rely on to index criminal sexual activity took place not in the closet (which also sometimes means a room—a bedroom, mayhap, or a rented boarding house room, or a suite in Haxell's Hotel), but in the very center of respectable society—in the center of the city, in the center of middle-class social circles, in the center of attention. The scandal of the case really came from the fact that the female personators weren't particularly scandalous at all until retroactively and suddenly reclassified as such by the arrest. As much as being part of a secretive "androgynous clique," they were also thoroughly integrated into middle-class (and higher) society.

The historical record does not furnish us with the details of what occurred in the closets of the female personators and their friends, nor do we have access to detail about how the members of the "hermaphrodite gang" perceived themselves, or whether they perceived their "campish undertakings" as constitutional truths, part of a shared identity as sodomites, homosexuals, or gay men. Eve Kosofsky Sedgwick declares,

> to alienate conclusively, *definitionally*, from anyone on any theoretical ground the authority to describe and name their own sexual desire is a terribly consequential seizure. In this century, in which sexuality has been made expressive of the essence of both identity and knowledge, it may represent the most intimate violence possible.[8]

Following Sedgwick's caveat, I want to avoid the violence of assigning any single definitive meaning to Boulton and Park's actions and behaviors now, especially considering that what I have always found most fabulous about them was their consistent flouting of concrete definitions. Judith Butler writes in the 1999 preface to *Gender Trouble*, "if there is a positive normative task in *Gender Trouble*, it is to insist upon the extension of . . . legitimacy to bodies that have been regarded as false, unreal, and unintelligible."[9] Without setting aside the pressing question of what legitimacy may mean and within which structures legitimacy is itself rendered legitimate, I see this work as part of the larger task of making life more livable for more individuals, even those whose deeply felt convictions have caused them to fall outside the limits of normative classification. Moreover, while the case certainly comprises a signal cataclysm in mid-Victorian understandings of homosexuality, indeed perhaps the very birth of modern notion(s) of homosexuality, the case also, I have been arguing and will demonstrate further, provides a key window for articulating how fashion and quotidian public performance conditioned the making of a great range of raced, gendered, sexed, and sexualized selves in the mid-Victorian period, not just a small, secretive "androgynous" underground in the capital. My desire to avoid assigning meaning or intention to my deceased interlocutors' actions (especially as they are almost entirely available to us solely through police, court, and news documents) does however pose a significant problem for the terminology I will have to use to convey the events and reasonings that occurred in 1870 and 1871. I have therefore followed the conventions of gender and sex assignment assumed by my nineteenth century interlocutors, while also seeking to expose all the places where these assumptions were (and are) stymied by the facts of the case. While Boulton and Park are rightly regarded as important gay ancestors as well as occasionally (and I suspect in future years more often) transgender ones, in this book they are recognized as forebears to anyone whose subjectivity has been delegitimized, questioned, or denied because of their failure to live up to societal rules of performance—or because they live in excess of normative expectations. After all, much of the scandal of the female personators case devolves onto fomenting mid-Victorian gender troubles: performativity, theatricality, and the intractable problem of the natural, albeit all haunted by the specter of nonnormative sexuality.[10] In this sense, attending to the antics of Stella and Fanny and the public discursive fallout from their tabloid trial offers insight not only into issues of queer and homosexual history but also into any number of other mid-Victorian identity issues, including those of gender, class, and nationalist discourses.[11] Boulton and Park's case activated many of the same societal concerns as the Girl of the Period (they were identified more than once as "Girls of the Period"), while adding additional valences of sexual deviancy to the Girl of the Period's perceived gender deviancy. (After all, the GOP herself was imagined to adopt mannish habits as much as excessively feminine ones.)

What if we were to place these beyond-the-pale "other Victorians" precisely in the center—in the center of the city, in the center of their respectable social circles, in the center of attention—which is exactly where they were when they were arrested? After all, as much as being part of a secretive "androgynous clique," they were also thoroughly integrated into middle-class (and higher) society. News of their arrest was not their first appearance in the newspapers; they'd been favorably reviewed in amateur theatricals. The respectable mingled with them at a ball in Haxell's Hotel; formed appreciative audiences in Scarborough, Essex, and London; hosted them in homes and offices; met them in theaters, restaurants, public amusements, and the Oxford-Cambridge boat race.[12] They counted the wealthy and well-connected among their friends, including gentlemen of leisure (Amos Gibbings and Hugh Mundell); professionals like lawyer Francis Kegan Cox, John Safford Fiske, the American consul at Edinburgh; and of course the aristocratic former MP Lord Arthur Clinton, third son of the Duke of Newcastle.

So my objective here is to look at the controversy Boulton and Park's arrest sparked, like the Girl of the Period and the Meiji clothing reforms, at the center of the status quo. While these may all be considered resistances or rebellions, they were not necessarily formulated as such—rather I submit that they are examples of individual attempts to get by within the system, balancing the urges of selfhood or personal identity with the requirements and demands of society or collective identity.

Boulton and Park as proto–gay icons obviously partake of queer sexuality's perpetual social abjection, yet this case reveals something more than the already obvious fact that same-sex sexual practices were abjured in Victorian Britain. Unlike some of the other British same-sex scandals up to and beyond this point, which contained evidence of private sexual behaviors among a secret group (eighteenth-century Molly Houses, the Cleveland Street scandal), the primary evidences arrayed against Boulton and Park were much more public, if, like the Girl of the Period, outré and occasionally rebuked or opposed. Obviously, such activities could be classified as tactically resistant, but by looking at other aspects of the case and trial, we can avoid binarizing our thinking into two homogeneous social groups of outsiders and insiders. Such a move allows us to articulate other nuances about how deviances from the (always ideal and never fully realized) rules, mores, taboos, and strictures of a society were dealt with and managed. Arraignment and trial testimony offers a window into dissensus within London's wider middle-class cultures of diversion, with occasional glimpses of the higher and lower classes. Boulton and Park's public self-performances, most of which had been tolerated and some applauded by the larger society, were only retroactively classified as unacceptable, violently suppressed through both criminal judicial and social power. In turn, the explicit relimning of boundaries precipitated by the Boulton and Park case helped to shift the dominant ideology about acceptable behaviors in the city.

In this chapter I focus in particular on how notions of theater and theatricality were deployed and debated by the legal counsels and the media to make sense of Stella and Fanny and their "epicene college" (*Times*, May 31, 1870). British society found itself wrestling with some of the primary issues of performance studies one hundred years in advance of such a designation in trying to draw lines about authenticity and theatricality in the performance of everyday life during a situation in which theater appeared to have run amok in reality (fig. 5). The prosecution pursued a novel attempt to identify sodomy as represented, performed, or enacted in nonsexual activities (like cross-dressing and gesture)—in contravention of centuries of Western discourse that defined same-sex sexual activity as peculiarly and particularly unspeakable, secret, or unrepresentable.[13] Such an attempt presages the advent of homosexual identity discourse in a way that perhaps adds additional importance to the coincidence of Stella and Fanny's day in court with Foucault's declaration of the birth of the homosexual. On the other side, the defense presented what I am calling the "theater defense"—a systematic emptying of the signifiers that the prosecution was attempting to read as signifying sodomy. I am not suggesting that theater is resistant to the status quo; as already noted, conceptions of resistance all too often coalesce an undifferentiated inside to a heroic yet futile outside. Rather, I demonstrate here that theater's position (admittedly a contested one) in the center of respectable society provided an alibi and an outlet for socially unsanctioned behaviors and desires, one which, because always remaining within the realm of the fictive, could be tolerated by the authorities invested in disciplining their unruly subjects.[14] As with the Girl of the Period controversy, theater proved a liminal organ by which society could contain its difference in place of (and in conjunction and collusion with) violent legal abjection.

In the remainder of this chapter, I use the Boulton and Park trial to further expand the complex of societal anxieties elicited by the Girl of

Fig. 5. One of several pamphlet covers that captured different popular speculations about the import of the Boulton and Park case. *The Unnatural History and Petticoat Mystery of Boulton and Park* (London: G. Clark, [1870]). Courtesy of Lilly Library, Indiana University.

the Period controversy, moving from the court of public opinion to an actual felony courtroom, and from concerns about (young) women's performances of gender and nation to young men, with the added sub-rosa concerns of same-sex sexual practices and nascent connections between sexuality and performances of gender. I will demonstrate how both prosecution and defense teams were forced to marshal their arguments in proto–performance studies terms, reading superficial performances of fashion as proofs of other bodily practices. By no means, either, did the fourth estate give up their claim to a stake in the regulation of society in this case, despite sharing jurisdiction with the Court of Queen's Bench. In the following, I consider the imbrication of this case with contemporary ideas about theater and theatricality, discuss the medical evidence and the rhetoric of sexual unspeakability that cloaked and undermined it, before moving on to discuss how the prosecution's pioneering attempt to collapse knowledge of private sexual behaviors into evidence from public acts elicited the "theater defense" from the defendants' side. From medical bodily evidence, the court was forced to move to clothing as proof, but the coexistence of a robust theater scene in London with pervasive antitheatrical societal anxieties rendered the courtroom a reluctant arbiter of some impossible paradoxes (and the periodical presses into active and exuberant commentators). My conclusion works through the various ramifications of the lawyers' gambit that I am calling the theater defense, in advance of our moving on to a new "stage"—Meiji Japan where Victorian fashions were rendered theatrical in novel ways.

Extraordinary Revelations of the Hermaphrodite Clique

Contemporary ideas about theater and theatricality followed Boulton, Park, and Mundell from the Strand straight to Bow Street Court, infusing news coverage by writers who were happy to note how the arraignment and later the trial unfolded like Boulton and Park's biggest two-act drama yet. The *Sun* reported that theater professionals were "taking a serious interest" in the case (May 6, 1870) and the *Globe* glibly reported that one such entrepreneur had recommended that the court "add another row of stalls and allow seats to be booked a fortnight in advance" (May 6, 1870). (Subsequent treatments of the case favor theatrical metaphor as well: Graham Robb calls the trial a "bedroom farce"; Morris Kaplan prefaces his account with a list of dramatis personae.[15]) Theater professionals joined a crowd of other "interested parties," which were reported to also contain aristocrats ("The Marquis of Grahame, Lord Verulam, and a great many other privileged figures"; *Sun*, May 6, 1870), "literary and theatre celebrities" (*Observer*, May 15, 1870), "fashionable people" (*Lloyd's*, May 29, 1870), and "briefless barristers" (*Illustrated Police News*, May

13, 1871, 4), leaving the room "crowded to excess" (*Sun*, April 29, 1870). Harry G. Cocks declares that "London's magistrates' courts in particular were treated as a form of popular theatre."[16] The descriptions in *Illustrated Police News* of the sold-out crowd seem to bear out the assertion: "The court was filled with aristocratic visitors, who at intervals laughed or applauded as their fancies dictated," albeit constantly reproved by court officials (June 4, 1870, 3). In contrast, London's actual theater-focused newspaper, the *Era*, hid their only postarrest mentions of the pair in two miscellaneous news items tucked beneath other larger items on "Freemasonry" (May 22, 1870, 4) and "Pigeon-Shooting" (June 12, 1870, 4). The first report noted only that at the ongoing arraignment "evidence produced was of a most disgusting nature, and quite unfit for a respectable paper to publish," and the latter named the defendants and confirmed the case would go to trial.

Outside the court another audience waited for the prisoners each day, even the morning after their arrest: "news of their capture drew thousands to the doors of the police-court," and as the prisoners (still in their evening finery) were taken from the station house to the court, on the opposite side of the road, they had to be hustled past cheering and jeering crowds (see fig. 6, *Sun*, April 29, 1870). The traffic-stopping crowds in the streets did not diminish even after the disappointment of the prisoners' subsequent appearances dressed in "ordinary fashionable morning dress" (*Sun*, May 6, 1870). One newspaper even suggested that the daily trip into the street "was more an ordeal for them than that they had to undergo in the court" (*Observer*, May 22, 1870). Arraignment took place over a month, from April 29, 1870, to their final examination before Justice Flowers of Bow Street police court in June, when they were "bound over" for trial, which was postponed repeatedly to allow time for the prosecution to gather evidence, until they finally went to trial May 9, 1871, before Lord Chief Justice Alexander Cockburn—over a year after the arrest outside the Strand.

Even larger crowds than those in Bow Street had access to the "extraordinary revelations" of the courtroom through the newspapers that began carrying extensive coverage of the case. The story was particularly popular with the *Illustrated Police News*, which published six engravings on its front pages between May 7, 1870, and May 20, 1871. These engravings, as well as others from the penny pamphlets that reprinted portions of testimony with brief commentaries, index shifting and contradictory attitudes about the "hideous mystery" being plumbed at Bow Street (*Telegraph*, May 23, 1870). The news outlets covering the trial maintained a dramaturgical interest in framing the proceedings as a cautionary tale (albeit one with a racy undercurrent of prurient fascination). The shifting visual portrayal of the defendants and their friends corresponds roughly with the revelations of the arraignment; sometimes the activities of the female

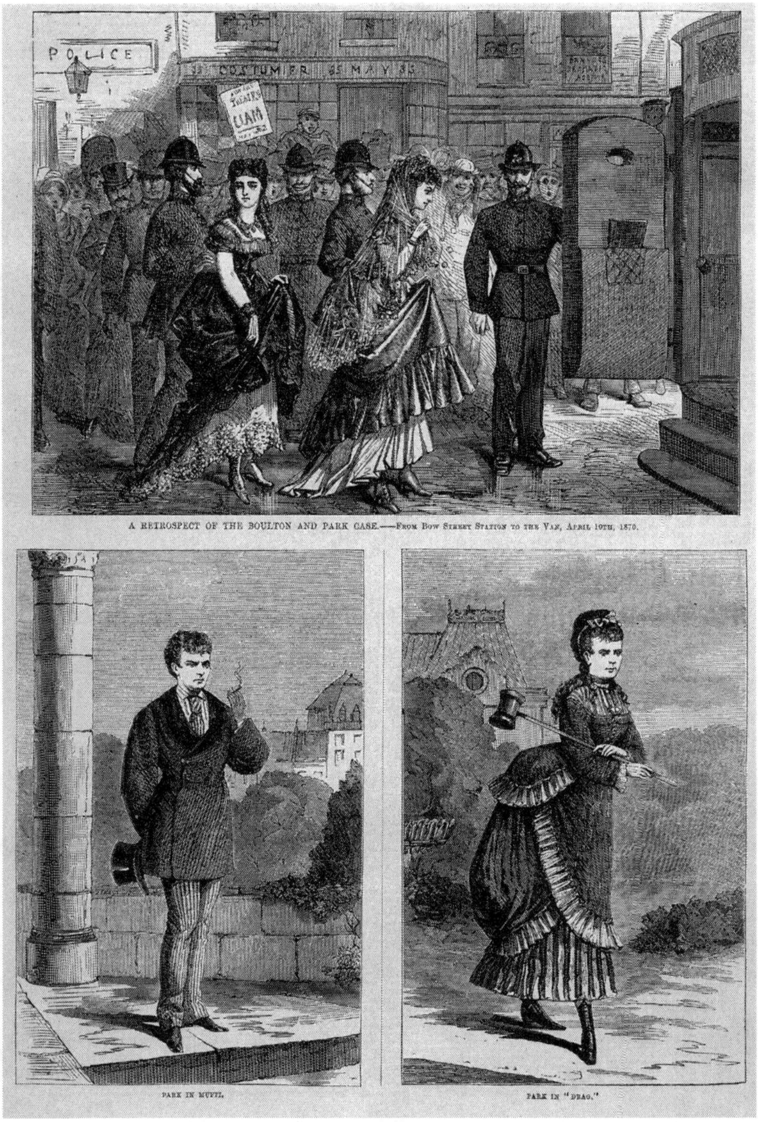

Fig. 6. "A Retrospect of the Boulton and Park Case," *Days' Doings*, May 20, 1871, 264, a rendition of Ernest Boulton and Frederick William Park's walk to the police van from the arraignment still in women's dress and copies of two photographs of Park from the trial evidence. Courtesy of Special Collections, Charles E. Young Research Library, UCLA.

Fig. 7. “The Boulton and Park Trial—The Commencement of the Story,” *Days’ Doings*, May 13, 1870, 248. This image dramatizes the feminized presentation of masculine dress witness that Hugh Alexander Mundell described in his first meeting with Boulton and Park when they appeared in men’s dress, but Mundell believed them to be women in drag. Courtesy of Special Collections, Charles E. Young Research Library, UCLA.

personators seem funny or unremarkable, at other times the defendants seem more menacing (and some more than others); sometimes Boulton and Park are indistinguishable from women, sometimes they absolutely don’t pass.

For example, in the earliest illustrations from a pamphlet and the *Illustrated Police News*, Boulton and Park are depicted as lovely ladies, but both feature the specter of surveillance in the form of a hovering policeman. He seems to see something that the viewer of the illustration cannot discern. The same surveillant aspect is doubled or even quadrupled in the first image published by the *Days Doings*, another weekly illustrated newspaper (see fig. 7). In this image, titled “the commencement of the Story,” Mundell’s testimony to having first met Boulton and Park in men’s dress, but accessorized in such a way that he believed them to be cross-dressed women is depicted, although in comparison to the way they are limned in the *Days’ Doings* other engraving (fig. 6), the artist seems to intend the viewer to doubt the two figures’ femaleness. While a rather elderly “Mundell” stands with Boulton and Park in the center, they are watched by two women, a policeman, and another male figure, probably meant to be the saloon manager.

An alternate cover of the pamphlet advances the case to an ambiguous postarrest scenario: in this picture we find "The Toilet at the Station" (fig. 8), which still depicts Boulton and Park as indistinguishable from cisgender women, even when stripped down to their undergarments, as the figure surrounded by three policemen is, two of whom are frankly leering.[17] While the half-dressed feminine figure seems to be fairly sanguine about the whole situation, the fully dressed feminine figure (I imagine this one to be Park—always the bridesmaid) has her hands raised in horror. Instead of Dr. Paul's pseudo-sodomitic "examination" of the prisoners' backsides, "The Toilet at the Station" stages a peculiarly heterosexual ravishment scene, with a feminine figure exposed to the leers of the gathered policemen and a displaced gesture of ineffectual feminine dismay. But, as the title indicates, this isn't the medical examination; this is a costume change. The center policeman is holding the trousers that will make the lady into the gentleman. Another pamphlet image crops the "Toilet at the Station" to show only the two central figures and makes the costume metaphor official—it is captioned "The Transformation Scene," a reference to the staple pantomime convention during which the characters magically change their appearances for the harlequinade, the singing, dancing extravaganza following the more strictly narrative portion of the performance.[18]

By the third and fourth weeks of *Illustrated Police News* coverage, the personators have taken on a distinctly more grotesque cast, far from the pretty figures whom the pamphlet had called "two fresh stars about to shine in the firmament of the demi-monde," whose "beauty, their fascinations, their paid for smiles, would before the London season expired, cause many a poor dupe to curse the hour in which he had been born" ("Lives," 3). In the June 16 edition are portraits of Park, Martin Luther Cumming, Amos Gibbings, and Boulton in ladies' attire. Cumming in particular looks frankly menacing, and Lord Arthur Clinton in male clothing makes up the center of the array; warrants had by this point been issued for the arrest of Clinton and Cumming for felony charges, but neither was in custody. Cumming fled and was never recovered to stand trial, and Clinton, with whom Boulton had lived at times and who had played husband to Boulton's wife in theatricals in London and Scarborough (and perhaps at home), turned up dead of "exhaustion brought on by scarlet fever" in rural Dorset (*Observer*, June 26, 1870, 4). He was buried in the presence of his solicitor and a few others on June 23, 1870, his thirtieth birthday (*Lloyd's*, June 26, 1870). Gibbings, who gets the most flattering portrait of the group, was the defense's star witness and the host of the heavily reported ball at Haxell's Hotel, which featured eight cross-dressed "ladies" as well as "several real ladies to avoid impropriety." Many newspapers devoted a line to the audience's display of "some little amusement . . . caused by the

THE TOILET AT THE STATION.

Fig. 8. An alternate cover of the George C. Clarke published pamphlet *The Lives of Boulton and Park: Extraordinary Revelations*, captioned "The Toilet at the Station" (1870). Courtesy of British Library / Granger.

very effeminate appearance he presented, and the slightly affected manner in which he gave his evidence" (*Reynolds's*, June 5, 1870).

In conjunction with the felony trial itself in 1871, the *Illustrated Police News* published just one engraving. (The trial was only six days long; in accordance with British law it couldn't last more than a week, so weekly papers only had one chance to exploit it in a timely manner.) In the 1871 engraving six of the eight defendants (only four of whom had been at trial)—Hurt, Fiske, Boulton, Park, Clinton, and Cummings—are depicted as men in suits, mustaches, and sideburns under the line "The Female Personators." Beneath the oval frame are shown theatrical masks, ladies' boots, a fan, a woman's hat, and a packet of letters. The defendants are no longer lovely ladies among male admirers, but are surrounded by the tools of their trade turned evidence (May 20, 1871). The defense team's work seems to have been sufficient to relegate the personators' fans, boots, and even their letters back into the sign of the stage symbolized by the theatrical masks. (Or, perhaps the stage was being reimbued with a fresh frisson of sin.)

Personation

As the "female personators" headlines highlight, official and public interpretations of the case hinged on the status of the theatrical in everyday life. The persistent use of the terms "personation" and "female personators" to describe the defendants referenced a common term for acting (a connotation borne out by the visual devices of the theatrical masks in the 1871 engraving, the pamphlet that labeled the "Toilet at the Station" scene with a pantomime term, and the newspapers' fondness for theatrical metaphors; "Lives"). For example, in a review of the very pantomime at which Boulton and Park were arrested, the *Era* wrote of one of eight cross-dressed performers: "Mr. Edward Terry discreetly personated the enchantress Kalyba" (April 3, 1870). But, according to the *Oxford English Dictionary*, the word "personation" carries within itself an ambivalence between the theatrical and the criminal in its two meanings:

> Personation
> 1. The dramatic or literary representation or depiction of a character; an instance or example of this. Now *rare*.
> 2. The action of assuming a character, or of passing oneself off as someone else, esp. for fraudulent purposes; *spec.* (*Criminal Law*) the action of casting a vote under a false name. Also: an instance of this.[19]

Like the closely related word "impersonation," the now-archaic term personation carries an ambivalent pejorative valence between mere representation (an "innocent" copy) and criminal false representation.[20] Thus, the choice of "personators" to describe the defendants did not necessarily betray the newspapers' opinions on the guilt of Boulton and Park. The illustrations oscillate (as shown above) between portraying the defendants as sinister criminals or harmless "actors." The prosecution and defense laid out their arguments over precisely the two forms of representation in the *Oxford English Dictionary* entry—was "personating women" in "real life" a harmless lark in the vein of a cross-dressed theatrical entertainment or did personation signify something criminal?

The misdemeanor charges alleged that the defendants

> unlawfully and wickedly did conspire confederate combine and agree together and with divers other persons whose names are to the said Jurors unknown to disguise themselves as Women and being so disguised to frequent and be present at divers places of public resort to wit public streets and highways Theatres Music Halls Licensed public houses and other places of public resort and then and there in public and in the presence and view of numbers

> of Her Majestys Liege subjects openly and publicly to pretend and hold themselves out and appear to be women and thereby to inveigle induce ^and incite^ divers of the male subjects of Her Majesty improperly ^lewdly^ and indecently to fondle and toy with them as women and thereby openly and scandalously to outrage public decency and to offend against public morals. (CRIM 4/777)[21]

Although there was debate as to whether cross-dressing was illegal under common law, the misdemeanor charge tied the act of gendered dressing explicitly to attempts to elicit sexual attention, thus tying people whose appearance blurred the conventions of gendered self-presentation to purposeful incitement of same-sex desire.[22] Even more disturbingly from a feminist point of view, the charge appears to take for granted that to appear to be a woman is automatically to "inveigle induce and incite divers of the male subjects of Her Majesty to improperly ^lewdly^ and indecently to fondle and toy with them" (i.e., no more than "to appear to be women" is "*thereby* to inveigle induce and incite"; emphasis added). No description of the defendants' behavior while in drag is described in the charge, so that strictly according to the charge's wording, it appears to require nothing more to invite sexual attention from men than to be or appear to be a woman.[23] (In contrast to the misdemeanor wording, the testimony in the arraignment and trial would provide multiple witnesses who described specific behaviors that might be construed as inviting or inciting male attention as well as attempts by witnesses to delineate respectable female appearance and disreputable, sexually inviting feminine display.)

But supposing a collapse between a feminine appearance and an invitation to male sexual attention, then the behavior outlined in the misdemeanor would seem to lead inevitably to the felony charge, that the defendants

> feloniously wickedly and against the order of nature had a venereal affair together the one with the other and then feloniously carnally knew each other and there feloniously wickedly and against the order of nature with each other did commit and perpetrate that detestable and abominable crime of buggery not to be named among Christians. (CRIM 4/777)

Later this charge was reduced to "conspiring to incite others" (and each other) to commit the crime of buggery.[24] But in both felony charges (sodomy and the lesser conspiracy to sodomy), street drag would come to be interpreted as a sign of the accused men's sexually deviant activities or identities. A perverse notion of authenticity in personation creeps back in when the prosecution begin to associate cross-dressing with sodomitic sexual activity; reading gender deviance as a sign of sexual deviance presages the nascent notion of sexual inversion in which homosexuality was defined as a female soul trapped in a male body (or vice versa), therefore reifying an ontological heteronormativity to all sexual desire and validating a certain truth value to homosexual cross-dressing.[25] Within a discourse of inversion, cross-dressing could performatively reestablish the legibility of the soul's gender on the exterior of the body—the truth of the clothes' represented gender would in some sense trump the sex characteristics presented by the body.

Unspeakable Secrets of the Darkest and Most Degrading Crimes

The prosecution's first attempt to tie illicit sexual activity to personation hinged on the testimony of two doctors who claimed the bodies of the defendants bore evidences of sexual crimes. Meanwhile, the doctors called for the defense consistently conflated ignorance with innocence and knowledge with criminality. It may very well have been the police surgeon, Dr. Paul, who initially precipitated this case into a felony when he exceeded his assignment to "determine the sex" of the defendants because he "wished to ascertain something more, that was of my own accord, and my own idea" (KB 6/3, 82). He deposed: "I took a desk stool, and said to the prisoner put yourself over that stool, without saying a word he did so, in the very way I had required him," and then he declared that both defendants' genitals and backsides displayed physical evidence of repeated anal intercourse with some parts "of inordinate length" and others "dilated, and dilatable to a very great extent" (KB 6/3, 79–81). Interpreting his observations, he contended, "the insertion of a man's person would cause the appearances I have described," going on to clinch the association: "I should examine any men in the same way if dressed in woman's clothes. I was told to examine those men, and I thought that was a justification for my examining them in any way I thought proper" (KB 6/3, 82–83).

To bolster the testimony of Dr. Paul, the prosecution deposed a physician named Barwell, who testified to treating Park for an anal syphilitic infection, whom he suggested had visited the hospital under an assumed name and disguised in shabby clothes.[26] Where Dr. Paul explicitly read drag as the signifier for sodomy by insisting he should examine any men in dresses for bodily proof of felonious sodomitic activity, and Dr. Barwell appeared to confirm Paul's suspicions, no fewer than eight doctors called for the defense (including Dr. Alfred Swaine Taylor, who wrote the book *Medical Jurisprudence*, the standard work on the subject in Britain from its appearance in 1842 through the twentieth century) examined the personators and testified to the contrary.[27] The defense doctors declared that they had no idea what sodomy looked like because they hadn't studied it ("I have abstained from studying the subject which is repulsive in half and not likely to be of any service to me professionally"; DPP 4/6, 726);[28] (paradoxically) the vice was unknown in England; and (paradoxically) the bodies not only of Boulton and Park but also virtually every other body they'd examined in their combined decades of experience did not reveal such marks.[29] Some disputed the claim that sodomy would be legible on the body at all (a fourth paradox). The array of defense doctors contended that the bodies of the defendants were perfectly "natural," which to them clearly meant "not engaged in sodomitical activity," and LeGros Clark went so far as to declare on the stand in the 1871 trial that Boulton's anus was "unusually [delicate and small] . . . in fact more like that of a female than a male of his age" (DPP 4/6, 737). William Cohen seizes on this moment to note that apparently "a female anus is a man's surest proof that he has not behaved sexually in a woman's position."[30] LeGros Clark declared that "he believed the perpetration of unnatural crimes to be of so uncommon occurrence, that no hospital surgeon would speak with certainty regarding them," for which he received a hearty round of applause from the galleries (KB 6/3, 149–55; *Reynolds's*, June 5, 1870).

As the defense built a correlation between ignorance and innocence, knowledge of the crime became confounded with the crime itself. The defense doctors, in claiming no knowledge nor signs of it on the defendants, effectively made Drs. Paul and Barwell look like the only two who bore any sodomitic taint, even if it was only in their thoughts. By the time of the trial, Lord Chief Justice Cockburn announced to the jurors since that "vice has not yet tainted the habits of the men of this country . . . the medical men here cannot give you as the result of their experience that perhaps medical practitioners in other and less happy countries in that respect could give" (DPP 4/6, 1001), and reprimanded Paul, who had "evidently been studying foreign works" on homosexual sex and then perpetrated an examination nearly as disgusting as the crime for which he was looking (DPP 4/6, 999).[31] By the time of Cockburn's speech on the last day of the trial, ignorance had been so thoroughly elided with innocence—and knowledge with guilt (along with a healthy dose of nationalist xenophobia)—that Dr. Paul was being castigated for his own learning in the international field of medical forensic science, not only by the defense but also by the Lord Chief Justice himself. Cockburn suggested that the true perpetrator of an "unnatural connexion" was Dr. Paul in the form of the rape of two defenseless youths when he declared of Paul: "If instead of two effeminate young men he had met with a man having the strength and energy to do it he would not have escaped summary punishment for proposing so revolting a thing" as his jailhouse rectal exam (DPP 4/6, 999).[32]

While the doctors had the relative luxury of speaking more plainly to their anatomical findings and suspicions in the interest of honesty, truth, and precision, unsavory truths posed a special problem for an age obsessed with truth and simultaneously with thwarting the potential mimetic power of immorality. The lawyer, the newspapers, and (to a lesser extent) the doctors' collective approaches to describing Boulton and Park's alleged activities amply illustrates the paradoxical dynamic of sex and unspeakability identified most famously by Foucault, who uses the Victorians as his paradigmatic case for the repressive hypothesis: "modern societies . . . dedicated themselves to speaking of [sex] *ad infinitum*, while exploiting it as *the* secret."[33] Remember, in "The Girl of the Period" Eliza Lynn Linton had called courtesans "a class of women whom we must not call by their proper—or improper—name." But more than sex as the secret, same-sex sexual activity holds a special position as the ne plus ultra of sexual secrets. Although Foucault's analysis of the "repressive hypothesis" treats homosexuality as only one part of the open secret of sexuality, numerous other scholars have zeroed in on the special relation of same-sex passion/homosexuality/sodomy.[34] Christopher Craft notes, "In its most general historical signification, sodomy denotes a more inclusive class or set of reprobated, nonreproductive sex acts whose correct name—the name for which 'sodomy' itself stands in as but an expedient and allusive alias—is, precisely, no name."[35] Although Craft rightfully points out that sodomy has been used to stand for a variety of forbidden sexual acts, by the period of which he and I write (Craft's book *Another Kind of Love* treats the period from 1850 to 1920), sodomy was specifically associated with male-male sexual acts, functioning synonymously with the term "buggery" (the word actually named in the original felony charge: "that detestable and abominable crime of buggery not to be named among Christians"; CRIM 4/777). Nor was the association of specifically same-sex sexual activity with unspeakability a new phenomenon, a fact attested to in that the 1870 indictment drags the longstanding Christian canonical designation *crimen inter Christanos non nominandam* into the secular realm of Victorian legalese.[36] Harry G. Cocks writes that "this particular form of namelessness . . . later came to be called the closet."[37] The Boulton and Park case, of course, both exemplifies and complicates Cocks's pithy designation of the closet as the practical, performed outgrowth of sodomy's unspeakable status, since they just wouldn't stay in it. Although their public words and actions were encoded in ways the straight newspapers declared incomprehensible (which we might note means not only not understood but also not included or not encompassed—i.e., abject), the "hideous mystery" being decided in court was precisely whether the nameless crime had escaped its bounds to appear, and potentially replicate, abroad in the city. Moreover, a consciously enforced absence can itself be an emphatic form of presence.[38] Within the Boulton and Park materials, numerous euphemisms pointed to sodomy through the veil of unspeakability with banal utilitarianism ("intent to commit a felony"; *Pall*

Mall Gazette, May 28, 1870) and sometimes with rivetingly breathless gothic horror:

> We only hint at the picture we could draw if we dare. We leave aside the common, and, by comparison, cleanly vices of our time: We are not speaking of broken commandments: of Belgravian mothers: but we point below our breath to other signs of commandments broken which are too sacred to be written; of man metamorphised, not to "beasts that perish," but to beasts procuring their own perishment, body and soul together, of abominations by which lust defies disease as well as heaven and all manly instinct; of houses————, but we cannot, indeed, tell the truth; and less than the truth is nothing in presence of the frightful vices that mock Christianity and poison society in our midst.[39]

Driving the rhetoric of sodomy's unspeakability is a fundamentally antitheatrical paranoia: the conviction that sodomy is irresistibly mimetic. Unspeakability and compulsive mimeticism are two halves of the same discourse; anxiety about the contagious, uncontrollable replication of sodomy brings down on sodomy an injunction to unspeakability and unrepresentability. (Or could an injunction to secrecy invite the commonsense retroactive explanation that sodomy must be contagious?) Further, the paranoia displayed by the news outlets over speaking their fears about Boulton and Park connected the "mere theatricality" of representation with the performative possibility that a representation could cause real changes in behavior. Far from being about inconsequence, the antitheatrical prejudice gives a name to a pervasive fear of and attempt to limit the performative power of theatricality.

In the case of Boulton and Park, the fantasy of identification of the sodomite through bodily evidence introduced by Drs. Paul and Barwell was systematically torn down by the doctors called for the defense; indeed, the medical men on both sides fought primarily on ideological rather than scientific grounds (proof positive of Samuels's concept of fantasies of identification at work). But the unspeakability of illicit sexual practice, especially beyond the realm of medical expertise, hampered the progress of the prosecution even as sodomy's obscured shadow threatened the defendants.

After the failure of the medical evidence to provide incontrovertible proof of felonious sexual activity, it fell to the prosecution to prove that sodomy, despite its longstanding status as unspeakable, secret vice, was in fact represented—encoded—in deviant gendered performance: communicable, decipherable, spoken, and public, identifiable in various activities, like cross-dressing and writing affectionate letters to other men. But, to the benefit of the defense, such an association was by no means a foregone conclusion. Surprise, confusion, and divergent opinions reigned in the news. "Whatever the result of the investigation, there is much in this matter which is very strange, and, indeed, almost unintelligible," wrote the *Times* (May 7, 1870). In contrast to the dark truths alluded to by the prosecution, the defense argued that theater and theater's ontological status as unmoored from truth or authenticity could explain away all the "dark features" of the case. In their version, the defendants' outfits were meaningless representations—merely theatrical illusions just like those seen pervasively on comic stages across Britain: Mr. Digby Seymour, one of Boulton's attorneys, explained at the trial, "when not engaged in theatricals of one kind they [the defendants] indulged in theatricals of another sort, and that for the purpose of having a laugh at those who were deceived by their appearance" (*Telegraph*, May 12, 1871).

In the staged theatrical charade of men playing women endemic to the era, Victorian audiences and producers acknowledged no frisson of sexual desire.[40] Men generally played female roles for comedy—especially the "dame role." Park was identified during the trial as a dame type—typically playing "dowagers and old women" (*Lloyd's*, May 22, 1870). Boulton's specialty was more unusual, apparently delighting audiences with his perfect semblance of ingénue femininity; Laurence Senelick identifies this as part of a new strain of cross-dressing he calls "glamour drag" in which "men frankly portrayed lovely women."[41] Articles frequently exclaim over the miracle of Boulton's femininity in a male body. In 1868 the *Scarborough Gazette* had declared "the 'make-up' of Mr. Boulton, as a lady, is something wonderful in its perfectly natural semblance of the part" (October 22, 1868). The *Essex Herald*'s review of the amateur theatricals both had performed in in 1869 was widely quoted during the arraignment:

> Looking at him with one's eyes both wide open, listening to his extraordinary voice, and criticizing, however narrowly, his wonderfully feminine appearance and manner, it is really difficult for a moment to believe that he is not a really charming girl. As the performance went on—and most highly amusing, as well as refined it was—one unconsciously felt impelled to speak of Mrs. Chillingstone, the fascinating widow whom Mr. Boulton personates so admirably, as if she were a veritable member of the weaker sex. Laugh! Who could help it? Few tried who were present at the Public Hall on Wednesday night. It was really one of the raciest and best things out. (*Illustrated Police News*, May 14, 1870)

These glowing provincial reviews of Boulton and Park's cross-dressed theatrical performances could be seen as drawing the public into collusion with the defendants—if, as the prosecution was arguing, cross-gendered dress and acting could be read for immorality, what would it mean that so many respectable men and women had applauded it?

To accurately read Stella and Fanny's public performances for their meaning or lack thereof (i.e., theatricality) became more vital as the medical evidence failed. As the proponents of unspeakability paranoically associated sexual knowledge (or representation) with its performative proliferation—uncontrollable mimetic contagion—the defense team would be systematically working to detach theatricality from suspicions of its performative efficacy to prove, just as they had with Drs. Paul and Barwell, that mysterious appearances meant nothing instead of something, that wrongness inhered in the thoughts of those who detected deviance rather than the so-called deviants themselves. The defense's affirmations of the harmlessness of theatricality and assertions that it was already endemic to British society would become a systematic antisemiotic effort: laboriously detaching signifiers from deviant signified ideas faster than the prosecution could attach them.

Frock Ontology

After Boulton and Park's bodies failed to confess alleged sexual crimes, the prosecution attempted to elicit answers from their clothes. One of the many novelties of the Boulton and Park trial seems to have been the introduction of a type of evidence apparently never before seen in the courts of Her Majesty's justice: more clothes than the jury cared to examine. The *Illustrated Police News* reported

> Mr. Poland then proceeded to read a summary of the articles mentioned in the list, and there were about sixteen dresses, thirteen petticoats—(laughter)—one crinoline, nine cloaks and jackets, about ten bodices, about eight pairs different boots, seven chignons—(laughter)—ten plaits, and a grey beard. (Laughter.)
>
> Mr. Flowers: I suppose you don't consider that as an article of female attire? (Laughter.)
>
> . . .
>
> Mr. Poland: It may be part of a disguise.
>
> The list also included curling-irons, sunshades, six pairs of stays, one lace cross-over, two tulle falls, chemisettes, garters, drawers, four boxes of violet-powder, one of bloom of roses—(rouge)—silk stockings, eight pairs of gloves, one bottle of chloroform, artificial flowers, and a great quantity of wadding—used apparently for padding. There were found also some articles of male apparel; and it was computed that the things seized were over £260 in value. (May 21, 1870)

Clothes were displayed until the jury actually asked for an end to the parade (*Times*, May 11, 1871). Despite the hilarity evoked in the audience by the defendants' cache of finery, the prosecution was attempting to make a serious ontological distinction between types of frocks, suggesting that theatrical dresses would signify different intents than ordinary female dresses. Unable to ask the wearers of the dresses (since defendants could not take the stand in British criminal trials) and cognizant that if indeed the dresses were disguises for felonious intentions, perjury would ensue, the prosecution was forced toward other methods of determining a dress's purpose, such as provenance, value, and condition. While the defense promised to prove that the dresses had been procured from theatrical costumers rather than ordinary shops, the *Illustrated Police News* declared that of thirty to forty seized gowns "there are not more than one, or at most two, costumes bearing any affinity to a masquerade or fancy dress" (May 7, 1870, 2).

Martha Stacey, Park's landlady, declared, "I thought the women's dresses were theatrical dresses, enabling them to represent female characters. They were ordinary female dresses." Justice Flowers replied, "We saw the dresses here, and they were not like ordinary theatrical dresses. People would not go to a boatrace in theatrical costume" (*Times*, May 14, 1870). But this exchange betrays the intense difficulty the theatrical introduced to the proceedings. Stacey's testimony conflates the ordinary with the theatrical (i.e., costume) in her declaration that the dresses she took for costumes were "ordinary female dresses," while the judge's reply explicitly discriminates between a theater costume and an everyday dress while simultaneously transposing the deceptive word "ordinary" to the theatrical—what is an ordinary theatrical costume and what about its ordinariness precludes it from appearing at a boat race? While Flowers's take seems rather comic now, the ontological status of the dresses as theatrical or ordinary (to leave aside the absolutely baffling ordinary theatrical) was a key issue. While the defense claimed that the dresses were all theatrical costumes, the prosecution sought to establish that (1) Boulton and Park's dresses were everyday women's dresses and (2) that donning ordinary female clothing was a very different undertaking than putting on a theatrical costume, even if the two were indistinguishable by sight (*Illustrated Police News*, May 21, 1870).[42] This inquiry seems rather backward: as the convoluted exchange between Mrs. Stacey and Justice Flowers indicates, the essence of the costume's purpose inheres much more strongly in an individual's use of the clothing than in the garment itself. Performance determines meaning: what someone does in an outfit obviously in this case actually determines whether the outfit is ordinary or theatrical. Mrs. Stacy appeared to grasp this in explaining that Boulton and Park used ordinary female dresses as theater costumes; Justice Flowers did not.[43]

The parade of dresses in evidence moved the *Telegraph* to a lengthy philosophical digression in their trial coverage:

> Yesterday, however, for the first time in its annals, the Court of Queen's Bench was turned into an old clothes shop. In the purlieus of London, more especially in the streets around and about Leicester-square, you may find scores of shabby-genteel shops devoted to the sale or hire of secondhand ladies' wearing apparel. In their windows you see displayed the ghosts of rich silks, the skeletons of dainty "mousseline de lainé," the poor relations, so to speak, of moire robes and velvet mantles. In the glare of gaslight you might fancy that at such places as these you could attire yourself—supposing you to be purchasers of female attire—in the height of fashion and elegance; and the class of customers who most frequent these marts of soiled finery are not as a rule particular to a grease-spot here, to a rent there, or to a few wine-stains. But if you are a philosopher of the streets, and peer into the windows of which we speak in the broad glare of day light, there are few more melancholy spectacles than these repositories of finery which has had its day. It seemed yesterday as though the outcasts of one of these Monmouth-street establishments had been scattered over the Court of Queen's Bench. Early in the course of the day's proceedings two large packages were brought in, containing various articles of wearing apparel, taken from the rooms of the defendants in Wakefield-street. The contents of the boxes were unpacked by the policemen in attendance, and silk petticoats, braided bodices, embroidered skirts, muslin wrappers, bonnets, parasols, boots, and all the paraphernalia of the "girl of the period" dress, were turned out ruthlessly upon the floor. Whether the articles thus displayed were "quite a lady's" costume may be doubted: To say that the "get up" of the "female personators," as estimated by this specimen of the wardrobes, was regardless of expense, would be to sacrifice truth to sensation. A dressmaker, who was called in to appraise the lot, assessed the whole, including some odd dozen dresses, as £170, an estimate which would make any one somewhat sceptical as to the richness of the toilettes in question. Still, the costumes when new must have looked handsome in saloons and theatres. (May 11, 1871)

The *Telegraph* took the introduction of this novel form of evidence as an opportunity to wax street philosophical about the uncanny nature of secondhand clothes[44]—likening the old gowns to ghosts and skeletons—but most importantly for the proceedings of the case was the article's implicit invocation of clothing's power of illusion. The entire passage is thoroughly disdainful of the defendants' feminine wardrobe: they are "sceptical as to the richness of the toilettes in question" and they mock-nobly invoke their truth-telling mission over the temptation to "sensation" in refusing to call the lot ladylike. Instead, the gowns are "soiled finery," the "poor relations" (i.e., poor genetic copies) or "ghosts" (i.e., psychic copies) of the truly fine materials real ladies' frocks are made of. The illusion here is *de*lusion—the purchaser of such clothes fancies him- or herself ladylike—and only in the last sentence does the author broach the possibility that such clothes as the ones in evidence could fool anyone else, and then only with the caveat that they might have "when new," in the dimness of saloons and theaters. Certainly, now it seems that the cold glare of the courtroom is as penetrating as the street philosopher and the simultaneously risible and pathetic subtext of the haunted clothes becomes evident to all.

The street philosopher is an apt figure to invoke. Where the *Times* wrote uneasily, "whatever the result of the investigation, there is much in this matter which is very strange, and, indeed, almost unintelligible," the street philosopher was a sophisticated observer who could interpret the encrypted appearances of the individuals who made up the crowd in the streets and public resorts of the city (May 7, 1870). The *Telegraph* invokes the street philosopher (whom Cocks equates with the flaneur) as the proxy figure who, even outside the clear-eyed glare of the courtroom, can penetrate the illusions of the street to see the melancholy spectacle of would-be ladies in their soiled finery or pick out the disguised members of the epicene college of cross-dressers.[45] The notion of the street philosopher offered ways of imposing a sense of order and legibility on the teeming crowds of the industrialized urban scene.[46] The street philosopher's mastery of the deceptive surfaces of the city assured the anxious that it was possible to, as Simon Gunn puts it, "make social difference visible, to assert control over public space and to define its uses."[47]

The jury was charged with the same tasks in attempting to make sense of Boulton and Park's cross-dressed antics, with the help of the prosecution and defense teams to decipher the meaning of the defendants' clothes and actions as relayed to them by the numerous witnesses, from boarding house maids and landladies, to studio photographers, shop owners, beadles, policemen, and theater staff. With the acumen of the street philosopher, commentators insisted that the clothes in evidence threatened no possibility of successful passing: the soiled finery could do no more than offer a self-evident charade of fashion and elegance. What's impossible for us to determine from our vantage point is to what extent these declarations of certainty, the confidence with which the street philosopher's ability to discern true representations from charade is confirmed, was itself a fantasized mode of containing the dangerous undecidability of theatricality. The street philosopher, his avatar the knowing newspaper columnist, and thus the informed newspaper reader, are all as much fantasies of identification as they could possibly be verifiable experts in parsing truth and pretense.

What's strikingly missing from the extended disquisition on clothing is anything at all about men. The *Telegraph* passes over the question of what it would mean for a man to dress as a woman or to pass as a woman, to focus on another form of personation: cross-class passing. Key to the *Telegraph*'s brief digression into the melancholy spectacle of lower-class mimicry of their betters was the choice of the word "finery" to describe the wardrobe. Mariana Valverde points out that finery usually

> connoted moral flaws on the part of the wearer. Finery in this pejorative sense meant clothes that were too showy, clothes that looked elegant and striking but were in some unspecified way cheap, if only because the woman wearing them was herself a cheap imitation of upper-class womanhood.[48]

But the difference between the cheap imitation constituted by soiled finery and the real lady was by no means as easy to discern as the *Telegraph*'s street philosopher and the cold scrutiny of the courtroom audience made it seem.

The prosecution sought to force the seized clothing to confess more than drag: they wanted to prove that the dresses were neither theater costumes nor ordinary women's clothes. The dresses, the prosecution argued, were uniforms: the uniforms of prostitutes. The personators were not just blurring the line between male and female, but also between woman and whore. The courtroom proceedings amply illustrate how difficult the job of deciphering the city's signs could be since respectable and "depraved" women mingled in certain public places like theaters and shopping arcades (*Lloyd's*, May 21, 1871). Gestures and fashions were construed as important yet vague indicators of virtue; prostitutes and other "loose women," for example, might be identified by their "gay and extreme" clothing (*Telegraph*, May 23, 1870; *Times*, May 11, 1871). But increasing mass production of fashion in the 1860s like "the production of cheap crinolines and ready-made suits, meant that dress itself no longer served as a reliable index of a person's class or status," leaving the decipherment of clothing's class or occupational meaning up to more subtle distinctions and gestural clues.[49] Boulton and Park dressed "very fast" according to landladies who saw them come and go. They were said to "move their shoulders," "look around," and "nod or speak to gentlemen in the street"—all signs of a prostitute. The defense lawyer Mr. Straight suggested that people might be distinguished because there was a "proper and an improper time" in the Burlington Arcade (*Times*, May 23, 1870). Yet these signs were far from conclusive: William Henry Martin, a merchant in the Burlington Arcade explained that he served anyone in his shop who behaved herself because "it is rather difficult now-a-days to tell who is loose and who is not," an offhand comment that recalls Eliza Lynn Linton's frustrations with the Girl of the Period (*Telegraph*, May 23, 1870).[50]

Sexual unspeakability exacerbated the trouble with identifying prostitutes. In the "Girl of the Period," Linton had called them "a class of women whom we must not call by their proper—or improper—name" (March 14, 1868, 340). Of course, such a show of obfuscation did not actually cloak meanings, but it did render it difficult to verbally point a whore out from respectable ladies (further echoes of the Girl of the Period controversy); witnesses and newspapers mentioned "depraved women" (*Lloyd's*, May 21, 1870), "women of the town" (*Telegraph*, May 7, 1870), "gay ladies" (*Reynolds's*, May 14, 1871), "loose characters" (*Times*, May 23, 1870), "ladies of a certain class" (*Illustrated Police News*, May 7, 1870), and "common women" (*Telegraph*, May 23, 1870). At least one arraignment witness, questioned about his vague terminology, was finally forced to say plainly, "I should call a prostitute a loose person" (*Lloyd's*, May 22, 1870). But of course, even with an exact word, public behavior and fashion remained inexact determiners of character.[51]

The retiring room attendant, Eleanor Coulton, "took them for gay ladies," but Mundell had "witnessed no impropriety" (*Reynolds's*, May 14, 1871; *Times*, May 10, 1870). George Smith, the beadle of the Burlington Arcade claimed he saw Boulton "wink at men and make a noise with his mouth, as women would to entice them," but William Henry Martin, the merchant in charge of security at the arcade said he had never seen the prisoners talk to any strangers (*Times*, May 14, 1870; *Telegraph*, May 23, 1870). When Mundell was asked if he had treated Stella "as a lady or as a woman of the town," the defense attorney Mr. Straight objected that they were "entering a metaphysical inquiry," flippantly indicating that there was no real line between a prostitute and a respectable woman (*Telegraph*, May 7, 1870).[52]

Attitudes of Affection

Another evidence marshaled toward determining costume's essence, or what the personators were doing with their costumes, were photographs—hundreds were reportedly seized from the defendants' rooms and admitted to evidence. Among the exhibits, the newspapers described a photo album with Ernest Boulton's initials on the cover "filled with portraits of young men of apparently good birth, and bearing the appearance in many cases of university men" and photos of the prisoners "in attitudes of apparent affection with men" (*Illustrated Police News*, May 7, 1870; *Globe*, May 6, 1870). And yet reading photographs as evidence was vulnerable to precisely the same confusions as the dresses. What, precisely, did the photographs document? Felonious affection between men or souvenirs of popular entertainments from around the country or boyish larks in which the entire point was to dress up for the camera? Some of the photos feature dresses that even the *Illustrated Police News* would surely recognize as bearing an affinity with fancy dress (fig. 9). Others were more ambiguous, such as Park perched on the arm of a chair holding another man whose arm encircles "her" waist (fig. 10) or Park alone in a dark dress.[53] Or a very similar shot taken in Scarborough of Boulton dressed in men's clothes on the arm of Lord Arthur Clinton's chair. In another Scarborough photograph Boulton and Clinton have traded spots, and Boulton has traded his brown suit for a high-necked day dress and a plaited chignon. In a heretofore unpublished photo, Park is in men's dress, but powders his face with a compact, next to another young man, who is probably his brother Harry (fig. 11). (Harry seemed to have his own gender troubles: shortly after his brother's arraignment concluded, the *Illustrated Police News* reported that Harry was arrested on a years-old charge of kissing a policeman; June 30, 1870).

Chelmsford photographer Frederick Spalding deposed that the personators frequently posed for pictures, that they conducted themselves freely but decorously in the studio, and that the prints sold "by the hundreds," as souvenirs from the plays (*Lloyd's*, May 21, 1871, 10; *Telegraph*, May 15, 1871). But even as the personators' portraits graced respectable middle-class drawing rooms, others ended up in an album hidden in an Edinburgh chimney by John Safford Fiske. Fiske was the American consul at Edinburgh, and eventually one of the defendants, accused of conspiracy to buggery on the basis of his adoring letters and that album of photos of Boulton. In one letter (addressed "à un ange qu'on nomme Erné Boulton") he wrote,

> I have eleven photographs of you (and expecting more tomorrow) which I look at over and over again—I have four little notes which I have sealed up in a packet. I have a heart full of love and longing—and my photographs, my four notes and my memory are all that I have of you—when are you going to give me more? (KB 6/3)

The attorney general declared bluntly, "Mr. Fiske was in point of fact in love with Boulton" (DPP 4/6, 70), but the defense argued Fiske wasn't queer, just American: "Our transatlantic cousins, whose homes were near the setting sun, were in the habit of using more fantastic imagery, farfetched metaphors, and extravagant language, than was common in this country" (*Telegraph*, May 13, 1871). While associating floweriness with Americanness is questionable at best, the trial transcripts demonstrate that

Fig. 9. Photograph of Ernest Boulton, Frederick Park, and C. J. Pavitt (?) in drag with two more unknown men. Courtesy of Essex Records Office, UK.

in 1871 at least the mainstream understanding of sodomy was still associated with coarse beastliness, rather than the effete, hypertrophied image it will come to have by the end of the century, even to the present day: "It is inconceivable," the lawyer argued of the Fiske letters, "that two Christians in the nineteenth century, having towards each other the relations that are imputed to the two young men, should express their mutual attachment in language savoring of sentiment, refinement or of respect" (DPP 4/6, 242).[54]

In both the photographs and the frocks there was a hidden code in play: appearances were deceiving—the poor looked rich, men looked like women, middle-class boys looked like lower-class prostitutes. The prosecution was painstakingly attempting to create new semiotic evidence of sexual deviance, where all these deceptive and strange inversions and appearances signified sexual deviancy. The defense would claim that this bizarre code whereby everything appeared to be otherwise than it truly was was no hideous mystery but instead could be deciphered within the

Fig. 10. Photograph of Frederick Park, in drag, with unknown man, C. J. Pavitt (?). Courtesy of Essex Records Office, UK.

code that everyone already knew—the code of theater: acceptable, popular, middle-class theater, occasionally in "execrable bad taste" but not morally wrong or criminal (*Observer*, May 14, 1871).

Theatricals of Another Sort

Theater provided the personators' alibi to the prosecution's accusations of both disguise and drag as a signifier of secret sodomy—Boulton and Park had not disguised themselves; they had simply "carried theatre into the streets" and their theatrical get up had proliferated out of control (*Telegraph*, May 13, 1871). Everyone could agree that theatricals were entirely innocent: the attorney general himself noted in his opening speech of the

Fig. 11. Frederick Park, powdering his face in men's attire, perhaps with his brother, Harry (?) Park. Courtesy of Essex Records Office, UK.

trial that to assume a woman's dress for theatrical purposes "is no offense whatever," continuing that even to "indulge" in an "occasional frolic or escapade" would have been foolish and tasteless, but not criminal (DPP 4/6, 8). The prosecution, thus acknowledging that there might be some slippage between the space of the stage and the stalls, asserted a temporal distinction between play and life: a lark is temporary and fleeting, and as a trivial pleasure it palls. A "frolic or escapade," the attorney general argued, would not happen repeatedly, for the defendants "would have got heartily tired of it." Instead, the prosecution argued, dressing up seemed to be "in a great degree the occupation and business of their lives" (DPP 4/6, 8). An occupation is fundamentally durational, repetitive, and serious. The serious is by definition not cross-dressed burlesque or the "foolish freak" of pretending to be women. It is the until recently capital offense felony:

sodomy. So, if Boulton and Park's charade was not temporary, but durational and repetitive, it follows (in the prosecution reasoning) that it was serious, it was an occupation, it was felony sodomy.

But, obviously, there was another place where dissemblance and occupation meet: acting. Where the prosecution fought to keep the theater out of the proceedings, the defense relentlessly dragged it in. The defense insisted, "All that [Boulton and Park] did was to parade their theatrical finery, acting a part as much as they did on the stage, indulging a passion for admiration—and no more" (*Telegraph*, May 12, 1871). And act on the stage they had, with their names in programs and newspapers for their entertainments from Essex to Scarborough to Edinburgh, and respectable ladies had invited them into their homes (even entreating them to come in drag) (*Illustrated Police News*, May 14, 1870, 2). Although most certainly not professional actors, neither were they making a living at anything else—in Boulton's case in particular, not having held a job in three years and supported by his family, he had the leisure to pursue theatricals nearly full time. (Park was articled to a lawyer in Chelmsford, but his father—a magistrate—deposed that he had been allowed to spend an additional 2,500 pounds of his family's money over the previous three years. While this declaration suggests Park had about as much leisure as Boulton, it was aired in court to refute the accusation that the defendants were earning their spending money through prostitution; *Times*, May 13, 1870.)

In their first article on the case, the *Illustrated Police News* weighed up the developing case in terms of temporality and labor:

> If they are amateur actors, and have indulged in this dangerous and highly improper folly in public on a few occasions only, probably the magisterial remand of seven days in the House of Detention may be considered sufficient atonement. But if, as the magnitude of their feminine wardrobe and its well-worn condition seems to indicate, they have been in the practice of visiting casinos and other public places of resort for many months past, and it should prove to be correct, as alleged by their co-accused, Mundell, that they have made the acquaintance of strangers, and under the pretence of being women in male attire have inveigled them to keep appointments, the charges may certainly assume a totally different character. (May 7, 1870, 2)

Like so many times before in the history of theater, the actor was in danger of being subsumed by the prostitute. Both the amateur status of the defendant actresses and the entertainment value of theater so eclipsed the work of the actor that the *Illustrated Police News* could not conceive of acting as a repetitive labor that might recur consistently and require significant amounts of costume, and that involved an amount and type of work that could lead to a costume's "well-worn" condition. There is an elision here: the felonious activities of going out and meeting men were not the only way gowns might become well worn. (As anyone who has worked in theater costume can attest, mere amateur acting can result in significant wear on a garment.) I don't mean to discount the possibility that Boulton and Park were doing precisely what the prosecution accused them of, only that their attempt to disambiguate acting from prostitution consistently failed to account for the material conditions of labor and temporality that go into theater making. (Not to mention, it failed to recognize that the defendants might very well have had the goal of simply dressing up and going out with friends.)

Where the prosecution laboriously attempted to reveal unspeakable sexual crimes represented in cross-gendered dress and role play, the defense systematically emptied those signs of deep meaning: they meant nothing beyond entertainment, they signified nothing beyond the signifying machine of the stage. The defendants were "guilty of nothing more heinous than a silly frolic" (*Telegraph*, June 21, 1870). Fiske's adoring letters were mere American rhetoric; the dresses were theater costumes; and the photographs were souvenirs from theatrical enterprises. The cross-dressed ball at Haxell's Hotel—rather than a gathering of an "association" of "foolish, if not unnatural young men"—was an elaborate theater game, deposed host Amos Gibbings: "The manner in which the party at the hotel originated was that some friends of mine, who had seen me act, wished to see if I could sustain the character as well in a room" (*Illustrated Police News*, May 9, 1870; *Lloyd's*, May 29, 1870). The cross-dressed trips to the theater, casino, boat race, Burlington Arcade, and so on, were all little theatricals of another sort as well.

Conspiracies of Meaning

But the defense's incessant assertions of theater's triviality oversimplifies the opposition between stage and life. Simultaneously with a determined exoneration of stage theater ("no offense whatsoever"), there also existed a robust and sustained concern in the public discourse about theater's moral effects. Stella and Fanny's reported escapades inflamed old Platonic antitheatrical fears: that second-order imitation, particularly of disreputable subjects, indeed meant that "there can be no doubt that to act often in burlesques and extravaganzas of the modern type has a distinctly demoralizing effect" (*Observer*, June 5, 1870). The June 5, 1870, issue of the *Observer* contained a lengthy article on the dangers of modern drama, while reserving a means of salvaging professional drama (obviously a central feature of British culture) by suggesting that, while the "amateur actor seldom knows when or where to stop," the professional was safe from "demoralization" because of "utter apathy" born of "long habit." Considering the prosecution's previous arguments about habit, duration, and repetition as proof of nonamateur prostitute status, this justification for professional acting's prophylactic effect against "demoralization" rings paradoxically. The *Observer* went on to suggest the danger of mimesis was of particular concern for those perceived as weaker in the face of vice (again, a direct crib from Plato's *Republic*):

> [It is not] any stretch of over-thought or of over-morality to say, that exactly as a man would be slow to allow his sister or his wife to play Ford's "Annabella," or Vanbrugh's "Berinthia," so, too, he ought to be chary of acting any part himself, which is other than he would be willing to bear in real life . . . If a man suffers who plays an unworthy part, what is to become of a mere boy, whose mind is not yet formed, and whose imagination is not yet sobered, and who yet lives from day to day in an unhealthy and unreal atmosphere? Can it be wholesome for a young lad, upon whom in most cases nature has already put the stamp of effeminacy, to forswear all manly pursuits, and to devote himself to mimicking women—and those, too, not women of the best type, until the mincing step and the affected voice [. . .] has become a second nature, and the assumed character has overgrown and choked the real? (June 5, 1870)

Once more then, the article founders on the problem of repetition—by which we might say performance. The amateur actor, and especially the young amateur, in direct contradistinction to the professional's inurement via repetition, is feared to performatively warp his young mind through repetitious mimeses. This passage betrays a particularly convoluted relation to the notion of the natural, since it locates the unnatural both in the artificial of theatrical second-order imitation and in young men's indulgence of their own natural effeminacy. The naturalness of masculinity is thus revealed to be a product of careful cultivation. (That femininity is a product of performative cultivation is of course a truism of feminist theory since at least Simone de Beauvoir's maxim, "One is not born, but rather *becomes* a woman."[55])

Moreover, theater itself comprises its own form of performative "second nature," an assertion that the defense also adopted in arguing precisely the opposite of the *Observer* article to explain away any suspicion of unnatural vice: "No doubt these young men carried on off the stage the assumption of female characters which had become so habitual to them on the stage; but what could be more natural?" one defense lawyer reasoned (*Times*, May 12, 1871). The material, real practice of theater making combined with the natural and inborn effeminacy of the defendants to prove that there was no taint of an unnatural crime about these two unfortunates who couldn't help but look like women. (Of Mundell's declaration that he was convinced Boulton and Park were women even though they were wearing men's clothes when he first made their acquaintance, defense lawyer Mr. Straight declared, "That is their misfortune, not their fault"; *Telegraph*, May 7, 1870.) Testimony from Boulton's mother about his childhood affinity for cross-dressing and playing a girl was brought forward by the defense, not the prosecution. The defense located an excuse for Boulton's conscious performance of femininity in his natural body: it was certain that Boulton was a man, yet the defense insisted that his soprano voice and effeminate nature, his youth, even his feminine posterior, were reason enough to treat a man like a young girl. Even the Lord Chief Justice declared in his final summary: "The friends and associates of this youth had got into the habit, from his feminine appearance, of treating him as a woman in their language and style of address" (*Times*, May 16, 1871).

Further, the theatrical sign might not be merely empty, but overloaded with signification: some of the viewers of the distinctly demoralizing modern extravaganzas observed a disturbing doubleness of meaning—precisely the coded message that Boulton and Park seemed to have ported from stage to street. Peter Bailey gives the name "conspiracies of meaning" to the attitude of knowingness that music-hall performers cultivated among their enthusiastic audiences, anxiously observed by Victorian critics: music hall, Bailey writes, generated "a resignification of everyday language which knowingly corrupted its conventional referentiality and required a certain competency in its decoding."[56] Bailey traces the performative means by which music-hall performers created in concert with audience members (i.e., in performance) a doubleness of meanings that resulted not only in pleasure but also in a resistive undercurrent to the authorities' insistence on truth, honesty, and being self-evident. For example, one critic in the 1880s described the style thus: "There was an unwritten language of vulgarity and obscenity known to music-hall audiences, in which vile things can be said that appear perfectly inoffensive in King's English."[57] Famous reformer Henry Mayhew thirty years earlier wrote, "It was absolutely awful to behold the relish with which the young ones jumped to the hideous meaning of the words."[58]

Because, as Bailey illustrates, the doubleness inhered in the performance and not in text, it was particularly difficult to capture unscripted, improvisational exchanges between performer and audience and prove double entendre ("witnesses were often bewildered by the audiences' convulsions over apparently pointless exchanges").[59] The apparent meaning of such exchanges provided an alibi against accusations of impropriety, and yet as Mayhew and the other observers report, even those who couldn't decipher them recognized a troubling sublayer to the discourse. Bailey points out the ways in which such a theatrically encoded knowledge—by definition exclusive—can operate as a resistance to authority.[60] By "theatrically" here, I mean that the meaning(s) appeared (1) in performance, emphasized and delivered via extratextual cues and (2) (at minimum) doubled and semi- or unattached to the regimes of reality that reigned outside the theater.

While Bailey focuses on subaltern uses of conspiracies of meaning, authorities themselves took advantage of the power that inhered in recondite doubled meanings. John Kucich's *The Power of Lies* articulates how the "centrality of truth-telling in Victorian culture" led to a paradoxical power and prestige that inhered in masculine middle- and upper-class "dexterity with the truth."[61] In the Boulton and Park coverage, precisely such a power game was blithely alluded to when the newspapers revealed their own conspiracies of meaning in euphemistically describing the indelicate court proceedings: "It will be sufficient for our purpose if grown men who are hardened to the world and the world's ways understand what is written," declared the *Telegraph* (May 31, 1870). Yet the *Pall Mall Gazette* worried that euphemism was not enough to protect those that ought to remain ignorant. Most articles referring to indecency, they wrote, "bear their character marked on their foreheads" so that

> no woman can be in any danger of reading about them unless she does so intentionally. But the heading "Men in Women's Clothes" need not in the first instance have served as an adequate warning of what was to follow; and a lady may have been left to make out the underlying filth for herself, or have had to be warned of its existence by some male relative. (May 31, 1870)

A week later, they speculated that fathers would have to lock up their newspapers to prevent them from falling into impressionable hands. The *Saturday* recommended that men would have to "burn the newspapers every morning after breakfast" to preserve their households from "contamination" (May 28, 1870). Such a masculinized, mainstreamed assumption of the privilege of trading in layered meanings precisely when talking about a felony trial against men for their truck in clothed performances of multiple meanings without acknowledging the resonance between the two modes suggests that another way of articulating Boulton, Park, and the other defendants' transgression was that they had appropriated tools of privilege to a subversive end: the furtherance of sexual (but, to be clear, still white, middle- and upper-class male) divergence from hegemonic societal norms.

Recognizing how the power of theatrically communicated, layered meanings can function equally as a tool of the privileged or oppressed reminds us that such powers of theatricality cannot be thought of as themselves resistant or inherently liberatory, but function within the flows and ebbs of power and in conjunction with other privileges and oppressions. It may very well be that it was precisely Boulton, Park, Fiske, and Hurt's own whiteness, maleness, and indubitably their monetary means that predisposed them as well as it did to resist the charges arrayed against them.

And to return to the theater's liminal status with and against the status quo in which it is embedded and the conspiracies of meaning it could safely harbor: Bailey notes that the resistance of his conspiracies of meaning may never reach beyond the fictive space of the stage, leaving "the counter-discourse of knowingness . . . limited to the infraction rather than the negation of the dominant power relationships."[62] But Boulton and Park's particular conspiracy of meaning relied specifically on the stage's reputation for fiction for its subversive power. When the personators were faced with the material consequences of presenting themselves in such an outrageous fashion, they retreated into a second meaning of their self-presentations, which was precisely theatrical meaninglessness.

Which brings me to camp. Like the music-hall conspiracy of meaning, camp is notoriously slippery and difficult to define, with fugitive meanings that resist text and archive, hiding sub rosa beneath more blatant and obvious meanings. The first entry for this sense of the word camp in the *Oxford English Dictionary* comes from 1909, but forty years earlier, Frederick Park had used the word in a letter addressed to Lord Arthur Clinton: "My 'campish' undertakings are not at present meeting with the success which they deserve; whatever I do seems to get me into hot water somewhere, but n'importe whats the odds so long as you're rappy" (KB 6/3).[63] Park's prose names camp but also performs it with aplomb in this letter that attracted baffled attention in both the courtroom and the newspapers where the straights attempted to decipher the message for its own potential multiple meanings. Obviously a different account of the Boulton and Park controversy could have focused entirely on the incredible object lesson in quotidian and stage camp presented by the female personators and their circle of admirers, from "Lady Stella Clinton's" never-paid-for calling cards to the Haxell's Hotel drag ball featuring "plenty of funning, but nothing coarse or improper" (as well as Boulton's performance of his signature song "Fading Away" in a soprano that the band leader reportedly refused to believe was not a woman's; *Observer*, May 22, 1870). There was Alexander Mundell's declaration that he believed the two powdered people he originally met in men's suits with open waistcoats and pink gloves were women (see fig. 6). There was the courtroom's amused warmth toward Amos Gibbings's "very effeminate appearance . . . and the slightly affected manner in which he gave his evidence" (*Reynolds's*, June 5, 1870). If we name these varied facts of the case as camp expressions, then camp could practically be a synonym for the theatricality that I have been arguing formed the liminal space in which Boulton and Park could have comfortably coexisted for as long as they did within middle-class society. As Susan Sontag declares in her famous (though not uncriticized) treatise "Notes on Camp," camp functions as a "fugitive sensibility"—"a private code, a badge of identity even"—all phraseologies that recall the music hall's conspiracies of meaning as well as the nascent (albeit disavowed by Sontag) coalescence of a gay male culture.[64] Stella and Fanny's visibility—camp-comic, doubled, encoded, and partial as it was—nevertheless comprises an ambivalent legacy: innocuous enough to have persisted for years with tacit (and sometimes roaringly supportive) approval, transgressive enough to ruin their lives with their arrest and trial. Certainly, Stella and Fanny's campish undertakings had indeed landed them in the hottest water of their lives, but the defense continued to bail dark suspicions out of the rocking boat, suppressing illicit sexual associations to focus on the camp silliness of pantomime cross-dressed hijinks and the everyday ordinariness of modern theatricals.

The Theater Defense

While the attorney general asked the jury to "stop this plague, which, if allowed to spread without check or hindrance, might lead to serious contamination of the public morals," Park's counsel, Serjeant Parry asked the jury "to perform a nobler and better function . . . to declare by their verdict that no such plague existed; that England was happily free from it, and was not yet tainted by its foul infection" (*Times*, May 12, 1871). Parry asked the jury to find the appearance of plague mere appearance without substance. He asked the jury to see a silly theatrical antic—and London was full of silly theatrical antics that were perfectly acceptable and amusing when contained by the proscenium, if not exactly admirable. Notably, both parties tied their appeals to the fate of the nation. The prosecution implicitly appealed to the pervasive rhetoric of sexual unspeakability and mimetic contagion through their invocation of a "plague" of immorality while the defense worked to systematically break the new semiotic links the prosecution posited between gender play and sexual behavior.

The defense team's theater defense proved persuasive: more than a year after their arrest and at the conclusion of a six-day trial, on May 15, 1871, the jury retired for fifty-three minutes before returning to deliver a verdict of not guilty. Ernest Boulton fainted. Upon his recovery, he, Frederick Park, John Safford Fiske, and Louis Charles Hurt left the court with their friends.[65]

Jeffrey Weeks suggests the acquittal occurred because "concepts of homosexuality" were still "extremely undeveloped" in 1871; Neil Bartlett and Charles Upchurch call this verdict a willful refusal to comprehend the unspeakable.[66] Alan Sinfield writes, of Bartlett's question, "who understood the personators?" "The answer, probably, is that some people heard same-sex passion loud and clear, whereas others could not conceive of it. It is through that indeterminacy that indirections and evasions—those of the court, and of Fanny and Stella—could flourish."[67]

I suggest that we could give another name to that indeterminacy: theatricality. The theater defense successfully decoupled, at least temporarily, the links beginning to tie nonnormative gendered behavior to the signified of deviant sexual behavior. The centrality, the very ingrainedness of theater and theatricality and society's inability to thoroughly abject it *or* to integrate it with a pervasive cultural obsession with truth telling provided a buffer zone wherein fashion choices and actions could be plausibly emptied of their perceived illegal meanings. The stage also provided a space wherein subordinated subjects could stage the forbidden—like a kiss between Ernest Boulton and Lord Arthur Clinton in the amateur comedy "A Morning Call"—not just with plausible deniability but with the approval of respectable society whose own doubled knowingness allowed space for transgression since it didn't really transgress out of the fictive at all (*Times*, May 13, 1871). The stage provided the special space that could allow everyone to enjoy the forbidden, precisely because it could be disavowed as just a play.

The female personators were declared innocent in the end of "conspiracy to incite others to commit the crime which must not be named among Christians," but this doesn't mean they were innocent of a conspiracy of meaning. Perhaps what was truly unspeakable for the gentlemen jury on May 15, 1871, was to acknowledge how all middle-class society had taken part in the conspiracy of meaning presented by the personators. Moreover, the personators' reprieve would be temporary—by the end of the century, the unsettled linkages being pioneered by the prosecution between mixed-up and inverted gendered self-presentation and sodomy would be concretized and the era of the closeted invert, unmasked instead of insulated by his own ineffaceable effeminate traits, would be underway.

Judith Butler writes in her groundbreaking article "Performative Acts and Gender Constitution" that the gender acts that happen on the stage are not revolutionary because "in the theatre, one can say, 'this is just an act,' and de-realize the act, make acting into something quite distinct from what is real."[68] This is of course why audiences can applaud any number of behaviors on the stage that would disturb and anger people in real life and this is of course what was so disturbing when Boulton and Park's "theatricals of another sort" broke through the proscenium and into the house. And yet, the very derealization of such acts provided a haven, at least for a while, for those who find their most cherished loves and desires forbidden in real life. Certainly, we know that to kiss on the stage is not necessarily to declare who can kiss in real life, but it is also not *not* a kiss in real life. Ernest Boulton and Arthur Clinton really did touch their lips together to the applause of a Scarborough audience. Boulton and Park / Stella and Fanny's successful theater defense provides an example of precisely how the realms of the unreal, the fictive—the theatrical—can exert serious material force. One of the powers of theater is precisely in its unreality, in its inefficacy, and this was the fugitive conspiracy of meaning that enabled Boulton, Park, and their "hermaphrodite gang" to beat the charge of felony conspiracy. As the *Essex Herald* declared in 1869, "taken as a whole these performances have been most satisfactory and successful, and it is to be hoped that the future appearances of the amateurs may be the reverse of 'few and far between' " (February 9, 1869).

Chapter 4

✦

"Great Mirrors"

Redressing Nation, Gender, and Modernity in Meiji Japan

In March 1868 the bombshell column the "Girl of the Period" and its fallout shared page space with news reports from Japan. Almost ten years after landmark treaties had "opened" the nation to foreign trade with the United States, Britain, and other European nations, the ensuing unrest had finally toppled the Tokugawa shogun and a new regime took power. Supported by a coalition of insurgent samurai leaders primarily associated with the domains of Satsuma and Chōshū (present-day Kagoshima and Yamaguchi prefectures, respectively), the fifteen-year-old emperor Mutsuhito became the new official head of state, adopting the name Meiji for his reign.[1] His first official photographic portrait shows the secluded teenager probably much as he must have looked to the few who would see him at the time of his coronation (fig. 12). He is wearing traditional imperial dress, the *sokutai* style, set and decided hundreds of years earlier: wide-legged white trousers mostly covered by a voluminously sleeved robe, and a black *kanmuri* cap with a black strip soaring straight up from his head.[2]

This photograph was taken in May 1872 by one of the first Japanese professional photographers, Uchida Kuichi, apparently as part of a plan to exchange photos of the emperor for photos of other nations' leaders during diplomatic missions abroad, but this seems not to have taken place, either because the prints weren't completed in time, or because the diplomat responsible for the activity didn't feel the emperor looked properly like a modern head of state.[3] Indeed, we know that the emperor's appearance was a source of concern, because within months of Uchida's first images, a new proclamation attributed to the emperor would appear:

> The national polity [国体 *kokutai*] is indomitable, but manners and customs should be adaptable. We greatly regret that the uniform of our court has been established following the Chinese custom, and

Fig. 12. Official portrait of Emperor Meiji, May 1872, photographed by Uchida Kuichi. Reprinted in Sudō, Kōki, *Meiji Tennō gyoden* (Tokyo: Kaneo Bunendō, 1912). Wikimedia.org.

> it has become exceedingly effeminate [軟弱 *nanjaku*] in style and character . . . The Emperor Jimmu (660–585 BCE) who founded Japan, and the Empress Jingu (201–69 CE) who conquered Korea, were not attired in the present style. We should no longer appear before the people in these effeminate styles, and we have therefore decided to reform dress regulations entirely.[4]

In conjunction with this declaration, emperor Meiji underwent a makeover, trading in court dress for a magnificent braid-covered military uniform (designed by a committee who studied and compared European monarchs' pictures in preparing their design), cutting his long hair, and growing a mustache and beard (fig. 13).[5] He was nineteen years old. Like the imagined teenage temptress Girl of the Period and the youthful (or childish, some said) Boulton and Park, another adolescent was being pushed to the fore as an overdetermined symbol of societal struggles over the proper presentation of gender, race, class, and nation. New photographs in 1873 documented Meiji's makeover and soon this photograph

Fig. 13. Uchida Kuichi, *Mutsuhito, the Meiji Emperor*, 1873. Albumen silver print from glass negative with applied color. The Metropolitan Museum of Art, New York, The Elisha Whittelsey Collection, The Elisha Whittelsey Fund, 1986. www.metmuseum.org.

of a modern, Europeanized Japanese figurehead would proliferate endlessly across Japan and abroad.

Taken only months apart, the two photographs of Mutsuhito before and after his makeover might be read as emblematic of Japan's official policy about-face from the emperor faction's precoup cry of *Sonno Joi* ("Honor the Emperor, Expel the Barbarian") to their postvictory slogan *Bunmei Kaika* ("Civilization and Enlightenment").[6] The diptych suggests a clean forward trajectory of primitive before and enlightened after (or, depending on your sympathies, a timeless, untainted before and a disagreeably debauched, "modernized" after). Of course, the emperor's new clothes were just one manifestation of *Bunmei Kaika*. Along with the official encouragement to the Japanese to adopt Western fashions and norms of self-presentation, the new government embraced Western imports and technologies both grand and minor, including transportation and communication technologies, political structures, foods, architecture, and academic, intellectual, and artistic ideas and practices. And, as the clothing proclamation's reference to Jingu and Jimmu indicates, the embrace of modernity necessarily encompassed a critical reworking of tradition as well, with patriotic reasoning as a pretext to adopting yet another foreign style. In the realm of clothing, the new imported styles received the collective name *yōfuku* (洋服 Western clothes), while native clothing, newly distinguished as sharing the quality of "Japaneseness," gained the term *wafuku* (和服 "Japanese clothing"). *Yō* (洋) and *wa* (和) are used to articulate many other cultural products in the same manner even today, such as *yōshoku* and *washoku* in cuisine or *yōshitsu* and *washitsu* for Western- and Japanese-style rooms, respectively.

The timing of Meiji's makeover coincides neatly with the fashion controversies of the Girl of the Period and Boulton and Park—barely a year after Boulton and Park's acquittal, the committee was confirming the details of the adolescent emperor's new clothes. The importation of Western fashions into Japan on a mass scale as part of a larger government campaign of civilization and enlightenment constitutes a very different kind of fashion controversy than the (apparent) minoritized resistances of the Girl of the Period, Boulton, Park, and their colleagues, fashionably resisting the pressure of the status quo. But, like those other controversies, this one hinged on overarching disputes about identity and its proper external expression—and, as we will see at the end of this chapter, looking at the controversy will also force us to question typical Anglophone doxa of what identity even is and where it resides to be expressed at all.

Further, the Meiji makeover was scandalous for many Japanese, as well as for foreign observers who observed it playing out. In this chapter I will highlight how attributions of theatricality were employed by both foreign and Japanese interlocutors in attempts to police the proper sartorial presentation of Japanese people. Just as Boulton and Park came to represent an "epicene college" of suspected underground deviants and the Girl of the Period seemed to indicate (to some) a growing crisis among young English women, so a small group of government elites were the progenitors of the makeover policy and its first adherents, along with their figurehead, the emperor. The initial outlandishness of redefining self-presentation across the nation thus came, like the cases of the Girl of the Period and Boulton and Park, from the center of the status quo. The difference, of course, is that their sartorial activities were not just centered, but had the hierarchical reach to become, over time, the hegemonic norm for Japanese society. But first we will see the ways in which this process was slowed, contested, adapted, and altered on its way to that eventuality. Resistance models of analyzing my three cases might see the Meiji makeover as directly opposed to the controversies sparked by the Girl of the Period and the Boulton and

Park case, but by setting aside an attachment to finding resistant heroes, we can see how all three might be more effectively recognized as working on wider norms in more ambiguous ways. While the Meiji makeover ideals eventually became the norm and the disruptions Boulton and Park's trial made visible were eventually abjected as acceptable behaviors, the debates over the Girl of the Period remain altogether more ambiguous, as the court of popular opinion failed to come to a consensus on what the Girl of the Period meant and whether she was a social menace or just a slightly saucy pleasure. (And, of course, public popular discourse lacked the mechanisms to coerce behavior that the British court system and Meiji legal apparatus possessed.) Yet, in all three cases, attributions of theatricality at the level of individual identity expression were employed to ease friction between individuals and the status quo, sometimes in attempting to alter the hegemonic norm, sometimes by way of sheltering deviant behaviors within society by designating them meaningless. Theatricality enabled Boulton and Park to escape the full force of the law and neutralized the threat of the Girl of the Period to respectable society, thereby shoring up the sense of cohesion and integrity attributed to the gender and sexuality norms of British society.

Because the Meiji makeover activities were pitched explicitly toward impression management of foreign treaty powers, Meiji elites remained constrained by external opinions. The Meiji government's intentions were by no means implicit: the official letter to the American president that accompanied the 1872 diplomatic mission to the United States to revise treaties plainly stated the goals of the state (as reported by *Macmillan's*): "It is our purpose to select from the various institutions prevailing among enlightened nations such as are best suited to our present condition, and adopt them, in gradual reforms and improvements of our policy and customs, so as to be upon an equality with them" (May 1, 1872, 495). But foreigners' reactions to these "enlightened adoptions" often failed to conform to Meiji elites' intentions, and the mode in which the failure registered for many foreigners was one of theatricality. Westerners repeatedly questioned the authenticity of Japanese experiments in performative Occidentalism by declaring them instead theatrical, superficial, or mindlessly imitative. "The Japanese are a strangely imitative people, and, like all imitative persons, are wanting in originality. They will adopt anything, whether it be a language, a manufacture, or an article of dress, but they can invent nothing," declares the *Saturday Review* (March 11, 1871, 318), almost exactly three years after unleashing the Girl of the Period. Eventually, the trope of Japanese imitativeness (always implying lack of depth or authenticity) became a recurring slight that continues to haunt Anglophone thinking about Japan even today. (This issue will reappear in chap. 5.) Yet, as I will demonstrate, these criticisms less index the mindless imitation of "children and monkeys" (and, as we will see, women) that they claim, than point to complex and compelling evidence of alternative modes of conceiving of the relation between appearance, identity, and selfhood.

The events that I consider in this chapter—longer, slower, and far more all-encompassing than the effects of either the Girl of the Period or Boulton and Park's tabloid trial—necessitated the extension of the temporal bounds of my research and the types of evidences available to me much farther than in the foregoing chapters. Rather than being able to focus on a tight one- or two-year time frame, as I did in chapters 2 and 3, I surveyed varieties of evidence from the 1850s through the early twentieth century, albeit anchored especially to the Meiji Restoration in 1868 and the proclamation on court dress in 1872, a major nexus in the longer, slower, messier transformation of Japanese sartorial self-presentation, and two dates nearly coincident with the Girl of the Period and Boulton and Park controversies.

Thus, with this chapter begins the diachronic slide that will rocket forward to a queerly Victorian twenty-first century in chapter 5. Moreover, it is appropriate to introduce temporality now since a fundamental concern of the Meiji makeover was both the instantiation and the appearance of modernity. Modernity appears at first in this chapter, as it must have to the Meiji elites who crafted these plans and policies, as a peculiarly Western invention, but one that was rapidly engulfing the world by 1868. Modernity appears as a philosophical avatar of Western imperialism, working at the level of intellectual discourse to organize and fix different nations and people into a timeline of greater or lesser advancement. And Japan's Meiji makeover, no matter how messy or partial the attempt, comprises an intervention in that system—it was not intended to change the structure itself, but foremost to play by the rules such a system encompassed (although some aspects of modernity's ideology may of course have been bent in the process). The game, however, was not only rigged, but also always more complex than simply civilized on top and barbaric below. Theatricality inheres in both of these dynamics: as one way of undercutting or neutralizing the Japanese bid to political and diplomatic equivalency through visual likeness, and by its elicitation of the affective modes of cross-cultural desire for the exotic other. A bolder way to say this might be to claim that theatricality infuses every cross-cultural encounter, in as much as encounters between unlike parties are always determined by appearances, previously encountered representations, and the inherently representational and painfully partial nature of linguistic communication and translation.

Modernity was, as many works have demonstrated, also a matter of great concern for Western interlocutors; after all, to be on top is always to have the most to lose.[7] To stay with examples from this book, recall how some writers anxiously identified the Girl of the Period as a proof of

Britain's moral decadence. Even if she was not such an issue at home, some advocated for hindering the education of women in India by insisting that modern, civilized girls were anything but. Similarly, both prosecution and defense in the Boulton and Park trial had claimed the well-being of the nation was at stake in either rooting out a "plague" or "to declare by their verdict that no such plague existed, that England was happily free from it" (*Times*, May 12, 1871). While the coconstitution of individual performances of modernity with the collective modernity of the nation was explicitly understood in *Bunmei Kaika*, the connection between collective national nature and individuals within the society had been claimed by the Girl of the Period and Boulton and Park commentators as well.

Moreover, modernity was, we should remember, far from necessarily a purely positive development in the eyes of many constituents of British society. While it is a truism in critiques of postcolonialism and Orientalism that Europeans positioned themselves at the apex of civilizations with modern technologies as one sinecure of the rightness of that position, such an understanding of global order was undermined by Europeans and Americans' own anxieties regarding the superiority of modernity. Looking at Euro-American interlocutors' heterogeneous reactions to Japanese culture and *Bunmei Kaika* efforts reveals a far more complex relationship between the British (and their imperialist colleagues and rivals) and the vast patchwork of colonizable others. The mid-Victorian period was, after all, suffused with waves of exoticist and nostalgic expressions of deep discomfort with the effects of modernity on society. Japan came to hold a privileged place in that imaginary, possibly not least because of how actively it bifurcated its efforts. It may very well be that the global mania for Japonisme was as much buoyed by Japan's simultaneous herculean effort to recalibrate society according to Western tastes as it was by its savvy promotion of its romantic, atavistic arts and crafts in the quintessential nineteenth-century forum of the international exhibition.[8]

It is not the place of this work to determine whether such a gambit as the makeover (and the cavalcade of other Occidentalisms adopted under the banner of *Bunmei Kaika*) was the only choice or the best choice for Japan; instead, my goal is to trace how the *Bunmei Kaika* fashion gambit played out and to point out how fashion's inherent theatrical ambivalence affected that project, at macro and individual levels. I treat two major parties in this chapter: the Japanese themselves and the foreign, especially British, interlocutors for whom the modern makeover was putatively staged. Although to the Meiji elites, the British were just one party among many treaty nations who tended to blend together in the foreign treaty ports, Yokohama foremost among them, the British Empire was undoubtedly the greatest sea power in east Asia and British citizens made up the majority of Yokohama residents.[9] While my emphasis on British voices helps to connect this chapter to the previous two, simultaneously, as the greatest imperial power of the nineteenth century and the preeminent diplomatic group of all the treaty nations (perhaps along with the United States), British interlocutors had a particularly loud voice in the integration of Japan into global politics.

The various strategies of the Meiji makeover, aimed alternately at the mass of new commoner "citizens," elites in positions of contact with foreign powers, and the nation's figurehead/mannequin(s) the emperor and the imperial family, constituted a battery of performative and theatrical tactics (and a key part of my contention will be that the performative functions here as one mode of the theatrical) aimed at both transforming the Japanese nation into a competitive world power and visually demonstrating that transformation (often in syncopation with the rate of actual transformation) as a key component to global competitiveness. These new practices of subject making and subject presentation aimed at making a homogeneous new Japanese national identity through (paradoxically) the creation of new liberal, self-possessed individuals.[10] But I will also consider how indigenous habits of thought regarding the location and nature of identity features like race, gender, modernness, class, and so on, cause subject formation to work in slightly different ways than the Cartesian formulations we've seen at work in the British context. And over the course of this chapter and the next, I will further be pushing some of these alternative modes of looking at the performativity of selfhood as potentially useful correctives to the ways in which Cartesian depth models of subjectivity fall short of accurately describing experiences of subjectivity, not only in Japan but beyond as well.

In the remainder of this chapter I will give a short history of the politics of fashion in Japan before the Meiji Restoration to establish a general sense of the indigenous cultural norms that would collide with imported Western ones over the course of the cross-cultural encounter. Next, I spend time describing the actual facts of the Meiji makeover, with special attention to both men's and women's clothing and hair, and some analysis of how clothing and images of clothing traveled together and separately to instantiate new norms of Japanese individual embodied subjectivity. Hairstyling and makeup norms play a large part in this chapter. Hair and other cosmetic modes of styling parts of the physical body function in a complex fashion middle space that may not feel fully like clothing, but in their malleability and subjection to imposed social norms are clearly not exempt from fashion's ideological penumbra. In the third section, I examine foreign reactions to the Meiji makeover and note how accusations based on theatricality, meaning empty imitation, formed a common refrain, while simultaneously foreign fantasies of Japanese exoticism were rarely recognized as themselves equally imaginary or contrived. This discussion feeds into the concluding section in which I weave together the ramifications of all the foregoing to ask whether examining alternative

Japanese conceptions of surface, depth, and efficacy might offer additional clarity not only to the Meiji controversy but also to cases beyond Japan.

A Brief History of the Tokugawa Politics of Fashion

Long before the new Meiji government decreed a vast makeover, political authority in Japan was especially concerned with both visibility and invisibility as strategies of exercising power. Robust systems of understanding and regulating the image of power and the power of image undergirded and complexly interacted with the one(s) that would be imported and adapted from the West. The Tokugawa shogunate (the samurai political faction that ruled Japan from 1603 until their overthrow in 1867–68) favored what Peter Duus calls "an iconography of absence":

> The Tokugawa shogunate was so intent on making politics invisible that it forfeited the opportunity to bind the ruler with his subjects through public and/or visual displays, as monarchs did in early modern Europe. The Tokugawa shoguns eschewed the public ceremonies staged by the Tudor/Stuart courts and the Bourbon kings as a "theater of power" intended to show their audiences that power and sovereignty resided not just in the royal office, but in the royal person. Nor did the shogunate erect any public monuments to living shoguns, hold public shogunal coronations, or mint any coins with the shogunal visage. Even when the shogun made one of his rare trips outside Edo castle, the streets were emptied of traffic and the second stories of houses along the way were vacated. The ruling elite did its best to remain invisible, hidden from public gaze behind towering gates and high walls that marked their presence but veiled their persons. In short, they relied on what Timon Screech has called "an iconography of absence" that buttressed their authority by concealing it rather than by revealing it.[11]

Of course, the absence of which Timon Screech and Peter Duus write is itself an emphatic form of presence, in that the swathes of forbidden territory and the injunctions to look away, close windows, and vacate the streets, themselves all signify in the public consciousness (a dynamic attested to by Screech's choice of the word "iconography"). Iconographies of absence linger in many aspects of Japanese culture today, in the anonymous public places like shops and restaurants, hidden behind blank or almost-blank facades with minimal or no signage and thus open only to those who know about them. We might recall Roland Barthes's perception of the Imperial Palace in Tokyo as the "empty center" of the capital, "forbidden and indifferent."[12] Indeed, for ten years of the Meiji era, the palace was literally absent, destroyed in a fire in May 1873.[13] The palace that comprised Barthes's "empty center" was not even built until the late 1880s. Barthes appropriately notices the use of opacity, but such opacity was by no means indifferent nor empty.

Concurrent and supplementary to the strategy of invisible power, the Tokugawa authorities also understood and regulated the power of appearances through extensive sartorial regulations and restrictions. Indeed, sensitivity to the potential power of clothing as a key visual means of materially enforcing divisions of status, obedience, and especially disobedience was deeply held by both Tokugawa and Meiji leaders; it was more that the contents of the dress codes were completely different.

During the Tokugawa period (1603–1867), imperial household and shogunate rulers had extensive wardrobes of ceremonial wear that had remained stable for centuries, built on Chinese modes imported around the seventh century CE. These dress codes were slightly different for men and women, but more emphatically they set apart all the members of the imperial household from other Japanese; both the emperor and the empress and their male and female retainers wore white lead makeup and blackened their teeth. They shaved their natural eyebrows, then painted "moth" eyebrows high on the forehead and wore voluminous layered silk clothing. (Remember the earlier of Emperor Meiji's first two portraits; figs. 12 and 13.) Samurai wore swords; nobles wore laminated caps.[14] Beyond the chambers of the imperial and shogunal estates, the remaining classes—farmers, *chōnin* (町人, merchants and artisans, literally "townspeople"), and *hinin* (非人, literally "nonpeople")—were subject to extensive sumptuary regulations. Different fabric, weaves, and patterns were restricted to different classes, while other sartorial markers like hairstyle or blackened teeth denoted other important demographic features, like age, marital status, or gender. Gregory Pflugfelder declares, "it is no exaggeration to say that for early modern Japanese such [tonsorial and sartorial] visible markers of identity constituted the primary signifier of belonging to a given social category."[15]

Trade and money making were considered particularly crass by the samurai (i.e., military) Tokugawa government, and merchants were accordingly technically ranked lowest in official hierarchies of classes (albeit still above the *hinin*, people of official nonstatus—actors, entertainers, itinerants, sex workers, beggars, convicts—and the *burakumin* [outcaste] groups).[16] Yet over the course of the Edo era the high-status samurai on fixed feudal incomes found themselves increasingly cash poor while merchants became increasingly rich.[17] Despite the divide between economic power and political-military-status power, visual regulation of the classes helped maintain social hierarchy, even though infrequently and unevenly observed. (Sumptuary regulations fell under the vernacular label of *mikka hatto* [three-day laws], an ascription that suggested how erratically they were enforced.[18]) Although officially restricted from luxurious display, wealthy merchants found ways around regulations by cultivating *iki* (粋 an understated sense of luxury), which featured sumptuous linings to plain outer clothes and the cultivation of an aesthetic that favored the muted and austere. *Iki* offers the potential for extensive material self-realization and luxury, as long as the expression remains personal and visually obscure: only the wearer of a haori (kimono jacket) will know what fabulous picture decorates the lining or can fully enjoy the feel of the richest silks while others only see the dim, dark color brown. *Iki* functions analogously to the negative theatricality of the iconography of absence, conserving power through its visual undetectability.

It should come as no surprise that zones wherein classes and sexes might mix or become confused were areas of special governmental concern since they served as popular grounds for transgression of the social boundaries that the Tokugawa government was so concerned with policing via visual means. Brothels and theaters, for example, were officially restricted to licensed areas called *ukiyo* (浮世, floating worlds) and staffed with people who fell outside the fixed and inherited class professions of *chōnin*, samurai, and farmers. The *hinin* were restricted to their *ukiyo* neighborhoods in a government effort to sequester and control the liminal members of society. Patronage of the déclassé activities of the floating world were supposed to be restricted to low-status *chōnin*, but of course the allures of the licensed quarter and the stage proved to be seductive also to samurai social elites.[19] For example, kabuki often restaged its own *ukiyo* milieu in ripped-from-the-headlines stories of the exploits and travails of a frequently noble but penniless samurai in love with an equally penniless geisha or *oiran* (high-ranking courtesan), generally ending in double suicide. Cross-class liaisons, disorderly reveling, and even the magnetic power of celebrity served to make the *ukiyo*, like fashion, a site of successive bans and regulations.[20] Further, fashion and the floating world overlapped to a great extent. Popular actors, although officially classed as *hinin*, used their stage celebrity (and circulation as subjects of ukiyo-e prints) to become fashion leaders and even purveyors of luxury goods and fashion.[21]

Some historians trace the very origin of kabuki to an early-Edo-period fringe of men and women from various classes who used fashion, leisure pastimes, and general eccentricity to set themselves apart from the status quo. Having abjected themselves from the class hierarchy by refusing their allotted roles and accoutrements, these people became known as *kabukimono*, derived from the verb *kabuku*: literally, "to slant" or to be off center, which some have translated as "queer."[22] The Tokugawa issued edicts not only against women's kabuki for mixing classes, genders, and sexualities on stage and off, but also against "strange clothing" worn by *kabukimono* which seemed to constitute the same intolerable boundary transgressions.[23]

The upshot of the Tokugawa government's obsession with regulating the superficial (read: visual) appearances of different types of subjects along class, gender, and age lines is that any deviation, even mere fashionable excesses like those of the *kabukimono*, could read as resistant, emphatically signifying against the regime's desire for clear visual demarcation of classes, types, and people.[24]

Overall, the *kabukimono*, Tokugawa sumptuary law, class and *hinin* segregation practices, and court dress regulations all demonstrate how deeply sartorial regulation was imbricated with the overarching project of social control. The Tokugawa and then Meiji authorities thus matched the Victorians' alarm over the social and political ramifications of fashionable appearances, but perhaps with less of the valence of triviality or silliness undercutting their concerns. Importantly, and perhaps paradoxically, extensive control over external appearances in Japan did not necessarily presume a model of identity that tied external appearances to inner essences in the same way that English interlocutors did in the previous chapters. David Howell writes,

> The Tokugawa authorities were more concerned with exteriority—the visible compliance with norms—than with the internalization of the principles behind those norms. This is revealed most obviously in their obsession with sumptuary regulation, which was primarily expressed by exhortations that people dress and behave in accordance with their social station . . . Lacking the means to intervene systematically in the inner lives of their subjects—and skeptical at any rate of most commoners' ability to comprehend the ethical and philosophical bases of governance—officials necessarily focused on the external performance of proper deportment.[25]

I will return to these underlying dynamics of understanding and enforcing fashion and personal appearance in this chapter's conclusion, particularly asking what a differing overarching sense of the location of identity and therefore its relation to visual representation might offer to the broken equation of fashion(ed) identity expression. The perpetual misfit between established Japanese emphases on superficial compliance and imported Cartesian depth models of meaning formed an oblique skew between dispositions toward fashioned identity rather than a clean inversion of approaches.

Extreme Meiji Makeover

In this section I survey the major material changes that happened in dress for Japanese people over the first half of the Meiji period. Meiji government leaders prolifically implemented rules, restrictions, and "encouragements" related to individuals' public self-presentations with the help of the arrayed social forces of media and press and groups allied to the political and social goals of the government. (But remember that this may be consonant with the previous regime's own emphasis on regulating appearances.) Varying tactics were aimed at the great mass of common people, with more specific requirements for elites and the men and women who interfaced directly with foreigners as avatars of the state, and particularly extensive attention to the emperor and later the empress, her retinue, and the rest of the imperial family as they transitioned from invisible icons to national emblems exhaustively circulated both at home and abroad. I will examine both sartorial changes materially implemented across society and representations of fashion, clothing, and modernized Japanese bodies. These performed, performative, and theatrical practices were intertwined and mutually constituting, but emphatically not the same thing. Here I articulate a historiographical and intellectual division: that real clothes and bodies did some things with clothing, and representations of clothing from this time did some other things, even as some representations were pitched toward changing material practices of clothing the body and most of what we know of material fashion practices must now be mediated by the archived remains of representations.

Although the maintenance of social class divisions was primary to the Tokugawa leadership, those classes were entirely dissolved and reorganized by the Meiji regime; but as the importance of class differentiation (supposedly) waned, gender differentiation, we will see, became quite important, along with gender's uncomfortable imbrication with notions of modernity. And although the nobility (and even deity) of the emperor was actively heightened, even as other social distinctions were abolished, the emperor and his family were simultaneously represented as templates and role models for the newly minted citizens of the renovated Japanese nation, inculcating a notion of domesticated modernity across classes through both popular imagery and recalibrated norms and institutions like compulsory education, reorganized military and political structures, and civil engineering.

I use the terms "makeover," "Meiji makeover," and "extreme Meiji makeover" to describe the battery of tactics and overall process of government-sanctioned and (slowly) culturally normalized change of sartorial, cosmetic, and tonsorial habits. This phraseology is chosen playfully but also under the necessity of having some catchall term to designate the innumerable ideas, injunctions, experiments, rules, and fads that made up the massive overhaul of the entire habitus of Japanese quotidian self-presentation that took place over the Meiji period (and beyond). The term "makeover" in twentieth- and twenty-first-century popular culture carries a feminine gendered valence that is here largely inverted (mostly men making over) but remains deeply concerned with the import of managing gender, and especially global perceptions of effeminacy or femininity in conjunction with the male rulers of Japan. (Remember the emperor's proclamation against effeminate styles.) Meiji elites recognized the gendered ramifications of imperial nations' Orientalist discourses a century in advance of Edward Said; but to make a play for globally recognized masculine authority on the basis of clothing change is to run the risk of escaping Orientalist effeminacy as exoticized subaltern only to be tainted by the feminizing superficiality of fashion.[26]

Thus, to return to where I began this chapter: the emperor's makeover stands as emblematic of both the material changes and semiotic representational tactics of the architects of the Meiji makeover. The emperor's individual makeover in 1872, bolstered by the proclamation intended for officials, led the way for mass wardrobe changes for all those officials who interfaced directly with foreigners, especially diplomats, although many had already begun adapting their wardrobes and public presentations, especially the diplomats who'd been abroad in 1859 and 1860 on the Iwakura missions to the US and then the UK and Europe.

In the early Meiji years innumerable little laws proliferated, especially around Tokyo, where the seat of government and the majority of foreigners (primarily in the foreign enclave of nearby Yokohama) were concentrated. These regulations and public campaigns were geared toward overhauling the appearance of Japan to eliminate the features that foreigners found ugly or backward. Due to the campaign architects' cosmetic intent, sartorial changes abounded: sword carrying for erstwhile samurai was banned; men were encouraged or even required to cut their long hair; habits of public nudity, urination, and mixed-gender bathing were banned; and the blackening of teeth and shaving of eyebrows for married women was discouraged.

Fukuzawa Yukichi, the famous foreign expert, translator, and education reformer, assisted in preparing Japanese readers for makeover by publishing numerous pedagogical works on foreign lifestyles in simple Japanese. Fukuzawa, who had accompanied the Iwakura mission to the US in 1859–60 and the 1862 mission to Europe, published the ten-volume *Seiyo jijo* (Western things) in 1866, just prior to the restoration.[27] Published at the same time, *Seiyo ishokuju* (Western clothing, food, and houses) is a slim volume with illustrations and short descriptions of how to wear the main (male) *yōfuku* garments, from underwear to hats, caps, and umbrellas, and how to eat meals at a table with descriptions and phonetic pronunciations of all the utensils down to the *tongusu* (トングス tongs) to use with the *shiugarubeesun* (シウガルベースン sugar basin). Fukuzawa's guides are simple and to the point, and apparently sold very well in both official and pirated editions, far in advance of actual changes of clothing, much less common people's acquisition of *tongusu* and *shiugarubeesun*.[28]

Perhaps most importantly, but rarely noted in standard histories, a sweeping makeover on a totally new model of clothing served a vital internal purpose for the nascent Meiji Republic: sweeping away all the lingering external mores and norms that had visually segregated the separate classes for centuries. In an abrupt about-face from the Tokugawa regime's focus on enforcing class divisions, the Meiji government immediately moved to abolish the classes, renaming them *heimin* (平民 ordinary citizens). Two years after merchants, farmers, and lower-ranking samurai were all designated *heimin*, the *hinin* and *burakumin* outcastes were also formally incorporated into the *heimin* (although social prejudice lingers against certain former *burakumin* even today).[29] As extensive sartorial conventions had visibly enforced the division of the classes, it is plausible that the wholesale importation of new fashions geared toward new semiotics of subjectivity (as imperfectly implemented as it may have been) relieved the vacuum that would otherwise have obtained.

A new (primarily masculine) makeover based on imported standards of appearance offered one means for the government to neatly sidestep and instantly render moot the problem of how to visually reconcile the newly homogenized *kazoku* (daimyo-ranking samurai and former *kuge* nobles) and *heimin*, so recently liberated from generations of sartorial stricture based on the class system. New laws and proclamations proliferated for the regularization and control of individuals' appearances, from haircutting regulations to sword carrying (heretofore restricted to samurai as a very literal status symbol) to the abolition of all sumptuary laws. Collectively these individual laws, rules, and movements helped to supersede and replace the old divisions through a modern drive to acquire new looks, even if the vast majority limited themselves to a few accessories and a haircut for years to come. Another way to say this is that mass costume changes semiotically marked (and perhaps even helped to performatively instantiate) the great mass of new *heimin* citizens, as much to each other and the rest of the Japanese nation as to observing foreigners.

Most *heimin*, lower on the (reorganized) social hierarchy and unburdened with frontline engagement with foreigners, were freer to take part in *Bunmei Kaika* as more of a fashion than a uniform. An 1871 print of a street scene in a rapidly changing Tokyo captures a changing landscape and populace, played for comedy (fig. 14).

In one spot, a man curses at the horse pulling a carriage that has intersected his path. One man in a rickshaw (itself a circa-1870, post-*sakoku* hybrid Japanese invention) has a fresh *zangiri* (cropped Western-style) haircut, *yōfuku*, and a red striped woolen scarf. Another man smiles directly at the camera (as it were) in kimono and *hakama*, with *yōfuku* hat, boots, and umbrella (the trifecta of modern accessories, possibly plus a pocket watch). At least four men are in scarlet-coated uniforms (three on foot and one driving a carriage) and another four seem to be depicted

Fig. 14. Ikkei, Shibaguchi Bridge scene: a lively and comedic slice of life image of the neighborhood now called Shinbashi, 1871. Author's collection.

in black frock or cutaway coats, the two in the background with top hats. This lively jumble indexes not just the hustle and bustle of a major new Tokyo intersection (Shinbashi, called "Shibaguchi Bridge" in the cartouche at the top center) but a whole urban society in flux. In contrast to the concerted efforts that turned the imperial court and government-involved samurai and nobles into a diplomatic international-facing contingent with extensive guidance, the street scene indicates disparate, individual choices on the ragged frontier of *Bunmei Kaika* as available fashion choices, with the potential to also signal one's personal attitude toward political events and incipient "modernization." It's important to note not just the full *yōfuku* ensembles depicted in the street scene, but also the eclectic mixes, like the man wearing a *hakama* and kimono with hat, umbrella, and boots.

The Shibaguchi print indexes some of the novelty of new goods, easier to obtain and incorporate into daily life than entire new suits of expensive and hard-to-tailor clothes, like pocket watches, hats, scarves, boots, and umbrellas. Although fashion dynamics, and more individualized interest, marks the practices of the *heimin* not caught up directly in international negotiations, political valence still attached itself to ordinary people's choices. Like hats, boots, and umbrellas, haircutting served as a means to quickly bring Japanese appearances closer in line with newly imported standards, long before *yōfuku* became de rigueur. *Yōfuku* were complicated to make and prohibitively expensive since the skilled labor and appropriate materials, especially wool, were still largely imports, but haircutting was cheap and didn't require any special materials. Encouraged, incentivized, and sometimes coerced by various local initiatives, newspapers reported that 13 percent of men had short hair in 1869, increasing to

60 percent by 1876, while in Tokyo, apparently 80 percent of men already had short hair by 1873.[30]

> Knock on a head with a *hanpatsu* hairstyle, and it makes the sound of "wavering indecision."
> Knock on a head with a *sōhatsu* hairstyle, and it makes the sound of "restoration of imperial rule."
> Knock on a head with a *zangiri* hairstyle, and it makes the sound of "civilization and enlightenment."[31]

This popular 1870s rhyme succinctly reads three haircuts semiotically for their wearers' political affiliations, while also capturing more than the simple binary (modern versus traditional) so often attributed to this era. Even with only three options, the "wavering indecision" of those who still shaved the tops of their heads in the old style contrasts obliquely with the *sōhatsu* faction, unshaved but still long-haired, associated with the Satsuma and Chōshū leaders who helped bring about the emperor's restoration under the slogan referenced here, "restoration of imperial rule," but later split from the Meiji rulers who had embraced *Bunmei Kaika*.[32]

It seems that in the early days of *Bunmei Kaika*, some confusion emerged as to who tonsorial "Civilization and Enlightenment" was actually for; *Shinbun Zasshi* reported, "there is a certain store in Asakusa where they try to be very Western. The owner's mistress and child have their hair cut Western-style. The owner's wife is very upset since her hair too may have to be cut this way. Her grief is in vain. Despite her pleading, she will be forced to have her raven locks cut" (although the article goes on to note the proprietor himself maintained his long traditional hairstyle).[33] David Howell reports that a Chiba newspaper at first praised women's short hair as an economical choice.[34] Another article writes of "a young woman who was seen in the Nihonbashi district in Tokyo wearing Japanese-style leggings, straw sandals, and a Western-style haircut. She said she was from the province of Shinshu and longed very much for Western learning, but since her parents would not hear of this she had run away and come to Tokyo. Now she was going to look up Mr. Fukuzawa and beg him to take her on as a pupil!"[35] The Shinshu girl's existence is unsubstantiated beyond this news item as far as I could determine, yet factual or imaginary, she strikes a painful grace note against the general masculine rush to *Bunmei Kaika*. Her misplaced (according to the authorities and the newspaper who expressed amusement at her) ambition reemphasizes the gendered dimensions of the Meiji makeover project; women would be exhorted toward a different set of goals under their own slogan of *Ryosai Kenbo* ("good wives, wise mothers"), which would always maintain a much more partial and complex relation to Westernization. Nevertheless, these scattered examples suggest the ways in which external markers of identity became

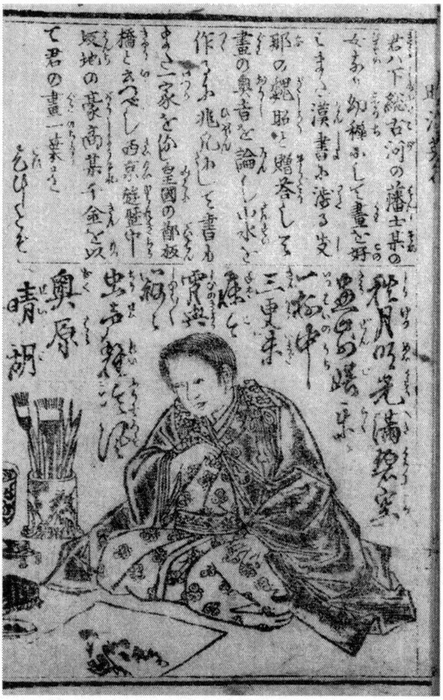

Fig. 15. Okuhara Seikō in *Meiji eimei hyaku'ei sen* (*A Collection of a Hundred Poems by the Eminent of the Meiji Period*), 1879. Courtesy of Joshua Mostow and University of British Columbia Library, Rare Books and Special Collections.

(temporarily) fluid in the liminal time while old mores were suspended and new ones had yet to clearly coalesce. *Shimbun Zasshi* tried to clarify the gender of enlightened haircutting once and for all in March 1872: "Recently in the city we have seen women with close-cropped hair. Such is not the Japanese custom and furthermore nothing of the sort is seen among the women of the West. The sight of this ugly fashion is unbearable" (March 14, 1872). Shortly thereafter, the government confirmed that tonsorial *Bunmei Kaika* was only for men and issued a ban against women wearing short haircuts.

Okuhara Seikō, one of the few Japanese professional women artists of the nineteenth century, was one of the women who had adopted the "ugly fashion"; she cut her hair into a *zangiri* style in 1871, concurrent with the proclamation allowing and encouraging samurai to cut their hair (fig. 15). (Okuhara was herself the fourth daughter of a samurai official of the Koga clan, living independently as an artist in Tokyo from 1865.) Martha

McClintock notes that Okuhara was close friends with Kidō Takayoshi, one of the architects of the samurai haircutting proclamation. But more importantly the thirty-four-year-old Okuhara kept her short hair for the rest of her life, until she died in 1913 at the age of seventy-six, and also habitually wore men's kimono. She successfully won a permission slip to keep her short hair after the ban—McClintock reports that the certificate Okuhara managed to get from the police in 1875 remains in the possession of the Koga clan. Inside a yellow silk pouch, it names the justification for Okuhara's short hair as "a fit of madness" (逆上の症 *gyakujō no shō*).[36] Like a latter-day *kabukimono*, Okuhara exploited the liminalities of life in a revolutionary period of social and political upheaval in conjunction with certain potential liberties available to artists and samurai, and even the relative superfluity of women to the political sphere, to carve out and maintain a woman-centric household and personal autonomy for nearly fifty years.

Sharon L. Sievers writes,

> The banning of short hair for women—however superficial the issue may seem—is one of the most important and revealing policies on women in the early Meiji period. To the extent that women cutting their hair can be viewed as a real, if spontaneous, attempt to join the progressive forces trying to create a new Japan, the government's denial of their right to do that was also a denial of their right to participate and contribute actively to that change. In fact, it can be seen as a symbolic message to Japan's women to become repositories of the past, rather than pioneers, with men, of some unknown future.[37]

It is true that women would be disproportionately tasked with the maintenance of tradition, although it's not clear that this is what the ban on women's haircutting signified, since of course short hair for women had no precedent in treaty nations, and simultaneously women were being encouraged to modernize in other ways, by giving up tooth blackening and eyebrow shaving, and later by streamlining and "rationalizing" their hair styles. Historian Oku Takemori argues that most women who were cutting their hair in the 1870s were not necessarily practicing masculinity or *Bunmei Kaika*, but rather older women doing devotional haircutting.[38]

The import here is not that either contemporary Meiji authorities or later historians were wrong about what was happening, but that cosmetic practices like haircutting were being conscripted by the Meiji authorities into singular scenographic labor (appearing civilized on a Western model) regardless of what other activities (such as Buddhist devotion) might have been competing for sartorial representation at the time. This conundrum of competing claims to sartorial representation occurs both in the early

1870s between individuals and the government and in the subsequent historical representations, like Sievers's, which follows the dominant voice of the Meiji government to reread women's haircutting as necessarily related to *Bunmei Kaika*, and further to a notion of personal freedom that may have as much to do with second-wave Anglophone feminism as nineteenth-century women's actual intentions.

David Howell writes of the foment of confusion:

> This fluidity gave modern Japan its dynamism, but at the same time it left people uncertain of their proper relationship to the state and to one another. Outcastes who thought they were commoners, Ainu who thought they were Japanese, women who thought they were free to cut their hair: such people were the obvious casualties of modernization, but the same uncertainties and ultimately ephemeral promises affected all Japanese to at least some degree. Indeed, the state itself was a victim of its own policies, for it constantly had to respond to its subjects' attempts to appropriate the symbols of modernity for their own purposes.[39]

Howell thus describes a semiotic crisis precipitated by the political crisis of regime change and the massive social engineering project of *Bunmei Kaika*. Remember the explicitness with which the authorities articulated their intentions to demonstrate Western-style civilization to treaty partners. In the parlance of this book, then, we can see how the makeover was pitched first as a theatrical demonstration—something to be seen that may or may not be able to guarantee a deep change. However, the makeover comprised a battery of theatrical changes which very well might turn out to be performative, not only appearing Westernized but also permanently changing the mindsets, values, and senses of self of the newly minted Japanese citizens.

Picturing *Bunmei Kaika*

Meanwhile, images and representations of new Western or modernized clothing circulated in excess, and often in advance, of actual material garments. Some representations functioned more as fantasies and others with more pragmatic aims to help instill various material changes in sartorial appearances. In this section I build on the description regarding material changes in Japanese people's sartorial norms from the preceding section by considering the ways clothing traveled as imagery, often farther and faster than physical clothing. From a historiographical perspective, such an articulation is somewhat arbitrary—for example, what makes the Shibaguchi Bridge print from 1871 (fig. 14) more documentary than artistic

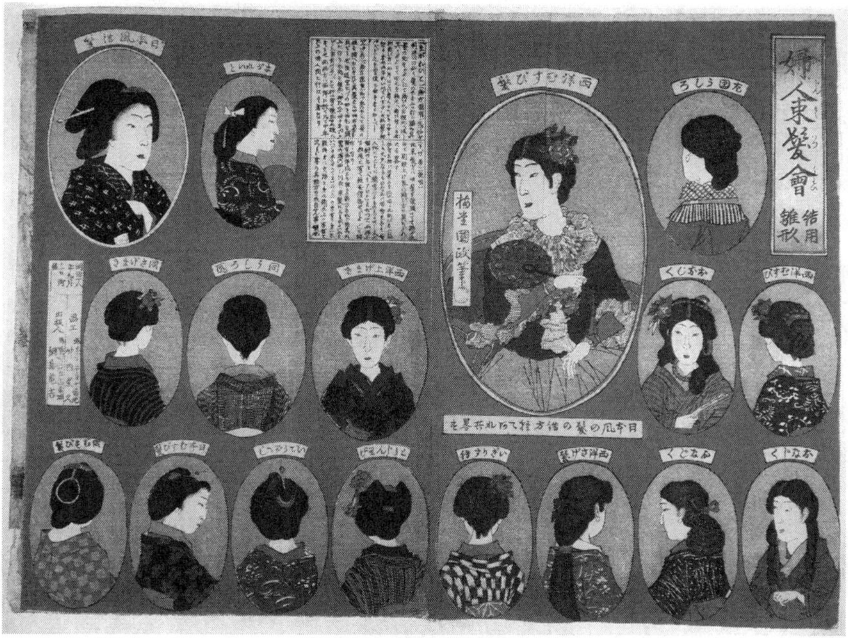

Fig. 16. "Fujin sokuhatsukai" (Women's swept-back hair group), 1885. Woodblock color print published by Tsunajima Kamekichi. Courtesy of Bunka Gakuen University Library, Tokyo.

in and of itself? Surely purchasers and viewers of that print must have read it as a comical commentary on the rapidly modernizing metropolis as much as they might have read it as I did, as an index of material changes happening in the early Meiji period. Other types of visual materials I will analyze function on a continuum from more pragmatic or pedagogical to more fantastical (or, if you will—theatrical) images clearly intended more as pleasurable diversions than blueprints to personal sartorial modernization; they offered up the modern for visual delectation, uninterested in securing an unquestionable relation to truth value.

To begin on the pragmatic end, one notable genre of pedagogical prints of the 1880s advanced women's traditional hairdressing reform through the formation of a club. As the eponymous print "Fujin sokuhatsukai" (Women's swept-back hair group) puts in its descriptive cartouche (fig. 16): "Japanese hairstyling has three disadvantages. First it is economically inefficient, second, it's not good for social occasions, and third, it's unhygienic. Hence, it should be reformed."[40] The note accompanies a catalogue of several hairstyles depicted in front and back views with descriptive names like *seiyo agemaki* (Western high roll), *seiyo musubi* (Western knot), and *igirisu musubi* (English knot); instructions for how to achieve the styles;

and descriptions about which female persons each style is most appropriate for. (The English knot is the "tightest" style and therefore good for working women; the *magarehito* is essentially a single braid left down, for teenage girls; and *agemaki* is best for middle-aged and older women, the text informs us.) Several variations of these prints survive with varying amounts of instruction included, often accented with women in *yōfuku* as well as in kimono.

In addition to pedagogical purposes, Western imports served as visual shorthand for imported culture in more abstractly discursive prints, against the increasing flood of which Japanese and traditional things were being rapidly rearticulated. These prints are certainly less concerned with inspiring material changes in viewers than they are in offering commentary on the social situation. In another 1885 print the new swept-back hair fad is recast as a literal dispute. "Kokon sokuai ketsu kyou" (Past and present hairdressing battle) depicts a massive brawl between two groups of women (fig. 17): one fighting under the banner of *sokuhatsuren* (swept-back hair division) and the others beneath the banner of *nabechō mage daiichiban* (pot-town hairdo no. 1).[41] In this print, from just before the empress's costume change proclamation and the height of elite women's *yōfuku* experimentation, we can assume that the conflict was heating up (literally, in the print!). The apparent leader of the swept-back hair division is a woman with a smooth European-looking coif, wearing a maroon European day dress, complete with gold upholstery-esque fringe and a hat tipped to tower over her face and exhorting arm. Next to her as a sort of lieutenant is an adolescent girl, dressed in the new school uniform of *hakama* over kimono. The women fighting in the *sokuhatsu* division, in one-on-one combat with the women of *nabechō mage*, are of course all wearing new hairstyles, in various varieties of modernized clothing; no one except the leader is wearing *yōfuku*, but another woman sports a *hakama*, and all are subtly distinguished from the *nabechō mage* brigade who are uniformly dressed in unmodernized city fashions with black collars and obi tied low and loose, although it's hard to tell in some cases whether the clothes' appearance is disheveled from fighting rather than style. Three male onlookers appear in the back: a Chinese man holding a cigarette, a man with cropped hair wearing a kimono and *hakama*, and a man with a mustache wearing a Western suit and bowler. While the kimono-wearing man seems quietly concerned, the other two men are yelling, either in support of their faction or perhaps in dismay at the fray.

The two women in *hakama* are particularly important as signs of the *sokuhatsuren*'s modernity, since the *hakama* had only just been adopted as a piece of womenswear; heretofore *hakama* were for men or imperial women, who wore a distinctive voluminous red *hakama* as part of court dress. Although the schoolgirl's *hakama* evolved into an iconic Meiji- and Taisho-era (1912–23) sign of the *shōjo* schoolgirl,[42] in contrast these

Fig. 17. "Kokon sokuai ketsu kyou" (Past and present hairdressing battle), 1885. Color woodblock print, three sheets, published by Ueki Rinnosuke. Courtesy of Bunka Gakuen University Library, Tokyo.

hakama are indistinguishable from men's *hakama*, worn low and in patterns often seen in menswear, but not typical of the higher, softer, and usually solid-colored school *hakama* that would later become standard.[43]

Another woman in the *sokuhatsu* brigade wears a *michiyuki* coat over her kimono; although the *michiyuki* is now considered quite old-fashioned among kimono enthusiasts, at the time of the "Kokon" print, it was another recent invention for women's changing kimono fashions. Thus, the "Kokon" print indexes a number of changes in a humorous way: while only some of them are inspired by the West (the *sokuhatsu* hairstyles and the *yōfuku*), even the *wafuku* on the *sokuhatsu* side pointedly illustrate changing norms of gender presentation that (as the sight of women violently scuffling itself) must have been quite striking.

Notably, I know of no prints about the conundrum of men's clothing. This discrepancy suggests the ambiguity of women's positions in the *Bunmei Kaika* project and how much more room for debate remained regarding the stakes and effects of a woman's makeover. Meanwhile, with uniforms for many professions paving the way, and in 1879 the Prussian military–inspired boys' school uniform, it seems there was significantly less sense of ambivalence about appropriate wardrobes for men.

Men's clothes do appear provocatively in a similar earlier print, using the same humorous battle format as the "Fujin sokuhatsukai" print to represent the cultural upheaval in Japan: "Kaika kyūhei kōhai kurabe" ("Comparison of the Destinies of the Enlightened and the Antiquated") by Utagawa Yoshifuji in 1873. In this print all kinds of everyday items then being replaced by imported Western versions are seen fighting furiously:

umbrellas; lamps, lanterns, and candles; latrines; barrels; mailboxes; and perhaps ironically, ukiyo-e versus photographs. To be fair, not all import items are winning. While the newly invented *jinrikisha* (rickshaw) appears the likely victor over two pole-carried palanquins, the ukiyo-e and photograph appear evenly matched. The leaders of the two factions command from beneath a traditional and a Western banner (the Western one has nonsense ABCs), each with a ship of his own on the horizon. The new Western imports sport bodies clothed in jackets and trousers reminiscent of the new civil and military uniforms while the Japanese traditional items fight in combinations of samurai armor, kimono, and *hakama*; one straw barrel of rice rests atop a sumo wrestler's burly body.

Not only do these two fight images humorously illustrate the wild ambivalence the average Meiji citizen must have felt amid the maelstrom of new influences, they also graphically demonstrate a coalescing sense of Japaneseness, formulated in opposition to "the West" as a composite image (despite the fact that by 1873 there were many treaty nations and *yatoi*, foreign consultants, of many nationalities already working for the Meiji government). As the rest of the world was elided into one homogeneous *gaikoku* (foreign land), a singular sense of Japanese identity emerged to reinvigorate old national rivalries (such as with Korea and China, as well as the Euro-American treaty nations). Importantly, both hegemonic conceptions of Japaneseness and imported culture factored into the sartorial modernity slowly coalescing in Meiji Japan. The meaning of tradition was reimagined and redefined precisely as part of forging a modern Japan, one in which foreign imports were laboriously justified with references to ancient signifiers, newly endowed with nationalist meaning, and women were increasingly associated with timeless Japanese essence, if only or especially in contrast to men's increasingly international obligations.

This bifurcated gendered allegiance to *wa* for women and *yō* for men is indexed in extant ukiyo-e that show the royal family and attendants in all kinds of documentary and imaginary scenes.[44] In these numerous images, emperor Meiji is recognizable in his signature military uniform while for the first eighteen years of her reign, the empress and her retinue of retainers appear in these prints standing out from the suited men in their voluminous, unreformed court dress.[45] It was not until 1886, fifteen years after the emperor's makeover, that Empress Haruko finally had a full makeover of her own. It is likely not a coincidence that the empress's new clothes were debuted just before she joined the emperor on official progresses through the country, seated next to the emperor in the English-style carriage topped with a golden phoenix.[46] This momentous change for women's *yōfuku* coincided with the swept-back hair reform and the most intensive period of elite experimentation with elite Western social culture (ca. 1883–87), inspiring a new subgenre of prints that combined aspects of the traditional *bijin* (beauty) genre of attractive women with tabloid-like documentation (or fantasies) about lifestyles of the royalty. Probably also inspired by imported European fashion plates, an exuberant series of prints places the empress, emperor, and female retinue in *yōfuku* frocks and suits at various events and locales, like the horse races, newly established Ueno Park, ladies' bazaars, factories, and in front of new bridges, buildings, and trains; sometimes they are playing music in a parlor or arrayed throughout fantasized Victorian gingerbread houses beside spectacular gorges or surrounded by snow.

Popular prints of the imperial family fulfilled many purposes: they supplemented the very few photographs of the emperor and empress with reports and speculations on the imperial family's doings; they posited the imperial family as national role models to help inculcate new ideologies of gender, family, and identity; and they were entertaining (along the lines of contemporary tabloid news of royals and celebrities). This increase in visual knowledge of the emperor and imperial family promulgated to the nation marks not just an increase in degree buoyed by new technology (photography and newspapers, but also aniline dyes for woodblock prints and broadening distribution networks), but a distinct pivot in the Japanese philosophy of power from an iconography of absence to one of emphatic presence. As Takashi Fujitani notes, innumerable new rituals symbolizing the emperor's "direct rule" were invented over the first half of Meiji's reign, including more than a dozen imperial progresses to various parts of the country (where the emperor was presented as observing and overseeing the citizens), new traditional ceremonies and holidays (like royal weddings and anniversaries, Constitution Day, and innumerable smaller observances), and the fostering of a cult of veneration of the emperor's (and empress's) portrait in the public schools (themselves a Meiji-era innovation).[47]

Strategies of the iconography of absence lingered on and modified certain aspects of the Meiji regime's otherwise relentlessly visual campaign of "exhibitory modernity" in interesting ways; Fujitani notes certain prints of Emperor Meiji progresses in which a strategically placed willow branch obscures his imperial person, making the carriage in which he rides the primary signifier.[48] Emperor Meiji allegedly did not like sitting for photographs or portraits, so although his image was relentlessly disseminated only a few official photographs of him exist, on which all the other representations are modeled (with varying degrees of imaginative license). Indeed, the second official portrait of the emperor from 1888 was a photograph taken by Maruki Toshiaki of a portrait drawn by Italian artist Edoardo Chiossone, a *yatoi* at the National Mint. The most official and recognizable image of the emperor for the second half of his reign was, as Fujitani describes it, "a copy of a copy of a representation of the emperor."[49]

The much-copied portraits themselves could thus function as surrogate stand-ins for the person of the emperor, offering a plausible effigy through which to circulate and consolidate the emperor as a unifying symbol of not only a coalescing national identity but also a model of new enlightenment looks and familial and social behaviors. Indeed, for the vast majority of Japanese subjects it would have been these images, verbal and textual representations, and maybe, just maybe, the passing imperial carriage and retinue around the capital or during one the many imperial progresses taken around the country over the first half of Meiji's reign, that stood in for the person of the emperor.[50] In the numerous prints documenting various activities of the emperor, empress, Prince Haru (destined to be the next emperor of the Taisho era), and ladies-in-waiting, it is precisely the emperor's consistent military uniform, coif, and facial hair that make him recognizable as the emperor in public, the emperor correspondent to his disseminated portrait. The uniform functions not as fashion (in the sense of irrationally changing styles signifying up-to-date modernity) but rather as a steady sign of the emperor's (newly established) global authority and iconicity.

And although it's coincidental that Emperor Meiji's new clothes were not merely *yōfuku* but a military-style uniform, the fact is also meaningful. Even before 1868's revolution, the Tokugawa government had begun experimenting with wool uniforms for soldiers from the 1850s, shortly after Commodore Matthew Perry's fleet's first arrival. Uniforms are a specifically nonfashion type of clothing—by definition they are calibrated toward accurately expressing otherwise invisible facts via semiotic messaging. Meiji's uniform comprises a particularly odd example then, since it semiotically communicated something like commander-in-chief but in a wholly invented way—the leaderliness of Meiji's uniform depended on a knowledge of other (European) nations' semiotics of monarchy, rather than on an integrated system wherein the monarch's military uniform gained meaning from its relation to the uniforms of the rest of the military ranged below him hierarchically. Meiji's 1872 costume change came in advance of the eventual reorganization of the Japanese military into a conscription model, as the restoration brought the official abolishment of the samurai as a hereditary military class.

Even as Emperor Meiji aged, supposedly coming to look less well in his *yōfuku* because he refused to have new measurements taken ever again after that first magnificent uniform made for him at the age of nineteen, in the ukiyo-e record he remains an eternal idealized monarch, tall and trim, sitting or standing in his unchanging gold-braid bedecked uniform.[51]

In the emperor's images in the 1880s he is increasingly overshadowed by the bevy of imperial women who, once they adopted *yōfuku* in 1886 along with Empress Haruko, dominate a fabulous array of scenes, especially in a series by Yōshū (Hashimoto) Chikanobu (1838–1912), one of the foremost Meiji-era ukiyo-e artists. In Chikanobu's prints, the empress and her ladies-in-waiting appear as a new twist on the classic ukiyo-e genre of *bijin* (beautiful women). Where the original *bijin* were courtesans

Fig. 18. Yōshū (Hashimoto) Chikanobu, *A Garden Refreshed by the Passing Rain* (*Ukasentei no zu*), July 1888. Woodblock print; ink and color on paper. The Metropolitan Museum of Art, New York, Gift of Lincoln Kirstein, 1959. www.metmuseum.org.

and geisha of the *ukiyo*, now the beauties are imperial entourage, offered up as edifying examples of feminine probity (under the doctrine of "Good Wives, Wise Mothers," which dominated Meiji-era ideologies of womanhood) and simultaneously as exquisite fashion plates in over-the-top 1880s European bustled fashions in color schemes no Parisian could have dreamed up. Like any fashion illustration, the images feature women in elaborate gowns against gorgeous, often unspecified or imaginary backgrounds. For example, "Illustration of the Garden Refreshed after Rain" places the emperor in a chair, back in the right corner of the triptych, surrounded by six ladies standing about in exuberantly colored day dresses that compete with a rainbow glimpsed over the spectacular cliffs, water, and distant hut beyond the party on the far left (fig. 18). Similarly, other Chikanobu prints place the emperor in the distance, inside a doorframe, with four more spectacular ladies out in front on a Western-style clapboard house veranda watching boys playing in the snow, or seated in the background of seven standing ladies and a lounging Prince Haru in a mini uniform (or a Prussian-style school uniform) enjoying cherry blossoms from an exuberantly carpeted veranda complete with hanging gas globe chandelier.

Even prints with ostensibly pedagogical purposes tend toward the fanciful. Witness "Jokan yōfuku saiho" ("Court Ladies Sewing Western Clothing") by Chikanobu and "Kiho saijo" ("Ladies sewing") by Adachi, both from 1887.[52] Here the ladies-in-waiting are busily demonstrating the activities of Western sewing, including detailed renderings of new Singer sewing machines. Chikanobu's print is garnished with substantial informational descriptions of how to do Western-style sewing, including how to measure and cut the fabrics to fit the clothes to specific bodies. A bit like Fukuzawa Yukichi's instructional manuals a decade earlier, the how-to instructions could travel far in advance of realities, yet must still have offered one form of domestication of foreign fashions by way of acquiring knowledge.

Notably (and surely not coincidentally), both these prints appeared in late 1887, a few weeks after the release of Empress Haruko's statement on changing clothes. Much like the emperor's proclamation almost twenty years earlier, the statement explicitly claimed that ancient native Japanese clothing styles were more similar to contemporary European fashion than Chinese-derived traditional costumes, presenting a specific, if rather unconvincing, nationalist justification for the change to bustles and bodices:

> From olden times there have been imperial regulations regarding women's clothing . . . if we look at contemporary Western women's wear, we find that it combines a top or jacket [kimono] and a skirt in the manner of our ancient Japanese system of dress. This is not only suitable for the formal standing bow but is also convenient for action and movement and makes it only natural to adopt the Western method of sewing. In carrying out this improvement, however, be especially careful to use materials made in our own country.[53]

A more poignantly ambivalent personal attitude toward her own makeover is revealed in the empress's personal writings. A circa 1887 verse collected in the official imperial records of Haruko's writings reads:

> から衣 / たちゐになれず / ともすれば / かざりの玉の / こぼれけるかな
>
> Karagoromo * (*With these new clothes*)
> Tachii ni narezu * (*I am not used to sitting or standing*)
> To mo sureba * (*What if*)
> Kazari no tama no * (*the beads of my necklace*)
> Koborekeru ka na * (*were to spill?*)

This poem is one of the few—maybe only—examples I can find of Meiji-makeover subjects' own feelings about changing clothes, and of course a poem destined for deposit in the public record is not disinterested. Nevertheless, in contrast to the confidence of the empress's public proclamation and the flamboyance of the visual presentations of new women's clothes, this poem punctuates the strangeness of such a major sartorial change with a touchingly vulnerable expression of uncertainty.

In another print from a few years later, after the popular swing away from the Rokumeikan-era height of Western appropriation, five women work diligently at sewing, three in kimono and two in *yōfuku*. One *yōfuku* wearer is at a sewing machine, while the other is standing next to a child-size dress on a dress form. The three kimono-clad women kneel while measuring and embroidering lengths of fabric, apparently making new kimono in the Japanese style of sewing (even today, a specific term—*wasou*—designates Japanese kimono tailoring techniques as distinct from Western techniques). In two other buildings in the background, women are assisting each other in dressing and making tea for each other, while two more adult women (one each in *yōfuku* and kimono) and one child in kimono enjoy the waterfowl in a pond lying beyond the wall of the foreground sewing room. Beyond showing a reasonably accurate rendering of dresses and a sewing machine, no other informative text instructs the viewer of the image about the making of *yōfuku*; rather, the activity is seemingly being folded into and normalized as a larger part of proper feminine activity, along with more traditional embroidery and possibly kimono sewing, dressing, grooming, and making tea.[54] Perhaps a more specific translation of the title (the only text besides the censor's mark of approval with date) helps to resituate this print: "Praise for education in handiwork" (*Kyoiku Homare no Shujutsu*).

These prints index attitudes toward (and, through their absence in certain periods, against) *yōfuku* for women. But, contained within the *bijin* category of prints, the adoption of women's *yōfuku* remains a much stronger air of fantasy or novelty than the *yōfuku*-clad men who appear in street scenes and journalistic prints of current events (like military actions, parades, and government affairs). Moreover, while the women in the imperial images dominate the emperor both in size and number, noble wives and daughters found themselves increasingly incorporated into the mechanisms of state display during the Rokumeikan era, and the empress's makeover was permanent for the rest of her life, but by no means should the reader assume that those events were an unadulterated step forward for women's rights.[55] The Rokumeikan era, which both ended in scandal and a general pendulum swing back away from the most elaborate practices of superficial Westernizing, also ended in the first constitution for Japan, finally promulgated in 1889, which also enshrined, for the first time, a ban on women emperors.[56] No matter whether invisible within the palace inner chambers or newly hypervisible as respectable and royal fashion plates, *Ryosai Kenbo* ideology still designated women as ancillary to political power, even if increasingly accepted in either Western dress or kimono.

I want to note that a significant refrain in the historical writing about women's lag behind men's sartorial *Bunmei Kaika* has hinged on accusing European women's fashion of backwardness. Toby Slade declares that European women's dress was useless for modernization, because "imported women's fashions of the 1870s were a profound reaction against modernity and were consequently immoderately ornamental, anatomically perfidious and formally arbitrary."[57] While such an argument regarding European women's costume is consistent with influential fashion historian Anne

Hollander's claim regarding gendered differentials of modernity, in my opinion it unnecessarily demonizes one subjugated group (European women) to valorize another (Japanese people).[58] Moreover, if women's fashions came to signify nonmodernity in both Europe and Japan, that is hardly a state of affairs women could bring about on their own. It is, of course, rather in distinction to the masculinized gendering of modernity that anything feminine can be rendered antimodern. And, in this case, even as such fashions persist in partaking of the endless teleology of the fashion system.

By way of wrapping up and summarizing this account of major points of "civilized and enlightened" makeover in Japan, we can see both the real material new clothes of (mostly) men and the explosion of representations of imported and adapted clothes that more fully encompassed both men and women as working theatrically and then, perhaps, performatively to instantiate new standard daily modes of embodiment. The emperor and empress, endlessly depicted in various milieus real and imagined, become emblematic of the larger performative task attempted by the whole nation of becoming through seeming. Although buying a print is manifestly different than getting and wearing new clothes or even changing hairstyles, we should not underestimate the potential impact that the steady promulgation of such images could have had: the Girl of the Period and Boulton and Park controversies were in many ways also cases of represented clothing as much and more than worn clothing. While Boulton and Park indubitably did exist and did wear the clothes they were so exhaustively described as wearing and photographed in, even they along with the Girl of the Period and these idealized Meiji royals also circulated extensively as image—as indeed most clothes circulate. We might imagine images of the imperial family and their sumptuously fantastical clothes a bit like the way that fashion magazines circulate images of high fashion to influence readers who will never have the financial means (or even inclination, perhaps) to buy the designer clothes pictured, but whose consumption and familiarization with such images goes on to influence trickle-down culture.

In the case of the Meiji makeover's explicit political goals, the theatrical can be said to have preceded the actual: clothing and other cosmetic norms were adopted rapidly by elites, and representations thereof were disseminated as strategically as possible with the aim of matching government representatives of Japan as closely as possible to Euro-American norms, along with sanitizing and adapting the common people's appearances to eliminate habits the foreigners found disagreeable. Meanwhile, domestic dissemination of new ideas, both politically mandated ones and those borne of faddish curiosity, prepared the ground for the rest of society to more slowly adopt and adapt imported fashions. We could even think of the Meiji makeover as an explicit experiment in Butlerian performativity: social identities like gender, class, and nationality were all intentionally reordered through the instantiation of new and altered behaved norms.

While Butler and other theorists are correct to caution that it's not the consciousness of performance that makes an identity performative, I suggest it's rather the sustainedness of the new norms of performance (even as they were altered and disputed) that eventually led to permanent shifts in the meanings and appearances of gender, sexuality, age, and especially race and nationality in Japan. In the concluding section of this chapter, I'll consider specifics from Japanese culture that may modify how we might think of performativity in Japanese subject formation, but for now we might note how the analyses of historians Howell and Fujitani begin to outline divergent interpretations. Howell, as noted in the discussion of Tokugawa politics of fashion, emphasizes the ways both Tokugawa and then Meiji authorities focused on exterior regulation with little regard for subjects' interior dispositions. Although written about a different geohistorical context, Michel Foucault's arguments about the absolutist state in *Discipline and Punish* correspond in the broad sense of the government's primary concern with the externalities of obedience. Fujitani goes on to posit that part of the Meiji regime's *Bunmei Kaika* project involved adopting aspects of the modern (European) system of internalized regulation. He writes,

> New Meiji rulers began to demand the active spiritual participation of the common people in the realization of national objectives . . . they hoped to reconstitute the people into more than simply objects of rule, so that they could become knowledgeable and self-disciplined subjects in the dual Foucauldian sense—that is, subjects who were not only subjected to "control and dependence" but who were also subjects possessed of their own identity by a "conscience or self-knowledge."[59]

Such a model relies inherently on a notion of identities as performative, in that the knowledges and practices imposed or offered, repeated and internalized, become identities through their sustained, repeated enactment and reenactment. The imaginary, nonessential, superficial enactment—the theatrical—thus precedes the performative instantiation of new norms. Whether such enactments truly penetrated to some collective subjective interior to create new identities or if they remained surface appearances, what we will see in the next section is how European antitheatrical suspicions of fashion's superficiality (such as those we've seen in chaps. 2 and 3) clashed with Meiji performative intentions.

Monkeys and Children

After all, the foreigners with front row seats to the performances being put on in part for their benefit were tough critics. Erwin Baelz, a German physician employed by the emperor, wrote in his diary on New Year's Day 1877:

> The Japanese government . . . thought fit to prescribe frock-coat and tall hat as the official dress for New Year visits. For this reason, today the streets have been full of figures more comical than you could possibly imagine. They look positively ridiculous, these unfortunate Japanese, in their incredibly ill-fitting frock-coats and trousers! On their heads are tall hats which look equally out of place. Their hands are adorned with white gloves, and hang stiffly by their sides, as if they were afraid of touching their "European" clothes. Not only full-grown men, but even boys of ten to twelve are sacrificed to this preposterous convention. You simply cannot imagine how absurd they look as they go about the streets or wait in antechambers. Yet these same Japanese have a very fine appearance, dignified and distinguished, when dressed for great occasions in their native finery.[60]

Baelz's sentiments were repeated endlessly over the decades: "The Japanese look most diminutive in European dress. Each garment is misfit, and exaggerates the miserable physique and the national defects of concave chests and bow legs," declared Isabella Bird in 1880.[61] "The Japanese figure was 'too dumpy and the legs too short to appear to advantage in this foreign dress,' " wrote Henry T. Finck, as late as 1895.[62] Certainly some photographers seem to have shared the idea that different clothing would reveal different things about the Japanese body, as an 1894 book suggests by juxtaposing two photographs of the same man in the same location and pose while wearing *yōfuku* and kimono (fig. 19).[63] It's difficult to identify anything particularly notable in the juxtaposition of this anonymous man's two outfits; by 1894, his knee-length wool coat, trousers, and bowler hat were no longer novel nor poorly fitted or coordinated, so whatever comedy earlier observers like Baelz or Charles Wirgman of the *Japan Punch* had witnessed is long gone from the photo in Palmer's book.

It is difficult to decide what to make of the recurring claim that *yōfuku* indexed inferior bodily constitutions. While it is generally understood that nineteenth-century Japanese people were significantly shorter on average than today and that both foreign and Japanese commentators looked to Western clothes and diets to "improve" the Japanese physique over time, examining extant photographs does not seem to reveal a nation of "miserable physiques."[64] Certainly the tourist trade in images of stripped-down rickshaw runners and messengers and tattooed people revealing much more skin and flesh than one's average *yōfuku* ensemble should have been a more likely index if there were anything typically unusual about

MAN IN FOREIGN DRESS. SAME IN JAPANESE DRESS.

Fig. 19. "Man in Foreign Dress, Same in Japanese Dress," from Henry Spencer Palmer, *Letters from the Land of the Rising Sun: Being a Selection from Correspondence Contributed to "The Times" between the Years 1886 and 1892 . . . with Seventy-Six Illustrations* (Yokohama: Japan Mail, 1894), 65.

Japanese bodies.[65] Rather it seems that commentators conflated unusual clothing combinations or fits (including, as Meech-Pekarik puts it, "ankles protruding from trousers, collars unfastened, and cravats askew") or combinations of kimono and *yōfuku* (such as hats, umbrellas, and leather shoes with kimono, or the fad for plaid shawls on both men and women) with physical unfitness.[66] For example, two plates attributed to the studio of early Yokohama photographer Baron Raimund von Stillfried and his business partner Herman Andersen show Japanese men in top hat, tails, gloves, and long shiny shoes. Although the two undated but apparently early to mid-1870s images look very similar, they seem to be different men. It's quite possible that both are wearing the same tailcoat, far too large for both of them, which, along with the white gloves, oversized top hat, and the subjects' bronzed skin, contributes to an uncomfortable sense of minstrel likeness in the black-and-white photos.[67] The images are hard to parse. Were these rental costumes and men who wanted to try *yōfuku* for a studio portrait? Did Andersen or Stillfried arrange and pose these portraits as photographers did many more conventional scenes, innumerable copies of which were then sold as standard tourist souvenirs over years? Even if they had been the former, they were certainly sold as the latter, since copies of these images appear in foreign museum collections now rather than with other Japanese individuals' personal portraits. And the open-mouthed expression of one and the contrived action with the gloves on the other image suggest novelty prints more so than portraits of individuals. Even more complications with interpreting these images will be presented near the end of this chapter when I return in detail to the activities of Yokohama tourist photographers and merchants like von Stillfried and Andersen.

Eliza Scidmore, travel author and first woman board member of *National Geographic*, described meeting a Nagoya *maiko* (an apprentice geisha) named Oikoto who mostly thrilled Scidmore and her party with her looks, kimono, and traditional dances, although not with the Western-style dance Oikoto and her colleagues had on the program. Scidmore explains, "when we begged the lovely Oikoto for her photograph, she proudly brought us one which showed that exquisite creature transformed into a dowdy horror by a foreign gown and bonnet, which the Nagoya photographer keeps on hand for the use of his customers."[68]

Despite the European notion of clothing as fundamentally, if not the most fundamental, artifice applied to the natural body, foreign observers obsessively described the unnaturalness of Western clothes on Japanese bodies and the natural fit of kimono. (This, of course, despite that kimono norms were in significant flux; shifts in kimono fashions tended to pass unnoticed by the foreigners enchanted with the beauty of what they imagined to be unchanging antiquity.)

In contradistinction to these foreigners' self-assured insistence that the fundamental physical inferiority of the Japanese was highlighted by their appearances in *yōfuku*, another key Meiji interlocutor troubled these accounts with a very different (if no less condescending) interpretation. Louis Marie-Julien Viaud, better known by his nom de plume Pierre Loti, was the French novelist and essayist now infamous for penning *Madame Chrysanthème*, a precursor to Giacomo Puccini's opera *Madame Butterfly*. Loti spent several years of the 1880s in Japan. In his disquisitions on his experiences in Tokyo, he describes not another fashion failure, but rather an unnerving success. In two essays Loti describes Western-style balls he attended:

> young ladies dressed all in white muslin, with gloves reaching above the elbow. They were seated on chairs, and assumed mincing, affected manners, as they toyed with their programmes. Then they danced polkas and waltzes in tolerably good time, to the tune of operetta music, notwithstanding the enormous difficulties all our unknown European rhythms and measures must have had for them.[69]

Loti veers back and forth between disdain for this performance and amazement, going on to identify the achievement of a European ball not as a genuine display of good breeding and culture but as a kind of trick:

> En somme, une fête très gaie et très jolie, que ces Japonais nous one offerte là avec beaucoup de bonne grâce. Si j'y ai souri de temps en temps, c'était sans malice. Quand he songe mème que ces costumes, ces manières, ce cérémonial, ces danses, étaient des choses apprises, apprises très vite, apprise par ordre impérial et peut-être à contre-coeur, je me dis que ces gens sont de bien merveilluex imitateurs et une telle soirée me semble un des plus intéressants tours de force de ce peuple, unique pour les jongleries.
>
> (Altogether, a very gay and pretty party, which these Japanese offer with abundant good grace. If I smiled occasionally, it was without malice. And when I think that these costumes, these manners, this elaborate etiquette, these dances, were something learned, and learned very quickly, learned on imperial command and perhaps against their will, I tell myself that these people are really marvelous imitators and a soiree such as this seems to me a most interesting tour de force on the part of people who are uniquely skilled at sleight of hand.)[70]

Loti was describing scenes from the Rokumeikan, the most infamous of all Meiji experiments in Western acculturation. The Rokumeikan "Deer Cry Pavilion" was a typical Japanese title given to an unprecedented building in Tokyo, designed by British *yatoi* Josiah Conder and completed in 1883. Intended as a centerpiece of foreign minister Inoue Kaoru and prime minister Ito Hirobumi's government experiments in escalating *Bunmei Kaika* by adopting European elite lifestyles, the Rokumeikan contained ballrooms and other public spaces intended for dancing, dinner parties, ladies' bazaars, and other typical bourgeois and aristocratic European social activities. It was as part of this brief period of hyper-intensive Westernization that the Empress Haruko completed her aforementioned makeover, eighteen years after her husband's. The series of *bijin*-cum-fashion plate ukiyo-e of the Empress and her retinue comprise part of this campaign by dramatizing her and her court's Western fashions as bright and exciting novelties. The Rokumeikan building is such a key part of this moment that the period is now simply referred to by historians as the Rokumeikan era.

Donald Keene describes the Rokumeikan as "a stage on which the Japanese might display to foreigners that, having turned their backs on the antiquated ways of the past, they had become masters of European table manners and the decorum of the ballroom."[71] Keene's choice of the word "stage" stands out here in emphasizing the theatrical, in the sense of intended for view by a specific audience. But this most intensive stage of the generation-long experiment in adapting Western culture would end ignominiously before the decade was out with social scandal and frustration over European powers' continued refusal to renegotiate the treaties. Historians typically describe the Rokumeikan period (approximately 1883–87) as the height of the *Bunmei Kaika* era whose end precipitated a swing back toward traditional lifeways, a swing further buoyed by the self-esteem boost of Japanese military victories in the Sino-Japanese War (1894–95) and then Russo-Japanese War (1904–5).[72]

Most importantly for my purposes was the fact that Inoue's gambit required elite women to dance, dine, and shop the bazaars in contradistinction to generations of Japanese social standards in which respectable wives and daughters were entirely excluded from official and social functions while professional women, like courtesans and geisha, presided over elite men's social functions. Despite the dancing lessons offered every Sunday for wives and daughters, apparently many events where foreigners mingled with Meiji government elites at the Rokumeikan were stocked with geisha, accustomed and trained to be social, charming, and discreet during high stakes events with important men.[73] While many elite Meiji men actually married geisha (including Ito, the prime minister) or took them into their households as concubines or mistresses, the uneasy attempt to initiate wives and daughters into public life remained fraught with the mixing of feminine types—an issue more of women from different status groups mixing in public than the social origins of the women physically present in the Rokumeikan.[74]

Illustrator Georges Bigot provided some of the most famous visual representations of the Rokumeikan, alongside fellow Frenchman Loti's essays.[75] Bigot's caricatures of women at the Rokumeikan diverge strongly from Loti's description of perfect semblance. Bigot's pen presumes to lay bare in its representation the truth of the geishas' low manners, showing them in ill-fitting day dresses and hats, ankles on view, awkward arms akimbo, stubbing out cigarettes and toting shamisen cases.

Another of Bigot's caricatures shows a couple, he in military uniform, she in a high-necked day dress, looking into a full-length mirror, which reflects them unmistakably as apes, barely anthropomorphic at all (fig. 20). Bigot's take is vicious in the animality of the reflection, but ambivalent in its meaning: has their clothing made this elite couple into subhuman monkeys, or does Bigot suggest only that they must feel like monkeys in new clothes prescribed by official edict? As cutting as the antitheatrical sentiment is, the caricature is stubbornly inconclusive.

What I want to focus on here, however, is the problem of appearances: Loti's take offers up a miracle of Japanese "sleight of hand" (*jonglerie*) perfectly mimicking European society, while Bigot promises that he sees

Fig. 20. Georges Bigot, "Monsieur et Madame vont dans le monde," *Tōbaé: Journal satirique*, 1, no. 6 (May 1, 1887). Miriam and Ira D. Wallach Division of Art, Prints and Photographs: Print Collection, New York Public Library Digital Collections.

through this facade, or possibly even suggests that everyone sees the poorness of the imitation: society ladies who are actually uncouth working girls, elites who feel like animals. Although they diverge on the quality of the Rokumeikan illusion, both Loti and Bigot agree that it is illusion. Loti's perfect semblance remains sleight of hand despite its perfection. Fail to appear to perfection, or execute flawlessly, the verdict from the foreign observers was the same: empty imitation.

Foreign interlocutors were not the only observers who used ape imagery to critique the methods and effects of makeover. Nomura Fumio, a government official who had spent time in Britain in the 1860s, quit his government position to found a satirical newspaper in 1877 on the model of English publications and Charles Wirgman's *Japan Punch*, which was so influential that it gave its name to the Japanese neologism for political

Fig. 21. Honda Kinkachiro, "Monkey Show," *Marumaru chimbun* (April 26, 1879). Courtesy of Cornell University Library.

cartoons: *Ponchi-e* ("Punch pictures").[76] Nomura's *Marumaru chimbun* obliquely referenced monkeys in its title page, which featured three men in *yōfuku*, one with huge ears, one with big eyes, and one with a big nose—who see, hear, and smell all evil in a parodic twist on the famous monkeys carved at Nikko who see, hear, and speak no evil. The *Marumaru chimbun* also used the monkey trope, particularly in relation to clothing, as in an 1879 cartoon showing three simian individuals, two men and a woman, completing *yōfuku* toilette under the title "Monkey-show" with a brief English caption, "All the monkeys dressed in European style, and in every respect trying to ape Foreigners" and a longer Japanese description laden with puns on the word "monkey" (fig. 21): "Morse declares humans come from monkeys, but they didn't just originate as monkeys, they are monkeys still and can't help aping Westerners. The world is just one great monkey show."[77] Monkeys are emblematic in both Euro-American and Japanese cultures, with differing valences. In Euro-American cultures, monkeys have recurred as caricatures of or even avatars for nonwhite and especially African or Black people.[78] In a post-Darwinian context, such elisions gained a veneer of scientific racism.[79] Meanwhile, monkeys also have a long history as symbols of human-animal-spirit liminality in Japan (and are actually endemic to the archipelago). Their almost-but-not-quite humanness has spawned notions of monkeys as gods and messengers to gods, as well as an extensive archive of imagery and texts that match the notions of monkeys as foolish imitators of humans found in Western cultures.[80]

The monkey trope thus tempers the performative potential of Meiji makeover ideals, undercutting the possibility that Japanese imitation of Western civilization could ever be truly commensurate with its models within a rhetoric of theatrical superficiality. And yet, European descriptions of Japan repeat this refrain of Japanese imitativeness endlessly with regular variations: imitation as brilliant (if of modern technologies) or silly and misguided (if of fashions), servile or cunning, laughably bad or disconcertingly perfect. As if observing apishness were itself infectious, the sheer repetitiveness of the claim of Japanese imitativeness itself seems to recur involuntarily. As the inseparable obverse of the trope of impossible difference ("fairyland" Japan, "contrary" Japan of roofs built before floors and shoes removed instead of hats), mimic Japan, commentators seemed to hope, could be held at bay with a careful parsing of mere aping from true civilization.[81]

The dynamic of theatricality—the failure of appearance to reliably reflect a perceived truth value—infected "serious" Orientalist discourse in addition to tourist and popular narratives: for example, William E. Griffis fears in his 1876 work *The Mikado's Empire* and its attendant excerpt in *Harper's New Monthly Magazine* for the US market that the Japanese might only achieve a "glittering veneer of material civilization and the corroding foreign vices" by appropriating only "the fruits of Christian civilization without its root."[82] Henry Norman, a journalist who published his book *The Real Japan* in 1892, repeated the same:

> It is, perhaps, open to inquiry, after all, how far the startling adoption of Western manners, methods, and institutions, upon which the universal admiration of Japan is chiefly based, is the result of intelligent appreciation, and how far it springs from a national quality of versatile imitation. The former is the condition of our education, whether of individuals or nations; the latter reaches its highest development in children and monkeys. "The Japanese think to raise themselves in Western estimation by donning tall hats and frock-coats," wrote even their most friendly critic. "They would rise more quickly by dressing their thoughts in European fashion."[83]

New clothes don't necessarily make a new man, however if there were not anxiety on the part of the upper-handed treaty powers about the menace of likeness and the power of a new suit to transform a Japanese man into a new sort of citizen, then there would be no impulse to relentlessly lampoon their efforts. I suggest that such slurs of theatricality, superficiality, and empty imitation thus belie their claim to identifying an absurdity (that Japanese person could never look right in Western clothes—read: could never rival Western imperial supremacy) with the sheer repetitiveness with which they insist. While Japanese efforts were aimed toward a combined theatrical and performative effect, the foreign interlocutors' interpretations relied on theatrical tropes to try to redefine these efforts (whether good or bad likenesses) as like Western norms, but not comparable and obviously ridiculous. I suggest that such repetitive representations that redefine, reiterate, and obsessively redraw the lines between West and

East, self and other, are required precisely because no such true divisions exist; such fantasies of essentially different identities are easily blurred and distinctions easily effaced.

The Meiji Japanese bid to attain power through mimicry of power and the (anti)theatrical Western response is clearly resonant with Homi K. Bhabha's description of the imposition of imperial power on colonial subjects as an injunction to mimicry. Bhabha writes, "Colonial mimicry is the desire for a reformed recognizable Other, as a subject of a difference that is almost the same but not quite."[84] According to Bhabha, although the colonial subject is required to become more like the imperial power, he or she will simultaneously be condemned to failure—to be "not quite" the same as the colonizer: "not white." Japan does not fit precisely into Bhabha's specific framework, because Japan was not colonized per se, but rather found itself in an unequal position vis-à-vis treaty status. Therefore, the Japanese were not so much coerced into conforming to a Western standard, but consciously and carefully chose Westernization as a strategy in a negotiation, albeit one with an unequal power differential.[85]

Nevertheless, the catch-22 Bhabha identifies in the impossible demands of colonial mimicry operates here: the "menace" Bhabha identifies in colonial mimicry is the otherness that continues to underlie the colonized other's "reformed" exterior—the menace of colonial mimicry is the menace of theatricality as duplicity, masquerade, disguise. In some sense, the potential subversive "menace" of the subaltern bid for power against the colonial was always explicit in Japan's case; the 1872 declaration made in the US president's letter is clear about its intentions to be seen "on an equality with" the "enlightened nations." The Western response of labeling such activities ridiculous monkey-like mimicries was a mode of maintaining colonial power by insisting on the authority to judge and judging Japanese performances of civilization and enlightenment empty or laughable.

In staking a part of their bid to masculine modernity in surface appearances, Japanese men played into that gendered trap of theatricality.[86] While Bhabha calls mimicry a menace to colonial systems of power, the very otherness within the copy also serves as a ground for derision in much imperial commentary. Miyake Setsurei (a conservative critic of the Meiji regime) wrote in 1891: "Westerners might laugh openly at the pigtail and robe of a Chinese, but inwardly they respected his independence; they might openly praise a Japanese for his Western clothing, but inwardly they mocked his unseemly imitation."[87] Miyake's claim is trenchant: not only is Japanese imitation deemed "unseemly" but the Westerners in this formulation are rendered equally theatrical, laughing at the ones they secretly respect and mouthing compliments for those they despise.

Meanwhile in the 1880s, while the cabinet danced in their new clothes, Miyake's sentiments saw material expression in other groups who resisted the government's call to *Bunmei Kaika* in old clothes. The term *sōshi* came to name what Jason Karlin calls a subculture of political dissidents especially associated with the Freedom and People's Rights Movement and the associated *Jiyūto* political party.[88] All of these groups took a critical view of the Meiji establishment's tactics, leadership, and increasingly tight rein on opposition as they led up to the 1889 ratification of the Meiji constitution and 1890s convening of the first National Diet. It may not be a surprise that especially during the years where the public face of the government was so heavily focused on harnessing *yōfuku* as a sign of its civilization, the *sōshi* reveled in adopting oppositional fashions: old, tattered *wafuku*, long hair, tied back kimono sleeves, and high wooden geta sandals. Influential late-Meiji journalist Tokutomi Soho wrote "that they are pusillanimous, narrow-minded, obstinate, and eccentric is not something for which they deserve special praise; but when one witnesses their righteous indignation, dauntless integrity and bounteous patriotic spirit, and when one sees them tuck up their sleeves, proud of being Japanese men (*Nippon danji*), they do become extremely appealing."[89] A bit like the *kabukimono* in generations past and Dick Hebdige's punks of the 1970s, fashion dissent fed and mirrored political dissent, albeit in a way that still cannot settle the question of the political efficacy of appearance.[90] Tokutomi's observation helps to capture the flickering possibility of political fashion: although he disagrees with the ideas espoused by the *sōshi*, he recognizes a simultaneous affective appeal.

Importantly, this battle for political power was playing out on the ground of gender, specifically, over the meaning and appearance of Japanese masculinity. Remember that the emperor's 1872 proclamation named erstwhile court dress as effeminate in advocating the change to *yōfuku*, while Tokutomi recognizes a rugged and honest masculinity in the unreformed dress of the *sōshi*. The Meiji elites inherently recognized over a century in advance Edward Said's future gendered critique of Orientalism when they grasped the importance of managing the Western perception of Japanese masculinity as part of competition on the world stage. But the materials at their disposal left their efforts toward sartorial *Bunmei Kaika* vulnerable to the gendered counterattack of the *sōshi*, who pitched their appeal toward a notion of masculine honesty and authenticity made visible by its contrast against superficial fashion and slavish or even apish imitation. Karlin traces an association of fashionability and imitativeness with feminization:

> In modernity . . . women are meant to represent origins and the immutability of identity in a way that makes the body of the female an important site for defining the nation. In contrast to the ephemerality of urban mass culture (to which women are often pejoratively aligned), women are expected to embody the timeless

> and eternal qualities of the past. In the denunciation of mass culture as feminine, the fear of emasculation through the triviality of fashion, imitation, and reproduction expresses anxiety about modernity.[91]

Karlin's prose betrays the bizarre oxymoronic nature of the gendered divide he is trying to describe: femininity appears on both sides of his equation, as representative of "origins" and the "immutability of identity" akin surely to both the Meiji (and beyond) values of *Ryosai Kenbo* and the Victorian era's "Cult of True Womanhood," as espoused in the negative by Eliza Lynn Linton's "Girl of the Period" and countless other antifeminists and conservatives. Karlin also is recalling specific colonial dynamics that bifurcated in a specifically gendered way. Imported imperial (Euro-American and white) modernity deeply penetrated the realm of native men who adapted and took on aspects of those imported forms of power and identity while native women were imbued with the aura of the native culture: awarded a certain kind of privilege as avatars of the original and traditional, but shut out from modernity and any other role than bearers of tradition.[92]

But this is where it gets weird: as Karlin's sentence betrays, femininity is simultaneously associated with the theatrical, what Karlin calls "the triviality of fashion, imitation, and reproduction."[93] Karlin's imitation is clearly the empty imitation of the monkeys and children—and now women—so derided by both Western and Japanese commentators in caricature and prose. The elision of women with such theatricality should remind us of previous chapters of this book, where, for example, the association of women and (empty) display added vehemence to Eliza Lynn Linton's and others' insistence that girls should be "content to be what God and Nature made them."

Looking closely at the negotiation of Meiji gender through the proxy of clothing reveals that the gender ideologies being instituted were hopelessly oxymoronic and irrational. That, however, is less important here than recognizing how central attributions of gender were to behavioral and representational changes. It's less that the *sōshi* recognized an inherent effeminacy in imitative Western fashions and reverted to a native, natural, virile masculinity than that resistant politics found a clear material mode of expression through resistant clothing and gender performance. That the resistant clothing could carry simultaneous messages of allegiance to tradition and native identity added positive, flattering gendered valences to a rebellious political stance.[94] Moreover, the *sōshi* (and Miyake's) discursive claim to naturalness tended to correlate disturbingly well with the desires of Western interlocutors, both sympathetic and critical, who preferred their Japanese people recognizably and comfortably foreign looking.

Theatricality of the Natural

What I am working to point out here is the conundrum that attended any choice of dress for modern Meiji citizens. Where political dissidents like the *sōshi* (to say nothing of later radicals like Miyake or Mishima Yukio) expressed their opposition through sartorial recourse to natural and traditional Japanese significations, many foreign commentators also interpreted the Meiji makeover as servile imitation. Such anti-Western adaptation stances may have been resistant to the Meiji status quo, but they were uncomfortably consonant with exactly the same "quaint, exquisite" desires Westerners had about Japan and Japanese people.[95] Any formula for Japanese resistance to global imperial pressures was thus stymied by a paradox articulated by Bhabha in conjunction with Rey Chow's theory of "coercive mimeticism."[96]

While Bhabha's foundational work on colonial mimicry obviously underwrites the reasoning of everything I've described in the Meiji makeover (albeit the Meiji elites recognized these dynamics a century and more before Bhabha described them for Anglophone academics), it is Chow's work, building on Orientalist critique, that helps to explain foreign interlocutors' antitheatrical response to Japanese people in *yōfuku*. Chow describes (following Foucauldian reasonings) how the more efficient means of controlling and hierarchizing cultures, races, or ethnicities is not to eliminate the stigmatized ones but to subtly delegitimize them through maintenance of hierarchized distinctions in which the subordinate need not be abjected or eliminated, but can simply be put "in its place."[97] One means of doing that is to insist on the primacy of the dominant culture's preconceptions of the subordinated culture and refuse to recognize ethnically marked subjects who don't fulfill expectations. This is a "coercive mimeticism" in which "the ethnic person is expected to come to resemble what is recognizably ethnic" to be recognized as a subject at all.[98]

Katherine S. Baxter exemplifies Chow's point in her 1895 travelogue, *In Bamboo Lands* (also published under the alternative title *In Beautiful Japan: A Story of Bamboo Lands*): "We thought it a piece of barbarism to discard the easy, graceful kimona [*sic*] for the stiff, ill-fitting European costume; for, with all our superior civilization, we cannot teach them anything about dress, and why, with all the world to choose from, they should choose ours is inscrutable."[99] One line later, she reveals the solipsism of her desire for the perpetuation of the "kimona": "I deplore the denationalization of nations, the breaking up, in short, of national life and customs; and instances of it are numerous—India rapidly becoming Anglicized, Hawaii [*sic*] a Republic, Japan imitating Europe. The times threaten to deprive these countries of their peculiar charm."[100] Baxter betrays the primacy of her allegiance to Japan (as well as India and Hawai'i) as exotic touristic spectacle over substantive trading partner or fully equal interlocutor in her singular emphasis on its responsibility to provide her with "peculiar charm." Such sentiments emphatically put Japan "in its place" as quaint, charming, romantic, and unthreatening to Western hegemonies of economic and political power.

Further, Baxter provocatively transposes two particularly laden terms in her lament for the kimono: to adopt the costume of "superior civilization" is deemed "barbarism" and to choose to wear garments intimately familiar to Baxter, "inscrutable." These two particular words, "barbarism" and "inscrutable," are so deeply imbricated in histories of Orientalist discourse that it nearly requires a psychoanalytic intervention to explain how they could be applied so oxymoronically to the very project of rendering Japanese people legible and equal in Western terms as human negotiators on the global stage. Obviously, the goals of *Bunmei Kaika* were hardly secret or disguised, despite Baxter's self-professed inability to decipher them. In another sense, Baxter's and her counterparts' mystification around other people's employment of superficial actions indexes their own cultural assumptions about both their own imperviousness to the illusory nature of appearances and the essentialized naturalness they attributed to the Japanese body in its proper kimono.

Travelogue authors sometimes even acknowledged the strange and limited ways in which Japan preexisted in Euro-American imaginaries primarily as quaint objects like doll-like people painted on porcelain export ware.[101] Augusta Campbell Davidson's first impression of Japanese people, male porters working the docks where she disembarked her ship, "were not my old friends, the quaintly gorgeous folk of the teacups, but still they were distinctly not European, and my hopes of the picturesque revived accordingly."[102]

Baxter's and Campbell Davidson's reactions, like Eliza Scidmore's disappointment with the geisha Oikoto's gift of her portrait in *yōfuku*, betray these women's dedication to a real and authentic Japan that had been itself carefully nurtured and arranged by a whole array of businesses, writers, and artists, both foreign and Japanese, who colluded to help create and maintain a cohesive image of Japan, under the pretense of only documenting it.[103] I do not argue that such a collusion was malicious, nor even conscious, but neither were the major forces behind the shaping and selling of narratives of real Japan disinterested or reflexive about the ways in which their documents would help to create the fairyland atavistic Orient that foreign markets found it so pleasant to consume. Accessing real Japan thus emerges as an epistemological and historiographical problem (not to say impossibility), especially in the Anglophone context. Even in Japan the avalanche of extant material created for foreigners and foreign markets (like the extensive documentation of Bigot's and Wirgman's imagery and overrepresentation of tourist photography in the archive of early Japanese photography) means that any history has to contend with the sheer preponderance of material intended to present a view of Japan defined from abroad.

Moreover, both the government and individual Japanese people have collaborated willingly with foreign markets to present the imagery of Japan that foreigners seemed most desirous of seeing. For example, Japan became an eager participant in the second half of the nineteenth-century's mania for international exhibitions, sending government-sponsored exhibits to the 1867 World Exposition in Paris, where the centerpiece was a teahouse with three women in kimono relaxing and smoking, and the 1873 World Exposition in Vienna, which featured a Shinto shrine and a garden complete with stone lanterns and an arched bridge. At the conclusion of the Vienna exhibition, the garden was purchased, down to the trees and stones, by one Alexander Park of London.[104]

Scidmore had surely expected a geisha portrait of Oikoto in the style of the Japan popularized by international exhibitions, export curios, and commercial photographers. Souvenir photographs of Japan were wildly popular among the tourists who tended to arrive first in Yokohama, where they could collect all their souvenir images of their trip from the commercial photographers' studios, sometimes picking à la carte, or buying handsome volumes of already compiled photos typically labeled "Native Costumes" or "Native Types," a companion to "Views of Japan."[105] Scidmore thus documents a divide between fantasies: where Oikoto offered her foray into Western semblance in honor of the Western visitors, Scidmore and her companions wanted souvenirs of a real Japan that was itself a carefully calibrated product of mostly foreign-born commercial photographers who were both shaping and reflecting representations of Japan that gratified non-Japanese visitors' desire (and expectations) for an exotic and strange fairyland.[106] Samurai, geisha, tattooed men, tattooed Ainu women, kimono, and curious artifacts like palanquins, chopsticks and handleless teacups served on low tables for floor sitting, wooden pillows, round bathing tubs, and rickshaws, all fill these staged studio images alongside the views of mostly person-free landscapes of temples, the Tokaido travel route between Tokyo and Kansai (the Kyoto-Osaka region), Mount Fuji, temples, seascapes, and so on.[107] Because it would be several decades before photographic equipment became cheap, easy, and portable enough for greater numbers of photographers to make more images with fewer studio constraints, the infinitely repeated standard scenes of early commercial photographers Felice Beato, Baron von Stillfried, and Kusakabe Kimbei dominate the photographic record (and, as a result, also the English language publications on early Japanese photography).[108] Photographers even bought each other's plates, copying and updating each other's images, which were also copied and adapted extensively by engravers, who provided the imagery for journalism and publications about Japan.[109] Some authors of travelogues and popular books on Japan openly discuss the process of acquiring sets of images from photographers or engravers, and certain photographic scenes can be found over and over again, from around 1860 when the first photographers set up in the new treaty port of Yokohama through the early twentieth century when personal, portable, amateur photography was finally able to displace the commercial photo in primacy. Often these images are inserted practically randomly in commercially published books, suggesting that the images of Japan were recognized as selling points separately from the texts they appeared alongside. For example, on a page from *In Bamboo Lands* a Tokugawa-era samurai with single-tooth geta wooden sandals and a *hanpatsu* haircut (the style that had been superseded twenty years earlier) appears alongside Baxter's description of riding the railway with, she declares, "samurai men," although they almost definitely no longer wore the clothes or hair of the illustration, and the very class of samurai had been abolished twenty years earlier as well.

Among innumerable examples, I'll offer only one more: in her 1904 travelogue *Present-day Japan*, Augusta Campbell Davidson's opinion that the status of women had not significantly advanced during Japan's Westernization campaigns is punctuated by an illustration of Empress Haruko based not on the portraiture released after her 1886 makeover, fully eighteen years before the book's publication, but on her first 1872 photographic portrait from thirty-two years earlier in, as the caption notes, "Japanese court dress." A more hilariously bastardized version of this portrait also appears in Griffis's *The Mikado's Empire*. In the Griffis version, the inner collar of the empress's robes have been turned into a white scarf that flows into the part of the image that was actually an open fan, simultaneously domesticating the ensemble with the recognizable form of a scarf around the neck even as the empress was exoticized by the choice of reprinting a twenty-year-old portrait in curious Japanese dress, rather than an eight-year-old portrait of the empress in the bustled frock she actually appeared in exclusively by that time.

There are any number of reasons for the perpetuation of the more foreign empress image rather than the Westernized one, but without speculating on intentions, we may note that the continued dissemination of the more exotic image, even if alongside the newer ones and even when embedded in prose that explicitly described the modernization of the imperial family's appearance among all the other innovations of "Young Japan," inherently gratified foreigners' preferred vision of "Old Japan." Such an affective and intellectual investment in otherness, both conscious and unconscious, highlights a fundamental way in which theatricality (representation untethered to truth value) precedes truth, thereby structuring which knowledges will be accepted as knowledge.

These images do not offer definitive proof of any mindset: it's not evidence of malice or intentional racism that the empress image in Griffis's book became bescarfed or that someone used an exotic, outdated image over the empress's new official portrait. Infinitely replicated photographic plates and engravings proliferated across publications and tourists' souvenirs; innumerable agents beyond the Japan expert authors were involved in the design and publishing of such mass-market books and audiences had to be wooed with appealing images. The empress's newer portrait may not have been as readily available for mass reproduction as an engraving (although it definitely is extant in other books) and the common assumption that Japan constituted an unchanging antiquated tradition would reassure many that there could be no need to look for a more recent portrait of the empress. Considerations such as these, and many more, thus temper the documentary truth value of factual works in English on Japan. While it's no revelation that (all) documents of history and culture are compromised and partial, what I want to emphasize here is that such exotifications need not be intentionally committed, cynically advanced, maliciously intended, or even conscious to nevertheless saturate Anglophone knowledge production about Japan.

The fact remains that even today the obvious fantasy of archival materials haunts our historical inquiries, especially in cross-cultural inquiries, and especially on a "fluffy" topic like fashion, already undercut by its association with irrationality, mere entertainment, femininity, and ephemerality. We need to do other work since a massive amount of Japanese photography and other visual imagery, especially that which made its way abroad, and which also formed the illustrations for innumerable contemporary (and even later) books on Japan, both scholarly and popular, was created in service of the market for pleasurable, exotic, and fantastical imagery. Today, these images are still largely extant, due to their massive dissemination around the world, posing a historiographical problem now just as it formed a clearly paradoxical problem of Japanese representation then. Even a small amount of humor in an otherwise balanced and serious approach to understanding Japan could have outsized effect. Early Japanologist Basil Hall Chamberlain was a comparatively sympathetic author who treated Japanese subjects relatively equitably. In *Things Japanese* (1890), he wrote at length about modernization and changes occurring in Japan, with one short chapter titled "Topsy-Turvydom" filled with "droll" observations on Japanese backwardness to Western norms, such as carrying babies behind instead of in front and removing shoes instead of hats as signs of respect. Chamberlain chose a sartorial oddity as his most odd "contrariety": "Another lady, long resident in Tokyo, says that the impulse of her Japanese maids is always to sew on cuffs, frills, and other similar things, topsy-turvy and inside out. If that is not the *ne plus ultra* of contrariety, what is?"[110] It is perhaps no surprise that it was excerpts from "Topsy-Turvydom" that most readily reappeared in newspapers across the Anglophone empires rather than any of Chamberlain's more serious

Fig. 22. Utagawa Yoshitora, England (*Igirisukoku*) (1865, detail, reversed), triptych of woodblock prints; ink and color on paper, 1865. An imaginary scene copied from imported images. Collection of the author.

writings that approached the Japanese people as rational actors on the world stage.

Fantasized imagery as a (perhaps even *the*) structuring mode of cross-cultural encounter was also not a one-sided operation. While Euro-Americans coveted curios of all kinds and albums of exotic images, the opening of the treaty ports sparked a new spike in fascination with the foreigners, newly allowed entry beyond the minuscule man-made island of Dejima, far away from the serious centers of population at the western tip of Kyushu. *Yokohama-e*, a new genre of woodblock print named after the largest new settlement and the one closest to the metropolis of Edo (later Tokyo), was a blanket title given to the outpouring of popular prints geared toward feeding public curiosity about both the new visitors and the wider world they represented. Just as treaty-port photographers peddled images that gratified the ideas tourists brought with them before arriving in Japan, woodblock printers freely mixed fact and fiction, eyewitness scenes, and adaptations of images gleaned from foreign publications to feed the imaginations of the Japanese market. Yoshitora's image of "England" comprises one such example from around 1865 (notice, before the restoration) (fig. 22). Cribbed from a combination of vague fashion silhouettes and ships along with carefully copied linear perspective images of European churches, Yoshitora's "London" gathers into a single fabricated image all kinds of interesting and exotic pieces of "English" culture juxtaposed in an imaginary single scene for domestic audiences to pore over: women and men in the foreground, ships at harbor in the middle, and architecture in the background.

As tenuously attached to reality as they were, many *yokohama-e* employed a pedagogical tone, offering up encyclopedic images of the different nationalities represented in the treaty ports, scenes of foreign buildings, ships, and customs like dining and socializing. *Yōfuku* fashion functions in a fascinating way in the *yokohama-e*: although the popular catalogue of foreigner images painstakingly label specimens of different nations, without the labels the foreigners would be mostly interchangeable, due to the homogeneity of skin tone and especially clothing among the European nations and the United States. At one point, I thought I could possibly detect evidence of France's global dominance in fashion production through finding two "French women" with comical hats featuring areolae of feathers, but later I found the same hat on an "American" woman astride a horse.[111] Except for the Black American sailors' skin color and the distinctive (and better known in Japan) clothing and queues of the Chinese merchants, the rest of the foreigners are largely indistinguishable except by their labels. The bell-like crinoline skirts, men's trousers, with the rest of the outfits rather fuzzily replicated, seem to be coalescing into a standardized notion of foreign that in turn helps to coalesce a standardized notion of "Japanese." Moreover, the transnational promiscuity of nineteenth-century European fashion rendered any Japanese attempt to distinguish foreigners by dress fairly impossible: Paris was the capital of European fashion, so Europeans and settler colonials tended to all be following the same trends, with only the minor differences of season-to-season change rippling out from the fashion capital to periphery and highest to lowest classes.[112]

Although I am here emphasizing that theatricality—fantasized imagery not necessarily attached, and often obviously unattached, to material realities—was a primary quality of a vast amount of both Euro-Americans' and Japanese people's information about each other, the impact of these two bodies of (theatrical) knowledge do not function as evenly weighted oppositions, since obviously the creators and consumers of each canon were not operating on equal footings in the global political ecosystem. Further, a significant difference obtained in Japan's bifurcated allegiance to makeover for men tasked with interfacing seriously at the global political level and as a national PR campaign on one hand, while shrewdly recognizing, as early as the 1850s, that Orientalist exoticism sold well on the global market. Through the export market and savvy participation in the nineteenth- and early twentieth-century mania for expositions, Japan employed both self-orientalizing and -occidentalizing modes of accumulating political and economic power in the face of Euro-American imperial maneuvering. Such a dual tactic was perhaps paradoxical, but government supported and debated at all levels, and, most importantly, both tactics were equally imbricated in networks of imperial subjugation.

Great Mirrors

The Bhabha-Chow oscillation names two troubling dynamics of representation that indebt themselves to theatricality as the fly in the ointment of intercultural relation. Together they reveal how both dynamics, in singular, are misleading. The Meiji situation reveals it: the Rokumeikan ukiyo-e celebrating ladies in impossible day dresses on white gingerbread verandas, or admiring a new steam engine, or steel bridge, or ladies' auxiliary bazaar would seem to be a totally different world than the "Views and Types" of a Yokohama-procured photo album. Certain images, primarily portraits of high-ranking individuals bridge that divide, but they are vastly outnumbered against the emperor's endlessly replicated image and the albums commercially sold under the title "Native Types" that traveled home with tourists.

Instead of settling into some sort of hybrid, a Hegelian synthesis perhaps, the two images—just the same, exactly the opposite—seem to oscillate in perpetual tension, both suffused with the nagging suspiciousness of theatricality. But here theatricality could simply mean the excess, the supplementarity of representation. These representations were pitched, some purposefully, some subconsciously, some unintentionally, toward producing and fixing knowledge, which is an inchoate and insubstantial form of power over Japan and Japaneseness, either in service of the Meiji government, seeking to bolster Japanese global equivalency through likeness, or by the altogether more vague, but effective and all-encompassing, "putting them in their place" Orientalism of absolute difference that suffused and enshrined "Views and Types" popular knowledge of Japan. And of course, the "Views and Types" infused even more theatrical—that is, just for fun, purposefully untied from truth claim—representations like Gilbert and Sullivan's Titipu in *The Mikado* and Oscar Wilde's Japan of "pure invention."[113]

Wilde's treatment of Japan in his essay "The Decay of Lying," merits more attention, not by way of either rehashing the racism of declaring a documented Asian nation nonexistent nor excusing a blithe Orientalist disregard for actual Japanese people, but because Wilde, and later Roland Barthes, both recognize the theatricality of the representations they have encountered. Wilde writes, "The actual people who live in Japan are not unlike the general run of English people; that is to say, they are extremely commonplace, and have nothing curious or extraordinary about them. In fact the whole of Japan is a pure invention. There is no such country, there are no such people."[114] This famous section of the essay acknowledges Japanese people as ordinary people before disavowing the narrator's (and by extension the author's and thus the reader's) ability to know anything at all about Japan except for the "pure inventions" of Orientalist fantasy, thereby erasing knowledge of the very existence of these "extremely commonplace" people immediately after describing it. Wilde's equation balances on a paradox: the ordinariness of the "real" Japan is declared unknowable (which might be to say unrepresentable) to Wilde's "Decay of Lying" avatar, Vivian, while it is the exquisitely rendered fantasized difference of Japan which is so well known and beloved in modern Britain. Perversely then, Wilde's camp erasure of Japan's or Japanese people's very existence might prove most humane in acknowledging the insufficiency of available representations of Japaneseness to say anything at all about real Japanese people.

How could difference be the known quantity and ordinariness unbelievable and unrepresentable? Like Baxter's "inscrutable" Japanese wearing *yōfuku*, the strength of the Anglophone canon of Japanese representations, shored up by fantasies of identification and the imperial Western paradigm of knowledge—theatrical because unmoored from a fixed relation to either truth or fantasy—could discount actual appearances. The bifurcation of Japan into a modern, almost-European nation, "The Great Britain of Asia" or the "Yellow Yankees of the East," and a "quaintly gorgeous" topsy-turvy fairyland, already well underway by the 1870s, has not abated in Japan or abroad.

The problem of Japanese sameness and difference recurs over and over again in Anglophone writing and theorizing on Japan. Jennifer Robertson asks, more than once, in the introduction to *Companion to the Anthropology of Japan*, "is Japan, like western Europe and the United States, somehow perceived as too much like 'us' to be recognized and appreciated as a worthwhile subject of anthropological inquiry?"[115] This question is necessarily a post–*Bunmei Kaika* one, in which the performative gambit of Westernization has been fully executed to leave Japan an industrialized, postimperial nation. And yet an oscillating binary still infuses attitudes about Japan both at home and abroad. Robertson identifies the sameness-difference conundrum with the twinned, dueling concepts of *Nihonjinron* ("theory of Japanese uniqueness") and *kokusaika* ("internationalization," the twentieth-century descendant of Meiji *Bunmei Kaika*): "the obsession today in Japan with cultural distinction mirrors a similar obsession with internationalization; in fact, the two obsessions can be understood as enantiomorphic: that is, the same impulse the other way around."[116]

A mirror flips everything, but a mirror also provides the perfect likeness; the mirror constitutes a mimesis that is simultaneously the opposite of what it reflects. Mirroring can be thought of as a theatricality that appears the same although it is putatively fake when the other is allegedly real, surface when the other is allegedly deep. Mirrors, moreover, are deeply significant in Japanese cosmology, as anthropologist Philip Swift points out: not only is "Mirror" or "Great Mirror" a set title phrase for classic Japanese literature, speaking to the mirror's fundamental association with representation, but mirrors are one of the three sacred items of Shinto shrines. Swift uses Robertson's thoughts on mirroring to articulate the paralyzing binary of same and different on the way to his larger argument regarding the "significance of superficiality in Japan."[117]

Taking the rituals of Shinto shrine worship as a primary example, including a scene of James Bond aping the set sequence in Ian Fleming's *You Only Live Twice* (1967), Swift effectively sets up the problem of thinking surface and depth in Japanese culture:

> Practices of prayer in Japan seem difficult to fathom because, at depth, there appears to be little there. In fact, such practices, we might feel, almost smack of the theatrical (what Kant would denounce as "pious play acting and nothing-doing"). But such feelings, I would hazard, are arguably the kinds of anxieties triggered when a "depth ontology," as Daniel Miller christens it, comes up against a counterforce of thought that takes surfaces seriously.[118]

Swift puts his finger on a recurring issue that I have also been trying to articulate in a very different aspect of Japanese history and culture: not the hollowness of the "smack of the theatrical" but the anxieties evoked in those invested in "depth ontology" when they encounter the potential efficacy of the shallow. This rearrangement, or recalibration, of the location of efficacy, I suggest, is what resonates with the surface-depth conundrum of the Meiji makeover. The primacy of the correctness of surfaces in Japan is indicated by Tokugawa and Meiji authorities' preoccupation with sumptuary and sartorial expressions, with maintaining clear demarcations between types of people (and concomitant anxieties where types mixed, such as professional and domestic women in the Rokumeikan).

Another example of an alternative mode of understanding the relation between surface and depth can be found in the pervasive cultural concept of *honne* (本音 inner feeling) and *tatemae* (建前 facade), most famously elucidated by prominent Japanese sociologist Doi Takeo. *Honne* denotes an individual's true inner feelings—the kanji literally translate to "true sound," while *tatemae* describes the outer behaviors a person executes. This may sound like a simple substitution for the surface-depth ontologies we saw so anxiously debated and regulated in the previous chapters, but importantly, *tatemae*, while distinct and often in conflict with *honne*, is not necessarily untrue. Rather, Doi emphasizes that *honne* and *tatemae* are mutually constituting.[119] I would choose to emphasize that the paired concepts can articulate more clearly the individual's obligations to societal, interpersonal behaviors and their frequent divergence from one's private, individual inclinations and desires. Doi references a fourteenth-century Buddhist story about people who, by way of trying to express their goodwill toward another group, promise a number of gifts they cannot actually deliver, while another group speaks roughly and only says what they mean. The first group, although technically liars, are the ones who express "real sincerity" toward others, while the latter people are unkind in their blunt truth telling.[120] This anecdote helps to elucidate how truth (or here "sincerity") does not lodge within one of the two terms, but rather can be located at either the surface of *tatemae* or the depth of *honne*. Truth becomes less important in this equation than recognizing how the interlinked system of *honne* and *tatemae* together "structuralize ambivalence" thereby making those ambivalences psychologically "tolerable."[121] While Doi notes that since World War II, *tatemae* has come to have more of the sense of falsity against the personal truth of *honne*, he argues that this new pejorative valence of "just" *tatemae* is a recent occurrence, one we might speculate only comes after sustained contact and influence from European notions of essence and antitheatricality.[122]

The continued importance of maintaining *tatemae* even as it has picked up pejorative associations with "mere" appearance or "empty" gesture corresponds with Swift's locating of Japanese ritual efficacy at the level of surface, Butlerian theories of performativity, and the Meiji elites' faith in their makeover project. "The mirror, as a device, is efficacious because it simulates," writes Swift.[123] While one may (or may not!) be deep, the reflection is shallow. But it is the shallow in this equation that is efficacious, because it creates something out of nothing, makes a nothing into a something, much like Butler's "performative acts" are shown to precede "gender constitution" and do the constituting. As Butler's oeuvre repeatedly emphasizes, performative acts of mimicry should not be imagined as freely chosen acts of individual will, but rather fenced and policed actions coerced under various forms of external and internalized pressures. And internalized pressures may look very like, or indeed be indistinguishable from, personal desire.

Over the years, various historians of the Meiji period have found themselves repeating the old saw of the "duplicitous Oriental" (as Bhabha put it) in trying to make sense of the bifurcating, unreconcilable streams of Japanese likeness and difference. As Meech-Pekarik put it: "In the end, it could be said that Meiji Japanese never really adopted European costume at all. It was worn only outside the house as a business or military uniform, 'protection by mimicry,' to use the words of nineteenth-century Japanologist Basil Hall Chamberlain. Japanese clothing still remained the center of private life."[124]

In 1879 the studio of the woodblock artist Tsukioka Yoshitoshi released a series called *Concise Illustrated History of Japan* (大日本史略図会 Dainihon shi ryakuzu e). One of those prints, "Empress Jingu Leading the Invasion of Korea" (第十五代神功皇后 "Dai jugo dai Jingu kogo"), depicted a mytho-historical event recounted in the *Kojiki* and *Nihonshoki*, that, if it happened, happened early in the third century CE (fig. 23).[125] One of nine empresses in the imperial history of Japan, Jingu was actually struck from the official history as the fifteenth emperor of Japan around the same time as Yoshitoshi's 1879 print, ten years before the Meiji constitution would definitively bar future empresses. (She had come after her husband Chuai's death, and before her son Ojin, who took her place as the fifteenth emperor and also now forms the putative first of the conjectured historical rather than legendary emperors.[126]) In the print Jingu stands on the shore of Korea, raising her bow toward the interior, which she is about to conquer. Her clothing, though, is unmistakably influenced by European women's fashions of the late 1870s: the red skirt billows behind her in a bustled lobster-tail shape, the plaited Japanese-style arm armor also looks like a fringed shawl, and a white gauze clings to the top half of her ensemble forming a bit of lacy collar and fichu and accenting the broadness of the skirt. Her hair is half up and half down in a style that may resemble other warrior prints, but simultaneously resembles some of the hairstyles of the *sokuhatsu* hairdressing reform prints as much as it recalls any archaic or Edo-era women's hairstyles. She is, in contradistinction to the imperial proclamation seven years earlier, literally dressed both effeminately and in the present style. Thus, Jingu stands in the far past, dressed as a civilized woman of the present, conquering Korea a millennium and a half in advance of Japan's full colonization of Korea that would happen a couple of decades after Yoshitoshi's print. And indeed, in 1876, just three years before Yoshitoshi committed a *Bunmei Kaika*–fied Jingu to aniline posterity, Japan had already successfully imposed an unequal treaty of its own on Korea, replicating many of the humiliating demands the Western powers had imposed on them (and still not revised) twenty years earlier.[127] Yoshitoshi's Jingu isn't just a jingoistic figurehead trotted out at a crucial time; she concentrates many of this chapter's concerns tightly into a single image, a single figure even. A woman, on the verge of being erased from the imperial lineage on account of her gender, yet still emperor enough to carry out the imperial conquest at which her husband had failed, she is simultaneously emblematic of Japan through reference to its most ancient origin myths and as the very archetype of the imperial—conquering other lands—appearing in the guise of the latest empire builders, the Europeans and Americans. Just as both Emperor Meiji's and Empress Haruko's original proclamations regarding clothing recalled ancient, indigenous Japanese sources as a (spurious) basis for adopting *yōfuku*, here Yoshitoshi puts that fusion of ancient and modern into aniline print, near the end

Fig. 23. Tsukioka Yoshitoshi 月岡芳年, *Dai jugo dai Jingu kogo* 第十五代神功皇后 (Empress Jingu Leading the Invasion of Korea), 1879. Color woodblock triptych print. © The Trustees of the British Museum.

of ukiyo-e's lifespan as a mainstream (nonarchaic) technology. Perhaps Jingu's modern dress helps reference the recently completed unequal treaty with Korea; it certainly cherry picks a (legendary) moment of Japanese-Korean history that could be imagined to swell national support for the decades-long incursion on Korean sovereignty that had just been set in motion and would culminate in about twenty years in Japan's own stint as colonial power at the apex of the euphemistically named "Greater East Asian Co-Prosperity Sphere."

In this sense the Meiji makeover gambit succeeded. In 1899 virtually the last of the unequal treaties would finally be revised. By the time Emperor Meiji, who was posthumously awarded his reign's name, died in 1912, Japan would already have become the first Asian nation to defeat a European one in war (Russo-Japanese War, 1904–5) and the first (virtually only) modern Asian colonial power having already occupied Korea and Taiwan and consolidated political and cultural control over Ainu populations in Hokkaido and the Ryukyuan people in Okinawa. Although Japan was eventually checked at the apex of their colonial aggression, in World War II against the United States and allies in the Pacific and mainland Asia, it nevertheless did not permanently forfeit a primary political and economic place among world nations in the late-twentieth and twenty-first century. In 2019 Japan had the third highest gross domestic product in the world, after the US and China, countries with massively more landmass and population.

This is an ambivalent legacy: nineteenth- and twentieth-century colonial—and contemporary neoliberal economic—might are no longer judged unadulteratedly "good" things, proofs of a forward-progressing civilization. It is rather as evidence that a nonwhite nation could compete on the amoral stage of world power that we can look at Japan's political career of the late nineteenth and first half of the twentieth century as impressive.

It is surely because Japan took the unusual step of voluntarily (if not *not* under duress) Westernizing both superficially and infrastructurally, embracing, adopting, and strategically mirroring the most powerful technologies and attitudes of their rivals (and potential colonizers) that they came to occupy such a favored position with their Euro-American treaty partners. Japan's bifurcated self-presentation: the maintenance and dissemination not only of the "reformed other" mimicking the colonizer (in Bhabha's parlance) but also the continued performance of oriental exoticism, tweaked and altered in response to foreign tastes, in tourist goods, exports, and world exhibitions perhaps proved a canny strategy of meeting multiple, paradoxically foreign demands, even as it may very well have led to the recurring Japanese identity crisis of *Nihonjinron* and *kokusaika*. It is telling that foreign interlocutors could so easily identify the theatricality of *Bunmei Kaika*, but so willingly believed in the fantastical authenticity of quaint, exotic Japan.

What did theatricality add to this legacy? We can't say that the Meiji makeover was necessary to the later legacy Japan would create for itself, but we can identify that theatrical dynamics flowed through everything that happened in the cross-cultural encounter of the Meiji period: Meiji elites bet on a spectacular makeover and primarily succeeded. The conundrum of thinking theatricality in conjunction with expression of assumed inborn national identity fed a persistent bifurcation in identity within Japan and in perceptions of the Japanese beyond. The efficacy of the superficial, which I have argued is conceived differently in Japan, suggests more than monkey-like imitativeness and might even point toward more precise or accurate ways of perceiving how identity and subject formation are formed from external and internal factors, even beyond Japan. In the next chapter I will close the circuit of my fashionable peregrinations from Britain to Japan by dragging Victorian fashions across the centuries to the early twenty-first century, where Japanese young women resurrected the Girl of the Period and her outré fashions as an antifashion protest and inspired enthusiasts across the globe. Gothic lolita subcultural fashion thus replays the Victorian as a fresh new Japanese fad, desirable in part in the twenty-first century because it savors of the Japanese modern-exotic, circulating new relations not only to history, race, ethnicity, and nationality but also to gender and sexuality across the ever more tightly connected planet.

Chapter 5

✦

"Returning to the Real Me"

Gothic Lolita Self-Fashioning

At the western edge of central Tokyo, delineated by the encompassing circle of the Japan Rail Yamanote train line, is a huge green space, home to Yoyogi Park and Meiji Jingū, a massive Shinto shrine dedicated to the memory of Emperor Meiji and Empress Haruko, the figureheads of the era that encompassed the massive cultural upheaval and shifts that changed the face of Japan from a "fairyland" of Western imagination and launched it toward modern economic superpower as the "Yankees of the East."[1] Across the road from Meiji Shrine lies the neighborhood of Harajuku, an area largely developed post–World War II, and since the 1960s and 1970s the epicenter of Japan's youth fashion subcultures.[2] The range of spectacular subcultures Tokyo has fostered is legendary. The throngs of spectacular youth—briefly poised between the conformist strictures of education and the narrow range of expectations at which they are aimed (salaryman corporate employment or compulsory marriage and motherhood for boys and girls, respectively) can each be seen as enacting a series of critiques of the ideologies from which they are briefly fugitive. *Ganguro* and *yamamba* girls ("black face" and "mountain witches," respectively), preeminent around the year 2000, inverted the classical Japanese beauty ideals of pale skin and inky black hair with their bleached manes and hypertanned faces enhanced with pale lipstick.[3] *Yankii* (or "Yankee") biker gangs (usually sex-segregated teams of either boys or girls) are frequently described as training grounds for the yakuza, induction into which forms a permanent transition from the ideological structures of hegemonic Japanese society to a shadowy mirror world, itself still rife with hierarchy and structured roles for each individual in the whole.[4] *Decora* and *fairy kei* kids have pursued the siren song of commodity consumption to its illogical conclusion, covering themselves entirely in the cheapest and cheerfullest of plastic bits and bobs, reflecting back to the roving camera lens of the "street snap" photographer the granular stakes of capitalist overconsumption: the world will end drowned gradually in dunes of microplastics, not destroyed by a singular cataclysm. And then there were gothic lolitas—overwhelmingly young women in their teens and twenties, and overwhelmingly girly in their outsized bows, platform Vivienne Westwood rocking horse shoes, and petticoat skirts—standing out even among the other style tribes.[5] Among a menagerie of rainbow variations, certain features are standard: lace and ruffle-decked blouses under jumpers, aprons, or high-waisted belled and crinoline knee-length skirts; more skin covered than bare; headwear including bonnets, miniature hats, or massive bows over ringlets and long tresses. So many ruffles; so much lace.

Most turn of the millennium Harajuku fashions have died out in keeping with a fad's typically short life cycle, but the gothic lolitas, although they have largely migrated from the confines of Harajuku and Meiji Shrine, nevertheless have failed to die the way fads are supposed to, traveling the mysterious paths of the internet, persisting and transmuting as they span the globe in a network of misfit girl aristocrats. Gothic lolita is the linchpin of this book—closing the circuit of transnational fashionable circulation between Europe and Japan, simultaneously crossing about a century and a half in the process. Where the foregoing chapters of this book looked synchronically at a number of fashion controversies that were taking place in Britain and Japan, looking for convergences that amplified certain aspects of performed and performative identity, particularly gender, sexuality, race, ethnicity, and nationality, and laid bare their imbrication with each other, now in this chapter I add the temporal consideration back into my analysis. I am calling on fashion and the gothic's own perennial returns—their special relationship with time—to license a claim to historiographical import for gothic lolita subcultural performances of embodied history. Although it is not often invoked by gothic lolitas or their academic observers, I read gothic lolita as one creative response to Japanese postcoloniality (a phrase by which I mean both Japan's semisubjugated status to Western powers in the nineteenth century and post–World War II *and* its foray into colonizing neighboring Asian nations in the early twentieth century).

I thus proceed on the hypothesis that we might read gothic lolita as a symptom of the continuing impact of the Meiji Restoration's sweeping *Bunmei Kaika* policies on individual Japanese psyches. This would entail setting aside, at least temporarily, a perennial habit of Western thought: the assumption that Japanese adoptions (and adaptations) of Western things are superficial copies, empty of meaning. More to the point, it will mean revisiting this recurring theme and deconstructing it, which I will attempt later in this chapter. It would suggest yet another way in which the personal is political and vice versa: how historical events reverberate and recur, appearing paradoxically repeated and transformed at the level of individual bodies, repetitions with differences. Such an understanding of the persistence and recrudescence of history at the level of individual bodies, their hobbies, and their habits (meaning, of course, both clothing and behaviors), might sound Freudian. But it's also quite gothic, and in the following I've taken the more speculative and less clinical approach, as I believe befits the practices of subcultural fashion that have alternately belied and been betrayed by depth analyses. The result is a methodological approach that follows the contours of gothic lolita practitioners' own reasonings about subject formation, tracing them backward through the looking glass of over the top "Victorian" finery, then forward to be transmuted by a Japanese pop cultural lens, to posit a culturally hybrid hyperfemininity decoupled from bodily gender and sex as a vehicle for group identification, no matter the nationality, race, gender, or sexuality of the wearer. I take further license for this approach from fashion theory like Caroline Evans's *Fashion at the Edge*, where Evans writes, "On the edge of discourse, of 'civilisation,' of speech itself, experimental fashion can act out what is hidden culturally. And, like a neurotic symptom, it can utter a kind of mute resistance to the socially productive process of constructing an identity."[6]

In chapter 4 I articulated the ways gender was mobilized in the East-West encounter of the Meiji Restoration. Meiji elites used fashion (as well as other bodily and behavioral changes) to alter their standards of masculinity to more closely align with European standards and then staked part of their claims to modernity and equality to other national players on the imperial stage (i.e., the world) on these shifting codes of masculinity. We see in chapter 4 how Japanese claims to modernity were staked on the grounds of masculine gender in compelling ways, thereby revealing modernness itself to be a gendered category, unevenly available to men and women. Women's and femininity's association with atavism, primitivity, and backwardness is of course a well-documented issue.[7] In this chapter, then, we will see the Victorian return with a feminine vengeance, staging if not a revolution then at least a spectacular rebellion on the strength of exactly those backward and anachronistic aspects that rendered Victorian femininity unsuitable for the Meiji project of Civilization and Enlightenment.

In this chapter I have two major concerns. First, how does gothic lolita function as a technology of the self, one which mutes typical markers of an individual's demographic identity (such as gender, age, race, class, nationality) under a banner of anachronistic femininity? Second, and intertwined with the first, how do we reconcile the distinct Europeanness of gothic lolita's historical, cultural, and aesthetic references with its indelible (and desirable) "odor" of Japanese cool?[8] Buttressing the inquiry into these questions, I provide a history of gothic lolita fashion and consider certain salient contexts for its invention, efflorescence, and possible decline.

Considering the work of this girl-powered, commerce-driven fashion rearranges typical models of globalization to put young women and gender-nonconforming individuals (ambivalently) at the center of networks of global capitalism and in the driver's seat of culture and identity formation, where they so rarely have been recognized. As I pointed out earlier the ways my previous chapters' subjects, the Girl of the Period, Boulton, Park, and the Meiji elites, also in fact can be seen as central figures, rendered scandalous or abject only retroactively by the community judgments passed on their transgressions, so now I am less performing an intellectual translocation of gothic lolitas so much as occupying the perspective from which we might recognize the ways girls, youth, weirdos, and their money are central to certain imbricated global flows of culture and capital. From another perspective, gothic lolitas might appear as marginal figures eking out a collective (and sometimes lonely) existence in small pockets of metropolitan capitals and the internet. Their medium, fashion, adds additional complexities. Theirs is a self-fashioning project that works primarily at the level of the fictive—or, we might say, the theatrical—and yet, as I argued in earlier chapters as well, performance, performativity, and theatricality interact deeply and strangely when it comes to clothing.

In the following I zigzag between the Japanese context and the ways in which gothic lolita fashion has been taken up in other geographical areas, primarily the Anglocentric, but by no means solely Anglophone, internet communities of non-Japanese lolitas. The United States hosts one of the largest populations of enthusiasts, but they are connected via the internet to active communities in Canada, across Europe, Mexico, Central and South America, Australia, New Zealand, South Africa, India, Indonesia, Malaysia, Singapore, the Philippines, Hong Kong, and mainland China.[9] Methodologically, I draw on a variety of sources and approaches, including the primary sources of internet communities, gothic lolita publications, especially periodicals online and in print, as well as my own participant observation at various in person events and locations in Japan, the US, and Europe, primarily the Rufflecon alternative fashion conference in 2015 and 2017 and two-day Paradiso event in 2019.[10] After initially discovering gothic lolita by picking up a *KERA* magazine during a two-week stay in Japan in 2000, I faithfully bought the magazine every month for the two years I lived in Japan from 2001 to 2003. I continued picking up back issues and magazine books like *Gothic & Lolita Bible* on every trip back to Japan and when I found them at US outlets. I visited Harajuku and the gothic lolita–dominated shopping mall *LaForet* every time I was in Tokyo and poked around Ikebukuro, the Tokyo district that hosts *Otome-rōdo*, "Maiden's Road," popularly considered the girl-otaku's alternative to Akihabara. I even treated myself to a butler café, where, for one set-price hour, I had my own butler who addressed me by my choice of honorific (Princess, Lady, Miss, etc.), served me tea and a beautifully composed sweets plate, and carried my bag to the washroom door before handing it off to me and awaiting my return. I was gently remonstrated with when I foolishly refilled my own teacup. Thus, while I've never considered myself a gothic lolita practitioner, my knowledge base has been compiled in an analog way to which I now apply my performance studies training. (And I may now own, but will not be admitting to, a few brand-name dresses.) Certainly, to have spent any time at all trying to chart out a coherent narrative of gothic lolita's visual spectacularity, worldwide spread, and simultaneous underground niche status (by no means is the fashion necessarily widely known even in Japan after more than twenty years) is to be forced to recognize the inadequacy of any one account. Thus, I proceed with the overt understanding that my arguments and conclusions are an exercise of power on a living dynamic, and that my arguments and conclusions are provisional. Like the work of any historian or theorist, we construct mirrors as much as we do windows. Here follows my own version of posing as a gothic lolita, anchoring fashion performance into discourse.

Both popular and academic accounts of gothic lolita frequently pursue either a taxonomy or a genealogy model of description; gothic lolitas themselves tend to value encyclopedic knowledge, dropping connoisseur information about brands, specific prints, and dress styles into highly specialized conversations.[11] For example, a major resource for Anglophone gothic lolitas is the website Lolilibrary, where volunteers catalogue every dress, blouse, accessory, shoe, headpiece, and bag they can from each brand (including recent fast-fashion "off-brand" Chinese retailers) with original selling prices, colorways, dates of release and rerelease, and notes like how quickly the run sold out in the preorder period. Dress types are further separated into specialized terminology for standard silhouettes, like "OP" ("one-piece" dress) and "JSK" ("jumper skirt," a sleeveless dress usually worn with a blouse). Indeed, the words "gothic lolita" don't name a discrete style so much as a family of associated aesthetics, practitioners, and brands that have been chronicled in specific magazines (especially *KERA* and *Gothic & Lolita Bible*) and sold next to each other in specific geographical areas (Harajuku's Takeshita Street, the LaForet and Marui 0I0I shopping malls in Shibuya, and KERAshops across Japan) and virtual shops, like the "EGL sales" community on Livejournal.com and lacemarket.us. Practitioners have a number of other abbreviations and terms they favor, including *gosu-rori* (ゴスロリ; goth-loli) or just *rori-ta* (ロリータ; lolita). In recent years as social media has become a bigger part of the subculture's life, the acronym EGL, coined by gothic lolita icon and male rock musician Mana, has become increasingly popular. EGL technically stands for "Elegant Gothic Lolita," but in practice is conveniently short to maximize character counts in hashtags, and not porn related to avoid getting caught up in automated sweeps of restricted content or targeted by internet denizens with more sexually explicit interests (more on this anon). Only some of the styles collected under these umbrella monikers have clear gothic tendencies. I use the phrase "gothic lolita" to denote this loose complex of aesthetics and practices; considerations of both the "gothic" and the "lolita" in the fashion's name will emerge in the course of the text.

By way of setting the stage, I will briefly stray down the well-worn path, offering a description of some of the gothic lolita substyles that proliferate like so many storybooks lined up next to each other, shared tropes in endless variations on a few themes, available for the right price. Imagine, if you will, a horizontal axis with the endpoints deemed darkness and light. On one end, you will find the gothically inclined styles like gothic lolita, *kuro-rori* (simply "black lolita") headed toward steampunk styles, classic lolita (in solid shades, with ribbons and trims), and country lolita (red, gingham, floral prints). At the opposite end, you will encounter sweet lolita, in baby pastels and sugary prints of things like cupcakes and teddy bears. On the vertical axis, you will see variations on the standard knee-length crinoline silhouette and puff sleeves. Foremost among these must be EGL and EGA ("Elegant Gothic Aristocrat," a more "mature" style with longer, slimmer skirts, darker, richer colors, maybe a corset); wa lolita (Japanese ruffly-kimono style) and the recent invention, qi lolita (Chinese style), and *ouji* (prince) or "boy style." *Ouji* names nominally masculine, Little Lord Fauntleroy–type outfits with knee breeches and capelets, occasional military accents, jackets, and vests, worn interchangeably by people of all gender identifications (as indeed all lolita styles are).[12]

The very tendency of gothic lolita fashions, and more to the point, most published attempts to understand them, to spread outward in proliferating lists and charts of elements and substyles draws attention to the ways gothic lolita may seem to resist or belie deep meanings. Although fashion has perennially excelled at selling repurposed signifiers apparently stripped of previous meanings, there is something about the extreme spectacularity of gothic lolita dress that excites speculation and indeed disbelief about the meanings and motives of wearers. The borders established by gothic lolita clothes may be superficial in the way that clothing is literally hollow—waiting to be filled out and completed by a body, whatever the body—but they are also dense, if not with precise and clear significations, then with inchoate ones: Meiji *Bunmei Kaika*, fearful Victorian inheritances, and imaginative eternal maiden wonderlands.

Gothic

I endeavor to set the stage of this chapter with two sections named after the two words of my subject: first gothic and then lolita. Under the rubric of gothic, I am invoking the gothic's special relation with temporality, particularly tangled, cyclical, and syncopated temporalities. Hallmarks of gothic aesthetics bear out forward-moving time's failure to keep marching through numerous tropes: fearful inheritances, haunting and revenants, ruins (of houses and people). Horrible premonitions—often born of some unburied past transgression—run the clock backward and forward simultaneously. The gothic then not only names a fundamental darkness in personal outlook (which I will touch on soon) but also creates an entry into the queer kind of relation with the past that I see in gothic lolitas' historically inflected aesthetics. In this section I will cover three major topics: first, a short general history of gothic lolita fashions themselves, then discussion of the larger, queerer (or more gothic) strands of historical thinking the subculture activates, and finally a discussion of gothic darkness and bad feeling in lolita subcultures.

From a fashion history perspective, the standard move in documenting gothic lolita is to recapitulate an origin story, tracing the evolution of gothic lolita's panoply from girly 1970s brands like Pink House and Milk, through 1980s Jane Marple (Milk and Jane Marple are still in business as gothic lolita–adjacent brands), to the 1990s and 2000s explosion of Harajuku youth fashions.[13] Facilitated by the weekend traffic closure of Omotesandō, the main road through Harajuku to create a *hokōsha tengoku* (歩行者天国 pedestrian heaven), teenagers, out of school and uniform, could loiter throughout the area on Sundays, forming "style tribes" and attracting the anthropological lenses of street snap fashion photographers like Aoki Shoichi and pop culture encyclopedists, who helped perpetuate their images across the globe.[14] Competing origin stories name Osaka as the birthplace of gothic lolita or focus on Visual Kei, a hard-rock popular music genre in which spectacular goth- and historical fantasy–inspired costumes were as important as sound—hence the name meaning "visual style."[15] The most important figure in Visual Kei history is Mana, the guitarist for Visual Kei band Malice Mizer, and later head of the band Moi-dix-Mois. Although Mana does not identify as transgender or queer, in public appearances he wears almost exclusively skirts and dresses in the gothic lolita style along with long hair and full-face makeup. Although he never speaks publicly (he mimes elegantly or whispers into the ears of bandmates or translators, he is nevertheless credited with coining the term "gothic lolita" as well as EGL and EGA to name related styles—all of which, incidentally, Mana also sells under his highly successful brand Moi-Même-Moitié, founded in 1999.[16] It seems that, in choosing the word "lolita," Mana did not intend to reference any aspect of Vladimir Nabokov's 1955 novel except youthful femininity, but more on that connection in the following section.[17]

Although American pop singer Gwen Stefani arguably made Harajuku style world famous with her 2004 solo album *Love Angel Music Baby* and the debut of her four Harajuku girl backup dancers who featured in live shows and videos for the album, hers was only the loudest (and not uncontroversial) paean to Japanese street style. The international growth of anime convention culture, "Cool Japan" campaigns, and a flurry of illustrated and photo-rich books also contributed to the international spread of Japanese pop culture, including gothic lolita. Foremost among the publications has surely been Aoki Shoichi's book compilations *Fruits*, *Fresh Fruits*, and *Gothic & Lolita*, released in 2001, 2005, and 2007, respectively by Phaidon (all culled from Aoki's street-style magazine *FRUiTS*), which set the stage for *Japanese Schoolgirl Inferno: Tokyo Teen Fashion Subculture Handbook* (2007), *Style Deficit Disorder: Harajuku Street Fashion Tokyo* (2007), *The Tokyo Look Book* (2007), *Japanese Goth* (2009), *Tokyo Street Style* (2008), *Japanese Street Style* (2012), and *Kawaii! Japan's Culture of Cute* (2013), among others.[18] Along with Bill Cunningham in New York and the seminal magazines *i-D* and *The Face* in the UK, Japanese street fashion photographers like Aoki presaged and inspired the internet-enabled explosion of street portraiture and fashion photography. The "street snap" (as it is ubiquitously called in Japanese, usually using English letters) format works powerfully to suggest that the fashionable subjects of the photo are individual creative geniuses, simply caught by chance and the photographer's luck on a street corner. The Japanese fashion magazines that foregrounded this format (*FRUiTs, KERA*, and others) therefore took on an aura of documentation of individual, amateur fashion masters, while in effect also creating a class of semi-professional models who appeared in the magazines' pages month after month, sometimes vaulting from there to the staged fashion spreads in the same magazines.[19] (*FRUiTs* is an advertising-free magazine of nothing but street snaps by Aoki and associates.) Although there are certainly a large number of fabulously fashionable regular people on the streets of Tokyo, the magazines and photographers had a powerful hand in framing, curating, and therefore defining the seemingly autochthonous style tribes of Harajuku. Magazines, individual enthusiasts, and fashion brands function together as an ecosystem devoted to the perpetuation of street styles.

Perhaps because of its spectacularity, maybe due to its familiar repetition of storybook European aesthetics (with an exotic difference), gothic lolita traveled far beyond Japan, more quickly and more effectively than any other Harajuku subculture—first through coveted *KERA* magazines and mook (magazine book, a common publishing format in Japan) series *Gothic & Lolita Bible*, brought from Japan or purchased at massive markups in Japanese bookstores in major US cities and scanned by kind, copyright-flouting souls to be posted in internet message boards and blog platforms. The clothes traveled too, more slowly than images, since the original Japanese brands are costly, expensive (or sometimes impossible) to ship abroad, produced in limited sizes, and hard to order for non-Japanese–speaking enthusiasts. As web communities have grown and evolved, English-speaking lolitas have congregated on LiveJournal, Tumblr, Facebook, and even 4chan and Reddit. This is not to suggest

Fig. 24. Coord reminiscent of Emperor Meiji's makeover uniform (fig. 13), from Chinese brand Lost Angel. Photo courtesy of Lolitawardrobe.com.

that gothic lolita lives primarily on the internet—it is, fundamentally, a clothing fashion that requires material bodies to get dressed; rather, new media technologies have facilitated in-person interactions at conventions, meetups, and teas, and in turn new communities have created new media presences.

Gothic lolita seems to have traveled especially as one part of the larger fad for Japanese cultural exports, particularly manga, anime, and cosplay in the 2000s, a wave helped along by the official government-backed "Cool Japan" campaign beginning in 2006.[20] As cute-culture ambassadors like pop idols and Sanrio characters buoyed up their influence, English-speaking gothic lolitas got access to Takemoto Novala's lolita novel *Shimotsuma monogatari* published in Japanese in 2002 and in English as *Kamikaze Girls* in 2008, along with the international release of the 2004 film adaptation, and the publication of five issues of the *Gothic & Lolita Bible* in English by manga translation and publishing company Tokyo Pop in 2008–9.[21] More recently, a number of independent brands and small business lolita dressmakers have sprung up around the world, and in the last few years the Chinese fast-fashion industry has transformed the market by offering their own styles and brands as well as knock-off replicas, often custom sized and directly shipped to consumers around the world, significantly undercutting the high resale values of costly and hard-to-procure name brands from Japan (see fig. 24). The diffusion of fashion production beyond the Japan-based name brands may eventually dilute the still-strong sense of gothic lolita as a distinctly Japanese export.

Meanwhile, I want to turn back the clock and rerun the past in a larger frame. What of the myriad past aesthetics that gothic lolitas revivify through creative reanimation and resignification? While the modifier "Victorian" is by far the most common period designation (and "rococo" the second), few lolita ensembles are actually mistakable for a Victorian silhouette. Rather, certain elements are cherry picked and reregularized as lolita accessories, such as the mid-nineteenth-century face-framing bonnet, the 1860s bell-shaped crinoline (only cut to knee-length), button-up boots, and parasols. Some supplementary gothic lolita publications do work to thicken the types of historical associations made sartorially, such as *KERA* magazine's articles on Lewis Carroll and *Alice's Adventures in Wonderland* (a perennially popular character in Japan also beyond gothic lolita circles) or European places of historical and touristic interest. Takemoto Novala, the self-avowed straight male writer declared the "lolitas' bard," opens his novel *Shimotsuma monogatari* (as with the film, titled *Kamikaze Girls* in English) with several pages of disquisition on French rococo—how it comprised a feminine counterpoint to the masculine baroque; how Madame de Pompadour makes a much better rococo icon than Marie Antoinette.[22] Sweet lolita-loving protagonist Momoko's fervent identification with the French rococo aesthetic is not a case of self-hate—it's a serious intellectual and philosophical engagement (even as it uses its knowledge to make a case for self-centeredness, pleasure, and a distinctly postmodern aesthetic) balanced by Momoko's devotion to the Japanese sweet lolita brand Baby, the Stars Shine Bright (often abbreviated as "Baby" or BTSSB). Momoko emerges as an active agent of understanding, employing (foreign) history in a project of negotiating a milieu she experiences as hostile.

Although gothic lolita has mostly been considered in ethnographic, pop culture, and fashion studies contexts, taking the possibility of historical redress seriously puts me in closer dialogue with neo-Victorian studies of literature and film. Elizabeth Ho writes that the "'neo-Victorian and other 'neo's' . . . do not simply look back to the past but reiterate and replay it in more diverse, complicated and troubled ways."[23] We could potentially read gothic lolita with Ho's treatment of neo-Victorian novels from postcolonial nations as emphasizing "a present still haunted and seduced by colonial structures or privilege"—a replaying, perhaps, of the Meiji Restoration.[24] To "reiterate and replay" the past is also a hallmark of fashion. In *Fashion at the Edge*, Caroline Evans elaborates Walter Benjamin's image of history as a labyrinth: "Distant points in time can become proximate at specific moments if their paths run close to each other."[25] Gothic lolitas' jumbled Victorian, rococo, and baroque (incidentally, also the name of a Korean lolita brand) references thus indicate an uncanny resonance between something past and a present need. According to Evans, "If late twentieth-century fashion looped back to earlier moments of modernity in specific formations, it was not because the moments of past and present were the same but because a visual link between them uncovered interesting things about the present that echoed the past."[26]

Meiji elites undertook the same painstaking processes of study and adoption as non-Japanese gothic lolitas do today. They went through their own *ita* phases, according to foreign observers, and sometimes amazed with the brilliance of their adaptations. (*Ita* is "ouch" or "pain" in Japanese and has been adopted into Anglophone gothic lolita to refer to embarrassingly bad coordinates, usually associated with newbies who haven't yet built a good wardrobe or internalized a strong sense of the aesthetics.) It is precisely the high Victorian fashions that were adopted into Japan then that are name-checked now in gothic lolita anachronistic references—no matter that the actual details and silhouettes of gothic lolita fashions are not particularly precise replications of historical Victorian garments. Notably, both the Meiji and gothic lolita projects are highly gendered: the Meiji makeover was, as is made clear in the emperor's proclamation, specifically a defeminizing fashion project, whereas gothic lolita is obviously the opposite. (Consider figs. 24 and 13 together.) And both projects have been dogged by foreign assertions about the emptiness of Japanese imitation. Where Pierre Loti interpreted the Rokumeikan ball he attended as a "marvelous" trick by a people "uniquely skilled at sleight of hand" and others suggested the Japanese imitated the West like "children or monkeys," *Gothic E-Zine* commentator David Graham echoed the same belief of Japanese gothic lolitas in 2009:

> The Gothic Lolita is another example of how Japan's popular culture has appropriated imagery without the content. Witness the past interest in Elvis and '50s American culture, for example. It was a superficial and accurate take on a cultural phenomenon, and the motivation was completely devoid of irony. Likewise, the Victorian costumes are huge signifiers in Western culture. We interpret the wearing of such clothing as infantalizing [*sic*] women, but the criticism is lost on the Tokyo Gothic Lolitas much the same as we would not understand the subtle meanings associated with various styles of kimonos.[27]

Leaving aside the fact that there is nothing particularly accurate about the Victorian costumes of gothic lolitas, Graham's take encapsulates the trouble with gothic lolita: costume, superficial accuracy, and (perceived) vacuity. I am less interested in critiquing the factual correctness of this commentator's claims than I am in using them to articulate a number of intertwined assumptions about transnational and transtemporal fashioning. Graham perceives gothic lolita appropriations as totally empty "imagery without the content," although he also apprehends them as "accurate." He further asserts that "we" Westerners interpret feminine Victorian costumes as infantilizing. (By this he may also have in mind gothic lolita practices of dressing like a child or doll, although he doesn't mention this specifically.)

Graham's statements are particularly interesting in a goth publication because they curiously mirror typical dismissals of goths themselves. On the one hand, according to sociologist Amy Wilkins, "goth style becomes such an effective means of drawing distinctions because it is assumed to speak for the real self."[28] But on the other hand, goths' spectacular appearances have been characterized as mere shock tactics, or "phases" that one grows out of—not true emanations from a dark interior.[29] Conundrums about proper attribution of authenticity and mere theatricality are perennial problems for spectacular subcultures, especially goth. But Graham identifies something specifically *Japanese* about the emptiness he identifies in gothic lolita's Victorian looks, as well as the rockabillies he compares them to.

How much depth a repurposed and redeployed signifier like gothic lolita's Victorian dresses contains is obviously of interest here, but that should not come at the expense of considering the potential of shallowness. Where David Graham characterizes gothic lolita's surfaces as lack, we might look back to Philip Swift's account of Japanese cosmetic cosmology, described in chapter 4. The potential efficacy of surfaces, regardless of the depths they may conceal, index, or not, might alternatively position the detachment of gothic lolita aesthetics from clear and confirmable interior truths as a strength and an excess of meaning. It may be precisely the flatness of the gothic lolita aesthetic that allowed it to travel so fluidly across oceans, language barriers, and networks to inspire new enthusiasts across the planet. The superficial distinctiveness of the Victorian silhouettes that gothic lolita fashions cribbed from dolls, children's book illustrations, and fantasized European pasts now have picked up valences from their reinvention as Harajuku fashion. This is where the Victorian transitions into public domain, as it were, freely available to any taker on the strength of the cultural hegemony that propelled it to global saturation in the first place. The emptiness identified by Graham is closely akin to overfullness, where now the look of the European doll comes across as unmistakably Japanese, an uncanny reincarnation of Victorian values in the persons of contemporary young Japanese women (and others). Here, though, gothic lolita girls adopt past modes associated with the suppression of women to declare their independence from contemporary regimes of heteronormative hegemony. Conceiving of gothic lolita hyperfemininity as potentially resistant belies any binary between acquiescence and resistance to the status quo; rather, gothic lolita spectacularity makes visible a web of competing and indeed often irreconcilable interpellative societal demands made on young women (and others). Fashion's common property of semiotic semiattachment renders the fashion subculture sticky—picking up more and more meanings where some people have repeatedly recognized only etiolation.

The stickiness of overfilled signifiers brings me back around to gothic's fearful inheritances and the ways such gothic tendencies erupt in the larger ecosystem of gothic lolita, not only as recognizably dark imagery. Explicitly gothic looks are now more or less a minority in the larger lolita panoply, eclipsed by the international popularity of sweet lolita (although 2020 reports that classic lolita styles are beginning to surpass a decade or so of sweet supremacy). But a current of gothic sensibility runs through even the pinkest, cutest strands of sweet lolita. As cute studies scholars have pointed out, the aesthetic of cute and its (if anything) more developed Japanese counterpart *kawaii* contains an ambivalence that can tip the dominant qualities of softness, sweetness, helplessness, and adorableness into aggression, destruction, and so on.[30] Frances Richards writes, "draw a circle, and ray out from it the *abject*, the *melancholic*, the *wicked*, the *childlike*. Now in the zones between add the *erotic*, the *ironic*, the *narcotic*, and the *kitsch*. Intersperse the *Romantic/Victorian*, the *Disney/consumerist*, and the *biologically deterministic*. At the center of this many-spoked wheel lies a connective empty space. Label it CUTE."[31] Richards goes on to point out how the stylized, cuteified mode can evacuate the negative valence of violence, using the example of a cute cartoon cat versus the real nastiness of cleaning up after the flesh-and-blood bird mauled to death by a real cat. Certainly such a confused ambivalence obtains in explicitly gothic lolita looks, where handbags masquerade as puffy coffins or skulls and bones are softened into cartoons.

As Nobuko Anan points out in her book on girls' aesthetics in Japanese theater, some aspects of girls' aesthetics in Japan manifest the same dichotomy: quests to thwart time and chrononormativity to remain young and cute forever leads to themes of suicide and death as the ultimate means of stopping the clock and refusing society's demands.[32] Momoko, the protagonist of the novel and movie *Shimotsuma monogatari*, is a sweet lolita, not a gothic one, but she narrates the darkness of her lolita tendencies by acknowledging how her willfulness put her at odds with not just her small town's social standards, but also moral ones, which in the Japanese context continue to emphasize filial care and family loyalty. Momoko steals her father's counterfeit goods to sell them to schoolmates herself to afford to buy her expensive name brand lolita dresses. "So what if I was deceitful?" she declares. "My happiness was at stake. It's not wrong to feel good. That's what Rococo taught me. But actually my soul is rotten."[33] Although fictional, Momoko elucidates a key *shōjo* and gothic lolita tenet, positing her fashion pursuits as a mode of individualistic self-fashioning that cannot be reconciled with her family and society's demands that she acquiesce to the strictures of the group. Indeed, the central plot line revolves around Momoko's belief that she cannot even make and maintain friends, much less the wildly different *yankii* (motorcycle punk) girl Ichigo. (Spoiler: Momoko actually can make friends.)

Jane Mai and An Nguyen used Momoko's word "rotten" to name their book of gothic lolita essays and comics: *So Pretty / Very Rotten*. Using this dichotomy between pretty and rotten, they muse on the bank-breaking expense of filling a lolita closet, mean-girl antics within the community, the apparent paradox of self-realization through commodity consumption, and issues of isolation, mental health, and depression. "How can something so beautiful also make you feel so sad, angry, and detached?" they ask.[34] The overall effect of the collection uses the two authors' experiences (and Nguyen's doctoral research) in gothic lolita fashion to reckon less with the details of the aesthetic and more with the existential work and angst of trying to forge a self, a word I choose for its dual valences of creation through hard physical labor and fakery. I will return to the labor of self-fashioning in the latter part of this chapter, after we take an important tour through specifically Japanese regimes of femininity, to which gothic lolita owes so much of its gendered display and ambivalent attitude toward gender norms.

Lolita

In its Japanese context, gothic lolita fashion is imbricated in a rich, varied, and controversial tapestry of Japanese girl-centric sensibilities grouped under the catch-all descriptor *shōjo* (少女). *Shōjo* is one of the primary terms used in Japanese to designate girls and girl culture, and it also articulates the sense of liminality so important to girlness—the characters directly translate to "not-quite-female female."[35] Foremost among *shōjo* cultural products are manga, anime, and of course fashion, although the long durée of Japanese *shōjo* culture stretches at least as far back as the 1910s and 1920s. The regularization of girls' education, other changes in girls' social status like increasing employment, and the 1910s and 1920s' invention of the *moga* (a contraction of "modern girl" rendered in phonetic Japanese) contributed to the emergence of a girl-student culture.[36] (In the twinned outrage and adoration she elicited, the *moga* very much resembles the Girl of the Period.) One allied and equally ambivalent development in girl culture could be the founding of the Takarazuka all-women's revue company by railroad magnate Kobayashi Ichizō in 1913.[37] The example of Takarazuka amply demonstrates the twined strands of apparent new freedom and gender-bending self-presentation offered to young women, simultaneous with tightly controlled commercial appeal and continued structures of patriarchal orchestration that ensured that the primary benefits of women's entertainment labor accrued to the institution and the men who controlled it.

Further, all these changes marked increasing visibility for women beyond the domestic space, but only for those not subsumed within a nuclear family as wives or mothers. Linguistic and especially orthographic innovations marked early schoolgirls' culture and continued over the intervening decades, notably with the 1980s fads for *koneko-* or *burikko-ji*, super-cutesy handwriting called alternately "kitten writing" or "fake-child writing," respectively.[38] As can be deduced from the inherent censure in a phrase like "fake-child writing," young women's effects on the broader culture have often been editorialized as deleterious, much like contemporary US American hand-wringing over feminine linguistic innovations "vocal fry" and "upspeak."[39] And further, the sobriquet "fake" in fake-child writing, along with the anthropomorphizing of kittens should activate attention to the role of an antitheatrical strain to these critiques of young women. Just as in the case of the Girl of the Period, girls failing to be what society has decided they are is the heart of the complaint.

Concurrent with recognition of their impact on the wider social sphere, *shōjo* have come to occupy a highly ambivalent place within Japanese discourse.[40] Specifically linked with commodity consumption and nonproductivity (both as un- or insignificantly employed and definitionally not yet part of a reproductive economy of parenthood), *shōjo* both constitute a key market for the consumption of goods and are singled out for scorn. "The *shōjo*, that new human species born of commodification, has today commodified everything and everyone," declared Horikiri Naoto.[41] Horikiri's claim is polemically negative and frankly ridiculous: in what way could teenage girls be capable of personally shifting the social reality of late capitalism? Nevertheless, it attributes great power (real or imagined) to the category of *shōjo*. Further, John Whittier Treat points out how, formulated by behavior, aesthetics, and consumption choices, the *shōjo* constitutes a discursive category much more than a figure necessarily tied biologically to specific young female bodies. The youth and femininity of the *shōjo* could thus come to function as a space within the status quo that—when entered and barricaded like a fortress, rather than moved through as a liminal stage—constitutes a sort of refusal of society's demands on the individual to submit to chrononormativity. Nobuko Anan identifies just such a dynamic in her book *Contemporary Japanese Women's Theatre and Visual Arts*, delineating girls as those who "reject stereotypically defined female material bodies," for example, through recourse to "strategic reconceptualization of the notion of female 'innocence'" to emblematize "nonconformity to the patriarchal, heteronormative social structure."[42] Note here how Treat's and Anan's explanations gesture toward the detachability of *shōjō* from female physical bodies; this is also crucial to my conclusions regarding gothic lolita self-fashioning.

Although gothic lolita only figures in three brief mentions in Anan's book, her analysis of what her book's subtitle calls *Performing Girls' Aesthetics* presents a list of congealed affects and desires that very closely mirror those exhibited by gothic lolitas. Many gothic lolitas certainly refuse to fall into line with hegemonic societal expectations. They escape, like many *shōjo*, not into strident opposition, but into themselves and an imaginative world removed from time and space where they can, as Anan puts it, "move freely across geographical, cultural, and historical borders"[43] In this context, the Victorian or rococo of gothic lolita fantasy is less important for what it is than for what it isn't: the contemporary landscape with attendant social and familial ties and obligations that face young women (and others). "Justine," a Japanese lolita, says, "normal things like getting married, having a child, having a household—that kind of future is something I can't completely imagine. I want to forever remain *otome* [a maiden]. What I consider normal is different."[44] If resistant, this is, however, a "weak" resistance—a mode of building up a repeatedly breached barrier between the self and societal expectations, what Anan calls "an imaginative reconfiguration of what is given rather than an attempt to overthrow the oppressive social structure."[45]

Although most gothic lolita practitioners eschew all connections to *Lolita*, Vladimir Nabokov's 1955 novel of adult male lust after the enigma of girlish flesh, we might instead consider the coincidence of the name as an example of Anan's contention of "imaginative reconfiguration." As the moniker *shōjo* is itself used in competing and contradictory ways by foes and friends of the *shōjo*, so Nabokov's eponymous nymphet has been alternately reckoned with and disavowed by gothic lolitas. Many Japanese lolitas have never heard of Nabokov's book and tend to be disgusted when they learn what it is about, whereas for Anglophone lolitas the question comes up fairly regularly, and answers range from complete disavowal of any connection between the two uses of "lolita" to rehabilitation of the character of Dolores Haze to emphasize her innocence of the latter connotations of the nymphet as seducing or leading on older men.[46]

Despite Japanese lolitas' ignorance of the provenance of the name, its excessive semiosis predates the rise of the fashion: in Japan "Lolita" had already been appended to the "Lolita complex," typically abbreviated *rori-con* (ロリコン). Adapted from a 1966 book by Russell Trainer, describing adult men who desire young girls, the term has acute applicability in Japan where the pornographic imaginary features a particularly large subsection of youth tropes.[47] Despite sharing a name, lolita fashion drastically diverges from typical *rori-con* aesthetics of standard-issue middle school uniforms that everyday status-quo pubescent girls wear, rather than outlandish, fairy tale frocks. The common denominator between lolita fashion and *rori-con* seems, however, to lie with a perceived essence, not any visual marker: a shared obsession with the girlish innocence attributed to *shōjo* or younger girls. Or to reverse the formulation, they both, as Vera Mackie writes, "share common roots in an anxiety about adult female sexuality."[48] Pornographic *rori-con* representations employ youth (middle-school uniforms, not high-school ones) and rape motifs to signify girlish innocence, whereas gothic lolitas are preserving innocence by strategically escaping to a different time and place (the past, fantasy Europe) to avoid the threat of defilement. Indeed, the very quotidian banality of *rori-con* porn tropes suggests a credible reason for Japanese girls to want to construct a delicious fantasy persona: when the trappings of daily life, like your required school uniform, have been appropriated into an extensive pornotopia with sadistic overtones for the gratification of older men, you may indeed prefer to escape your quotidian milieu.

In the shared space of the internet, linguistic anthropologist Isaac Gagné has even documented alternate phonetic spellings (ロリイタ and ロリヰタ) that Japanese lolitas invented to avoid unwanted overlaps during web searches.[49] Until recently, I thought the struggle for internet supremacy had been settled in favor of gothic lolita fashionistas, but in the few years leading to the publication of this book, the internet's battles over control of pornography and the pervasiveness of seekers of sexual specificities have led to a number of chronic new troubles for gothic lolitas online. By 2018, even without safe-search functions, basic Google searches for ロリータ turned up all gothic lolitas, not *rori-con* pornographic sites, but meanwhile the word "lolita" in Romaji (ABCs) has become increasingly fraught. Lolitas on Anglophone internet outlets have also increasingly had to negotiate the growing popularity of a subset of BDSM culture called "DDlg" (Daddy Dom / little girl) on platforms like Instagram and Reddit. While DDlg play is consensual and definitionally occurs between role-playing adults (not children or anyone under the age of consent), the overlap in imagery, tags, and search terms makes certain locations into battlegrounds between lolitas who want to eschew any sense of sexual fetish to their Japanese fashion habit and kink seekers who may reblog, friend, or follow fashion lolitas, or share search terms and tags. For example, until the end of 2018, Tumblr was widely known as an image-centric blogging mecca for both teenage and youth blogs and NSFW (not safe for work, sexually explicit and pornographic) channels. Although Tumblr's ban on explicit content in December 2018 might ostensibly have helped lolita fashion practitioners gain an upper hand in their battles to keep their fashionable practices separate from others' sexual predilections, in practice many lolita fashion bloggers discovered that their blogs disappeared overnight, caught in the porn cull. The battles continue on Instagram, where gothic lolitas are sometimes harassed or, at the very least, forced to deal with unwanted DDlg advances or misuse of their photos.[50]

Lolitas discuss unwanted encounters and both malicious and clueless interactions online and in person and virtually every Facebook group for lolita fashion is protected by moderators to keep out creeps—those who can't answer a few questions demonstrating basic knowledge about the fashion are barred from joining. Like their Japanese counterparts, Anglophone lolitas spend significant amounts of time and effort policing the boundaries between their fashion and the pornographic practices that rub up against it in nonconsensual ways. In 2012 an independent filmmaker from Belgium ignited fury within the community with the poster for his documentary *Are All Men Pedophiles?* Much to lolitas' dismay, one of the two posters featured a young blonde woman wearing a pink Angelic Pretty brand coordinate. The model herself, a sweet lolita enthusiast, later apparently claimed that she had been deceived at the photoshoot, as the filmmakers had said the shoot would be for a feature on J-Fashion (Japanese subcultural fashions), not a documentary defending pedophiliac and more specifically hebephilic (sexual attraction to adolescents) heteromasculine desire.[51]

Isaac Gagné describes an earlier moment of this struggle among Japanese lolitas as a "fear of being appropriated not as a 'figure of identity,' expressing their own idea of their authentic self, but instead recirculated as a sexualized, pornographic 'figure of desire,' a costume-fetish 'character' addressed to the desires of an indefinite population."[52] The trick, of course, is that this isn't a problem of having chosen a wild outfit; this is a liability of being an embodied human, and particularly a feminine embodiment. It's hard to tell whether lolitas face more unwanted sexual advances than "normie" (non-lolita) femme-presenting people, but lolitas do frequently discuss their run-ins and resistance to such behaviors. Anecdotally, it certainly seems that daring to dress in a spectacular way runs the risk of attracting more attention and evokes more reckonings with the fallacious attitude that confuses visual notability with an invitation to unsolicited interaction. Such an attitude recalls the language of the Boulton and Park indictment, which elided the appearance of womanness with an invitation to personal interference. Feminine embodiment thus remains a matter of public struggle, inherently demonstrating that, at least in modern Euro-American and Japanese societies, many consider femininity, perhaps especially youthful femininity, to be a personal subjectivity liable to external and group regulation.

Technologies of Girly Counteridentity

"I feel like I'm returning to the real me when I wear Gothic Lolita clothes," explains Kana, an eighteen-year-old who works in a gothic lolita boutique.[53] Anglophone gothic lolitas in particular extensively debate and describe the stages of their fashion as identity, albeit rarely in so many words. One website for lolitas in English declares, "whether lolita is a fashion or a subculture is a matter of some discussion among followers. Many women wear the style only on weekends and for concerts, possibly as a form of escape from their more prosaic everyday lives and of course, simply because it's 'cute.' Other women say that lolita is a lifestyle, and even when not wearing the clothes, they try to incorporate the lolita ethos into their everyday lives."[54] The key word in this passage is "simply." Here again, at the center of a forum dedicated to a fashion trend, remains the question of whether a visual appearance is merely a fashion or a subculture, presupposing that a fashion is somehow less—less significant, less meaningful—than a lifestyle or subculture. But lifestyle and subculture as physical manifestations are themselves unstably poised between theatricality and authenticity. Another problem with identity alluded to in the quotation is that of self-sameness and consistency: if something is worn "only on weekends and for concerts" then could it be an identity? The logic of identity as monolithic, unchanging, or emanating from within legislates against the possibility of a sometimes activity or sometimes appearance sufficing for an identity. But fashion constantly offers the possibility of identity as shifting—one of the reasons fashion is always a suspect signifier; we can change our clothes quite easily. The clothes may make the man, but the identity established via fashion is temporary, contingent, and therefore suspect to the claim of theatricality—of impersonation or poseurism or mere appearance.

Much of Mai and Nguyen's *So Pretty/Very Rotten* eloquently questions the stakes and state of gothic lolita as a form of community and self-fashioning, and asks whether a fashion that disproportionately appeals to individuals who feel like misfits could possibly simultaneously be a sound forum for group identifications. Although both enthusiasts and academics have debated whether gothic lolita can sustain the designation of subculture by indexing the amount of music, literature, and other shared cultural products necessary to rise beyond fashion, my focus is rather on interrogating how a fashion or subculture contributes to subject formation. Like other minoritarian identifications, defining the boundaries of gothic lolita is a perennial matter of concern and debate for adherents of the fashion. Gothic lolitas fight to define and explain themselves to each other and outsiders; to define the boundaries of lolitaness suggests a meaningful form of self-making. As one member of the Facebook forum Rufflechat asked in August 2018:

> At what point are you considered a lolita? I've heard some people say you have to actually have Lolita clothing in order to be Lolita. If so what is the right amount? One item or one dress/main piece or one full coord [short for "coordinate," meaning full outfit] or is it having a functional wardrobe? Can you be Lolita and not be wearing the fashion (like you have an interest in it and know alot [*sic*] about it but currently lack garments)? What makes you Lolita?[55]

Nearly two hundred comments over the next few days generally agreed that one should own and wear lolita clothes, but also ran through the differences between brand-name clothes, off-brand clothes, and "loli-able" clothes (garments considered sufficiently frilly or poufy enough to pass as lolita fashion, but not originally manufactured or marketed as such); how many outfits one should own; and how often one should wear them and to where (only to anime conventions once a year was a bit suspect). "I consider lolita something I wear, not something I am," one commenter wrote, pithily articulating a tension in all performative modes of identity formation. It is less the details of the definition that emerges than that the boundaries of the group are being negotiated constantly that performatively coalesces gothic lolitas as a subculture or even an identity group. Their clarity as a recognizable group is hardly assured. There are many competing forces that both Japanese and global lolitas have to contend with: aesthetic overlap with cosplay, another clothing-based Japanese cultural export, unwanted sexualization and cooptation into otaku and pornographic aesthetics, infighting and gatekeeping around who is and is not a lolita, and the pure incomprehension of outsiders, within but especially beyond Japan.

In taking up gothic lolita as a form of self-fashioning, it can be instructive to look at the allied practice of cosplay. Although gothic lolita traveled extensively overseas along with cosplay and other anime- and manga-related fan practices, most gothic lolita fashion adherents are adamant about drawing a boundary between cosplay and true gothic lolita fashion. Quite simply, cosplayers are dressing up as someone else—a character—whereas gothic lolitas are dressing as themselves.[56] Short for "costume play," cosplayers construct or purchase the getups of their favorite characters from popular culture, especially anime and manga characters, but also musicians and video game and movie characters.[57] Because gothic lolita has inspired a number of fictional popular representations, now there are many cosplayers who dress as gothic lolita characters without themselves identifying as gothic lolita.[58] In Tokyo, cosplayers and gothic lolitas tend to favor different areas of the city (cosplayers are more prominent in Akihabara, the electronics district famed as an otaku culture mecca, while gothic lolita shops and hangouts are concentrated in Harajuku, Shibuya, and Ikebukuro), but elsewhere it might be difficult to tell who is really a gothic lolita and who is impersonating a gothic lolita character.

The thin and repeatedly breachable difference between a costume and an expression of selfhood is further indexed by attempts to draw a line between "conlitas" (convention dress-up lolitas) and real lolitas. Gothic lolitas have typically shored up this boundary marker through additional articulations of difference, such as the claim that cosplayers wear cheap, simple costumes, whereas gothic lolitas' ensembles are detailed and expensive. But policing this divide is made more complicated by the fundamental slippages that happen not only due to the burgeoning market for cut-rate and knockoff lolita fashions, the increasing number of gothic lolita anime and manga characters that exist to be cosplayed, and the number of people who alternate between practices, but also by a deeper and more fundamental ambiguity about how identities are formed and manifested. Indeed, we might use the coincidence of cosplay, fan cultures, and international lolita fashion to ask pointed questions about technologies of self-making in a context of transnational cultural and capital flows. After all, why wouldn't dressing up as a fictional character constitute an act of identity formation any more or less than dressing to performatively instantiate yourself as a loner princess exiled from her era? Or just dressing up as a girl who loves ruffles and bows? The spectacularity of lolita looks also incites policing from the mainstream where hegemonic norms for gender, race, and age self-presentation undergird the hostile or disbelieving reactions many lolitas encounter. I am emphatically not arguing that the existence of cosplay gothic lolitas shows that real gothic lolitas are more authentic, but rather pointing to the successive layers and permutations of the theatricality-authenticity binary to show the absurdity of such a question. If a cosplayer produces the authenticity of his identification with a character or series through donning a costume, while a gothic lolita produces the special, out-of-time nature of herself through donning a frilly dress, while a goth constitutes their worldview through black clothes, and everyone else expresses the theatricality of their associations—occupational, gender, sexual, racial, and so on—through their clothes, then there is surely no ground from which to legislate the authenticity of fashion statements.

Another commonly debated border case for lolita identity is the "lolita at heart," an enthusiast who own no lolita clothing at all, often because of financial constraints or because she is embarrassed or afraid her body won't fit or suit lolita clothes, but she still consumes images and information regarding the style. The lolita at heart thus marks a limit case for where and how lolita as an identity resides and is instantiated; for most lolitas, the obviously discriminatory barriers of sizeism and financial means are not enough to counteract their conviction that one must own and wear the clothes to performatively instantiate oneself as a real lolita.

Thus, like many or most other identity categories, the borders of lolita are demonstrably porous, provisionally established via discursive means, with two strong camps juxtaposing some internal, invisible kernel of identity which really counts versus insistence on actions and behaviors that must be present to performatively establish an identity, regardless of some internal truth from whence such actions may emanate.

At the opposite end of the spectrum from the lolita at heart is the "lifestyle lolita," a predominately Euro-American term for a lolita who always dresses in lolita fashion (not just at events, teas, and conventions, or in her bedroom for Instagram and webcams) and who "loli-fies" her life by decorating her house, cooking, and eating in lolita-appropriate, ladylike, and cute ways, and practicing lolita-like hobbies like embroidery, tea drinking, arts and crafts, and book reading (not the novel *Lolita*, of course). It is notable that, while Japanese magazines have frequently featured the loli-fied bedrooms and apartments of lolita adherents, the notion of going all in on a 24/7 lifestyle is a peculiarly Western one. Although most lolitas deem lolita at heart "not a thing," that does not mean that lifestyle lolitas are by contrast the best lolitas—the far end of the spectrum hosts a number of other identity conundrums like, "Are you still lolita if you change into jeans to change a car tire?" "How can you be a lifestyle lolita if you're not a princess and have to go to work in a non-frilly uniform?" and "I was a lifestyle lolita before I even knew what lolita was."[59]

Accounts of gothic lolita self-fashioning then might throw into relief the contradictory ways in which we conceive of all kinds of demographic identities like race, gender, sexuality. For instance, in a roughly analogue way to lolitas' debates over internal or externally demonstrated lolita identity, quotidian notions of race or ethnic identity also frequently revolve around people's inborn identities (say, Black or Latina/o/x/e) and how those do or do not match outward indicators. Black comedian Phoebe Robinson's self-professed, unabashed love of the band U2 is played for laughs because of its perceived incongruence with Black culture, or Rachel Dolezal's self-presentation of Blackness through appearance and actions took her to presidency of a Spokane, Washington, NAACP branch before she was unmasked as a "transracial" white woman.[60] Gothic lolita accounts of the dialectical working of what identity is and how it functions at the quotidian level parallel, overlap, and diverge from poststructural theoretical accounts of subjectivity. Gothic lolita clearly adheres to some poststructural recognitions of subjects as provisionally, contingently in process as formations, rather than formed and fixed, even as many adherents clearly also retain the sense of an inborn kernel of authentic selfhood. Or an observer may simply observe how gothic lolitas themselves habitually talk about their own identifications in casually identificatory statements like "I am a lolita," "I met some lolitas at the anime con," and so on.[61] The question of whether lolita is an identity and how it is expressed is of as much fascination to lolita enthusiasts as it is to academics and Anglophone communities of gothic lolitas (as in many Western subcultures) who continuously debate what a gothic lolita identity must entail to be real. In a certain sense, I suggest that it is precisely the vigor with which this question is continuously reworked, at least by Anglophone lolitas, that suggests it is a variety of identity, one which is intersectional with other identity markers, like gender, sexuality, nationality, race, class, and so on.

The notion of forging an identity through fashion—we could say *fashioning* an identity—is inherently paradoxical, since identity presumes, at least etymologically, a fixed and unchanging selfsameness, one which in Western thought paradigms ask subjects to be themselves unfailingly in every situation. This conception of identity is both culturally bounded—we have already broached some ways in which Japanese notions may contradict these models of identity—and also becoming outmoded in poststructuralist and postmodern theories.

In Japanese, the word for "self" is *jibun. Jibun* is made up of the kanji 自分 (self-part): the part of the whole that can be labeled as an individual, but which is by no means a whole, or to be considered self-contained or self-sufficient. The self, that thing enshrined at the center of so much of Western thought—"all men are created equal," "I think therefore I am," "the self-made man"—that thing is not distinguishably unique or separate; it's part of a greater network. Nancy R. Rosenberger, in the introduction to *Japanese Sense of Self*, describes it thus: "the self is not an essentiality apart from the social realm . . . Self attains form through relating to others, but . . . by relating in a variety of ways. It is in this multiplicity of relationships that meaning and power emerge."[62] This etymological interpretation of an alternatively constituted individuality is corroborated by other Japanese anthropological, sociological, and psychological models. For example, the concepts of *honne* and *tatemae* (inner feeling and external face, introduced in chapter 4), describe a dualistic understanding of individuals' selves. While this dualism may at first seem to correspond to a notion of true inner essence and its superficial mask, importantly *tatemae* could also be thought of as equally true or intrinsic to the individual. Recognition of the equal potential truth of a surface as an interior should remind us of Swift's location of efficacy at the level of the "cosmetic" in Japanese cosmology (chap. 4). We could perhaps think of *tatemae* as more like the superego to a *honne* id than like an artificial imposition upon an otherwise unified individual.[63] *Tatemae* also corresponds neatly with Erving Goffman's sociological concept of "front" in the *Performance of Self in Everyday Life*.[64] All these models recognize individual selfhood as made of riven and contradictory threads and recognize the truth of externally imposed factors interacting with possible internally generated ones; fashion theorists have too. In his 1904 treatise "Fashion," Georg Simmel articulated one of the paradoxes of fashion: that it satisfied two opposing human traits simultaneously—both the desire (we might even say need) for conformity and the desire for differentiation:

> Fashion is the imitation of a given example and satisfies the demand for social adaptation; it leads the individual upon the road which all travel, it furnishes a general condition, which resolves the conduct of every individual into a mere example. At the same time, it satisfies in no less degree the need of differentiation, the tendency toward dissimilarity, the desire for change and contrast.[65]

Simmel's fashioned subject is simultaneously an individual and an imitation, and that subject makes herself thus with each iteration, which is to say, in performance. Simmel touches on the social necessity of "imitation" (which may be to say: on the performative constitution of society through imitation and conformity to various norms). Simmel's imitation is simultaneously a difference. It is a repetition and a revision, a copy and a new creation. Indeed, this entire book has been more or less concerned with this process—identifying what and how of so many discursive and performative ways people in the nineteenth century and today have used the means at their disposal to become and maintain selves. Clothing is authentic and theatrical, self and other, it constitutes a self that is only a part. Simmel's model implies a theatricality through imitation that is constitutive of not only clothing fashion but also subjectivity. Visibility is a part of selfness, neither superior nor subordinate to the invisible.

Transnational gothic lolita communities actively engage in concerted, if incomplete, performative and discursive efforts to redraw the boundaries and limitations of gender, race, nation, size, color, sexuality, and so on, all under the aegis of a fantasized transnational, transtemporal, frilly femininity that is made equally available to all by virtue of affective affinity and fashion. Gothic lolitas performatively instantiate a femininity that is increasingly untethered to gender and reflects (especially in US and European contexts) a core belief that femininity could be for everyone.

In both online forums and in-person conventions, like Rufflecon and Paradiso, the majority of participants make concentrated efforts to create inclusive spaces coalesced around outfits and interest and not around individual demographic factors like gender, race, or sexuality. Gothic lolitas use a number of performative technologies to overwrite usual divisions of identity: one is certainly clothing and modes of dressing. Expertise regarding dress patterns, where to buy, how to size, and how to perfect coordinates is liberally traded in convention panels and in internet fora. A popular format for these discussions consists of an uploaded photo of a person in a coord, which other users comment on with compliments and critiques. In Facebook and LiveJournal fora, these discussions are usually instigated by the subject of the photo uploading her own image with a request for "concrit" (constructive criticism) and the ensuing discussion is heavily moderated for kindness. There are also more outlaw groups, particularly on Reddit and 4chan, dedicated to trash talking *ita* (ouch!) coordinates. Another technology is gesture and pose. One of Rufflecon's most popular events was the posing workshop where participants worked to master a vocabulary of cute and romantic poses for photos and fashion shows.[66] Gothic lolitas have ample opportunities to study vocabularies of posing and expression in photos of both models and enthusiasts that circulate freely on the internet. Kind and cruel discussions alike serve to continuously map and remap the shifting edges of what and who will count as lolita.

The tension between the self-fashioning valence of establishing oneself as a figure of identity versus being apprehended by an onlooker as a figure of desire, while surely pressing in most feminine modes of embodiment, seems to be exacerbated by the spectacularity of gothic lolita self-fashioning. While fetishists, or even just the skeptical, tend to argue, "surely you wanted attention when you dressed in an eye-catching way," Vera Mackie points out, "frills and decoration actually draw attention away from the body, obscuring rather than accentuating the shape of the body . . . making the clothes into an especially dense border between the body and the outside world."[67] In the introduction I noted how clothing functions as a border, but only here does the question of that border's depth emerge. Some fashions might constitute deeper surfaces than others. There is a certain literal truth to Mackie's comment, as lolita outfits require many layers—a blouse, bloomers and petticoat or crinoline, a dress or jumper-skirt, and no coord is considered complete without jewelry, headgear, and often wrist cuffs; in recent years wigs have increasingly been considered a requirement.

The protective or ameliorative function of a thick border between the self and the rest of the world is articulated poignantly by lolitas who describe how they use fashion to treat body dysmorphia. As one Rufflechat member says, "lolita makes me feel like i have agency over my body. i suffer really heavily from dysmorphia and through the extreme sense of control lolita gives me over everything from the shape of my body to how my hair is colored and laid out i've been able to really develop an actual sense of what -I- look like and how i look to the world. i know exactly what people see when i'm in lolita, but in other clothes i don't feel that same sense of control." Another concurs: "I feel a lot of awkward out in public, but when I wear lolita, I feel confident, I guess because I know people stare because of my clothing and not because of me." Also, "I feel too self-conscious about my body to wear the typical urban clothing which is close to the body and revealing and thin. So being hidden under ruffles and petticoats makes me feel safer." And

> Lolita makes me feel in control of my own life and destiny, as corny as that sounds. Even when I wore bland normie clothes to try to blend in and disappear, I still always got comments about my hair (it's really long) or awkward stares or gross comments about my body (short, big . . . features). I would get in trouble in middle and high school for showing too much cleavage, even when the same shirt wouldn't have shown cleavage on someone taller or more average-breast-sized. So alt fashion in general, and particularly lolita, felt like it gave me back some control over how I present myself and how people see me. Even when I wanted to blend in I couldn't, so might as well give people something to look at that I've chosen on my own terms.[68]

Perhaps it is also the thickness of the border, the amount of space of negotiation and, indeed, the layer of artifice—which is not to say fakery, but perhaps theatricality—with which a lolita persona is presented, that also makes the subculture such a haven for people with nonnormative affiliations to gender and sexuality. By theatricality I mean precisely the layer of identity insulation that the foregoing interlocutors describe primarily in body-consciousness terms: the clear consciousness with which the lolita's appearance has been composed, and the outfit's ambiguous relationship to identity in the normative demographic sense. This is a paradoxical claim, as I also have reported that lolitas are not in costume, but rather dressed as their true selves. Nevertheless, the picture of a true self limned by practitioners tends to be a complex and paradoxical one.

For example, a large proportion of the discussants in a question posed about an intersection between queer identities and lolita fashion in 2018 both self-identified as gay, bisexual, nonbinary, or trans (among many other nonstraight identifications) *and* declared there was no intersection between their sexual or gender orientation and their allegiance to lolita fashion. While many, about half, of the 180 replies on this thread claimed no relation between their queerness and their lolitaness, the other half, also mostly claiming queer identifications, argued that the sheer coincidence of queer, nonbinary, and trans people in the lolita subculture surely meant there was some specific connection between the two. By virtually every estimate (I have not been able to find any systematic attempts to conduct a gender and/or sexuality census of lolita communities), the proportion of queer, gay, nonbinary, and trans lolitas is exponentially larger than estimates for national populations. The closest attempt I've seen to estimate US lolitas is 33 percent queer identifying and about 15 percent nonbinary and trans. Several discussants in various threads on Rufflechat report that their local "comms" (communities) are 75 percent or even 90 percent queer.[69] (As this book goes to press, current estimates of queer/gay populations in the US are 4–5 percent and the best estimate of trans populations in the US is from 2016, reporting .6 percent of the US adult population—1.4 million people—identify as trans.[70]) Among discussants who did articulate a connection, some appreciated lolita as a mode of reclaiming gender: "As a lesbian, I've always had a strenuous [*sic*] connection to femininity and fashion. I loved feminine clothing, but I hated that much of it was made to appeal to men and that feminine women were always expected to be meek, caring, motherly, and straight. Lolita fashion is a way for me to dress femme strictly on my own terms, and it lets me feel beautiful without worrying about being seen by men as something they can sexualize." Reply: "i hated how much i exuded so many feminine traits that seemed to cater to the male gaze but wearing what i want and in my own way made me reclaim my confidence in being femme."

Although the vast majority of participants in Japan and beyond are ciswomen, there are enough cisgender men who dress occasionally in lolita fashions that they have acquired their own affectionate (and controversial) term: "bro-lita." There are also a number of trans and nonbinary people who participate, like Andrea Nicole Baker, a long time Atlanta-area lolita enthusiast, who uses the financial assets she's built to support areawide events, even organizing a lolita convention in Atlanta for two years. There are even a number of lolita participants who otherwise shun conventional modes of feminine self-presentation. Geraldine Fahr Sindram is a long-time sweet lolita wearer and active participant in online lolita communities. Fahr identifies as FTM (female-to-male) trans but declares he has no intention of giving up lolita fashion as he continues with his transition. Jane Mai explains that she came to gothic lolita fashions as an inveterate tomboy. She became a fan of the fashion by observing male Visual Kei musicians, whose avowedly straight, cis-male bodies in feminine frills helped her to recognize the performance of gothic lolita fashioned femininity as untethered to any specific body, sexual orientation, or personal disposition.[71] The most famous and important of these male musicians is undoubtedly Mana, the enigmatic guitarist for the bands Malice Mizer and Moi-dix-Mois (his solo project) who appears almost exclusively in gothic lolita-esque skirts and dresses, full-face makeup, and long hair, and who is credited with naming at least two substyles of lolita fashion, EGL and EGA (Elegant Gothic Lolita and Elegant Gothic Aristocrat), partially through his own gothic lolita fashion brand, Moi-Même-Moitié. Takemoto Novala, the author generally hailed as the "lolitas' bard," has expressed similar sentiments: "I am . . . a Rococo writer who has been racing headlong in full-blown Lolita mode for years, in spite of being a straight male."[72] It's worth noting that, although there are trans and male gothic lolitas in Japan and abroad, in general there is more hostility and distrust of bro-litas within Japanese communities. This is a state of affairs that mirrors more general attitudes toward gay and queer acceptance in Japan and may also be attributable to the strength of the *rori-con* pornographic aesthetic there.[73] In rambling online discussions, Anglophone lolitas also discuss the difficulties of balancing a welcoming community for everyone with the need to neutralize sexualized threats and discomforts aimed particularly at girls and women who have dared to stand out in public.[74] Thus, gothic lolitas use varieties of performative means to make over-the-top femininity a category available to the self-selected—replacing demographic diversity with fashionable diversity: "prince" and "boy" styles for girls and boys and everyone else alike, dresses in pink or black or teddy-bear print for all.

To be clear, when I suggest thinking through subcultural fashion as a technology of fashioning a self, I am not in any way disregarding or discounting the coercive interpellative power of performative norms to instantiate identity characteristics on individuals. I'm thinking here of Judith Butler's work on gender performativity or (to name just one relevant theorist) Rey Chow's trenchant observations on how raced subjects are compelled to conform to stereotypes to be intelligible at all.[75] Indeed, despite advances in making a greater variety of gendered expressions available to a greater variety of bodies, transnational gothic lolita communities have been beset by microcosmic—we might even say heterotopic—issues of discriminatory bullying that mirror the vagaries of the societies they draw from, such as sizeism, ageism, and colorism. Gothic lolitas track patterns of "mean girl" hierarchizing and policing, despite (or perhaps directly leading to) direct, concerted efforts to make gothic lolita a welcoming community for all genders, body shapes, income levels, and so on. The infamous website 4chan, for example, hosts the dark side of Facebook's heavily moderated (albeit still frequently contentious) lolita community discussion; users grab images from other sites like Instagram and repost them with disparaging comments regarding the taste level or looks of the individual in the image. At a longer running site, "Behind the Bows" on LiveJournal, moderators collate email contributions, anonymize them, and post them weekly. These are sometimes calling individuals ugly or fat but more often insulting individuals for bad taste in outfits or tagging pictures as lolita when they aren't. Many more of the anonymously posted "secrets" are about frustrations with brands, outsiders, and occasional debates about whether wearing lolita when you're not Asian is cultural appropriation.[76]

Of course, there could be a limit to the coalition-building prowess of an eclectically gathered group of girls (broadly defined) who generally pride themselves on being self-centered loners and princesses. Princesses, after all, are hardly neutral political figures. Despite the dark pockets of the online community, gothic lolita constitutes an inversion of social hierarchy toward the feminine and an extension of the possibility of community formation under a frilly, feminine, youthful, anachronistic banner by obscuring—literally covering over—other aspects of identity like nation, masculinity, age, and temporal era. But there are additional caveats to add to this (literally) rosy picture, beyond the existence of mean-girl backbiting. For instance, those who materially benefit the most from the propagation and capitalization on girl culture are not necessarily girls. For the most part, magazine publishers, fashion manufacturers, and even two of the most prominent lolita culture makers—Takemoto Novala and Mana—are not young women. Just as girlishness is available to a variety of bodies on the consumer end of things, so is it potentially exploitable or producible by any number of bodies; gothic lolita femininity is an eminently alienable quality. Indeed, it seems likely that people like Mana, Takemoto Novala, and male fashion designers get ahead precisely because of conventional markers of privilege—male bodies, relative age—in the larger dynamics of Japanese economics and society. The persistence of societal inequities, negative feelings, and bad behaviors within the gothic lolita subcultural heterotopia available only to those who can pay the internet bill or the dressmaker emphasizes that this is not a heroic resistance narrative, wherein girly ruffles cover over human difference resulting in world peace, but potentially a more modest, or maybe brash, notion that subcultural affinities, characterized by deep affect and obsessive study and creation, might point toward methods of thinking identity past essentialism.

Here then are the unanswerable questions that unite all the topics of this book: when does fashion encapsulate or display a true self and when is it something else? Why has spectacularity so often inspired contempt and fear? Is it possible that fashion spectacles too easily show up the theatricality of all identities? I would not say the Girl of the Period, Boulton and Park, the Meiji elites, or gothic lolitas were (or are) performing their true selves (nor would I say that they were not). Perhaps I would declare that these examples show us the undecidability, the fundamental impossibility of anything like a true self. Is it not more that the Girl of the Period revealed the nondifference between a respectable middle-class girl and a whore, that Boulton and Park revealed the indistinction between a man and a Girl of the Period, and that the Meiji-era Japanese were far too close to demonstrating the lack of a material reason why the English should rule the nineteenth century?

It is here then that I want to return to the notion of gothic lolita self-fashioning as insulation from identity rather than expression of it. While it has been a doxa of Anglophone thought to assume that self-expression is a moral good even as we valorize individual resistances to hegemonic powers, a viewpoint that reexamines this habit from the point of view of clothing's dual-identity valence—emanating from within or imposed from without—might find holding these two views at once oxymoronic. Taken together, the case studies in this book begin to suggest that identity is, first, not an interior essence, but rather has been attributed as essence by the power of performativity; second, and following from the foregoing, that individual freedom might indeed look more like systematically minimizing and recalibrating personal expressions of social identity norms. Gothic lolita and other chosen, performative allegiances, as well as Japanese models of subjectivity, might both offer more accurate modes for understanding the multifarious forces at work in creating individual subjectivities. And theatricality remains a salient dynamic by which all these subjective operations are eased along or sometimes gummed up.

Endings for Goths

Evolution and indeed decline are part of the typical life cycle of a fashion trend. My work here is bound to become outmoded even upon publication, as recent events have heralded the death of lolita fashion, after record longevity that far outlasted and outtraveled other Harajuku trends. In 2017 the seminal Japanese street-style magazines *FRUiTs, KERA*, and *Gothic & Lolita Bible* all ceased print publication, although *KERA* persists as a website and complex of online and brick-and-mortar shops in cities across Japan. Rather than pointing to the dire financial state of print periodical media, Aoki, the founder of *FRUiTS*, declared the magazine was folding because "there are no more fashionable kids left to photograph."[77] Although the decline of swanning in the street around Harajuku is confirmed by many sources ("Harajuku is dead, long live Uniqlo," declares one headline), the styles continue to ripple out across national borders via social media outlets Facebook, Instagram, and Twitter; online fashion sites, like *FRUiTS*-esque website Tokyo-Fashion.com; and internet meeting places into and out of physical spaces (the shopping streets of Harajuku and adjacent Yoyogi Park), cons, and meetups. Rufflecon, North America's one "alternative fashion" conference (which was founded and dominated by lolita fashion adherents) also announced its dissolution in early 2018, after its final event in November 2017.

Endings, however, are complicated when it comes to the gothic, which precisely thrives on death, revivification, fearful inheritances, and the revisitation of the repressed past on the unsuspecting or unwelcoming present. The longtime Japanese brand Victorian Maiden announced its closure in the last days of 2017, before reviving and resuming operations later in 2018. After the demise of Rufflecon, a new annual event called Paradiso in Kansas City, Missouri, founded in 2016, grew to attract nationwide visitors in 2018 and 2019, before being postponed by the global pandemic in 2020 (see fig. 25). Nevertheless, after two years of remote events in 2020 and 2021, Paradiso rose again in 2022, where they announced that there would not be any more future Paradiso events.

Fig. 25. Jordin Manning (they/he), winner of the Paradiso 2019 Ouji (Prince style) Pageant (Kansas City, MO), with consort Rue Estelle (they/them). Photo courtesy of Jordin Manning.

Just like other irrepressible gothic returns of the irrational, we have seen how the gothic lolita look has largely failed to obey the cyclical, regular, rationalized dictates of fashion commercial production in its own self-nourishing subcultures, growing and shifting over the years, and especially seeing adherents come and go from the fashion in their own microcosmic lifecycles.[78] Although we may concede that doubling down on modesty, girliness, spectacle, and anachronism is a weak resistance, gothic lolita's excessive fashions congeal and materialize the excess of feeling, particularly feminine feeling, desire, and darkness unattended to and uncontained by rational modernity and patriarchy. The sumptuous black blot of the gothic erupting in the now critiques the present in its very remaining.

In this book I have foregrounded dynamics of theatricality: how they appear in everyday life by means particularly of fashion and clothing, and how they both suture and unsettle fantasies of identification about gender, sexuality, race, nationality, class, and age.[79] I suggested that the very lack of apparent efficacy (the fictiveness) of their fashion representation made it possible for Boulton and Park to escape a sodomy conviction. I suggested that the theatricality of the Girl of the Period made her irresistible to the consuming public even though the possibility of performative change engendered in her performance seemed threatening. I suggested that the attempts of Meiji-era Japanese to dress for success on the world stage were challenged and undercut by theatrical discourses of seeming. In this concluding chapter I offered subcultural self-fashioning as a mode not of identity formation, but of identity insulation, wherein an individual might find more freedom, not the closer they embody an identity, but for how they might diffuse and distance themself from socially assigned (and admittedly personally internalized) identity factors. Gothic lolita's amplification of fashion's potential protective margin might in turn cast new light on the previous cases. In what ways is gothic lolita's thick border between self and other related to the Girl of the Period's awarishness—the self-aware separation that Lydia Thompson's burlesque Girl of the Period charmed and disturbed audiences with? For Meiji elites, the change of clothes functioned perhaps as protection by mimicry, even as foreign commentators called the makeover an empty imitation. And it was precisely the detachability and plausible deniability of their theatrical gender transgressions that Boulton and Park's theater defense provided that enabled the defendants to escape the force of the law in 1871. Clothing as a performance is made of both performative possibility and representational power, but both are tempered by the fluid force of theatricality to confirm or undermine any given appearance. Gender, as well as nationality, race, and sexuality, remain today prerequisites to attribution of full subjectivity, and as such remain grounds of struggle and dissent. In what ways can we use different means of thinking gender, race, nation, sexuality, and identity—perhaps along the lines of *jibun*—to more faithfully represent how identity works, how it is theatrically constituted, how it might prove something more than merely authentic?

NOTES

Acknowledgments

1. A. B., "The Girls of the Period," in *Drawing Room Plays and Parlour Pantomimes*, collected by Clement Scott (London: S. Rivers, 1870), 341–60.

Chapter 1

1. Anonymous [Eliza Lynn Linton], "Girl of the Period, The," *Saturday Review of Politics, Literature, Science, and Art*, March 14, 1868, 339–40.

2. The translation of this proclamation that I will be using can be found in Keiichiro Nakagawa and Henry Rosovsky, "The Case of the Dying Kimono: The Influence of Changing Fashions on the Development of the Japanese Woolen Industry," *Business History Review* 37, nos. 1/2 (Spring–Summer 1963): 63. The original text can be found in the online archives of the National Diet Library; see, e.g., *Meiji shouchokushu* (明治詔勅輯 Meiji imperial edicts), compiled by Nakamura Sadakichi, https://dl.ndl.go.jp/info:ndljp/pid/759506.

3. Mario Perniola, "Between Clothing and Nudity," in *Fragments for a History of the Human Body, Part Two* (New York: Zone, 1989), 237. Quoted in Ruth Barcan, *Nudity: A Cultural Anatomy* (Oxford: Berg, 2004), 12.

4. Elizabeth Wilson, *Adorned in Dreams: Fashion and Modernity* (London: Virago, 1985), 3.

5. Alexandra Warwick and Dani Cavallaro, *Fashioning the Frame: Boundaries, Dress and the Body* (London: Bloomsbury, 1998).

6. For example, Ernest Crawley, "Dress: Its Origins, Forms, and Psychology, with Special Emphasis on the Sexual Psychology" (1931), *The Anthropology of Dress and Fashion: A Reader*, ed. in Brent Luvaas and Joanne B. Eicher (London: Bloomsbury, 2019), 28–29.

7. Karl Kraus, "The Eroticism of Clothes," in *Rise of Fashion: A Reader*, ed. Daniel Leonhard Purdy (Minneapolis: University of Minnesota Press, 2004), 242.

8. Anne Hollander, *Seeing through Clothes* (New York: Viking Press, 1978).

9. Susan Bordo, *Unbearable Weight: Feminism, Western Culture, and the Body* (Berkeley: University of California Press, 1993).

10. Roland Barthes, *Erté* (New York: Rizzoli International Publishers, 1975), 26.

11. Wilson, *Adorned in Dreams*, 1.

12. Roland Barthes, "The Death of the Author," in *Image, Music, Text*, trans. Stephen Heath (New York: Farrer, Strauss, and Giroux, 1977), 146.

13. Keith Jenkins, *Rethinking History* (New York: Routledge, 1991).

14. See, e.g., Hanne Blank, *Straight: The Surprisingly Short History of Heterosexuality* (Boston: Beacon Press, 2012).

15. See also Noel Ignatiev's influential work *How the Irish Became White* (New York: Routledge, 1995).

16. David L. Howell, *Geographies of Identity in Nineteenth-Century Japan* (Berkeley: University of California Press, 2005), 12, italic in the original.

17. Coined in 1930, "The Great Masculine Renunciation" is J. C. Flügel's charming sobriquet for this shift in men's fashion, which has massive implications for the primary meaning of clothing for the nineteenth, twentieth, and twenty-first centuries, from class distinction to gender and sexual distinction. J. C. Flügel, *The Psychology of Clothes*, 3rd ed. (London: Hogarth Press, 1950), 110.

18. For a thorough critique of the lopsidedness of the woman-consumer and man-producer binary, see Christopher Breward, *The Hidden Consumer: Masculinities, Fashion and City Life, 1860–1914* (Manchester: Manchester University Press, 1999).

19. See Ellen Jean Samuels, *Fantasies of Identification: Disability, Gender, Race* (New York: New York University Press, 2014).

20. Patricia A. Cain, "Litigating for Lesbian and Gay Rights: A Legal History," *Virginia Law Review* 79, no. 7 (1993): 1551–641. See also Marjorie Garber, *Vested Interests: Cross-Dressing and Cultural Anxiety* (New York: Routledge, 2011), 141.

21. Nyong'o, *Amalgamation Waltz* (Minneapolis: University of Minnesota Press, 2009), 10–11.

22. Anne Anlin Cheng, *Ornamentalism*, illustrated ed. (New York: Oxford University Press, 2019), 3.

23. Christopher Bush, "The Ethnicity of Things in America's Lacquered Age," *Representations* 99, no. 1 (August 2007): 74–98.

24. Thomas Dekker and Edward Arber, *The Seven Deadly Sins of London, Drawn in Seven Several Coaches, through the Seven Several Gates of the City; Bringing the Plague with Them. October 1606* (London: E. Arber), 36–37, http://archive.org/details/sevendeadlysinso00dekkuoft.

25. Ann Jones and Peter Stallybrass, *Renaissance Clothing and the Materials of Memory* (Cambridge: Cambridge University Press, 2001), 66.

26. Anon. [Eliza Lynn Linton], "Girl of the Period, The," 339–40.

27. Modern fashion's largely unchallenged devolution into almost exclusively youthful representations raises another book's worth of considerations. I will only offer one speculation for now: is perhaps the fleetingness of youth the perfect unattainable (or unrecapturable) object of desire to power the late-capitalist fashion machine?

28. Thorstein Veblen. *Theory of the Leisure Class: An Economic Study of Institutions* (1899; New York: Modern Library, 1934).

29. Georg Simmel, "Fashion," *International Quarterly* 10 (1904): 133.

30. Sheila Rowbotham, *Hidden from History: Rediscovering Women from the 17th Century to the Present* (New York: Pantheon Books, 1973). Sheila Rowbotham, *Hidden from History: 300 Years of Women's Oppression and the Fight Against It* (London: Pluto Press, 1977). Martin Duberman, Martha Vicinus, and George Chauncey, eds., *Hidden from History: Reclaiming the Gay and Lesbian Past* (New York: NAL Books, 1989).

31. Jennifer Helgren and Colleen Vasconcellos, "Introduction," in *Girlhood: A Global History* (New Brunswick, NJ: Rutgers University Press, 2010), 4.

32. Most of these other works will be addressed in the course of the text. For Girl of the Period, see, e.g., Kristine Moruzi, "Fast and Fashionable: The Girls in *The Girl of the Period Miscellany*," *Australasian Journal of Victorian Studies* 14, no. 1 (2009): 9–28. For Boulton and Park, see Neil McKenna, *Fanny and Stella: The Young Men Who Shocked Victorian England* (London: Faber and Faber, 2013), as well as others referenced in chap. 2. For Meiji, see Toby Slade, *Japanese Fashion: A Cultural History* (Oxford: Berg, 2009); and gothic lolita, Isaac Gagné, "Urban Princesses: Performance and 'Women's Language' in Japan's Gothic/Lolita Subculture," *Journal of Linguistic Anthropology* 18, no. 1 (2008): 130–50; or Theresa Winge, "Undressing and Dressing Loli: A Search for the Identity of the Japanese Lolita," in *Limits of the Human*, ed. Frenchy Lunning, 47–63 (Minneapolis: University of Minnesota Press, 2008).

33. Anne McClintock, *Imperial Leather: Race, Gender, and Sexuality in the Colonial Contest* (New York: Routledge, 1995).

34. Fernand Braudel, *Capitalism and Material Life, 1400–1800* (New York: Harper Colophon, 1975), 226.

35. Thomas Richards, *The Imperial Archive: Knowledge and the Fantasy of Empire* (London: Verso, 1993), 1.

36. Richards, *Imperial Archive*, 17.

37. "Information" and "knowledge" are distinct terms in Richards's *Imperial Archive*: "Information is knowledge fractured into bits and pieces that can be moved around easily but never really assembled successfully into an integrated whole" (76).

38. The polite, official phraseology is honorific guest working foreigner, although many at the time and in contemporary scholarship employ the abbreviation "*yatoi*" as I will too. H. J. Jones, *Live Machines: Hired Foreigners and Meiji Japan* (Tenterden, UK: Paul Norbury Publications, 1980), xv.

39. Janes's school ended when he converted most of the students to Christianity and was forced to leave Kumamoto; he and the students relocated to Kyoto where they joined the fledgling Christian university Doshisha. See Leroy Lansing Janes, *Kumamoto, an Episode in Japan's Break from Feudalism* (Kyoto: Dōshisha Shashi Shiryō Henshūjo, 1970); and F. G. Notehelfer, "L. L. Janes in Japan: Carrier of American Culture and Christianity," *Journal of Presbyterian History* 53, no. 4 (1975): 313–38. For more on Griffis, see Edward R. Beauchamp, *An American Teacher in Early Meiji Japan* (Honolulu: University of Hawai'i Press, 1976).

40. John Gardiner, *The Victorians: An Age in Retrospect* (London: Hambledon Continuum, 2002), 4.

41. "Global Victorianisms" have been subject to increasing attention in the twenty-first century, perhaps particularly in conjunction with the rise of Neo-Victorian studies. See the open access journal *Neo-Victorian Studies* and the work of Elizabeth Ho, such as *Neo-Victorianism and the Memory of Empire* (New York: Bloomsbury, 2012).

42. Dallas Finn, *Meiji Revisited: The Sites of Victorian Japan* (New York: Weatherhill, 1995), 3.

43. Similarly, the second most common descriptor in gothic lolita is "rococo"—often with just as little intentional indication of eighteenth-century France as "Victorian" has with the United Kingdom.

44. Takashi Fujitani discusses the "monarch's two bodies" concept explicitly in connection with the Meiji emperor in *Splendid Monarchy: Power and Pageantry in Modern Japan* (Berkeley: University of California Press, 1998). Joseph Roach provides a performance studies usage of the concept in *It* (Ann Arbor: University of Michigan Press, 2007).

45. At the copyediting stage of this book's writing I was made aware that Michael Fried had made "to-be-seenness" a key term in a work that I hadn't read: *Why Photography Matters as Art as Never Before* (New Haven, CT: Yale University Press, 2008). My use of the phrase here is not intended to be referencing Fried's.

46. See, e.g., Regina Bendix, "Moral Integrity in Costumed Identity: Negotiating 'National Costume' in 19th-Century Bavaria," *Journal of American Folklore* 111, no. 440 (Spring 1998): 142; and Alexander Maxwell, *Patriots against Fashion: Clothing and Nationalism in Europe's Age of Revolutions* (London: Palgrave Macmillan, 2014), 157–58.

47. Henrik Ibsen, *A Doll House (Ibsen's Selected Plays)* (New York: W. W. Norton, 2004).

48. Braudel, *Capitalism and Material Life*, 231–32; Wilson, *Adorned in Dreams*, 16. Recent turns in fashion studies identify in this particular strain of earlier fashion history reasoning an indebtedness to racist and colonialist notions of fashion as modern and therefore necessarily uniquely European (read: white) while other cultures were perceived as being fashionless and unchanging, behind or outside of time. We will see much more about this dynamic in the nineteenth century in chapter 4. For my own thoughts on this debate about who "has" fashion when, I find it more important to interrogate how different definitions of fashion, or preoccupations with different aspects of clothing and change, are elucidated in the choices made by different scholars. Linda Welters and Abby Lillethun, *Fashion History: A Global View* (London: Bloomsbury Visual Arts, 2018).

49. See, for example, Quentin Bell, *On Human Finery*, 2nd ed. (New York: Schocken Books, 1976), 17; J. C. Flügel, *The Psychology of Clothes*, 137–39; Anne Hollander, *Sex and Suits: The Evolution of Modern Dress* (New York: Kodansha, 1994), 15; Lars Svendsen, *Fashion: A Philosophy* (London: Reaktion Books, 2006), 23.

50. Indeed, fashion serves as yet another example of how the postmodern can be identified in activities and processes that predate even the modern. Moreover, such circumvention itself performs a certain postmodern critique of linear temporal narrative.

51. *Oxford English Dictionary*, s.v. "fashion, v.," https://oed.com/view/Entry/68390. Fashion is further related to "faction" and "fact"; "a doing."

52. Wilson, *Adorned in Dreams*, 56, 60; Slade, *Japanese Fashion*, 22.

53. Svendsen, *Fashion*, 157.

54. Judith Butler, "Performative Acts and Gender Constitution," *Theatre Journal* 40, no. 4 (December 1988): 520.

55. The "Antitheatrical Prejudice" is of course cribbed from Jonas Barish's magisterial eponymous monograph; it will be cited again. Jonas Barish, *The Antitheatrical Prejudice* (Berkeley: University of California Press, 1981).

56. *Oxford English Dictionary*, 2nd ed. (1989), s.v. "investiture," https://www.oed.com/oed2/00120588.

57. *OED Online* 2nd ed. (1989), "Invest, v., definition 4," https://www.oed.com/oed2/00120566. For example, at the end of my dissertation work, which formed the basis of this book, I was "hooded" and performatively turned via investiture into a doctor of philosophy.

58. Jones and Stallybrass, *Renaissance Clothing*, 3, emphasis in the original.

59. J. L. Austin, *How to Do Things with Words* (Cambridge, MA: Harvard University Press, 1962), 43.

60. Samuels, *Fantasies of Identification*, 2, original emphasis.

61. Butler, "Performative Acts," 523.

62. This binary is of course finally giving way to other gender options as we enter the third decade of the century. I leave this phrasing now as an index of the standard choices available to my nineteenth-century interlocutors as well as to most of us today, although certainly much has changed in popular definitions of and attitudes toward gender identity even in the time since I began writing this book.

63. Butler, "Performative Acts," 519.

64. Kendall Gerdes, "Performativity," *Transgender Studies Quarterly* 1, nos. 1/2 (2014): 148.

65. See, e.g., Wilson, *Adorned in Dreams*, 12. Glaringly missing from my analysis here is sustained attention to the way in which fashion operates as an agent of commodity capitalism. While this aspect of fashion is addressed from time to time in this work, another volume and another author are required for this important topic.

66. Butler, "Performative Acts," 525.

67. Tracy C. Davis and Thomas Postlewait, "Theatricality: An Introduction," in *Theatricality* (Cambridge: Cambridge University Press, 2003), 1.

68. Alison Lurie, *The Language of Clothes* (New York: Random House, 1981), 3.

69. Roland Barthes, *The Fashion System* (Berkeley: University of California Press, 1983), 4–5.

70. Richard Schechner, *Between Theater and Anthropology* (Philadelphia: University of Pennsylvania Press, 1985), 112.

71. James Laver, *Costume and Fashion: A Concise History* (1969; New York: Thames and Hudson, 1982), 256.

72. Svendsen, *Fashion*, 29; Linda Welters and Abby Lillethun, *Fashion History: A Global View* (London: Bloomsbury Visual Arts, 2018), 33.

73. For example, consider Michael Fried's famous antitheatrical screed on contemporary sculpture, "Art and Objecthood," in which he declares, "art degenerates as it approaches the condition of theatre." Importantly for Fried, theatricality and theatre involve a viewer's awareness of his (almost definitely a "his" for Fried) body in relation to the artwork, instead of, I presume, a detached and disembodied sublime experience of the art. Michael Fried, *Art*

and Objecthood: Essays and Reviews (Chicago: University of Chicago Press, 1998), 164.

74. Such an argument thus contradicts Richard Schechner's famous "entertainment-efficacy braid" as described in *Performance Theory* (New York: Routledge, 1988), 103–46, helped along by the incisive critique of this binary made by Stephen J. Bottoms. What I most distilled from these works is an awareness of how theater, to the extent that it is elided with entertainment in Schechner's 1960s formulation, is definitionally excluded from potential efficacy. See Stephen J. Bottoms, "The Efficacy/Effeminacy Braid: Unpicking the Performance Studies / Theatre Studies Dichotomy," *Theatre Topics* 13, no. 2 (2003): 173–87.

75. On the surrogational logic of performance, see, e.g., Joseph Roach, *Cities of the Dead* (New York: Columbia University Press, 1996) or Marvin Carlson, *The Haunted Stage* (Ann Arbor: University of Michigan Press, 2003).

76. Kirk Williams, "Anti-Theatricality and the Limits of Naturalism," in *Against Theatre: Creative Destructions on the Modernist Stage*, ed. Alan Ackerman and Martin Puchner (London: Palgrave Macmillan, 2006), 95.

77. Michel Foucault, *The History of Sexuality, Volume One* (New York: Vintage Books, 1990) 43, emphasis in the original.

78. Quoted in Davis and Postlewait, *Theatricality*, 145; Thomas Carlyle, *The French Revolution* (Leipzig: Bernhard Tauchnitz, 1851), 2:59.

79. Among important thinkers on surface studies, this book is most inspired by Anne Anlin Cheng's *Ornamentalism*, although for another key work and overview, see also Stephen Best and Sharon Marcus, "Surface Reading: An Introduction," *Representations* 108, no. 1 (Fall 2009): 1–21.

80. Sean Metzger, *Chinese Looks: Fashion, Performance, Race* (Bloomington: Indiana University Press, 2014), 5.

81. Kimberlé Crenshaw, *On Intersectionality: Essential Writings* (New York: New Books, 2019).

82. Elizabeth K. Helsinger, Robin Lauterbach Sheets, and William Veeder, *The Woman Question: Society and Literature in Britain and America, 1837–1883* (New York: Garland, 1983), 125.

83. Nakagawa and Rosovsky, "The Case of the Dying Kimono," 63.

84. Koichi Iwabuchi, *Recentering Globalization: Popular Culture and Japanese Transnationalism* (Durham, NC: Duke University Press, 2004), 23; R. H. P. Mason and J. G. Kaiger, *A History of Japan: Revised Edition* (Boston: Tuttle Publishing, 1997), 362, chapter 2

85. Warwick and Cavallaro, *Fashioning the Frame*, xvii–xviii.

Chapter 2

1. Merle Mowbray Bevington, *The Saturday Review, 1855–1868: Representative Educated Opinion in Victorian England* (New York: Columbia University Press, 1941), 25.

2. "Novels with a Purpose," *Westminster Review* 84 (1864): 40.

3. Quoted in Nancy F. Anderson, *Woman against Women in Victorian England: A Life of Eliza Lynn Linton* (Bloomington: Indiana University Press, 1987), 120; quoted in Bevington, *The Saturday Review*, 108–14.

4. Eliza Lynn Linton, "Such Things Are" (book review), *Saturday Review*, February 14, 1863, 215 (possibly also published two weeks earlier in the *London Review*, January 31, 1863, 126); Eliza Lynn Linton, "Rose Blackett and Her Lovers," *London Society*, vol. 6, November 1864, 474. This earlier girl of the period comes off far better than her younger sister in the *Saturday Review*: Rose Blackett "was altogether a 'girl of the period,' after the best models of her kind; just a little too jaunty, perhaps, and a shade too indifferent, but evidently a fine-natured, pure-minded, high-hearted creature, as yet in the block, and unawakened."

5. A cursory Google Ngram charting of the phrase "of the period" reveals a singular spike in printed usage of the phrase beginning around 1860 and peaking by 1870, with nearly as steep a drop off from 1870 to 1880. As a phraseology, then, "of the period" was itself as faddish as the various things it sought to describe.

6. "The Girl of the Period" and "Modern Mothers" were among over fifty *Saturday Review* articles Linton contributed between 1866 and 1868, and she continued to contribute until at least 1877. Herbert van Thal, *Eliza Lynn Linton: The Girl of the Period: A Biography* (London: Allen and Unwin, 1979), 229.

7. John Stuart Mill, *The Subjection of Women* (New York: D. Appleton, 1870).

8. T. H. S. Escott, *Platform, Press, Politics, and Play* (Bristol, UK: J. W. Arrowsmith, 1895), 262. Quoted in Bevington, *The Saturday Review*, 112; and *Fun*, June 12, 1869, 138.

9. Escott, *Platform, Press, Politics, and Play*, 262.

10. Remember this phrase, because it also comes back in chapter 3.

11. The parent periodical of both the *Miscellany* and *Almanack*, *Echoes from the Clubs* appears to have changed its title to the more capacious the *Period* at the beginning of 1870, although it too folded not long after. I concluded this from examination of extant copies of all three journals, although my surmise is corroborated in George Somes Layard, *Mrs. Lynn Linton: Her Life, Letters, and Opinions* (London: Methuen, 1901), 143.

12. Three major accounts are found within the three biographies of Eliza Lynn Linton: Layard, *Mrs. Lynn Linton* (1901), published shortly after her death in 1898; van Thal, *Eliza Lynn Linton*; and Anderson, *Woman against Women*.

13. Layard, *Mrs. Lynn Linton*, 88.

14. Anderson, *Woman against Women*, 121. Biographer Herbert van Thal bases the designation of "first professional woman journalist" because she is the first known woman to draw a salary from a "famous daily newspaper," and many historians have followed suit. See van Thal, *Eliza Lynn Linton*, 1.

15. Eliza Lynn Linton, *The Girl of the Period and Other Social Essays* (London: R. Bentley and Son, 1883).

16. Escott, *Platform, Press*, 262. Quoted in Bevington, *The Saturday Review*, 112.

17. Nana Rinehart, "'The Girl of the Period' Controversy," *Victorian Periodicals Review* 13, nos. 1/2 (1980): 2–9.

18. Moruzi, "Fast and Fashionable," 9–28; Christina Boufis, "'Of Home Birth and Breeding': Eliza Lynn Linton and the Girl of the Period," in *The Girl's Own: Cultural Histories of the Anglo-American Girl, 1830–1915*, ed. Claudia Nelson and Lynne Vallone, 98–123 (Athens: University of Georgia Press, 1993). See also Ronald Pearsall, *The Worm in the Bud: The World of Victorian Sexuality* (London: Weidenfeld and Nicolson, 1969). Pearsall mentions the Girl of the Period briefly in conjunction with his examination of fashion and sexuality.

19. Helsinger, Sheets, and Veeder, *The Woman Question*, 125.

20. Lurie, *Language of Clothes*.

21. Jonas Barish, *The Antitheatrical Prejudice* (Berkeley: University of California Press, 1981).

22. Alan Ackerman and Martin Puchner, eds., *Against Theatre: Creative Destructions on the Modernist Stage* (London: Palgrave Macmillan, 2006), 15.

23. Nina Auerbach, *Private Theatricals: The Lives of the Victorians* (Cambridge, MA: Harvard University Press, 1990), 4.

24. Linton, "The Girl of the Period," 340.

25. Wilson, *Adorned in Dreams*, 11.

26. Amy Milne-Smith, *London Clubland: A Cultural History of Gender and Class in Late Victorian Britain* (New York: Palgrave Macmillan, 2011), 5–6; Seth Alexander Thévoz, *Club Government: How the Early Victorian World Was Ruled from London Clubs* (London: I. B. Tauris, 2018), 4–5.

27. See also "Reviewer of the Period," *Tinsley's Magazine*, July 1868, 621; "'The Girl of the Period' Defended," *Sheffield and Rotherham Independent*, March 28, 1868, 4; "Painted by a Prurient Prude," *Tomahawk*, April 4, 1868, 139; "The Past and Future of the Girl of the Period." *London Society*, November 1869; and "Girls of the Period," *Nottinghamshire Guardian*, February 12, 1869, 6.

28. See, e.g., Jon Sternglass, "Cheating, Gender Roles, and the Nineteenth-Century Croquet Craze," *Journal of Sport History* 25, no. 3 (Fall 1998): 398–418.

29. "Mrs. Punch's Letters to Her Daughter," *Punch*, October 24, 1868, 180; "A Lady's Remonstrance," *Star*, August 19, 1869 [reprinted from *Girl of the Period Miscellany*]; "The Origin of the 'Girl of the Period,'" *Penny Illustrated Paper*, October 16, 1869, 254; "The Latest Crusade," *Victoria Magazine*, July 1868, 193–201; and "The Man of the Period" (London: Robert Hardwicke, 1868), 4.

30. M. E. Braddon, "Whose Fault Is It?" *Belgravia Magazine* 9 (August 1869): 214–15.

31. This author has been identified as Penelope Holland, an Anglican clergyman's wife. See Anderson, *Women against Women*, 124; and Janet Horowitz Murray, *Strong-Minded Women and Other Lost Voices from Victorian England* (New York: Pantheon, 1982), 45.

32. Eliza Lynn Linton, *Modern Women and What Is Said of Them* (New York: J. S. Redfield, 1868). "Modern Women and What Is Said of Them" review, *Atlantic Monthly* 22, no. 132 (November 1868): 640; "The Latest Crusade," *Victoria*, 193; "The Girl of the Period," *Tomahawk*, 136.

33. The notion of the Anglican clergy constituting a distinct third gender is a fascinating concept, but, alas, must be saved for another work.

34. Bevington, *The Saturday Review*, 111–12; *Ladies Treasury*, April 1, 1869, 61.

35. Bevington, *The Saturday Review*, 112

36. Linton, *Girl of the Period*, vii–viii.

37. Layard, *Mrs. Lynn Linton*, 145; quoted in Bevington, *The Saturday Review*, 111.

38. "'The Girl of the Period' Defended," 4.

39. Louisa May Alcott, *An Old-Fashioned Girl* (Boston: Roberts Brothers, 1870), v–vi.

40. The *Englishwoman's Domestic Magazine* controversies on whipping girls and tight lacing are beyond the scope of this work, but briefly, over the few years that also saw the Girl of the Period fad, Beeton's *Englishwoman's Domestic Magazine* published a series of letters from readers on these two matters, which attracted notoriety for their frank discussion of fetishistic sexual behaviors. The whipping letters were compiled into a pamphlet reprint: *Letters Addressed to the Editor of the Englishwoman's Domestic Magazine on the Whipping of Girls and the General Corporal Punishment of Children* (London: Office, Warwick House, Paternoster Row, 1870; very rare, but available at the British Library) and the corset letters were eventually incorporated into a book: William Barry Lord, *The Freaks of Fashion: With Illustrations of the Changes in the Corset and the Crinoline from Remote Periods to the Present Time* (London: Ward, Locke, and Taylor, 1870). This book was later reprinted as *The Corset and the Crinoline*. This latter title is also available as a facsimile reprint edition as W. B. Lord, *The Corset and the Crinoline: An Illustrated History* (New York: Dover Publications, 2007).

41. See, e.g., *London Society*, "The Past and Future of the Girl of the Period," November 1869.

42. Eliza Lynn Linton, *The Autobiography of Christopher Kirkland* (1885; New York: Garland Publishing, 1976).

43. McClintock, *Imperial Leather*, 5–9.

44. See also the "Parsee Girl of the Period" in forthcoming work by Kellen Hoxworth.

45. Chapter 4 will spend much more time working through race, nationalism, gender, and their awkward imbrication in popular cultural discussion.

46. See Efrat Tseëlon, *The Masque of Femininity: The Presentation of Woman in Everyday Life* (London: Sage, 1995); Rebecca Schneider, *The Explicit Body in Performance* (New York: Routledge, 1997); and Rita Felski, *The Gender of Modernity* (Cambridge, MA: Harvard University Press, 1995).

47. Burlesque did not yet resemble twentieth- and twenty-first-century burlesque, but instead retold well-known stories or plays in a broadly comic form, almost always in verse, featuring a wealth of satirical contemporary references. But another popular feature of burlesque were attractive women, playing both men's and women's roles, and eventually the "leg show" aspect of the burlesque became its overriding feature, squeezing out plot-driven plays, and eventually even the supplementary humor acts by men. See, e.g., Robert

Clyde Allen, *Horrible Prettiness: Burlesque and American Culture* (Chapel Hill: University of North Carolina Press, 1991).

48. Francis Cowley Burnand, *The Girls of the Period, or the Island of Nowarpartickilar: A Folly in Two Scenes of Prose, Rhyme, Dance and Song* (London: Phillips, 1869), 13.

49. Burnand, *Girls of the Period*, 16–17, emphasis in the original.

50. "Mr. Edward Terry, made up as a caricature on that wonderful creature the Girl of the Period performs Sister Ann, and humorously embodies all that young lady's fast tendencies, as exhibited in amorous advances to Blue Beard and Selim" (*Era*, April 4, 1869). *Daily News*, March 30, 1869; *Liverpool Mercury*, April 26, 1869.

51. Maria-Elena Buszek, "Representing 'Awarishness': Burlesque, Feminist Transgression, and the 19th-Century Pin-up," *TDR: The Journal of Performance Studies* 43, no. 4 (Winter 1999): 147.

52. For more on the cigar shop mannequin and picture, see Paul D'Ambrosio, "Girl with a Squirrel." *American Folk Art at Cooperstown* (blog), June 27, 2010. https://folkartcooperstown.blogspot.com/2010/06/girl-with-squirrel.html.

53. Allen, *Horrible Prettiness*, 18.

54. The stump speech is filled with malapropisms and faux pomposity, satirizing public-speaking formats like the scientific lecture and the political speech from which it takes its name. Robert C. Toll, *Blacking Up: The Minstrel Show in Nineteenth-Century America* (New York: Oxford University Press, 1974), 56.

55. Further, the article suggested that satire frequently fostered or even birthed more elaborate street fashions, using examples from Thomas Rowlandson and James Gilray in the eighteenth century, and *Punch*'s send-ups of the crinoline in the previous decade as examples.

56. A. B., "The Girls of the Period" in *Drawing Room Plays and Parlour Pantomimes*, collected by Clement Scott (London: S. Rivers, 1870), 341–60.

57. Anonymous [Eliza Lynn Linton], "Girl of the Period, The," 340.

58. One notable way in which these anxieties arise is as a recurring plot issue in Victorian fiction: innumerable novels hinge on worries about money and social standing, and for female characters, how to secure these things through marriage and romance.

59. See Judith Walkowitz, "The Contagious Diseases Acts, Regulationists and Repealers," in *Prostitution and Victorian Society: Women, Class, and the State* (Cambridge: Cambridge University Press, 1982), 67–148. For the most extensive treatment of this issue in the theater history context, see Tracy C. Davis, *Actresses as Working Women: Their Social Identity in Victorian Culture* (London: Routledge, 1991).

60. "The pretty housebreakers" is a play on "the pretty horsebreakers," a euphemism applied to the 1860s courtesans and kept mistresses whose horseback riding pastime in London parks, especially Rotten Row, showed them off at one leisurely margin of bourgeois and aristocratic society. Just like "The Girl of the Period," the phrase was coined from an 1861 satirical poem published in a popular journal. "A Belgravian Lament," *Times* (London) June 27, 1861, 6. See Katie Hickman, *Courtesans: Money, Sex, and Fame in the*

Nineteenth Century (New York: HarperCollins, 2003), 284; Cyril Pearl, *The Girl with the Swansdown Seat* (Indianapolis: Bobbs-Merrill, 1955), 128–29; and Erica Munkwitz, *Women, Horse Sports, and Liberation* (London: Routledge, 2021).

61. Bevington, *The Saturday Review*, 111.

62. See Sara Ahmed's treatment of later iterations of this evergreen figure in *The Promise of Happiness* (Durham, NC: Duke University Press, 2010), 65–67.

63. Moruzi, "Fast and Fashionable," 11.

64. Moruzi, "Fast and Fashionable," 25.

65. See, e.g., Catherine Driscoll, *Girls: Feminine Adolescence in Popular Culture and Cultural Theory* (New York: Columbia University Press, 2002), 281.

66. Among other references, see, e.g., Ariel Levy, *Female Chauvinist Pigs: Women and the Rise of Raunch Culture* (New York: Free Press, 2006).

67. Deeply unfortunately, the full text of the "Marriage Market" stump speech seems not to be extant; the closest I've come is the complete handwritten promptbook for the Thompson Troupe's *Sindbad*, held in the Tams-Witmark special collection at the University of Wisconsin, Madison. In that document, a large heading announces "The Marriage Market" with a short blank before the text continues with the lines that came after the conclusion of the speech. The evidence thus speaks to the probable shifting and improvised nature of the stump speech, but sadly doesn't give us more of Thompson's provocative presentation. The phrase containing "awarishness" is quoted in a glowing review of Thompson in the *Galaxy* 8, no. 2 (August 1869): 260.

68. Buszek, "Representing 'Awarishness,'" 155.

69. Joan Rivière, "Womanliness as Masquerade." In *International Journal of Psycho-Analysis* 9 (1929): 303–13.

Chapter 3

1. Public Record Office, National Archive, Kew, London, Court of King's Bench deposition files for the Boulton and Park arrest and arraignment, hereafter cited in text by its shelf mark KB 6/3. "Offences Against the Person Act, 1861," in Chris White, ed., *Nineteenth-Century Writings on Homosexuality: A Sourcebook* (London: Routledge, 1999), 44.

2. "Lives of Boulton and Park" (London: George Clarke, 1870), 3–4, hereafter cited as "Lives"; Wayne R. Dynes, ed., *Encyclopedia of Homosexuality* (New York: Garland Publishing Company, 1990), 256.

3. Eve Kosofsky Sedgwick, *Epistemology of the Closet* (Berkeley: University of California Press, 1990), 44.

4. Foucault, *History of Sexuality*, 43; Christopher Craft, *Another Kind of Love: Male Homosexual Desire in English Discourse, 1850–1920* (Berkeley: University of California Press, 1994), 35.

5. Foucault, *History of Sexuality*, 43.

6. Chris White, "General Introduction: Strategies for Liberation," in White, *Nineteenth-Century Writings on Homosexuality*, 4. I could say the "much maligned" word homosexuality, disdained even at the time of its coining not least because of its promiscuous mixing of Latin and Greek roots.

7. The *Oxford English Dictionary*'s first quotation for "drag" in the sense of cross-dressing comes from newspaper coverage of the arraignment. The first entry for "camp" (in the sense pertinent to sexuality) is from 1909, making Park's use of the word "campish" in a seized letter all the more notable.

8. Sedgwick, *Epistemology of the Closet*, 26, emphasis in the original.

9. Judith Butler, *Gender Trouble: Feminism and the Subversion of Identity* (New York: Routledge, 1990), xxiii.

10. Our very vocabulary constantly highlights the difficulty of articulating the epistemic differences between Victorian self-conceptions and contemporary vocabularies of identity. To wit, what might a term like sexuality presuppose about consistency, regularity, self-sameness—identity—in sexual activities, as opposed to more performative models (à la Foucault and Butler) that would suggest that sexuality's appearance as monolithic and consistent is an illusory one created and maintained through repeated acts. And all this is to say nothing of how rapidly the contemporary discourses on sexuality and gender change. Because I've been working on this research since 2004, I've constantly needed to update it particularly in conjunction with changes in trans theory and norms of terminology, although it is certainly a bit dated already due to its own mid-aughts "temporal drag." Herewith, I will be attempting to step out of such a stream of dialectical "advancement" to spend some time in an eddy of gender and sexuality discourse. (Here I am dragging Elizabeth Freeman's term. See Elizabeth Freeman, *Time Binds: Queer Temporalities, Queer Histories* [Durham, NC: Duke University Press, 2010].)

11. The temerity of my claim that this apparently niche tabloid scandal is and should be of interest to the wider social historiography of the Victorian era owes something to Sedgwick's groundbreaking work *Epistemology of the Closet*, in which she, bolder than I, argues that the homo-heterosexual binary has underwritten all of twentieth-century epistemology. Sedgwick, *Epistemology of the Closet*, 1.

12. Haxell's Hotel was absorbed into the Strand Palace Hotel in 1909, a much larger hotel built on its site and adjoining lots at 372 Strand. The Strand Palace is still in business today and now has a restaurant named Haxells after the earlier hotel. Today, the luxury Savoy Hotel stands directly across the street from the former site of Haxell's, but in 1870, that was an empty lot, awaiting redevelopment by Richard D'Oyley Carte as the Savoy Theatre and Hotel in 1880–81.

13. Among a wealth of potential citations for sodomy as the unspeakable vice, the "mute sin," and the "nameless offence," consider Carolyn Dinshaw, *Getting Medieval: Sexualities and Communities, Pre- and Postmodern* (Durham, NC: Duke University Press, 1999), 5; White, "General Introduction," 1; and Harry Cocks, *Nameless Offences: Homosexual Desire in the 19th Century* (London: I. B. Tauris, 2003), 1.

14. I am indebted to Shannon Jackson's *Lines of Activity* for this understanding of the fictive as "temporarily suspended from other modes of social reality," a status that Jackson points out "prompts many to call [aesthetic forms and performances] expendable." Jackson, *Lines of Activity: Performance, Historiography, Hull-House Domesticity* (Ann Arbor: University of Michigan Press, 2000), 17.

15. Graham Robb, *Strangers: Homosexual Love in the Nineteenth Century* (New York: W. W. Norton, 2004), 100; Morris Kaplan, *Sodom on the Thames: Sex, Love, and Scandal in Wilde Times* (Ithaca, NY: Cornell University Press, 2005), 191.

16. Cocks, *Nameless Offences*, 87.

17. In 2023, during the copyediting stage of this work, I have altered this phraseology to better reflect current terminology about gender identification, but the changes in consensus on best language even during the fifteen years I've been living with this research until this book's publication—not even touching the total lack of coherent discourse much less ethically elaborated terminology during the era of which I speak—leaves descriptions like these fraught and bound to sound wrong or offensive. The fact that there is no comfortable or uncontested way to describe the gender mysteries the *Illustrated Police News* was plumbing in its imagery is indeed a main focus of this chapter.

18. Laurence Senelick, "Pantomime," in *The Cambridge Guide to Theatre*, ed. Martin Banham, 751–52 (Cambridge: Cambridge University Press, 1992).

19. *Oxford English Dictionary*, s.v. "Personation," https://oed.com/view/Entry/141498.

20. Because "personation" and "personators" were the terms overwhelmingly used in the news media to describe Boulton, Park, and their associates, I choose to focus on this term, and hesitate to fully elide it with impersonation as synonymous. In contrast, in his work on the trial, Harry G. Cocks uses exclusively the term "impersonation" to describe Boulton and Park's actions and the interpretations others made of them. Since female impersonation or male impersonation is now common for stage cross-dressed performance, it is probably worthwhile to consider this phraseology. Cocks cites Laurence Senelick in charting a shift in the usage of impersonation over the nineteenth century, from "the personification of certain qualities or characteristics" before mid-century to later referring to "the assumption of a character in its modern sense of imitation or mimicry" (Cocks, *Nameless Offences*, 99). The term in relation to Boulton and Park could refer to either usage, since female could refer to qualities coded as female or to the imitation of females. Neither of these usages cited by Cocks via Senelick carries a negative connotation, although in my opinion, impersonation seems to carry slightly more pejorative weight than personation due to the ambivalence of the meaning of the prefix "im" derived from the Latin for either "not" or "into." Although impersonate uses the prefix for into (as in to invest with personality), I believe it currently tends to (and in Victorian usage tended to, as Senelick gestures toward) simultaneously carry the connotation of negation, in that an impersonator is manifestly not the thing he or she imitates, but a fraudulent copy.

21. Public Record Office, National Archive, Kew, London, official criminal charges, handwritten on vellum, pierced and bound on a cord along with all other criminal charges for the term in 1870, hereafter cited in text as CRIM 4/777. The carets in the text correspond to additions inserted into the handwritten text of the indictment (on an irregularly sized piece of parchment stored in a roll with the other indictments from the term at the Public Record Office)—as if after writing the initial charge out, "inveigle induce" did not seem sufficiently precise or "improperly and indecently" sufficiently condemnatory.

22. At the very least, the prosecution suggested, men dressing as women might have been fooling other men and then blackmailing them; one penny pamphlet called this "merely a felony" as opposed to the yet more horrifying possibility of an "unnatural crime of a dreadful description" ("Lives," 3).

23. This is of course consonant with centuries or even millennia of discourse on women's sexual objectification and particularly with Victorian notions of men's inability to control their sexual appetites. Combined notions of men's inability to control their lusts and women's inability not to incite desire presents a grim catch-22 to anyone hoping to avoid sexual assault or sexual immorality.

24. Although the charge was reduced to a conspiracy felony rather than a buggery felony, this was a frequent tactic for prosecuting sodomites, since in British law sodomy convictions had traditionally required an eyewitness who was not a participant, obviously not an easy witness to find. See Cocks, *Nameless Offences*, 34; and William A. Cohen, *Sex Scandal: The Private Parts of Victorian Fiction* (Durham, NC: Duke University Press, 1996), 83. There seems to be little precedent in English law for Dr. Paul's claim that he could identify physical evidence of sodomitic activity on the body and this claim was thoroughly contested by the defense doctors.

25. Craft, *Another Kind of Love*, xii.

26. Although according to his signature in the original deposition transcripts he was Richard Barwell, some sources erroneously called him Dr. Barlow: KB 6/3, 147; *Lloyd's*, May 22, 1870, 7; *Globe*, May 20, 1870; *Sun*, May 20, 1870.

27. L. Rosenfeld, "Alfred Swaine Taylor (1806–1880), Pioneer Toxicologist—and a Slight Case of Murder," *Clinical Chemistry* 31, no. 7 (1985): 1236.

28. Public Record Office, National Archive, Kew, London, Department of Public Prosecutions, complete handwritten trial transcript, hardbound, hereafter cited in text as DPP 4/6.

29. Although there is much to be discussed about the medical portion of the trial, it falls beyond the scope of this book. See my other work on the trial, "Performers in the Audience: The Boulton and Park Case of 1870–1871," (MA thesis, University of Colorado Boulder, 2006), as well as Cohen, *Sex Scandal*; and Kaplan, *Sodom on the Thames*.

30. Cohen, *Sex Scandal*, 109.

31. Paul had admitted to reading some medical books by the French pathologist August Ambroise Tardieu and the German forensic scientist Johann Ludwig Casper (DPP 4/6, 282–83).

32. Under apparently hostile cross-examination at the arraignment, Dr. Paul insisted: "I did not use my hand with violence, I used both hands. I do not use the speculum, in ordinary cases, I did not use it on this occasion, I could see without . . . When I made the examination no one could see but myself, I made it decently and in every way carrying out my professional duty as I always do and they made no objection or protest against my doing so" (KB 6/3, 84, 86). The arraignment depositions are not written in verbatim dialogue form. The questions asked are not recorded, only the witness's statements; answers to questions are generally separated by commas, causing the somewhat rambling appearance of quotations from this document. I have altered some punctuation to assist the flow of the quotations.

33. Foucault, *History of Sexuality*, 35, original emphasis.

34. See especially Sedgwick, *Epistemology of the Closet.*

35. Craft, *Another Kind of Love*, 6

36. The long association of same-sex practices and unspeakability in Christian practice are attested to by Carolyn Dinshaw's tracing of clerical injunctions to silence on same-sex sexual immorality in fourteenth-century England. Dinshaw, *Getting Medieval*, 5.

37. Cocks, *Nameless Offenses*, 1. For more on homosexuality and unspeakability, see, e.g., Cocks, *Nameless Offenses*; and Craft, *Another Kind of Love.*

38. This is of course a restating of Foucault's "repressive hypothesis," and we will see this dynamic again in chap. 4 under the phraseology "iconography of absence" in Meiji Japan.

39. "Men in Petticoats," 7. Remember from chap. 2 that Belgravian mothers had been accused of doing on behalf of their daughters what Girls of the Period were accused of doing to themselves. It's worth musing on how and why the moral disapproval of mercenary matrimonial behaviors seemed, at least to this polemic pamphleteer, comparable to the shadowy accusations against Boulton, Park, and company.

40. Significantly, this was not (and is not) true in the reverse situation of women playing male roles, in which it is a doxa of theater history that breeches roles, popular from virtually the moment women first appeared on the "legitimate stage" in Britain, served the purpose of displaying women performers' anatomies more explicitly to the audience's (male) gaze for their sensual delectation. There is much more to be made of this asymmetry of viewers' desiring practices in varieties of gender performance that exceeds the limits of this book. Obviously, the intertwining structures of homophobic paranoia and heteropatriarchy underwrite the situation.

41. Laurence Senelick, "Boys and Girls Together," in *Crossing the Stage: Controversies on Cross-dressing*, ed. Lesley Ferris (London: Routledge, 1993), 85. Of course, glamour drag has finally more or less become the dominant mode of drag in the twenty-first century and achieved a mainstream popularity surely inconceivable to Boulton, Park and their contemporaries. Much of this remarkable transformation seems to be thanks to the reality television show *RuPaul's Drag Race* (2009–present).

42. Note the odd transposition of gender from a body to a piece of clothing, so that the gender appears to inhere in the garment instead or as well as in the person wearing the clothing. Clothing is so heavily imbricated with gender (and the body) that garments are constantly metonymically invoked to stand for gender. For instance, "petticoat" was a favored term at the time for femininity, in headlines about Boulton and Park ("men in petticoats" or "the unnatural history and petticoat mystery of Boulton and Park") as well as shorthand for women, as in discussing women's first forays into the professions as "petticoat doctors" and "petticoat lawyers" ("Men in Petticoats," 1870; "Unnatural History," 1870); see also *Englishwoman's Domestic Magazine*, August 1, 1868, 98, or *New York Medical Gazette* 7 (1856): 219. Possibly not unrelated: British English usage persists in a slightly different habit of gendering inanimate objects than commonly seen in American English even today. Witness that public facilities tend to be labeled "female toilet" and "male toilet" as if the gender designation inhered in the rooms themselves rather than their usage.

43. Adding to the trouble with distinguishing between theater and the ordinary was the instability of the terms available to describe clothing. For instance, although costume was used in the manner we use it now to describe the outfits actors and performers donned on stage—clothing donned expressly to be not oneself, related to disguise but generally considered openly legible to viewers that the wearer is pretending to be someone else—it was also used to describe everyday clothing. (To give but one example of costume used in a theater context: an 1870 ad for Miss Azalia Sharp's appearance in Liverpool announces "New costume for the occasion"; *Liverpool Mercury*, February 3, 1870.) A more common term for theater stage clothing was the curiously colloquial "get up" (sometimes with hyphen or without the space) and this phrase also appeared in descriptions of Boulton and Park's "get up" as we will soon see. In contemporary fashion magazines, costume was a favored term to describe any clothing, for instance, attached to physical description or description of function as in "spring costume of buff alpaca," "morning costume," or "promenade costume." (The fashion plates I reference here as representative of the period are contained in the Victoria and Albert Museum Art Library fashion plate collection.)

44. Remember, Barthes and Elizabeth Wilson will both also dwell on clothing's uncanny relation to deceased and absent bodies a century later.

45. Cocks, *Nameless Offences*, 95–96.

46. Cocks, *Nameless Offences*, 96.

47. Simon Gunn, *The Public Culture of the Victorian Middle Class: Ritual and Authority and the English Industrial City, 1840–1914* (Manchester: Manchester University Press, 2000), 77.

48. Mariana Valverde, "The Love of Finery: Fashion and The Fallen Woman in Nineteenth-Century Social Discourse," *Victorian Studies* 32, no. 2 (1989): 168.

49. Gunn, *Public Culture of the Victorian Middle Class*, 66.

50. It is well documented that police generally avoided interfering with suspected prostitutes unless they were causing some disturbance for precisely the reason that they could easily make a mistake in identifying them. See Peter Bailey, "Conspiracies of Meaning: Music-Hall and the Knowingness of Popular Culture," *Past and Present* 144 (August 1994): 161. This, several historians have argued, surely assisted Boulton and Park in avoiding arrest for up to four years. See Charles Upchurch, "Forgetting the Unthinkable: Cross-Dressers and British Society in the Case of the Queen vs. Boulton and Others," *Gender and History* 12, no. 1 (2000): 134.

51. In a Victorian precursor to Supreme Court Justice Potter Stewart's (in)famous declaration of pornography that it could not exactly be defined but "I know it when I see it," one witness declared that Boulton and Park had been witnessed "assuming a number of airs and gestures, which one cannot exactly describe, but those who saw them knew perfectly well what they meant" (DPP 4/6, 11). Paul Gewirtz, "On 'I Know It When I See It.' " *Yale Law Journal* 105, no. 4 (1996): 1023–47.

52. Yes, the lead defense lawyer was named Mr. Straight. And there was a Justice Flowers and a Lord Chief Justice Cockburn.

53. This is probably C. J. Pavitt, the organizer of the Essex amateur theatricals, who appears in several of the more obviously posed photos.

54. For more on the historicization of effeminacy's elision with homosexuality, see Alan Sinfield, *The Wilde Century: Effeminacy, Oscar Wilde, and the Queer Moment* (New York: Columbia University Press, 1994).

55. Simone de Beauvoir, *The Second Sex*, trans. Constance Borde and Sheila Malovany-Chevallier (New York: Vintage Books, 2011), 283.

56. Bailey, "Conspiracies of Meaning," 158.

57. Quoted in Bailey, "Conspiracies of Meaning," 158.

58. Quoted in Bailey, "Conspiracies of Meaning," 150.

59. Bailey, "Conspiracies of Meaning," 156, 158.

60. Bailey's conspiracies of meaning thus could be considered as an analogue to James C. Scott's well-known concept of hidden and public transcripts. See James C. Scott, *Domination and the Arts of Resistance: Hidden Transcripts* (New Haven, CT: Yale University Press, 1992).

61. John Kucich, *The Power of Lies: Transgression in Victorian Fiction* (Ithaca, NY: Cornell University Press, 1994), 3.

62. Bailey, "Conspiracies of Meaning," 168.

63. As obvious as the word seems to be in conjunction with Stella and Fanny, it was baffling enough that no less a queer eminence than Rictor Norton misprints the word as "caw fish" in his anthology of gay love letters. Rictor Norton, ed. *My Dear Boy: Gay Love Letters Through the Centuries* (San Francisco: Leyland Publications, 1998), 157–62. This is presumably a misreading of the handwritten copies of letters in the Public Record Office or (more charitably) a quote from one of the handful of newspapers that reported the word incorrectly.

64. Susan Sontag, "Notes on Camp," in *Susan Sontag: Essays of the 1960s and '70s*, ed. David Reiff (New York: Library of America, 2013), 260, 259.

65. Ernest Boulton and Frederick Park both appear to have emigrated to New York City, where Laurence Senelick turned up evidences that both returned to the music-hall stage. Senelick reports that Park died at age 33 in 1881. Boulton seems to have done somewhat better on stage; a few cartes de visite of Boulton survive under the name Ernest Byne from 1875. His diplomatic career ruined by the trial, John Safford Fiske did spend some time back in the United States but lived out most of the rest of his life (a long one) around Europe, as befitted a nineteenth-century sexual misfit of means. As far as I can tell, Louis Charles Hurt obtained a post as a professor of English in Vienna a few years after the trial and spent the rest of his life abroad as well (d. 1936).

66. Jeffrey Weeks, *Sex, Politics, and Society*, 2nd ed. (London: Longman, 1989), 101; Neil Bartlett, "Evidence: 1870," in *Reclaiming Sodom*, ed. Jonathan Goldberg (New York: Routledge, 1994), 298; and Charles Upchurch, "Forgetting the Unthinkable," 151.

67. Alan Sinfield, *The Wilde Century: Effeminacy, Oscar Wilde, and the Queer Moment* (New York: Columbia University Press, 1994), 8.

68. Butler, "Performative Acts," 527.

Chapter 4

1. Naming conventions of elite Japanese people tend to be complex. The emperor posthumously known as Emperor Meiji was known during his entire

reign (1868–1912) as Mutsuhito, although his name given at birth was Sachinomiya. At the ceremony officially declaring him the crown prince and heir of the throne, he became Mutsuhito. Meiji was the name given to the era of Mutsuhito's reign and, unusually, it was then also chosen as his posthumous designation. Following standard academic conventions, this work uses the name Meiji to refer to the emperor and the era. Donald Keene, *Emperor of Japan: Meiji and His World, 1852–1912* (New York: Columbia University Press, 2002), 14, 52, 706.

2. Some reproductions of this image in photographs and engraved copies of the photograph crop the black rod out of the image, making a more compact portrait and presumably a less odd-looking ensemble for those unfamiliar with traditional court dress of Japan. Keene, *Emperor of Japan*, 194, 237, 773; Takashi Fujitani, *Splendid Monarchy: Power and Pageantry in Modern Japan* (Berkeley: University of California Press, 1998), 175–76.

3. Keene, *Emperor of Japan*, 237, 774. A note on Japanese names in this book: in accordance with current conventions on names in English language work on Japan, I have put Japanese family names first and given names second as is typical in east Asia (in this sentence, the first name written in this way is Uchida Kuichi). The exceptions to this convention are those authors whose English language works are being cited, like Katsuya Hirano and Takashi Fujitani. In hopes of avoiding confusion for readers unfamiliar with Japanese names in the notes and bibliography all author names are given in concert with English conventions (family name last in the endnote and alphabetized first in the Bibliography). Fun fact about the difficulty with names: one of the books I consulted from the UCLA library does indeed have the author's given name printed on its ca. 1950s library buckram spine: MASAAKI. As my tiny contribution toward clarifying a long history of misunderstanding, I sharpied the author's surname Kōsaka into place above.

4. Nakagawa and Rosovsky, "Case of the Dying Kimono," 61.

5. Keene, *Emperor of Japan*, 237.

6. Both these phrases were used by the Satsuma-Chōshū faction of samurai who overthrew the Tokugawa samurai government and instated their own with the emperor as figurehead. I use them here to metonymically describe overarching attitudes toward the foreign intruders who had managed to complete extensive treaties with the US and UK in 1858 and 1859, and then several other European nations whose treaties were based on those initial agreements.

7. David Cannadine, *Ornamentalism: How the British Saw Their Empire* (Oxford: Oxford University Press, 2002).

8. Ellen P. Conant, "Refractions of the Rising Sun" in *Japan and Britain: An Aesthetic Dialogue 1850–1930*, ed. Tomoko Sato and Toshio Watanabe (London: Lund Humphries, 1991), 79.

9. Tomoko Sato and Toshio Watanabe, eds., *Japan and Britain: An Aesthetic Dialogue, 1850–1930* (London: Lund Humphries, 1991), 15.

10. Fujitani, *Splendid Monarchy*, 19–21.

11. Peter Duus, "Presidential Address: Weapons of the Weak, Weapons of the Strong; The Development of the Japanese Political Cartoon," *Journal of Asian Studies* 60, no. 4 (November 2001): 969. See also Timon Screech, *The*

Shogun's Painted Culture: Fear and Creativity in the Japanese States, 1760–1829 (London: Reaktion Books, 2000).

12. Roland Barthes, *Empire of Signs* (New York: Hill and Wang, 1982), 30.

13. Fujitani, *Splendid Monarchy*, 40.

14. Mikiko Ashikari, "The Memory of the Women's White Faces: Japaneseness and the Ideal Image of Women," *Japan Forum* 15, no. 1 (2003): 58.

15. Gregory M. Pflugfelder, "The Nation-State, the Age/Gender System, and the Reconstitution of Erotic Desire in Nineteenth-Century Japan," *Journal of Asian Studies* 71, no. 4 (2012): 963. Pflugfelder is writing particularly with attention to the social distinctions between youth and man, a confluence of age and gender specifications that, while only fuzzily related to physical realities, constituted such major social differences as to comprise practically two different genders. Those who teach the broad outlines of kabuki will easily recognize this distinction from the successive bans placed on *onna* (women's) kabuki, then *wakashu* (youth) kabuki, leaving only *yarō* (adult men's) kabuki.

16. Marius B. Jansen, *The Making of Modern Japan* (Cambridge, MA: Belknap Harvard Press, 2000), 117, 122–23.

17. Amy Stanley, *Stranger in the Shogun's City: A Japanese Woman and Her World* (New York: Scribner, 2020), 116; Katsuya Hirano, *The Politics of Dialogic Imagination: Power and Popular Culture in Early Modern Japan* (Chicago: University of Chicago Press, 2014), 73.

18. Hirano, *Politics of Dialogic Imagination*, 43; Toby Slade, *Japanese Fashion: A Cultural History* (Oxford: Berg, 2009), 35, 37; Donald Shively, "Sumptuary Regulation and Status in Early Tokugawa Japan," *Harvard Journal of Asiatic Studies* 25 (1964): 124.

19. Satoko Shimazaki, *Edo Kabuki in Transition: From the Worlds of the Samurai to the Vengeful Female Ghost* (New York: Columbia University Press, 2016), 88; Hirano, *Politics of Dialogic Imagination*, 43.

20. Slade, *Japanese Fashion*, 37; Hirano, *Politics of Dialogic Imagination*, 57.

21. Donald Shively, "The Social Environment of Tokugawa Kabuki," in *Japanese Aesthetics and Culture: A Reader*, ed. Nancy G. Hume (Albany: State University of New York Press, 1995), 225.

22. Maki Isaka, *Onnagata: A Labyrinth of Gendering in Kabuki Theater* (Seattle: University of Washington Press, 2016), 5; Hirano, *Politics of Dialogic Imagination*, 170; Loren Edelson, *Danjūrō's Girls: Women on the Kabuki Stage* (New York: Palgrave Macmillan, 2009), v; Katherine Mezur, *Beautiful Boys / Outlaw Bodies: Devising Kabuki Female-Likeness* (New York: Palgrave Macmillan, 2005), 14.

23. Hirano, *Politics of Dialogic Imagination*, 170–71.

24. Hirano covers the disruptive potential of urban popular culture extensively in *Dialogic Imagination*.

25. Howell, *Geographies of Identity*, 16.

26. Edward Said, *Orientalism* (New York: Vintage Books, 1979).

27. Yukichi Fukuzawa, *Seiyo Jijo* (Tokyo: Shōkodō, 1866).

28. Keio University (Tokyo) has made digital copies of Fukuzawa's works available online at https://dcollections.lib.keio.ac.jp/en/about. A digital version

of *Seiyo ishokuju* can be found at https://iiif.lib.keio.ac.jp/FKZ/F7-A06/pdf/F7-A06.pdf.

29. Hirano, *Politics of Dialogic Imagination*, 200–1.

30. Howell, *Geographies of Identity*, 165; Kunio Yanagida, *Japanese Manners and Customs in the Meiji Era* (Tokyo: Ōbunsha, 1957), 28.

31. Suzanne O'Brien, "Splitting Hairs: History and the Politics of Daily Life in Nineteenth-Century Japan," *Journal of Asian Studies* 67, no. 4 (2008): 1309. O'Brien's article provides an excellent analysis of both the uses of this rhyme and Meiji haircutting in general as an overdetermined object of historiographical fascination. Most importantly, she marshals significant evidence to complicate the apparent steady forward trajectory of progress celebrated in the rhyme.

32. Keene, *Emperor of Japan*, 237–47; and Jansen, *Making of Modern Japan*, 369–70.

33. *Shinbun* Zasshi 1873, 47, https://dl.ndl.go.jp/pid/898142/1/47. Translated in Masaaki Kōsaka, *Japanese Thought in the Meiji Era*, trans. David Abosch (Tokyo: Pan-Pacific Press, 1958), 58. The Kōsaka/Abosch excerpt does not contain the article's further note about the shop owner's own uncut hair. Thanks to Mariko Takano who assisted with the legwork of finding these original publications in the NDL online archives and translation.

34. Howell, *Geographies of Identity*, 160.

35. Translation from Kōsaka, *Japanese Thought in the Meiji Era*, 58. The original article can be found in the *Shinbun Zasshi* (1873) in the National Diet Library online archives: http://dl.ndl.go.jp/info:ndljp/pid/1920332.

36. Martha McClintock, "Okuhara Seiko (1837–1913): The Life and Arts of a Meiji Period Literati Artist" (PhD diss., University of Michigan, 1991), 29. Yurika Wakamatsu translates *gyakujō no shō* as a "rush of blood to the head," although "fit of madness" is a typical meaning of this phrase, and McClintock (in contrast) has translated it as such. It's interesting to consider both of these possibilities as reasons to allow a woman to cut her hair short. Yurika Wakamatsu, "Painting in Between: Gender and Modernity in the Japanese Literati Art of Okuhara Seiko (1837–1913)" (PhD diss., Harvard University, 2016), 4.

37. Sharon L. Sievers, *Flowers in Salt: The Beginnings of Feminist Consciousness in Modern Japan* (Stanford, CA: Stanford University Press, 1983), 15. Howell discusses this passage in *Geographies of Identity*, 160.

38. Oku Takenori, *Bunmei kaika to minshū: Kindai Nihon seishinshi no danshō* (Tokyo: Shinhyōron, 1993), 18–20. Glossed in David L. Howell, "The Girl with the Horse-Dung Hairdo," in *Looking Modern: East Asian Visual Culture from Treaty Ports to World War II*, ed. Jennifer Purtle and Hans Bjarne Thomsen (Chicago: Art Media Resources, 2009), 204.

39. Howell, *Geographies of Identity*, 168.

40. Presumably by "unhygienic," the activists are referring to the oils required for the lacquered appearance of traditional hairstyles coupled with the infrequent washing this entailed. Translations of this print and most others were primarily done by Mariko Takano, with additional translation, confirmation, assistance, and editing by Michelle Liu Carriger and Ken Shima.

41. "Pot-town hairdo" is overly comic, although it is the literal translation of the characters for *nabechou mage*. The *nabechou mage* was a popular hairstyle in the 1860s, albeit closely related to other traditional styles like *shimada*

mage. See, e.g., Yasutaka Kanazawa, *Edo keppatsushi* (Tokyo: Seiyabō, 1961), 285; Ryūen Hiromatsu, *Kurokami to bijo no nihonshi* (Tokyo: Suiyōen, 2012); or Rieko Ōhara, *Kurokami no bunkashi* (Tokyo: Tsukiji Shokan, 1988).

42. *Shōjo* more or less means "girl" but the *shōjo* has come to occupy a highly evocative place in Japanese culture, both for those who may be named *shōjo* but also for those who will never be *shōjo*. Much more on this in chapter 5. Nobuko Anan, *Contemporary Japanese Women's Theatre and Visual Arts: Performing Girls' Aesthetics* (London: Palgrave Macmillan, 2016); John Whittier Treat, "Yoshimoto Banana Writes Home: *Shōjo* Culture and the Nostalgic Subject," *Society for Japanese Studies* 19, no. 2 (Summer 1993): 353–87.

43. Rebecca Copeland, "Fashioning the Feminine: Images of the Modern Girl Student in Meiji," *U.S.-Japan Women's Journal*, nos. 30/31 (2006): 18; Tomoko Namba, "School Uniform Reforms in Modern Japan," *Fashion, Identity, and Power in Modern Asia*, edited by Kyunghee Pyun and Aida Yuen Wong (Cham, Switzerland: Springer International, 2018), 91–113.

44. I will continue to use the word ukiyo-e here since in English it has come to describe all Japanese woodblock prints, but strictly speaking a better term would be *nishiki-e* (brocade pictures) which in Japanese more accurately describes all woodblock prints, while *ukiyo-e* refers more narrowly to pictures that depict the courtesans and theaterfolk of the *ukiyo* floating world.

45. To be fair, a few concessions to new looks sometimes appear, such as European-style umbrellas or (in one eyewitness report) in the form of the empress's incongruous boots and pink European parasol worn with ceremonial dress. Howell, "Girl with the Horse-Dung Hairdo," 205.

46. Fujitani, *Splendid Monarchy*, 110.

47. Fujitani, *Splendid Monarchy*, 13, 97; Morris Low, *Japan on Display: Photography and the Emperor* (London: Routledge, 2006), 14.

48. "Exhibitory modernity" comes from Morris Low's *Japan on Display*, although Low is developing the term from Qin Shao, *Culturing Modernity: The Nantong Model, 1890–1930* (Stanford, CA: Stanford University Press, 2003). Fujitani, *Splendid Monarchy*, 166.

49. Fujitani, *Splendid Monarchy*, 177.

50. Low, *Japan on Display*, 14. Low describes the treatment of the imperial portraits of Emperor Meiji and Empress Haruko in the newly organized public schools: "Schools were required to provide a safe, fixed home for the sacred pictures and imperial rescript on education. Teachers took turns at safeguarding them as if their very lives depended on it. While the words of the emperor contained in the imperial rescript were seen as important, it was the images of the imperial couple that were treated with special care. The photographs were seen as shadows of the emperor and empress, their bunshin (their other selves). Both female and male teachers were involved in protecting the sacred portrait, with men in particular assigned the job at night. It was only after the Second World War that such guard duty came to an end in schools" (*Japan on Display*, 14).

51. Donald Keene, *Japan at the Dawn of the Modern Age: Woodblock Prints from the Meiji Era, 1868–1912, Selections from the Jean S. and Frederic A. Sharf Collection at the Museum of Fine Arts, Boston* (Boston: Museum of Fine Arts, 2001), 4.

52. Digital images of these prints are both available from the Metropolitan Museum of Art online database: https://www.metmuseum.org/art/collection/search/55499 and https://www.metmuseum.org/art/collection/search/55345.

53. The empress's proclamation was published in the January 17, 1887, issue of the *Chōya Shimbun.* This translation comes from Julia Meech-Pekarik, *The World of the Meiji Print* (New York: Weatherhill, 1986), 129.

54. Note that the tea depicted in this image is the matcha format of brazier-made tea in a tatami room. While today a hospitable practice like tea seems overwhelmingly feminine, and currently about 90 percent of tea ceremony practitioners in Japan are women, this was a new innovation in 1893, when the orthodox schools of tea study were rebranding from upwardly mobile gentlemanly and samurai distinction to a form of ladylike cultivation. For more on women and tea, see Rebecca Corbett, *Cultivating Femininity: Women and Tea Culture in Edo and Meiji Japan* (Honolulu: University of Hawai'i Press, 2016); Michelle Liu Carriger, "ElasticiTEA? Preliminary Theses on Cross-Cultural (re)Presentation and the Japanese 'Way of Tea,'" *GPS: Global Performance Studies* 4, no. 1 (2021); or Etsuko Kato, *The Tea Ceremony and Women's Empowerment in Modern Japan* (London: Routledge, 2004).

55. Sally Hastings, "The Empress' New Clothes and Japanese Women, 1868–1912," *Historian* 55, no. 4 (Summer 1993): 678.

56. Fujitani, *Splendid Monarchy*, 180.

57. Slade, *Japanese Fashion*, 41; portions of Slade's book stray extremely close to text by Meech-Pekarik in *World of the Meiji Print*, who discusses the same interchange, 137–43.

58. The relevant Hollander tome is Anne Hollander, *Sex and Suits* (New York: Knopf, 1994).

59. Fujitani, *Splendid Monarchy*, 19.

60. Erwin O. E. von Baelz, *Awakening Japan: The Diary of a German Doctor; Erwin Baelz* (Bloomington: Indiana University Press, 1974), 30–31.

61. Isabella Bird, *Unbeaten Tracks in Japan*, reprint (1880; London: Virago Press, 1984), 15.

62. Henry T. Finck, *Lotos-Time in Japan* (New York: Charles Scribner's Sons, 1895), 112.

63. Henry Spencer Palmer, *Letters from the Land of the Rising Sun: Being a Selection from Correspondence Contributed to "The Times" between the Years 1886 and 1892 . . . with Seventy-Six Illustrations* (Yokohama: Japan Mail, 1894), 65.

64. I consulted Meiji-era photography books like the following, but with little sense that national defects could be detected in the bodies depicted: Ozawa Takeshi, *Shashin de miru bakumatsu Meiji* (Tokyo: Sekai bunkasha, 1990); Keishō Ishiguro, *Meiji Taishō Shōwa Tōkyō shashin daishūsei* (Tokyo: Shinchōsha, 2001); Toshio Takebe and Kazunori Nakamura, eds., *Meiji no Nihon: Kunaichō Shoryōbu shozō shashin* (Tokyo: Yoshikawa Kōbunkan, 2000); Mainichi shinbunsha, *Shashin Meiji Taisho 60-nenshi* (Tokyo: Mainichi shinbunsha tosho henshūbu, 1956).

65. In addition to the photography books listed in the previous note, books on tourist imagery which contain the types of images I describe include Sebastian Dobson, *Art and Artifice: Japanese Photographs of the Meiji Era:*

Selections from the Jean S. and Frederic A. Sharf Collection at the Museum of Fine Arts, Boston. (Boston: Museum of Fine Arts Publications, 2004); Nicole Coolidge Rousmaniere and Mikiko Hirayama, eds., *Reflecting Truth: Japanese Photography in the Nineteenth Century* (Amsterdam: Hotei Publishing, 2004); Christine Guth, *Longfellow's Tattoos: Tourism, Collecting, and Japan* (Seattle: University of Washington Press, 2004); Eleanor M. Hight, *Capturing Japan in Nineteenth-Century New England Photography Collections* (Farnham, UK: Ashgate, 2011).

66. Meech-Pekarik, *World of the Meiji Print*, 112.

67. The two images of which I speak here pop up in various histories and collections. The three-quarter-profile image is an albumen silver print with applied color attributed to von Stillfried with the title [Studio Portrait of a Japanese Man in Western Clothing], https://www.metmuseum.org/art/collection/search/287979. The second print, not attributed to von Stillfried, is a direct facing figure without background (Peabody Museum of Archaeology and Ethnology, Harvard University, http://www.luminous-lint.com/app/image/09456623531210923955173/.%20%3c%3cMR; a copy from a private collection, printed in Meech-Pekarik, *The World of the Meiji Print* (182), is attributed to him and dated 1870s. In his monograph on von Stillfried, Luke Gartlan discusses the former image of the man's ill-fitting costume in some detail, further pointing out that this image does not appear in von Stillfried's oeuvre until after his business partnership with the German expatriate Herman Andersen failed, von Stillfried left Japan, and Andersen appropriated the Stillfried name (and library of negatives) to continue selling prints to tourists and Yokohama locals familiar with the Baron's name. Gartlan considers the image "part of broader hostilities" toward Japanese adoptions of *yōfuku*, but feels these inclinations should be attributed to Andersen, not von Stillfried whose primary attitude toward *Bunmei Kaika* in his photographic work was to carefully excise its evidence from his imagery (*A Career of Japan*, 245). The pair of images thus not only index a derisive attitude toward Japanese bodies in *yōfuku* dress, they also reveal a thorny historiographical problem of how to evaluate images which endlessly replicated into tourist albums and publications that sailed off to innumerable locations around the globe, promiscuously trading hands not only after the point of sale, but also before as Yokohama photographers partnered and split in a messy dance, selling and trading their collections of plates and negatives, altering and adding to the images and their contexts over decades. (This tendency also explains why the images can bear date ranges up to twenty years apart [and more]). The Peabody date, circa 1870, is too early in my opinion, as I concur with Gartlan's estimate of 1879—and the Metropolitan Museum image is dated 1880s.)

68. Eliza Ruhamah Scidmore, *Jinrikisha Days in Japan* (New York: Harper and Bros., 1902), 216.

69. Pierre Loti, "Japanese Women in 1890," in *Carmen Sylva and Sketches from the Orient*, trans. Fred Rothwell (New York: Macmillan, 1912), 187.

70. Pierre Loti, "Un bal à Yeddo," in *Japoneries d'automne* (Paris: Calman Lévy, 1898), 105–6. Translated by the author in consultation with partial translation in Meech-Pekarik, *World of the Meiji Print*, 151.

71. Keene, *Emperor of Japan*, 392.

72. Sally Hastings, "A Dinner Party Is Not a Revolution," *US-Japan Women's Journal*, no. 18 (2000): 112.

73. See, e.g., Sukehiro Hirakawa, *Japan's Love-Hate Relationship with the West* (Folkestone, UK: Global Oriental, 2005), 117–48.

74. Hastings, "Dinner Party," 120.

75. Georges Bigot seems to be largely unknown in Anglophone literature, but is very prominent in Japanese histories of the Meiji period, meriting multivolume series on his work as a foreign correspondent who provided extensive drawn and painted imagery to the European press for their publications on Japan throughout the latter nineteenth and early twentieth centuries. See Tadayasu Sakai, *Bigō gashū: Fūshi fūzoku sobyō* (Tokyo: Iwasaki Bijutsusha, 1973); Tōrū Haga, *Bigō sobyō korekushon*, vols. 1–3 (Tokyo: Iwanami Shoten, 1989); Isao Shimizu, *E de kaita Nihonjin ron: Joruju Bigō no sekai* (Tokyo: Chūō Kōronsha, 1981).

76. Duus, "Presidential Address," 977.

77. The Morse referenced here is Edward S. Morse, a prominent American *yatoi* who served as the first professor of zoology at Tokyo Imperial University from 1877 to 1880. The gist of the cartoon about being descended from monkeys suggests Morse had been teaching Darwinian theories of evolution, a notion corroborated by another *Marumaru Chimbun* cartoon that explicitly namechecks "Professor Morse" in conjunction with Darwinism in the February 15, 1879, issue. Translated and edited by Mariko Hirano and Michelle Liu Carriger.

78. See, e.g., McClintock, *Imperial Leather*, 216; Brett A. Berliner, "Mephistopheles and Monkeys: Rejuvenation, Race, and Sexuality in Popular Culture in Interwar France," *Journal of the History of Sexuality* 13, no. 3 (2004): 306–25; and Sophie Chao, "We Are (Not) Monkeys": Contested Cosmopolitical Symbols in West Papua," *American Ethnologist* 48, no. 3 (2021): 274–87.

79. Leila May, "Monkeys, Microcephalous Idiots and the Barbarous Race of Mankind," *Victorian Newsletter* (Fall 2002): 20–27.

80. Emiko Ohnuki-Tierney's book *The Monkey as Mirror* (Princeton, NJ: Princeton Unversity Press, 1987) traces multiple uses of monkey tropes across Japanese history, as well as their special association with *burakumin* (Ohnuki-Tierney uses the term "special status people") and the use of living monkeys in folk street performances associated with *burakumin*.

81. Charles Wirgman founder and nearly sole publisher of the *Japan Punch* has so far managed to largely escape my text. In line with its British forebear, the *Japan Punch* was a long running Yokohama publication that provided fairly equal opportunity satire on Yokohama expatriates and the Japanese. Amongst a handful of cartoons and articles lampooning Japanese experiments in *yōfuku*, there are no monkey references, but there is a drawing of a parrot from 1872. The parrot is labeled "Young Japan" and is eating a lump labeled "beef" next to a bottle labeled "Bass Pale Ale" (with Bass's logo). The caption reads, "Portrait of a foolish bird who thought he could become a man by eating beef and drinking beer." Wirgman's cartoon functions in an analogue manner to the fashion critiques I have been describing while aimed at another aspect of *Bunmei Kaika* and using another animal famed for "empty" imitation. See the parrot cartoon in Josef Rogala, *The Genius of Mr. Punch*, trans.

Hitomi Yamashita (Tokyo: Yurindo, 2004), 147; Tōru Haga, *Wāguman sobyō korekushon* (Tokyo: Iwanami Shoten, 2002), 1:118.

82. Griffis's work was reprinted and expanded through several editions after first publication in 1876. The easiest to access now is William E. Griffis, *The Mikado's Empire* (New York: Harper and Brothers, 1896) and "The Mikado's Empire," *Harper's New Monthly Magazine*, September 1876, 514.

83. Henry Norman, *The Real Japan: Studies of Contemporary Japanese Manners, Morals, Administration, and Politics* (London: T. Fisher Unwin, 1892), 354.

84. Homi K. Bhabha, *The Location of Culture* (London: Routledge, 2004), 122.

85. Charles Fisher put it, "Japan was in effect already playing the West at its own game in reverse, for instead of succumbing to the familiar imperialist tactic of divide and rule it was initiating what proved to be a highly effective counter policy of select and survive." Fisher, "The Britain of the East? A Study in the Geography of Imitation," *Modern Asian Studies* 2, no. 4 (1968): 351.

86. See, e.g., Donald Roden, "Thoughts on the Early Meiji Gentleman," in *Gendering Modern Japanese History*, ed. Barbara Molony and Kathleen Uno, 61–98 (Cambridge, MA: Harvard University Press, 2008). On the gender of theatricality: Efrat Tseëlon, "The Lady Is a Fake," in Tseëlon, *Masque of Femininity*, 33–53.

87. Quoted in Hastings, "Empress' New Clothes," 691.

88. Jason G. Karlin, *Gender and Nation in Meiji Japan: Modernity, Loss, and the Doing of History* (Honolulu: University of Hawai'i Press, 2014), 43.

89. Quoted in Karlin, *Gender and Nation in Meiji Japan*, 44.

90. Dick Hebdige, *Subculture: The Meaning of Style* (London: Routledge, 1979), 106–12, 114–27.

91. Karlin, *Gender and Nation in Meiji Japan*, 15.

92. Uma Narayan, *Dislocating Cultures: Identities, Traditions, and Third-World Feminism* (New York: Routledge, 1997).

93. Karlin, *Gender and Nation in Meiji Japan*, 15.

94. The *sōshi*, along with the related Freedom and People's Rights Movement, more or less faded away after the successful ratification of the Meiji Constitution in 1889 and the convening of the National Diet in 1890. Jansen, *Making of Modern Japan*, 380; Karlin, *Gender and Nation in Meiji Japan*, 9–10, 236.

95. "Quaint and exquisite" names two recurring modifiers for the status of Japanese things and sometimes people in Victorian Britain and is reflected in the title of Grace Lavery's book on that topic: *Quaint, Exquisite: Victorian Aesthetics and the Idea of Japan* (Princeton, NJ: Princeton University Press, 2019).

96. Rey Chow, *The Protestant Ethnic and the Spirit of Capitalism* (New York: Columbia University Press, 2002), 107–8.

97. Chow, *Protestant Ethnic*, 37.

98. Chow, *Protestant Ethnic*, 107.

99. Katharine Schuyler Baxter, *In Beautiful Japan: A Story of Bamboo Lands* (1895; New York: Hobart, 1904).

100. Baxter, *In Beautiful Japan*, 355.

101. See Bush's compelling article "The Ethnicity of Things in America's Lacquered Age," 74–98.

102. Augusta Campbell Davidson, *Present-Day Japan* (Philadelphia: J. B. Lippincott, 1904), 4.

103. For more authors who think through the touristic production of an "authentic" Japan, see Philipp March and Claudia Delank, eds., *The Adventure of Japanese Photography 1860–1890* (Heidelberg: Kehrer Verlag, 2003), 14; Luke Gartlan, *A Career of Japan: Baron Raimund von Stillfried and Early Yokohama Photography* (Leiden: Brill, 2016); Christine Guth, *Longfellow's Tattoos*; Eleanor M. Hight, *Capturing Japan*; and Allen Hockley, "Packaged Tours: Photo Albums and the Implications for the Study of Early Japanese Photography," in *Reflecting Truth: Japanese Photography in the Nineteenth Century*, ed. Nicole Coolidge Rousmaniere and Mikiko Hirayama, 64–83 (Leiden: Brill, 2004).

104. "Vienna International Exposition and Japonism," *Expositions: where the modern technology of the times was exhibited* online exhibition, National Diet Library. Last modified April 17, 2017, https://www.ndl.go.jp/exposition/e/s1/1873-2.html.

105. Guth, *Longfellow's Tattoos*; Hight, *Capturing Japan*; March and Delank, *Adventure of Japanese Photography*, 10–11; and Hockley, "Packaged Tours."

106. Numerous recent works treat the wealth of tourist imagery extant from the 1860s to the 1900s. See, e.g., Dobson, *Art and Artifice*; Guth, *Longfellow's Tattoos*; Hight, *Capturing Japan*; March and Delank, *Adventure of Japanese Photography*; and Gartlan, *A Career of Japan*.

107. Rickshaw is the bastardization of *jinrikisha* ("person-powered vehicles"). For all their quaintness today, rickshaws are in fact a modern innovation that combined the traditional pole-suspended palanquin with new influences, appearing first in Japan around 1870.

108. See Gartlan, *A Career of Japan*; or March and Delank, *Adventure of Japanese Photography*.

109. Gartlan, *A Career of Japan*; Dobson, *Art and Artifice*.

110. Basil Hall Chamberlain, *Things Japanese: Being Notes on Various Subjects Connected with Japan* (London: Kegan Paul, Trench, Trübner, 1890), 354–55.

111. Representative images can be found reprinted in Kanagawa Prefectural Museum of Cultural History, *Yokohama kaikou 160nen Yokohama ukiyo-e* (Yokohama: Kanagawa Prefectural Museum of Cultural History, 2019), 81, 119; Ann Yonemura, *Yokohama: Prints from Nineteenth-Century Japan* (Washington, DC: Smithsonian Institution, 1990), 119.

112. Maxwell, *Patriots against Fashion*, 5.

113. See Josephine Lee's *The Japan of Pure Invention: Gilbert and Sullivan's The Mikado* (Minneapolis: University of Minnesota Press, 2010) for an exhaustive account of *The Mikado*'s relationship to Victorian Orientalism and Japan.

114. Oscar Wilde, "The Decay of Lying" (1889), in *Intentions* (Leipzig: Heineman and Ballestier, 1891), 38.

115. Jennifer Robertson, "Introduction: Putting and Keeping Japan in Anthropology," in *A Companion to the Anthropology of Japan*, ed. Jennifer Robertson (Malden, MA: Blackwell Publishing, 2005), 5.

116. Robertson, "Introduction," 7.

117. Philip Swift, "Cosmetic Cosmologies in Japan: Notes Toward a Superficial Investigation" (Working Paper Series 4, Open Anthropology Cooperative Press, October 10, 2010), 2, http://openanthcoop.net/press/2010/10/09/cosmetic-cosmologies-in-japan/.

118. Swift, "Cosmetic Cosmologies in Japan."

119. Takeo Doi, *The Anatomy of Self: The Individual Versus Society* (Tokyo: Kodansha USA Publishing, 1985), 37.

120. Doi, *Anatomy of Self*, 43.

121. Doi, *Anatomy of Self*, 45.

122. Doi, *Anatomy of Self*, 35.

123. Swift, "Cosmetic Cosmologies in Japan."

124. Meech-Pekarik, *World of the Meiji Print*, 143.

125. The *Kojiki* (*Record of Ancient Matters*) and *Nihonshoki* (*The Chronicles of Japan*) are considered the two oldest literary works in Japanese. Completed within about ten years of each other near the beginning of the eighth century CE, they record historical and mythological accounts of gods, cosmology, emperors and assorted strange tales up until about the sixth century CE.

126. The replacement of Jingu is apparently justified by declaring that Ojin was gestated by Jingu for somewhere around fifteen years. Ojin receives credit for the conquest of Korea by these parasitic fetal means in the revised history and Jingu can be excised from the lineage. See H. Paul Varley, trans., *A Chronicle of Gods and Sovereigns: Jinnō shōtōki of Kitabatake Chikafusa* (New York: Columbia University Press, 1980), 101–3.

127. Peter Duus, *The Abacus and the Sword: The Japanese Penetration of Korea, 1895–1910* (Berkeley: University of California Press, 1998), 48.

Chapter 5

1. William Eleroy Curtis, *The Yankees of the East: Sketches of Modern Japan* (New York: Duffield, 1906), https://catalog.hathitrust.org/Record/006535094.

2. Tiffany Godoy, *Style Deficit Disorder: Harajuku Street Fashion, Tokyo* (San Francisco: Chronicle Books, 2007), 11.

3. Izumi Evers, Patrick Macias, and Kazumi Nonaka, *Japanese Schoolgirl Inferno: Tokyo Teen Fashion Subculture Handbook* (San Francisco: Chronicle Books, 2007), 58–85.

4. Ikuya Sato, *Kamikaze Biker: Parody and Anomy in Affluent Japan* (Chicago: University of Chicago Press, 1998), 114, and "Play Theory of Delinquency: Toward a General Theory of 'Action,'" *Symbolic Interaction* 11, no. 2 (1988): 202; Evers, Macias, and Nonaka, *Japanese Schoolgirl Inferno*, 34–45.

5. This is Ted Polhemus's not-uncontroversial phrase for fashion subcultures. See Polhemus, *Streetstyle: From Sidewalk to Catwalk* (London: Thames and Hudson, 1994).

6. Caroline Evans, *Fashion at the Edge: Spectacle, Modernity and Deathliness* (New Haven, CT: Yale University Press, 2003), 6.

7. Hollander, *Sex and Suits*; Schneider, *The Explicit Body in Performance*; Felski, *Gender of Modernity*.

8. Here I am following Koichi Iwabuchi's theorization of Japanese cultural exports in *Recentering Globalization*.

9. A 2018 Rufflechat post by Asma Ab, December 17, 2018, indexed a "lone-lita" (lolita practitioner without a local community) in Turkey, another unidentified Middle Eastern country, and several other locations: https://www.facebook.com/groups/rufflechat/permalink/1929338613828147. English-speaking lolitas have also compiled a Google spreadsheet of known lolita communities (usually called "comms") that gives a general overview of the international reach of the subculture: https://docs.google.com/spreadsheets/d/1evXegSoFbfEXn8o0joeA-KFvolNKPKllgvaYqNgvOiw/edit?usp=sharing.

10. As I prepared this book for print in 2020–21, lolita fashion's "con" (convention) culture sustained a serious blow, as so many other culture industries built on in-person gathering did during the global COVID-19 pandemic. All big meetups, cons, and most smaller tea parties and other gatherings migrated online, and the global circuits of fashion shipping were heavily curtailed; Japan in particular restricted international shipping and circuits between China and the rest of the world were severely disrupted. At the point of copyedits in 2023, shipping had been largely restored and in person gatherings are returning, but it's currently unclear whether they'll ever regain their prepandemic levels.

11. A representative popular media article on gothic lolita fashion would be Kai-Ming Cha, "Sweet and Sour in a Frilly Dress: Gothic Lolita Hits the U.S.," *Publishers Weekly*, January 3, 2005.

12. For more encyclopedic treatments, see Winge, "Undressing and Dressing Loli"; Evers, Macias, and Nonaka, *Japanese Schoolgirl Inferno*; and An Nguyen, "Maiden's Fashion as Eternal Becomings: Victorian Maidens and Sugar Sweet Cuties Donning Japanese Street Fashion in Japan and North America" (PhD diss., University of Western Ontario, 2012).

13. Yuniya Kawamura, *Fashioning Japanese Subcultures* (New York: Berg, 2012), 72.

14. Kawamura, *Fashioning Japanese Subcultures*, 29.

15. Valerie Steele, Patricia Mears, Yuniya Kawamura, and Hiroshi Narumi, *Japan Fashion Now* (New Haven, CT: Yale University Press, 2010), 96; Don Cameron, "Off-the-Rack Identities: Japanese Street Fashion Magazines and the Commodification of Style." *Japanese Studies* 20, no. 2 (September 2000): 179–87, https://doi.org/10.1080/713683780.

16. "Moi-Même-Moitié: Elegant, Gothic Lolita, Aristocrat, Vampire, Romance," https://moi-meme-moitie.com/.

17. Vladimir Nabokov, *Lolita*, ed. Alfred Appel (New York: Vintage Books, 1991).

18. Shoichi Aoki, *Fruits* (New York: Phaidon, 2001) *Fresh Fruits* (New York: Phaidon, 2005); *Gothic & Lolita* (New York: Phaidon, 2007); Izumi Evers, Patrick Macias, and Kazumi Nonaka, *Japanese Schoolgirl Inferno: Tokyo Teen Fashion Subculture Handbook* (San Francisco: Chronicle Books, 2007); Tiffany Godoy, *Style Deficit Disorder: Harajuku Street Fashion Tokyo*

(San Francisco: Chronicle Books, 2007); Tiffany Godoy, Ivan Vartanian, Keiko Hirayama, and Tetsuya Suzuki, *Tokyo Street Style: Fashion in Harajuku* (London: Thames and Hudson, 2008); Philomena Kent and Yuri Manabe, *The Tokyo Look Book: Stylish to Spectacular, Goth to Gyaru, Sidewalk to Catwalk* (Tokyo: Kodansha USA, 2007); Tiffany Godoy and Ivan Vartanian, *Japanese Goth* (New York: Universe, 2009); Pat Lyttle, *Japanese Street Style* (London: A&C Black, 2012); and Manami Okazaki and Geoff Johnson, *Kawaii! Japan's Culture of Cute* (Munich: Prestel, 2013),

19. We might think of this process as roughly analogue and preceding the phenomenon of the social media celebrity, many of whom, of course, have also created their own spaces not just through the knack of crafting viral images, but through savvy combinations of institutional assistance and framing, which are usually obscured.

20. There is much to be said about Japan's "Cool Japan" and other soft power campaigns. See Laura Miller, "Cute Masquerade and the Pimping of Japan," *International Journal of Japanese Sociology* 20 (2011): 19–20; and Iwabuchi, *Recentering Globalization.*

21. *Kamikaze Girls* is a choice of translation which has nothing to do with gothic lolita fashion or Takemoto's narrative. Shimotsuma is a town in Ibaraki prefecture, about two hours outside Tokyo by rail, and "Shimotsuma monogatari" simply means "Shimotsuma story" and comes off as a tongue-in-cheek nod to classical Japanese titling conventions—that is, *Genji monogatari* for *The Tale of Genji.* Presumably translators and marketers of the English language book and movie felt "Kamikaze" was a more recognizable and saleable word than Shimotsuma.

22. Takemoto Novala, *Kamikaze Girls*, trans. Masumi Washington (San Francisco: VIZ Media, 2008), 1.

23. Ho, *Neo-Victorianism*, 9.

24. Ho, *Neo-Victorianism*, 11.

25. Evans, *Fashion at the Edge*, 9.

26. Evans, *Fashion at the Edge, 11.*

27. David Graham, "Gothic Lolitas: Goth Girls Just Wanna Have Fun!," *Gothic E-Zine*, December 31, 2012, http://gothic.lilithezine.com/gothic_lolitas.html.

28. Amy Wilkins, *Wannabes, Goths, and Christians: The Boundaries of Sex Styles and Status* (Chicago: University of Chicago Press, 2008), 44.

29. For example, Amy Wilkins and Paul Hodkinson, *Goth: Identity, Style and Subculture* (Oxford: Berg, 2002), 79; Lauren M. E. Goodlad and Michael Bibby, "Introduction," in *Goth: Undead Subculture* (Durham, NC: Duke University Press, 2007), 12–13; and Gavin Baddeley, *Goth Chic* (London: Plexus, 2002), 19.

30. I won't spend very much time here on *kawaii* which has its own robust set of scholarship. See Anne Allison, "Cuteness as Japan's Millennial Product," in *Pikachu's Global Adventure: The Rise and Fall of Pokemon*, (Durham, NC: Duke University Press, 2004), 34–49, https://doi.org/10.1215/9780822385813-003.

31. Frances Richards, "Fifteen Theses on the Cute," *Cabinet Magazine* 4 (Fall 2001), http://cabinetmagazine.org/issues/4/cute.php, emphasis in the original.

32. "Chrononormativity" is adopted from Elizabeth Freeman's work in *Time Binds: Queer Temporalities, Queer Histories*, (Durham, NC: Duke University Press, 2010); Anan, *Contemporary Japanese Women's Theatre and Visual Arts*, 22–23.

33. *Kamikaze Girls*, directed by Tetsuya Nakashima (Tokyo: Tōhō Kabushiki Kaisha / VIZ Media, 2004), DVD.

34. Jane Mai and An Nguyen, *So Pretty / Very Rotten: Comics and Essays on Lolita Fashion and Cute Culture* (Toronto: Koyama Press, 2017), 9.

35. Jennifer Robertson, *Takarazuka: Sexual Politics and Popular Culture in Modern Japan* (Berkeley: University of California Press, 1996), 66; Anan, *Contemporary Japanese Women's Theatre*, 33.

36. For more on moga and shōjo culture and history, see Indra Levy, *Sirens of the Western Shore: The Westernesque Femme Fatale, Translation, and Vernacular Style in Modern Japanese Literature* (New York: Columbia University Press, 2006); Rebecca Copeland, "Fashioning the Feminine: Images of the Modern Girl Student in Meiji," *U.S.-Japan Women's Journal*, nos. 30/31 (2006): 13–35; Laura Miller and Jan Bardsley, eds., *Bad Girls of Japan* (Basingstoke, UK: Palgrave Macmillan, 2011); Frenchy Lunning, "Under the Ruffles: Shōjo and the Morphology of Power," *Mechademia* 6 (2011): 3–19; and Jaqueline Berndt, Kazumi Nagaike, and Fusami Ogi, eds., *Shōjo Across Media: Exploring "Girl" Practices in Contemporary Japan* (Basingstoke, UK: Palgrave Macmillan, 2019).

37. Robertson, *Takarazuka*, 4. For more on *moga*, see, e.g., Alisa Freedman, Laura Miller, and Christine Reiko Yano, *Modern Girls on the Go: Gender, Mobility, and Labor in Japan* (Stanford, CA: Stanford University Press, 2013), 6.

38. Isaac Gagné's 2008 article on linguistics and the gothic lolita contains much more on the subject of language, writing, and gothic lolitas. See Gagné, "Urban Princesses."

39. Douglas Quenqua, "They're Like, Way Ahead of the Linguistic Currrrve," *New York Times*, February 27, 2012, https://www.nytimes.com/2012/02/28/science/young-women-often-trendsetters-in-vocal-patterns.html.

40. The plural of Japanese nouns is the same as the singular: one *shōjo*, two *shōjo*.

41. Quoted in Treat, "Yoshimoto Banana Writes Home," 363; Naoto Horikiri, "Onna wa dokyō, shōjo wa aikyō," in *Shōjo ron*; ed. Naoto Honda et al. (Tokyo: Aoyumi Sha, 1991), 108–9.

42. Anan, *Contemporary Japanese Women's Theatre and Visual Arts*, 22.

43. Anan, *Contemporary Japanese Women's Theatre and Visual Arts*, 18.

44. Quoted in Nguyen, "Maiden's Fashion as Eternal Becomings," 213.

45. Anan, *Contemporary Japanese Women's Theatre and Visual Arts*, 9.

46. Mai and Nguyen, *So Pretty / Very Rotten*, 15; Kayla Daniéll Robinson, "Empowered Princesses: An Ethnographic Examination of the Practices, Rituals, and Conflicts within Lolita Fashion Communities in the United States," (MA thesis, Georgia State University, 2014), 96; P. R. Hinton, "Returning in a Different Fashion: Culture, Communication, and Changing Representations of Lolita in Japan and the West," *International Journal of Communication* 7 (2013): 1582–602; Kathryn Hardy Bernal, "The Lolita Complex: A Japanese

Fashion Subculture and Its Paradoxes" (MA thesis, Auckland University of Technology, 2011).

47. Russell Trainer, *The Lolita Complex* (New York: Citadel Press, 1966). Trainer's book appeared in Japanese in 1969. Nguyen, "Maiden's Fashion as Eternal Becomings," 190.

48. Vera C. Mackie, "Transnational Bricolage: Gothic Lolita and the Political Economy of Fashion," *Intersections: Gender and Sexuality in Asia and the Pacific*, no. 20 (2009), http://intersections.anu.edu.au/issue20/mackie.htm.

49. Gagné, "Urban Princesses," 135.

50. The popular lolita vlogger Tyler Willis of the YouTube channel *ScarfingScarves* has made a cottage industry of calling out sissy and DDlg harassment, as well as all kinds of other predatory behaviors exercised toward lolitas.

51. The anonymous model's account does not seem to be substantiated, but achieved the status of truth among lolita fashion communities online. See "The Documentary About You-Know-What," *F Yeah Lolita: A Lolita Fashion and Lifestyle Blog*, http://www.fyeahlolita.com/2012/02/documentary-about-you-know-what.html.

52. Gagné, "Urban Princesses," 140. Gagné attributes "figure of identity" and "figure of desire" to a 2005 article by Deborah Cameron and Don Kulick, "Identity Crisis?" *Language and Communication* 25 (2005): 107–25; however, these terms actually do not appear in the article. They do discuss two modes of linguistic use corresponding to "identity" and "desire" however.

53. Sheila Burgel, "Dark and Lovely," *Bust* 44 (April/May 2007): 77.

54. Nessa Neko, "Lolita and Japanese Society," Lolita Fashion—For Lolitas of All Styles, December 31, 2012, 2, http://www.lolitafashion.org/lolita_culture.php. This website has since disappeared, but the 2011 version—identical to what I referenced—is archived at https://web.archive.org/web/20111227002309/http://www.lolitafashion.org/lolita_culture.php.

55. Michelle MacKay, Rufflechat Facebook post, August 21, 2018, https://www.facebook.com/groups/rufflechat/permalink/1778728848889125/.

56. See Nguyen, "Maiden's Fashion as Eternal Becomings, 262–63; Hiro Muramoto, "Lolita Goes Victorian, Goth in Japan Cosplay Trend." *Reuters*, September 29, 2008, https://www.reuters.com/article/us-lolitas-japan/lolita-goes-victorian-goth-in-japan-cosplay-trend-idUSTRE48S1Z220080929; Akiko Sugawa-Shimada, "Grotesque Cuteness of Shōjo: Representations of Goth-Loli in Japanese Contemporary TV Anime," in *Japanese Animation: East Asian Perspectives*, edited by Masao Yokota and Tze-yue G. Hu, (Jackson: University Press of Mississippi, 2013), 199–222.

57. Gagné, "Urban Princesses," 141. See also, Therèsa M. Winge, *Costuming Cosplay: Dressing the Imagination* (London: Bloomsbury Visual Arts, 2018).

58. Gagné, "Urban Princesses," 141–42. To name just one representative manga with gothic lolita tendencies, see Mitsukazu Mihara's manga series *Doll* (English translation) (Los Angeles: TokyoPop, 2000).

59. One relevant Rufflechat discussion can be found posted by Mushi Rose on February 19, 2017, "What do you consider yourself as? A lifestyle lolita, or a hobby lolita?" https://www.facebook.com/groups/rufflechat/permalink/1211752355586780.

60. Phoebe Robinson, *You Can't Touch My Hair: And Other Things I Still Have to Explain* (New York: Plume, 2016), 54–55.

61. These are paraphrases from the Rufflechat community on Facebook; the same dynamics typically hold everywhere where lolitas get together to discuss. A convenient ethnographic bonus to the rise of the internet is how many frank conversations among subjects are now preserved complete with timestamps. Rufflechat Private Group, Facebook, https://www.facebook.com/groups/rufflechat/.

62. Rosenberger, *Japanese Sense of Self*, 4.

63. Doi, *Anatomy of Self*. See also Dorinne Kondo, *Crafting Selves* (Chicago: University of Chicago Press, 1990).

64. Erving Goffman, *The Presentation of Self in Everyday Life* (New York: Anchor Books, 1959), 22–30.

65. Simmel, "Fashion," 133.

66. Although numerous videos offering specific gothic-lolita advice for posing exists if you search YouTube, here is one that recaps the 2015 Rufflecon posing workshop: Milkbox, "Lolita Posing 101: Tips for Posing For Photos!" April 11, 2017, YouTube video, 6:17, https://www.youtube.com/watch?v=LQtHTI6oG_E.

67. Mackie, "Transnational Bricolage."

68. All comments from the Rufflechat Group, Facebook, July 4, 2019, Dee Clover post "When a character was asked why," https://www.facebook.com/groups/rufflechat/permalink/2224507207644618. These lolitas' sentiments resonate with accounts from wheelchair and other mobility device users who decorate their equipment in personalized ways so that when able-bodied strangers inevitably pay attention to them, they "gain control over the stare by making it happen on their own terms." Emily Smith, "Pimp My Wheelchair: The Supply and Demand for Personalized Wheelchairs," *Explorations: The UC Davis Undergraduate Research Journal 8* (2005): 25. Loli-fying of mobility devices, canes, and specialized footwear is a not-uncommon topic of conversation on Rufflechat as well. For more on disability and visibility, see also Rosemarie Garland-Thomson, "Staring at the Other." *Disability Studies Quarterly* 25, no. 4 (September 15, 2005), http://dsq-sds.org/article/view/610.

69. Shay Merker, "Do you feel like there's some intersection between Lolita fashion and queer identity?" Rufflechat Group, Facebook, March 4, 2018, https://www.facebook.com/groups/rufflechat/permalink/1570909126337766/.

70. Andrew R. Flores, Jody L. Herman, Gary J. Gates, and Taylor N. T. Brown, "Report: How Many Adults Identify as Transgender in the United States?" UCLA School of Law: Williams Institute, June 2016, http://williamsinstitute.law.ucla.edu/wp-content/uploads/How-Many-Adults-Identify-as-Transgender-in-the-United-States.pdf.

71. The aforementioned thread featured many more accounts of similar sentiments: Merker, Facebook ("Lolita fashion and queer identity"), March 4, 2018.

72. Kathryn Hardy-Bernal, "*Kamikaze Girls* and Loli-goths," conference presentation, Fashion in Fiction: An International Transdisciplinary Conference, University of Technology, Sydney, Australia, May 26–27, 2007.

https://www.academia.edu/3990474/Hardy_Bernal_K_2007_May_26_27_Kamikaze_girls_and_loli_goths_conference_paper_presentation_full_text_Fashion_in_Fiction_An_International_Transdisciplinary_Conference_University_of_Technology_Sydney_Australia?f_ri=358270.

73. Nguyen, "Maiden's Fashion as Eternal Becomings," 275.

74. Jamison Long, "So a major question," Rufflechat Group, Facebook, January 19, 2018, https://www.facebook.com/groups/rufflechat/permalink/1527284090700270/. Unfortunately, at some point after 2019, comments were turned off for this post. The discussion is lost, though the original question remains: "So a major question, its difficult enough for the female lolitas, and those who wear male lolita to be able to be accepted as they pursue the life style, but what about the Brolitas, the males whom the female fashion speaks to thier soul? do you all think they tend to have it even harder. people see them and think oh its a fetish they are getting excitement from wearing, when its often just not so. Also i know that the community claims to accept the brolitas, but do you as females in the lifestyle find the males like myself who love the female fashion to be creepy?"

75. See Butler, *Gender Trouble*; and Chow, *Protestant Ethnic*.

76. Secrets Post #239, "Behind the Bows," LiveJournal, https://behind-the-bows.livejournal.com/177501.html#comments.

77. "'Osharena koga torenakunatta' snappushi 'Fruits'ga gekkan hakkou o shuuryoushita riyu." Fashionsnap, February 3, 2017, https://www.fashionsnap.com/article/2017-02-03/fruits-stop/. Quoted in English in Marc Bain, "Japan's Wild, Creative Harajuku Street Style is Dead: Long Live Uniqlo," *Quartz* (blog), February 22, 2017, https://qz.com/909573/japans-wild-creative-harajuku-street-style-is-dead-long-live-uniqlo/.

78. See, e.g., numerous "Leaving Lolita"–tagged sales albums on internet sales sites.

79. Samuels, *Fantasies of Identification*.

BIBLIOGRAPHY

Archives Consulted

Beinecke Library, Yale University, New Haven, CT
British Library, London
British Library Newspapers, Colindale, London
Brown University Hay Library, Providence, RI
Bunka Gakuen Library, Tokyo
Harvard University Fine Art and Houghton Libraries, Cambridge, MA
John Johnson Collection, Bodleian Library, University of Oxford (via Visual Arts Data Service)
London Low Life Collection, Lilly Library, Indiana University, Bloomington
Mills Music Library, University of Wisconsin–Madison, Madison
National Diet Library, Tokyo
Nichibunken (International Research Center for Japanese Studies), Kyoto, Japan
Paul Mellon Centre for British Art, London
Public Record Office (British National Archive), Kew, London
Victoria and Albert Museum Library, London

Periodicals

Belgravia Magazine (London)
Bell's Life in London and Sporting Chronicle
Berrow's Worcester Journal
Birmingham Daily Post
Bradford Observer
Bristol Mercury
Bury and Norwich Post
Daily Mail (London)
Dundee Courier and Argus (Scotland)
Echoes from the Clubs (later *Period*) (London)
Englishwoman's Domestic Magazine (London)
Examiner (London)
Fun (London)
Era (London)
Freeman's (Dublin)
Girl of the Period Almanack 1869 (London)

Girl of the Period Almanack 1870 (London)
Girl of the Period Miscellany (London)
Globe (London)
Illustrated Police News (London)
Jackson's Oxford Journal
Judy (London)
Ladies Treasury (London)
Liverpool Mercury
Lloyd's Newspaper (London)
London Review
London Society
Macmillan's (London)
Morning Post (London)
New York Clipper
Nottinghamshire Guardian
Pall Mall Gazette (London)
Penny Illustrated Paper (London)
Period (see *Echoes from the Clubs*) (London)
Preston Guardian
Punch (London)
Observer (London)
Queen (London)
Reynolds's Newspaper (London)
Saturday Review of Politics, Literature, Science, and Art (London)
Sheffield and Rotherham Independent
Shinbun Zasshi (新聞雑誌) (Tokyo)
St. Paul's (London)
Star (St. Peter Port, UK)
Sun (London)
Telegraph (London)
Times (London)
Tinsley's Magazine (London)
Tomahawk: A Satire Journal of Satire (London)
Trewman's Exeter Flying Post
Victoria Magazine (London)
Young Englishwoman (London)

Books and Articles

Ackerman, Alan, and Martin Puchner, eds. *Against Theatre: Creative Destructions on the Modernist Stage*. London: Palgrave Macmillan, 2006.

Ahmed, Sara. *The Promise of Happiness*. Durham, NC: Duke University Press, 2010.

Alcott, Louisa May. *An Old-Fashioned Girl*. Boston: Roberts Brothers, 1870. http://archive.org/details/oldfashionedgirl00alco2.

Allen, Robert Clyde. *Horrible Prettiness: Burlesque and American Culture*. Chapel Hill: University of North Carolina Press, 1991.

Allison, Anne. "Cuteness as Japan's Millennial Product." In *Pikachu's Global Adventure: The Rise and Fall of Pokemon*, edited by Joseph Tobin, 34–49. Durham, NC: Duke University Press, 2004. https://doi.org/10.1215/9780822385813-003.

Anan, Nobuko. *Contemporary Japanese Women's Theatre and Visual Arts: Performing Girls' Aesthetics*. London: Palgrave Macmillan, 2016.

Anderson, Nancy F. *Woman against Women in Victorian England: A Life of Eliza Lynn Linton*. Bloomington: Indiana University Press, 1987.

Aoki, Shōichi. *Fresh Fruits*. New York: Phaidon, 2005.

———. *Fruits*. New York: Phaidon, 2001.

———. *Gothic & Lolita*. New York: Phaidon, 2007.

Ashikari, Mikiko. "The Memory of the Women's White Faces: Japaneseness and the Ideal Image of Women." *Japan Forum* 15, no. 1 (2003): 55–79.

Auerbach, Nina. *Private Theatricals: The Lives of the Victorians*. Cambridge, MA: Harvard University Press, 1990.

Austin, J. L. *How to Do Things with Words*. Cambridge, MA: Harvard University Press, 1962.

B., A. "The Girls of the Period." In *Drawing Room Plays and Parlour Pantomimes*, collected by Clement Scott, 341–60. London: S. Rivers, 1870.

Baddeley, Gavin. *Goth Chic*. London: Plexus, 2002.

Baelz, Erwin O. E. *Awakening Japan: The Diary of a German Doctor: Erwin Baelz*. Bloomington: Indiana University Press, 1974.

Bailey, Peter. "Conspiracies of Meaning: Music-Hall and the Knowingness of Popular Culture." *Past and Present* 144 (August 1994): 138–70.

Bain, Marc. "Japan's Wild, Creative Harajuku Street Style Is Dead: Long Live Uniqlo." *Quartz* (blog), updated March 14, 2017. https://qz.com/909573/japans-wild-creative-harajuku-street-style-is-dead-long-live-uniqlo/.

Barcan, Ruth. *Nudity: A Cultural Anatomy*. Oxford: Berg, 2004.

Barish, Jonas. *The Antitheatrical Prejudice*. Berkeley: University of California Press, 1981.

Barthes, Roland. *Empire of Signs*. New York: Hill and Wang, 1982.

———. *Erté*. New York: Rizzoli International Publications, 1975.

———. *The Fashion System*. Berkeley: University of California Press, 1983.

———. *Image, Music, Text*. Translated by Stephen Heath. New York: Farrer, Straus and Giroux, 1977.

Bartlett, Neil. "Evidence: 1870." In *Reclaiming Sodom*, edited by Jonathan Goldberg, 288–99. New York: Routledge, 1994.

Baxter, Katharine Schuyler. *In Beautiful Japan: A Story of Bamboo Lands*. 1895. New York: Hobart, 1904.

Beauchamp, Edward R. *An American Teacher in Early Meiji Japan*. Honolulu: University of Hawai'i Press, 1976.

Bell, Quentin. *On Human Finery*. 2nd edition, revised and expanded. New York: Schocken Books, 1976.

Bendix, Regina. "Moral Integrity in Costumed Identity: Negotiating National Costume in 19th-Century Bavaria." *Journal of American Folklore* 111, no. 440 (Spring 1998): 133–45.

Berliner, Brett A. “Mephistopheles and Monkeys: Rejuvenation, Race, and Sexuality in Popular Culture in Interwar France.” *Journal of the History of Sexuality* 13, no. 3 (July 2004): 306–25.

Bernal, Kathryn Hardy. “The Lolita Complex: A Japanese Fashion Subculture and its Paradoxes.” MA thesis, Auckland University of Technology, 2011.

Bevington, Merle Mowbray. *The Saturday Review, 1855–1868: Representative Educated Opinion in Victorian England*. New York: Columbia University Press, 1941.

Bhabha, Homi K. *The Location of Culture*. London: Routledge, 2004.

Bird, Isabella. *Unbeaten Tracks in Japan*. 1880. Reprinted with new introduction by Pat Barr. London: Virago Press, 1984.

Blank, Hanne. *Straight: The Surprisingly Short History of Heterosexuality*. Boston: Beacon Press, 2012.

Bordo, Susan. *Unbearable Weight: Feminism, Western Culture, and the Body*. Berkeley: University of California Press, 1993.

Bottoms, Stephen J. “The Efficacy/Effeminacy Braid: Unpicking the Performance Studies / Theatre Studies Dichotomy.” *Theatre Topics* 13, no. 2 (2003): 173–87.

Boufis, Christina. “‘Of Home Birth and Breeding’: Eliza Lynn Linton and the Girl of the Period.” In *The Girl’s Own: Cultural Histories of the Anglo-American Girl, 1830–1915*, edited by Claudia Nelson and Lynne Vallone, 98–123. Athens: University of Georgia Press, 1993.

Braddon, Mary Elizabeth. “Whose Fault Is It?” *Belgravia Magazine* 9 (August 1869): 214–15.

Braudel, Fernand. *Capitalism and Material Life, 1400–1800*. New York: Harper Colophon, 1975.

Breward, Christopher. *The Hidden Consumer: Masculinities, Fashion and City Life, 1860–1914*. Manchester: Manchester University Press, 1999.

Burgel, Sheila. “Dark and Lovely.” *Bust* 44 (April/May 2007): 77.

Burnand, Francis Cowley. *The Girls of the Period, or the Island of Nowarpartickilar: A Folly in Two Scenes of Prose, Rhyme, Dance and Song*. London: Phillips, 1869.

Bush, Christopher. “The Ethnicity of Things in America’s Lacquered Age.” *Representations* 99, no. 1 (August 2007): 74–98. https://doi.org/10.1525/rep.2007.99.1.74.

Buszek, Maria Elena. “Representing ‘Awarishness’: Burlesque, Feminist Transgression, and the 19th-Century Pin-Up,” *TDR: The Journal of Performance Studies* 43, no. 4 (Winter 1999): 141–62.

Butler, Judith. *Gender Trouble: Feminism and the Subversion of Identity*. New York: Routledge, 1990.

———. “Performative Acts and Gender Constitution.” *Theatre Journal* 40, no. 4 (December 1988): 519–31.

Cameron, Deborah, and Don Kulick. “Identity Crisis?” *Language and Communication* 25 (2005): 107–25.

Cameron, Don. “Off-the-Rack Identities: Japanese Street Fashion Magazines and the Commodification of Style.” *Japanese Studies* 20, no. 2 (September 2000): 179–87. https://doi.org/10.1080/713683780.

Cannadine, David. *Ornamentalism: How the British Saw Their Empire*. Oxford: Oxford University Press, 2002.

Carlson, Marvin A. *The Haunted Stage*. Ann Arbor: University of Michigan Press, 2003.

Carlyle, Thomas. *The French Revolution*. Vol. 2. Leipzig: Bernhard Tauchnitz, 1851.

———. *Sartor Resartus*. Oxford: Oxford University Press, 1987.

Carter, Ilise. "Beneath the Frills at Ruffle Con." *Racked*, October 28, 2015. https://www.racked.com/2015/10/28/9623030/ruffle-con-lolita-dresses.

Carriger, Michelle Liu. "ElasticiTEA? Preliminary Theses on Cross-Cultural (re)Presentation and the Japanese 'Way of Tea.'" GPS: *Global Performance Studies* 4, no. 1 (2021). https://gps.psi-web.org/.

———. "Performers in the Audience: The Boulton and Park Case of 1870–1871." MA thesis, University of Colorado Boulder, 2006.

Chamberlain, Basil Hall. *Things Japanese: Being Notes on Various Subjects Connected with Japan*. London: Kegan Paul, Trench, Trübne, 1890.

Chao, Sophie. "We Are (Not) Monkeys": Contested Cosmopolitical Symbols in West Papua." *American Ethnologist* 48, no. 3 (2021): 274–87.

Cheng, Anne Anlin. *Ornamentalism*. Illustrated edition. New York: Oxford University Press, 2019.

Chow, Rey. *The Protestant Ethnic and the Spirit of Capitalism*. New York: Columbia University Press, 2002.

Cocks, Harry. *Nameless Offences: Homosexual Desire in the 19th Century*. London: I. B. Tauris, 2003.

Cohen, William A. *Sex Scandal: The Private Parts of Victorian Fiction*. Durham, NC: Duke University Press, 1996.

"Colourful Past, A." *Nature* 440, no. 7083 (2006): 384. http://dx.doi.org/10.1038/440384a.

Copeland, Rebecca. "Fashioning the Feminine: Images of the Modern Girl Student in Meiji." *U.S.-Japan Women's Journal*, nos. 30/31 (2006): 13–35.

Craft, Christopher. *Another Kind of Love: Male Homosexual Desire in English Discourse, 1850–1920*. Berkeley: University of California Press, 1994.

Crenshaw, Kimberlé. *On Intersectionality: Essential Writings*. New York: New Books, 2019.

Curtis, William Eleroy. *The Yankees of the East: Sketches of Modern Japan*. New York: Duffield, 1906. https://catalog.hathitrust.org/Record/006535094.

D'Ambrosio, Paul. "Girl with a Squirrel." *American Folk Art at Cooperstown* (blog), June 27, 2010. https://folkartcooperstown.blogspot.com/2010/06/girl-with-squirrel.html.

Davis, Tracy C. *Actresses as Working Women: Their Social Identity in Victorian Culture*. London: Routledge, 1991.

Davis, Tracy C., and Thomas Postlewait, eds. *Theatricality*. Cambridge: Cambridge University Press, 2003.

de Beauvoir, Simone. *The Second Sex*. Translated by Constance Borde and Sheila Malovany-Chevallier. New York: Vintage Books, 2011.

Dekker, Thomas, and Edward Arber. *The Seven Deadly Sins of London, Drawn in Seven Several Coaches, through the Seven Several Gates of the City; Bringing the Plague with Them. October 1606*. London: E. Arber, 1879. http://archive.org/details/sevendeadlysinso00dekkuoft.

Dinshaw, Carolyn. *Getting Medieval: Sexualities and Communities, Pre- and Postmodern*. Durham, NC: Duke University Press, 1999.

Dobson, Sebastian. *Art and Artifice: Japanese Photographs of the Meiji Era: Selections from the Jean S. and Frederic A. Sharf Collection at the Museum of Fine Arts, Boston*. Boston: Museum of Fine Arts Publications, 2004.

Doi, Takeo. *The Anatomy of Self: The Individual Versus Society*. New York: Kodansha USA Publishing, 1985.

Driscoll, Catherine. *Girls: Feminine Adolescence in Popular Culture and Cultural Theory*. New York: Columbia University Press, 2002.

Duberman, Martin, Martha Vicinus, and George Chauncey, eds. *Hidden from History: Reclaiming the Gay and Lesbian Past*. New York: NAL Books, 1989.

Duus, Peter. *The Abacus and the Sword: The Japanese Penetration of Korea, 1895–1910*. Berkeley: University of California Press, 1998.

———. "Presidential Address: Weapons of the Weak, Weapons of the Strong; The Development of the Japanese Political Cartoon." *Journal of Asian Studies* 60, no. 4 (November 2001): 965–97.

Dynes, Wayne R., ed. *Encyclopedia of Homosexuality*. New York: Garland Publishing Company, 1990.

Edelson, Loren. *Danjūrō's Girls: Women on the Kabuki Stage*. New York: Palgrave Macmillan, 2009.

Escott, T. H. S. *Platform, Press, Politics, and Play*. Bristol: J. W. Arrowsmith, 1895.

Evers, Izumi, Patrick Macias, and Kazumi Nonaka. *Japanese Schoolgirl Inferno: Tokyo Teen Fashion Subculture Handbook*. San Francisco, CA: Chronicle Books, 2007.

Felski, Rita. *The Gender of Modernity*. Cambridge, MA: Harvard University Press, 1995.

Finck, Henry T. *Lotos-Time in Japan*. New York: Charles Scribner's Sons, 1895.

Finn, Dallas. *Meiji Revisited: The Sites of Victorian Japan*. New York: Weatherhill, 1995.

Fisher, Charles A. "The Britain of the East? A Study in the Geography of Imitation." *Modern Asian Studies* 2, no. 4 (1968): 343–76.

Flores, Andrew R., Jody L. Herman, Gary J. Gates, and Taylor N. T. Brown. "Report: How Many Adults Identify as Transgender in the United States?" UCLA School of Law: Williams Institute, June 2016, http://williamsinstitute.law.ucla.edu/wp-content/uploads/How-Many-Adults-Identify-as-Transgender-in-the-United-States.pdf.

Flügel, J.C. *The Psychology of Clothes* 3rd ed. London: Hogarth Press, 1950.

Foucault, Michel. *The History of Sexuality, Volume One*. New York: Vintage Books, 1990.

Freeman, Elizabeth. *Time Binds: Queer Temporalities, Queer Histories*. Durham, NC: Duke University Press, 2010.

Freedman, Alisa, Laura Miller, and Christine Reiko Yano, eds. *Modern Girls on the Go: Gender, Mobility, and Labor in Japan*. Stanford, CA: Stanford University Press, 2013.

Fried, Michael. *Art and Objecthood: Essays and Reviews*. Chicago: University of Chicago Press, 1998.

Fried, Michael. *Why Photography Matters as Art as Never Before*. New Haven and London: Yale University Press, 2008.

Fujitani, Takashi. *Splendid Monarchy: Power and Pageantry in Modern Japan*. Berkeley: University of California Press, 1998.

Fukuzawa, Yukichi. *Seiyou jijo* [*Things Western*]. Tokyo: Shōkodō, 1866. Freely available at Digital Collections of Keio University Libraries. http://dcollections.lib.keio.ac.jp/ja/fukuzawa/a02/3.

Gagné, Isaac. "Urban Princesses: Performance and 'Women's Language' in Japan's Gothic/Lolita Subculture." *Journal of Linguistic Anthropology* 18, no. 1 (2008): 130–50.

Garber, Marjorie. *Vested Interests: Cross-Dressing and Cultural Anxiety*. New York: Routledge, 2011.

Gardiner, John. *The Victorians: An Age in Retrospect*. London: Hambledon Continuum, 2002.

Garland-Thomson, Rosemarie. "Staring at the Other." *Disability Studies Quarterly* 25, no. 4 (September 15, 2005). http://dsq-sds.org/article/view/610.

Gartlan, Luke. *A Career of Japan: Baron Raimund von Stillfried and Early Yokohama Photography*. Leiden: Brill, 2016.

Gerdes, Kendall. "Performativity." *Transgender Studies Quarterly* 1, nos. 1/2 (2014): 148–50.

Gewirtz, Paul. "On 'I Know It When I See It.'" *Yale Law Journal* 105, no. 4 (1996): 1023–47.

Godoy, Tiffany. *Style Deficit Disorder: Harajuku Street Fashion, Tokyo*. San Francisco, CA: Chronicle Books, 2007.

Godoy, Tiffany, and Ivan Vartanian. *Japanese Goth*. New York: Universe, 2009.

Godoy, Tiffany, Ivan Vartanian, Keiko Hirayama, and Tetsuya Suzuki. *Tokyo Street Style: Fashion in Harajuku*. London: Thames and Hudson, 2008.

Goodlad, Lauren M. E., and Michael Bibby, eds. *Goth: Undead Subculture*. Durham, NC: Duke University Press, 2007.

Graham, David. "Gothic Lolitas: Goth Girls Just Wanna Have Fun!" *Gothic eZine*, December 31, 2012. http://gothic.lilithezine.com/gothic_lolitas.html.

Grant, Richard White. "The Age of Burlesque." *Galaxy* 8, no. 2 (August 1869): 260.

Griffis, William E. "The Mikado's Empire." *Harper's New Monthly Magazine*, September 1876.

———. *The Mikado's Empire*. 1876. 6th ed. New York: Harper and Brothers, 1896.

Gunn, Simon. *The Public Culture of the Victorian Middle Class: Ritual and Authority and the English Industrial City, 1840–1914*. Manchester: Manchester University Press, 2000.

Guth, Christine. *Longfellow's Tattoos: Tourism, Collecting, and Japan*. Seattle: University of Washington Press, 2004.

Haga, Tōrū. *Bigō sobyō korekushon*. Vols. 1–3. Tokyo: Iwanami Shoten, 1989.

———. *Wāguman sobyō korekushon*. Vols. 1–2. Tokyo: Iwanami Shoten, 2002.

Haijima, Agnese. "Japanese Popular Culture in Latvia: Lolita and Mori Fashion." *Regioninės studijos*, no. 7 (2013): 31–56.

Hastings, Sally. "A Dinner Party Is Not a Revolution." *US-Japan Women's Journal*, no. 18 (2000): 107–32.

———. "The Empress' New Clothes and Japanese Women, 1868–1912." *The Historian* 55, no. 4 (Summer 1993): 675–91.

Hebdige, Dick. *Subculture: The Meaning of Style*. London: Routledge, 1979.

Helgren, Jennifer, and Colleen Vasconcellos, eds. *Girlhood: A Global History*. New Brunswick, NJ: Rutgers University Press, 2010.

Helsinger, Elizabeth K., Robin Lauterbach Sheets, and William Veeder. *The Woman Question: Society and Literature in Britain and America, 1837–1883*. New York: Garland, 1983.

Hickman, Katie. *Courtesans: Money, Sex, and Fame in the Nineteenth Century*. New York: HarperCollins, 2003.

Hight, Eleanor M. *Capturing Japan in Nineteenth-Century New England Photography Collections*. Farnham, UK: Ashgate, 2011.

Hinton, P. R. "Returning in a Different Fashion: Culture, Communication, and Changing Representations of Lolita in Japan and the West." *International Journal of Communication* 7 (2013): 1582–602.

Hirakawa, Sukehiro. *Japan's Love-Hate Relationship with the West*. Folkestone, UK: Global Oriental, 2005.

Hirano, Katsuya. *The Politics of Dialogic Imagination: Power and Popular Culture in Early Modern Japan*. Chicago: University of Chicago Press, 2014.

Hiromatsu, Ryūen. *Kurokami to bijo no nihonshi*. Tokyo: Suiyōen, 2012.

Ho, Elizabeth. *Neo-Victorianism and the Memory of Empire*. New York: Bloomsbury, 2012.

Hollander, Anne. *Seeing through Clothes*. New York: Viking Press, 1978.

———. *Sex and Suits*. New York: Knopf, 1994.

Horikiri, Naoto. "Onna wa dokyō, shōjo wa aikyō." In *Shōjo ron*, eds. Honda et al. Tokyo: Aoyumi Sha, 1991.

Howell, David L. *Geographies of Identity in Nineteenth-Century Japan*. Berkeley: University of California Press, 2005.

———. "The Girl with the Horse-Dung Hairdo." In *Looking Modern: East Asian Visual Culture from Treaty Ports to World War II*, edited by Jennifer Purtle and Hans Bjarne Thomsen, 203–19. Chicago: Art Media Resources, 2009.

Hyde, H. Montgomery. *The Love That Dared Not Speak Its Name: A Candid History of Homosexuality in Britain*. Boston: Little, Brown, 1970.

Ibsen, Henrik. *A Doll House (Ibsen's Selected Plays)*. New York: W. W. Norton, 2004,

Ignatiev, Noel. *How the Irish Became White*. New York: Routledge, 1995.

Isaka, Maki. *Onnagata: A Labyrinth of Gendering in Kabuki Theater*. Seattle: University of Washington Press, 2016.

Ishiguro, Keishō. *Meiji taishō shōwa tōkyō shashin daishūsei*. Tokyo: Shinchōsha, 2001.
Iwabuchi, Koichi. *Recentering Globalization: Popular Culture and Japanese Transnationalism*. Durham, NC: Duke University Press, 2002.
Jackson, Shannon. *Lines of Activity: Performance, Historiography, Hull-House Domesticity*. Ann Arbor: University of Michigan Press, 2000.
Janes, Leroy Lansing. *Kumamoto, an Episode in Japan's Break from Feudalism*. Kyoto: Dōshisha Shashi Shiryō Henshūjo, 1970.
Jansen, Marius B. *The Making of Modern Japan*. Cambridge, MA: Belknap Harvard Press, 2000.
Jenkins, Keith. *Rethinking History*. London: Routledge, 1991.
Jones, Ann Rosalind, and Peter Stallybrass. *Renaissance Clothing and the Materials of Memory*. Cambridge: Cambridge University Press, 2001.
Jones, H. J. *Live Machines: Hired Foreigners and Meiji Japan*. Tenterden, UK: Paul Norbury Publications, 1980,
Kanagawa Prefectural Museum of Cultural History. *Yokohama kaikou 160nen Yokohama ukiyo-e* (160th Anniversary of the Opening of Yokohama Port: Yokohama Woodblock Prints). Yokohama: Kanagawa Prefectural Museum of Cultural History, 2019.
Kanazawa, Yasutaka. *Edo keppatsushi* (History of Edo Hairdressing). Tokyo: Seiyabō, 1961.
Kaplan, Morris. *Sodom on the Thames: Sex, Love, and Scandal in Wilde Times*. Ithaca, NY: Cornell University Press, 2005.
Karlin, Jason G. *Gender and Nation in Meiji Japan: Modernity, Loss, and the Doing of History*. Honolulu: University of Hawai'i Press, 2014. http://public.eblib.com/choice/publicfullrecord.aspx?p=3413776.
Kato, Etsuko. *The Tea Ceremony and Women's Empowerment in Modern Japan*. London: Routledge, 2004.
Katz, Jonathan Ned. *Love Stories: Sex between Men before Homosexuality*. Chicago: University of Chicago Press, 2001.
Kawamura, Yuniya. *Fashioning Japanese Subcultures*. London: Berg, 2013.
Keene, Donald. *Emperor of Japan: Meiji and His World, 1852–1912*. New York: Columbia University Press, 2002.
Keene, Donald, Anne Nishimura Morse, Fredric A. Sharf, and Louise E. Virgin. *Japan at the Dawn of the Modern Age: Woodblock Prints from the Meiji Era, 1868–1912, Selections from the Jean S. and Frederic A. Sharf Collection at the Museum of Fine Arts, Boston*. Boston: Museum of Fine Arts, 2001.
Keet, Philomena, and Yuri Manabe. *The Tokyo Look Book: Stylish to Spectacular, Goth to Gyaru, Sidewalk to Catwalk*. Tokyo: Kodansha USA, 2007.
Kondo, Dorinne. *Crafting Selves*. Chicago: University of Chicago Press, 1990.
Kōsaka, Masaaki. *Japanese Thought in the Meiji Era*. Translated by David Abosch. Tokyo: Pan-Pacific Press, 1958.
Kraus, Karl. "The Eroticism of Clothes." In *Rise of Fashion: A Reader*, edited by Daniel Leonhard Purdy, 239–44. Minneapolis: University of Minnesota Press, 2004.
Kucich, John. *The Power of Lies: Transgression in Victorian Fiction*. Ithaca, NY: Cornell University Press, 1994.

Laver, James. *Costume and Fashion: A Concise History*. New York: Thames and Hudson, 1982 [1969].

Layard, George Somes. *Mrs. Lynn Linton: Her Life, Letters, and Opinions*. London: Methuen, 1901.

Lee, Josephine D. *The Japan of Pure Invention: Gilbert and Sullivan's "The Mikado."* Minneapolis: University of Minnesota Press, 2010.

Levy, Ariel. *Female Chauvinist Pigs: Women and the Rise of Raunch Culture*. New York: Free Press, 2006.

Levy, Indra. *Sirens of the Western Shore: The Westernesque Femme Fatale, Translation, and Vernacular Style in Modern Japanese Literature*. New York: Columbia University Press, 2006.

Linton, Eliza Lynn. *The Autobiography of Christopher Kirkland* (1885). New York: Garland Publishing, 1976.

———. "The Girl of the Period." *Saturday Review of Politics, Literature, Science, and Art*, March 14, 1868, 339–40.

———. *The Girl of the Period and Other Social Essays*. London: R. Bentley and Son, 1883.

———. *Modern Women and What Is Said of Them*. New York: J. S. Redfield, 1868.

———. "Rose Blackett and Her Lovers," *London Society*, vol. 6, November 1864, 472-480.

———. "Such Things Are" (book review), *Saturday Review of Politics, Literature, Science, and Art*, vol. 15, no. 381, February 14, 1863, 214-5.

"Lives of Boulton and Park." London: George Clarke, 1870.

Lord, William Barry. *The Freaks of Fashion: With Illustrations of the Changes in the Corset and the Crinoline from Remote Periods to the Present Time*. London: Ward, Locke, and Taylor, 1870.

Loti, Pierre. "Japanese Women in 1890." In *Carmen Sylva and Sketches from the Orient*, 177–214. Translated by Fred Rothwell. New York: Macmillan, 1912.

———. "Un bal à Yeddo." In *Japoneries d'automne*, 77–106. Paris: Calman Lévy, 1898.

Low, Morris. *Japan on Display: Photography and the Emperor*. London: Routledge, 2006.

Lunning, Frenchy. "Under the Ruffles: Shōjo and the Morphology of Power." *Mechademia* 6 (2011): 3–19.

Lurie, Alison. *The Language of Clothes*. New York: Random House, 1981.

Luvaas, Brent, and Joanne B. Eicher, eds. *The Anthropology of Dress and Fashion: A Reader*. London: Bloomsbury Visual Arts, 2019.

Lyttle, Pat. *Japanese Street Style*. London: A & C Black, 2012.

Mackie, Vera C. "Transnational Bricolage: Gothic Lolita and the Political Economy of Fashion." *Intersections: Gender and Sexuality in Asia and the Pacific*, no. 20 (2009). http://intersections.anu.edu.au/issue20/mackie.htm.

Mai, Jane, and An Nguyen. *So Pretty / Very Rotten: Comics and Essays on Lolita Fashion and Cute Culture*. Tokyo: Koyama Press, 2017.

Mainichi shinbunsha. *Shashin Meiji Taisho 60-nenshi*. Tokyo: Mainichi shinbunsha tosho henshūbu, 1956.

"The Man of the Period: A Companion to The Girl of the Period." London: Robert Hardwicke, 1868.

March, Philipp, and Claudia Delank, eds. *The Adventure of Japanese Photography 1860–1890*. Heidelberg: Kehrer Verlag, 2003.

"Marriage Market and Belgravian Intelligence." *Saturday Review of Politics, Literature, Science and Art*, July 9, 1861, 9–10.

Mason, R. H. P., and J. G. Kaiger. *A History of Japan: Revised Edition*. Boston: Tuttle Publishing, 1997.

Maxwell, Alexander. *Patriots against Fashion: Clothing and Nationalism in Europe's Age of Revolutions*. London: Palgrave Macmillan, 2014.

May, Leila. "Monkeys, Microcephalous Idiots, and the Barbarous Races of Mankind: Darwin's Dangerous Victorianism." *Victorian Newsletter* (Fall 2002): 20–27.

McClintock, Anne. *Imperial Leather: Race, Gender, and Sexuality in the Colonial Contest*. New York: Routledge, 1995.

McClintock, Martha. "Okuhara Seiko (1837–1913): The Life and Arts of a Meiji Period Literati Artist." PhD diss., University of Michigan, 1991.

McKenna, Neil. *Fanny and Stella: The Young Men Who Shocked Victorian England*. London: Faber and Faber, 2013.

Meech-Pekarik, Julia. *The World of the Meiji Print*. New York: Weatherhill, 1986.

"Men in Petticoats." London: George Clarke, 1870.

Metzger, Sean. *Chinese Looks: Fashion, Performance, Race*. Bloomington: Indiana University Press, 2014.

Mezur, Katherine. *Beautiful Boys / Outlaw Bodies: Devising Kabuki Female-Likeness*. New York: Palgrave Macmillan, 2005.

Mihara, Mitsukazu. *Doll*. Vol. 1. Translated by Yuki N. Johnson. Los Angeles: TokyoPop, 2000.

Mill, John Stuart. *The Subjection of Women*. New York: D. Appleton, 1870.

Miller, Laura and Jan Bardsley, eds. *Bad Girls of Japan*. Basingstoke, UK: Palgrave Macmillan, 2011.

Miller, Laura. "Cute Masquerade and the Pimping of Japan." *IJJS: International Journal of Japanese Sociology* 20, no. 1 (2011): 18–29.

Milne-Smith, Amy. *London Clubland: A Cultural History of Gender and Class in Late Victorian Britain*. New York: Palgrave Macmillan, 2011.

Monden, Masafumi. "Being Alice in Japan: Performing a Cute, 'Girlish' Revolt." *Japan Forum* 26, no. 2 (2014): 265–85.

———. *Japanese Fashion Cultures: Dress and Gender in Contemporary Japan*. London: Bloomsbury Academic, 2018.

———. "Transcultural Flow of Demure Aesthetics: Examining Cultural Globalisation through Gothic and Lolita Fashion." *New Voices* 2 (December 2008): 21–40. https://doi.org/10.21159/nv.02.02.

Moruzi, Kristine. "Fast and Fashionable: The Girls in *The Girl of the Period Miscellany*." *Australasian Journal of Victorian Studies* 14, no. 1 (2009): 9–28.

Munkwitz, Erica. *Women, Horse Sports, and Liberation: Equestrianism and Britain from the 18th to the 20th Centuries*. London: Routledge, 2021.

Muramoto, Hiro. "Lolita Goes Victorian, Goth in Japan Cosplay Trend." *Reuters*, September 29, 2008. https://www.reuters.com/article/us-lolitas-japan/lolita-goes-victorian-goth-in-japan-cosplay-trend-idUSTRE48S1Z220080929.

Murray, Janet Horowitz. *Strong-Minded Women and Other Lost Voices from Victorian England*. New York: Pantheon, 1982.

Nabokov, Vladimir. *Lolita*. Edited by Alfred Appel. New York: Vintage Books, 1991.

Nakagawa, Keiichiro, and Henry Rosovsky. "The Case of the Dying Kimono: The Influence of Changing Fashions on the Development of the Japanese Woolen Industry." *Business History Review* 37, nos. 1/2 (Spring–Summer 1963): 59–80.

Nakashima, Tetsuya, dir. *Kamikaze Girls* (*Shimotsuma monogatari*). Tokyo: Tōhō Kabushiki Kaisha / VIZ Media, 2004. DVD.

Namba, Tomoko. "School Uniform Reforms in Modern Japan." In *Fashion, Identity, and Power in Modern Asia*, edited by Kyunghee Pyun and Aida Yuen Wong, 91–113. Cham, Switzerland: Springer International, 2018.

Narayan, Uma. *Dislocating Cultures: Identities, Traditions, and Third-World Feminism*. New York: Routledge, 1997.

Neko, Nessa. "Lolita and Japanese Society." *Lolita Fashion—for Lolitas of All Styles*. December 31, 2012. Accessed March, 14 2023. https://web.archive.org/web/20111227002309/http://www.lolitafashion.org/lolita_culture.php.

Nguyen, An. "Maiden's Fashion as Eternal Becomings: Victorian Maidens and Sugar Sweet Cuties Donning Japanese Street Fashion in Japan and North America." PhD diss., University of Western Ontario, 2012.

Norman, Henry. *The Real Japan: Studies of Contemporary Japanese Manners, Morals, Administration, and Politics*. London: T. Fisher Unwin, 1893.

Norton, Rictor, ed. *My Dear Boy: Gay Love Letters through the Centuries*. San Francisco, CA: Leyland Publications, 1998.

Notehelfer, F. G. "L. L. Janes in Japan: Carrier of American Culture and Christianity." *Journal of Presbyterian History* 53, no. 4 (1975): 313–38.

"Novels with a Purpose," *Westminster Review* 84 (1864): 24–49.

Nyong'o, Tavia. *The Amalgamation Waltz: Race, Performance, and the Ruses of Memory*. Minneapolis: University of Minnesota Press, 2009.

Nyong'o, Tavia. "TRAPPED IN THE CLOSET WITH EVE." *Criticism* 52, no. 2 (2010): 243–51.

O'Brien, Suzanne. "Splitting Hairs: History and the Politics of Daily Life in Nineteenth-Century Japan." *Journal of Asian Studies* 67, no. 4 (2008): 1309–39.

Ōhara, Rieko. *Kurokami no bunkashi*. Tokyo: Tsukiji Shokan, 1988.

Ohnuki-Tierney, Emiko. *The Monkey as Mirror: Symbolic Transformations in Japanese History and Ritual*. Princeton, NJ: Princeton University Press, 1987.

Okazaki, Manami, and Geoff Johnson. *Kawaii! Japan's Culture of Cute*. Munich: Prestel, 2013.

Oku, Takenori. *Bunmei kaika to minshū: Kindai Nihon seishinshi no danshō*. Tokyo: Shinhyōron, 1993.

"'Osharena koga torenakunatta' snappushi 'Fruits'ga gekkan hakkou o shuuryoushita riyu." Fashionsnap, February 3, 2017. https://www.fashionsnap.com/article/2017-02-03/fruits-stop/.

Ozawa, Takeshi. *Shashin de miru bakumatsu Meiji*. Tokyo: Sekai bunkasha, 1990.

Palmer, Henry Spencer. *Letters from the Land of the Rising Sun: Being a Selection from Correspondence Contributed to "The Times" between the Years 1886 and 1892 . . . with Seventy-Six Illustrations*. Yokohama: Japan Mail, 1894.

Pearl, Cyril. *The Girl with the Swansdown Seat*. Indianapoli: Bobbs-Merrill, 1955.

Pearsall, Ronald. *The Worm in the Bud: The World of Victorian Sexuality*. London: Weidenfeld and Nicolson, 1969.

Pflugfelder, Gregory M. "The Nation-State, the Age/Gender System, and the Reconstitution of Erotic Desire in Nineteenth-Century Japan." *Journal of Asian Studies* 71, no. 4 (2012): 963–74.

Polhemus, Ted. *Streetstyle: From Sidewalk to Catwalk*. London: Thames and Hudson, 1994.

Quenqua, Douglas. "They're Like, Way Ahead of the Linguistic Currrrve." *New York Times*, February 27, 2012. https://www.nytimes.com/2012/02/28/science/young-women-often-trendsetters-in-vocal-patterns.html.

Richards, Frances. "Fifteen Theses on the Cute." *Cabinet* 4 (Fall 2001). http://cabinetmagazine.org/issues/4/cute.php.

Richards, Thomas. *The Imperial Archive: Knowledge and the Fantasy of Empire*. London: Verso, 1993.

Rinehart, Nana. "'The Girl of the Period' Controversy." *Victorian Periodicals Review* 13, nos. 1/2 (1980): 2–9.

Rivière, Joan. "Womanliness as Masquerade." *International Journal of Psycho-Analysis* 9 (1929): 303–13.

Roach, Joseph. *Cities of the Dead: Circum-Atlantic Performance*. New York: Columbia University Press, 1996.

———. *It*. Ann Arbor: University of Michigan Press, 2007.

Robb, Graham. *Strangers: Homosexual Love in the Nineteenth Century*. New York: W. W. Norton, 2004.

Robertson, Jennifer, ed. "Introduction: Putting and Keeping Japan in Anthropology." In *A Companion to the Anthropology of Japan*, 3–16. Malden, MA: Blackwell Publishing, 2005.

———. *Takarazuka: Sexual Politics and Popular Culture in Modern Japan*. Berkeley: University of California Press, 1996.

Robinson, Kyla Daniéll. "Empowered Princesses: An Ethnographic Examination of the Practices, Rituals, and Conflicts within Lolita Fashion Communities in the United States." MA thesis, Georgia State University, 2014.

Robinson, Phoebe. *You Can't Touch My Hair: And Other Things I Still Have to Explain*. New York: Plume, 2016.

Roden, Donald. "Thoughts on the Early Meiji Gentleman." In *Gendering Modern Japanese History*, edited by Barbara Molony and Kathleen Uno, 61–98. Cambridge, MA: Harvard University Press, 2008.

Rogala, Jozef. *The Genius of Mr. Punch: Life in Yokohama's Foreign Settlement: Charles Wirgman and the Japan Punch 1862–1887*. Translated by Hitomi Yamashita. Yokohama: Yūrindo, 2004.

Rosenberger, Nancy Ross. *Japanese Sense of Self*. Cambridge: Cambridge University Press, 1992. http://catdir.loc.gov/catdir/toc/cam031/91026271.html.

Rosenfeld, L. "Alfred Swaine Taylor (1806–1880), Pioneer Toxicologist—and a Slight Case of Murder." *Clinical Chemistry* 31, no. 7 (1985): 1235–36.

Rousmaniere, Nicole Coolidge, and Mikiko Hirayama, eds. *Reflecting Truth: Japanese Photography in the Nineteenth Century*. Amsterdam: Hotei Publishing, 2004.

Said, Edward. *Orientalism*. New York: Vintage Books, 1979.

Sakai, Tadayasu. *Bigō gashū: fūshi fūzoku sobyō*. Tokyo: Iwasaki Bijutsusha, 1973.

Samuels, Ellen Jean. *Fantasies of Identification: Disability, Gender, Race*. New York: New York University Press, 2014.

Sato, Ikuya. *Kamikaze Biker: Parody and Anomy in Affluent Japan*. Chicago: University of Chicago Press, 1998.

———. "Play Theory of Delinquency: Toward a General Theory of 'Action.'" *Symbolic Interaction* 11, no. 2 (1988): 191–212. https://doi.org/10.1525/si.1988.11.2.191.

Sato, Tomoko, and Toshio Watanabe. *Japan and Britain: An Aesthetic Dialogue, 1850–1930*. London: Lund Humphries, 1991.

Schechner, Richard. *Between Theater and Anthropology*. Philadelphia: University of Pennsylvania Press, 1985.

———. *Performance Theory*. Revised and expanded edition. New York: Routledge, 1988.

Schneider, Rebecca. *The Explicit Body in Performance*. New York: Routledge, 1997.

Scidmore, Eliza Ruhamah. *Jinrikisha Days in Japan*. New York: Harper & Bros., 1902.

Scott, James C. *Domination and the Arts of Resistance: Hidden Transcripts*. New Haven, CT: Yale University Press, 1992.

Screech, Timon. *The Shogun's Painted Culture: Fear and Creativity in the Japanese States, 1760–1829*. London: Reaktion Books, 2000.

Sedgwick, Eve Kosofsky. *Epistemology of the Closet*. Berkeley: University of California Press, 1990.

Senelick, Laurence. "Boys and Girls Together." In *Crossing the Stage: Controversies on Cross-Dressing*, edited by Lesley Ferris, 80–95. London: Routledge, 1993.

———. *The Changing Room: Sex, Drag and Theatre*. London: Routledge, 2000.

———. "Pantomime." In *The Cambridge Guide to Theatre*, edited by Martin Banham, 751–52. Cambridge: Cambridge University Press, 1992.

Shao, Qin. *Culturing Modernity: The Nantong Model, 1890–1930*. Stanford, CA: Stanford University Press, 2003.

Shimazaki, Satoko. *Edo Kabuki in Transition: From the Worlds of the Samurai to the Vengeful Female Ghost*. New York: Columbia University Press, 2016.

Shimizu, Isao. *E de kaita Nihonjin ron: Joruju Bigō no sekai*. Tokyo: Chūō Kōronsha, 1981.

Shively, Donald H. "The Social Environment of Tokugawa Kabuki." In *Japanese Aesthetics and Culture: A Reader*, edited by Nancy G. Hume, 193–244. Albany: State University of New York Press, 1995.

———. "Sumptuary Regulation and Status in Early Tokugawa Japan." *Harvard Journal of Asiatic Studies* 25 (1964): 123–64.

Sievers, Sharon L. *Flowers in Salt: The Beginnings of Feminist Consciousness in Modern Japan*. Stanford, CA: Stanford University Press, 1983.

Simmel, Georg. "Fashion." *International Quarterly* 10 (1904): 130–55.

Sinfield, Alan. *The Wilde Century: Effeminacy, Oscar Wilde and the Queer Moment*. New York: Columbia University Press, 1994.

Slade, Toby. *Japanese Fashion: A Cultural History*. Oxford: Berg, 2009.

Smith, Emily. "Pimp My Wheelchair: The Supply and Demand for Personalized Wheelchairs." *Explorations: The UC Davis Undergraduate Research Journal* 8 (2005): 17–32.

Sontag, Susan. "Notes on 'Camp.'" In *Susan Sontag: Essays of the 1960s and '70s*, 259–74. Edited by David Reiff. New York: Library of America, 2013.

Stanley, Amy. *Stranger in the Shogun's City: A Japanese Woman and Her World*. New York: Scribner, 2020.

Steele, Valerie, Patricia Mears, Yuniya Kawamura, and Hiroshi Narumi. *Japan Fashion Now*. New Haven, CT: Yale University Press, 2010.

Sugawa-Shimada, Akiko. "Grotesque Cuteness of Shōjo: Representations of Goth-Loli in Japanese Contemporary TV Anime." In *Japanese Animation: East Asian Perspectives*, edited by Masao Yokota and Tze-yue G. Hu, 199–222. Jackson: University Press of Mississippi, 2013.

Svendsen, Lars. *Fashion: A Philosophy*. London: Reaktion Books, 2006.

Swift, Philip. "Cosmetic Cosmologies in Japan: Notes Toward a Superficial Investigation." Working Paper Series 4, Open Anthropology Cooperative Press, October 10, 2010. http://openanthcoop.net/press/2010/10/09/cosmetic-cosmologies-in-japan/.

Takebe, Toshio, and Kazunori Nakamura, eds. *Meiji no Nihon: Kunaichō Shoryōbu shozō shashin*. Tokyo: Yoshikawa Kōbunkan, 2000.

Takemoto, Novala. *Kamikaze Girls* (*Shimotsuma monogatari*). Translated by Masumi Washington. San Francisco, CA: VIZ Media, 2008.

Thévoz, Seth Alexander. *Club Government: How the Early Victorian World Was Ruled from London Clubs*. London: I. B. Tauris, 2018.

Toll, Robert C. *Blacking Up: The Minstrel Show in Nineteenth-Century America*. New York: Oxford University Press, 1974.

Treat, John Whittier. "Yoshimoto Banana Writes Home: *Shōjo* Culture and the Nostalgic Subject." *Society for Japanese Studies* 19, no. 2 (Summer 1993): 353–87.

Tseëlon, Efrat. *The Masque of Femininity: The Presentation of Woman in Everyday Life*. London: Sage, 1995.

"The Unnatural History and Petticoat Mystery of Boulton and Park." Lilly Library Archive, Indiana University. https://collections.libraries.indiana.edu/lilly/exhibitions_legacy/offthepedestal/otp10.html

Upchurch, Charles. "Forgetting the Unthinkable: Cross-Dressers and British Society in the Case of the Queen vs. Boulton and Others." *Gender and History* 12, no. 1 (2000): 127–57.

Valverde, Mariana. "The Love of Finery: Fashion and The Fallen Woman in Nineteenth-Century Social Discourse." *Victorian Studies* 32, no. 2 (1989): 168–88.

van Thal, Herbert. *Eliza Lynn Linton: The Girl of the Period: A Biography*. London: Allen and Unwin, 1979.

Varley, H. Paul, trans. *A Chronicle of Gods and Sovereigns: Jinnō shōtōki of Kitabatake Chikafusa*. New York: Columbia University Press, 1980.

Veblen, Thorstein. *Theory of the Leisure Class: An Economic Study of Institutions*. 1899. New York: Modern Library, 1934.

"Vienna International Exposition and Japonism." Expositions: *Where the Modern Technology Of The Times Was Exhibited*, National Diet Library (Japan) website. Modified April 17, 2017. https://www.ndl.go.jp/exposition/s1/1873–2.html.

Wakamatsu, Yurika. "Painting in Between: Gender and Modernity in the Japanese Literati Art of Okuhara Seiko (1837–1913)." PhD diss., Harvard University, 2016.

Walkowitz, Judith. "The Contagious Diseases Acts, Regulationists and Repealers." In *Prostitution and Victorian Society: Women, Class, and the State*, 67–148. Cambridge: Cambridge University Press, 1982.

Warwick, Alexandra, and Dani Cavallaro. *Fashioning the Frame: Boundaries, Dress and the Body*. London: Bloomsbury, 1998.

Weeks, Jeffrey. *Sex, Politics, and Society*. 2nd ed. London: Longman, 1989.

Welters, Linda, and Abby Lillethun. *Fashion History: A Global View*. London: Bloomsbury Visual Arts, 2018.

White, Chris, ed. *Nineteenth-Century Writings on Homosexuality: A Sourcebook*. London: Routledge, 1999.

Wilde, Oscar. *Intentions*. Leipzig: Heineman and Ballestier, 1891.

Wilkins, Amy. *Wannabes, Goths, and Christians: The Boundaries of Sex Styles and Status*. Chicago: University of Chicago Press, 2008.

Wilkins, Amy, and Paul Hodkinson. *Goth: Identity, Style and Subculture*. Oxford: Berg, 2002.

Williams, Kirk. "Anti-Theatricality and the Limits of Naturalism." In *Against Theatre: Creative Destructions on the Modernist Stage*, edited by Alan Ackerman and Martin Puchner, 95–111. London: Palgrave Macmillan, 2006.

Wilson, Elizabeth. *Adorned in Dreams: Fashion and Modernity*. London: Virago, 1985.

Winge, Theresa. *Costuming Cosplay: Dressing the Imagination*. London: Bloomsbury Visual Art, 2018.

———. "Undressing and Dressing Loli: A Search for the Identity of the Japanese Lolita." In *Limits of the Human*, edited by Frenchy Lunning, 47–63. Minneapolis: University of Minnesota Press, 2008.

Yanagida, Kunio. *Japanese Manners and Customs in the Meiji Era*. Translated and adapted by Charles S. Terry. Tokyo: Ōbunsha, 1957.

Yonemura, Ann. *Yokohama: Prints from Nineteenth-Century Japan*. Washington, DC: Smithsonian Institution, 1990.

Yoshinaga, Masayuki, and Katsuhiko Ishikawa. *Gothic and Lolita*. London: Phaidon Press, 2007.

INDEX

Numbers in italic refer to figures.